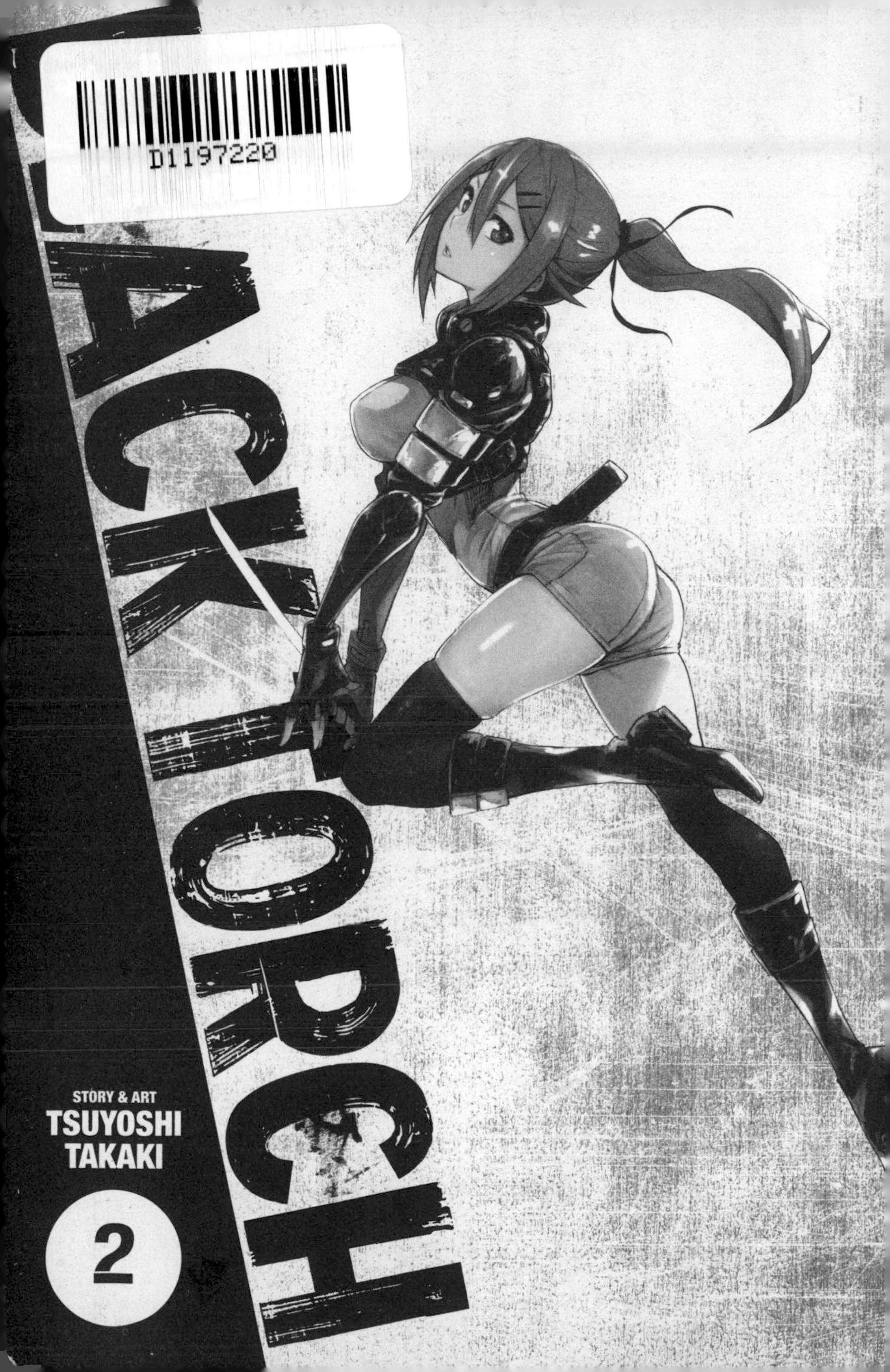

ACK TORCH

STORY & ART
TSUYOSHI TAKAKI

2

CHARACTER

Ninja, Bureau of Espionage

JIRO AZUMA

A ninja who can talk to animals. His grandfather trained him in martial arts since childhood. He joined the Bureau of Espionage after he fused with Rago, a mononoke.

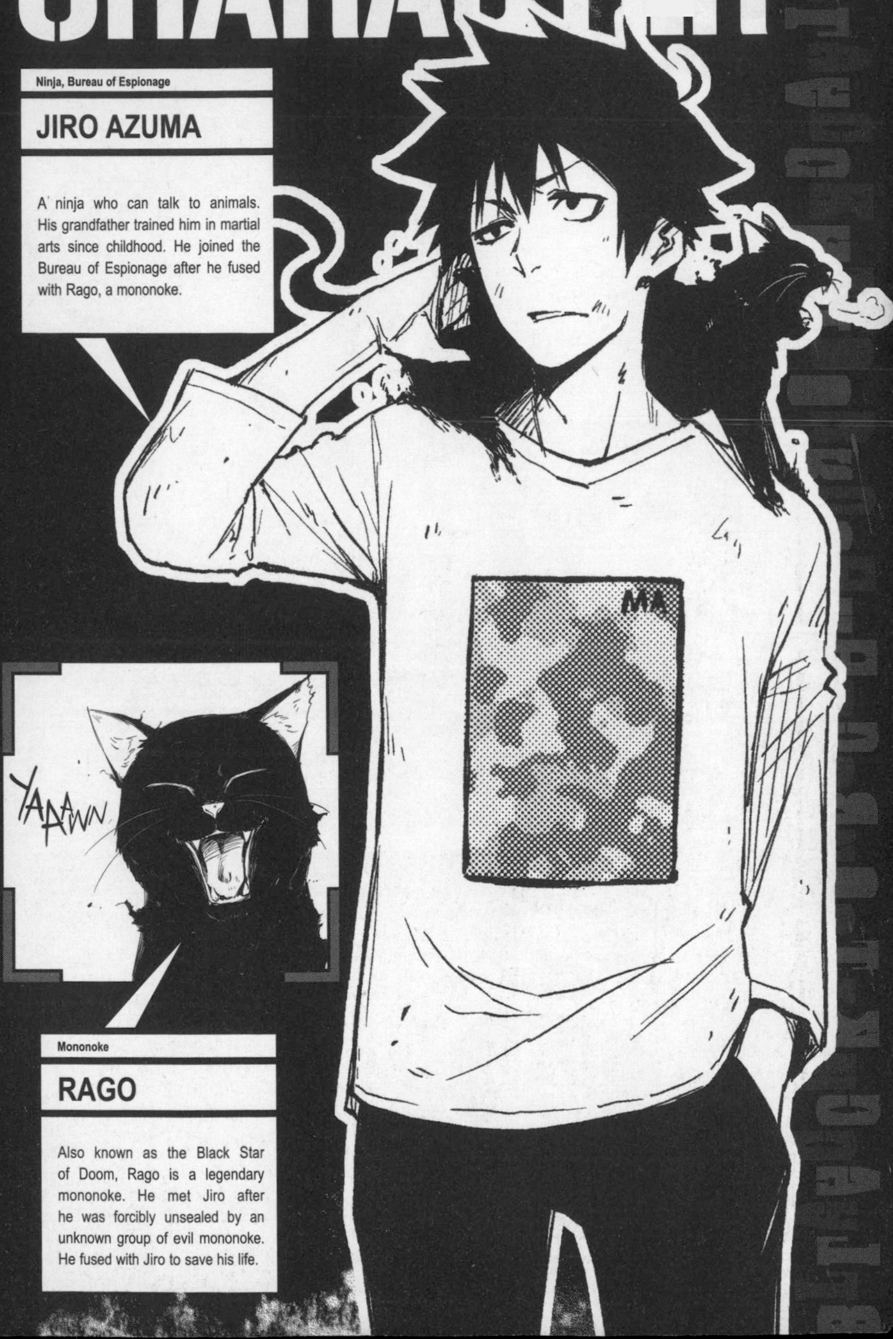
YAAAWN

Mononoke

RAGO

Also known as the Black Star of Doom, Rago is a legendary mononoke. He met Jiro after he was forcibly unsealed by an unknown group of evil mononoke. He fused with Jiro to save his life.

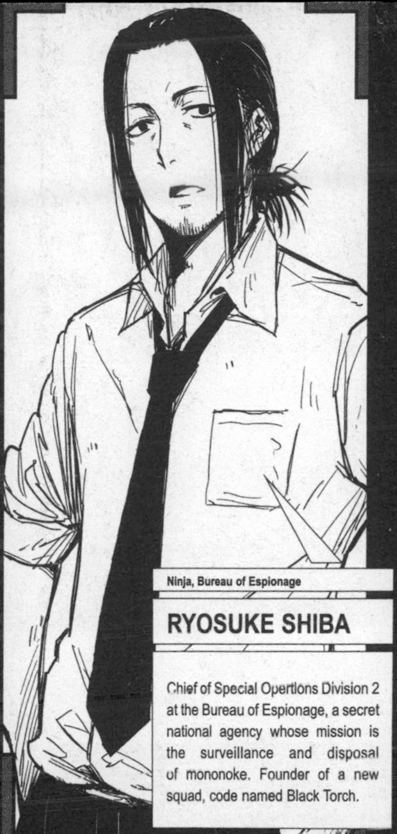

Ninja, Bureau of Espionage

RYOSUKE SHIBA

Chief of Special Opertions Division 2 at the Bureau of Espionage, a secret national agency whose mission is the surveillance and disposal of mononoke. Founder of a new squad, code named Black Torch.

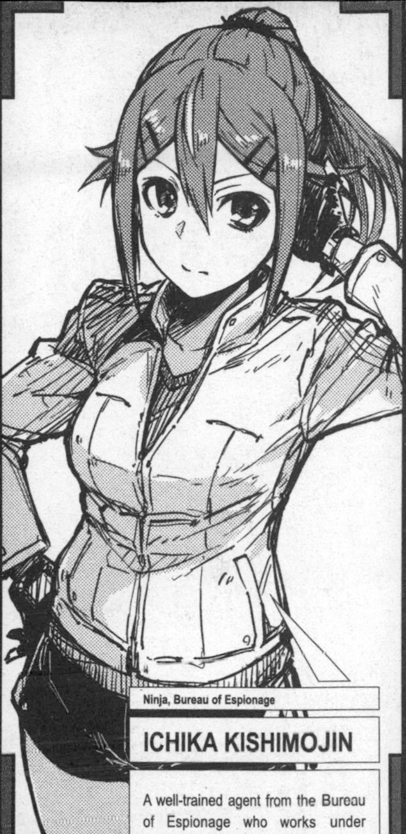

Ninja, Bureau of Espionage

ICHIKA KISHIMOJIN

A well-trained agent from the Bureau of Espionage who works under Shiba. She's the only daughter of the Kishimonjin clan, a famous clan of onmitsu.

STORY

Jiro Azuma, a ninja who can talk to animals and was raised by his grandfather, meets a mononoke named Rago. Mononoke are immortal demons with extraordinary, supernatural powers. Rago is badly injured and Jiro, who has a soft spot for the animals he can talk to, treats Rago's wounds. Another mononoke attacks Rago and Jiro dies protecting him. Rago returns the favor by fusing with Jiro, bringing him back from death but forever changing his life. This fusion gives Jiro the power to crush his opponents with Rago's power, but in exchange, he is no longer human.

Immediately after defeating the evil mononoke, Jiro is detained by Ryosuke Shiba and Ichika Kishimojin, government employed ninja from the Bureau of Espionage. The Bureau was pursuing Rago after he was freed by a mysterious group of mononoke during a raid on the Bureau. Jiro, no longer considered human by the Bureau due to his irreversible bond with Rago, is forcibly put under surveillance and protection, effectively becoming their prisoner.

Jiro manages to escape from the Bureau to return home to his grandfather only to learn that his grandfather is a former member of the Bureau! After a bitter fight, Jiro decides to return to the Bureau on his own to fight against the mononoke and humans who now want to use him. However, on his way back, Jiro and his escort, Ichika, are attacked by mononoke who want to use Rago's power for their own evil ends! Jiro and Ichika manage to defeat the mononoke together. Meanwhile, Shiba meets with his higher-ups and establishes a new onmitsu—government-employed ninja—squad to put Jiro to work. Code name: Black Torch!

CONTENTS

2

BLACK TORCH

BLACK TORCH

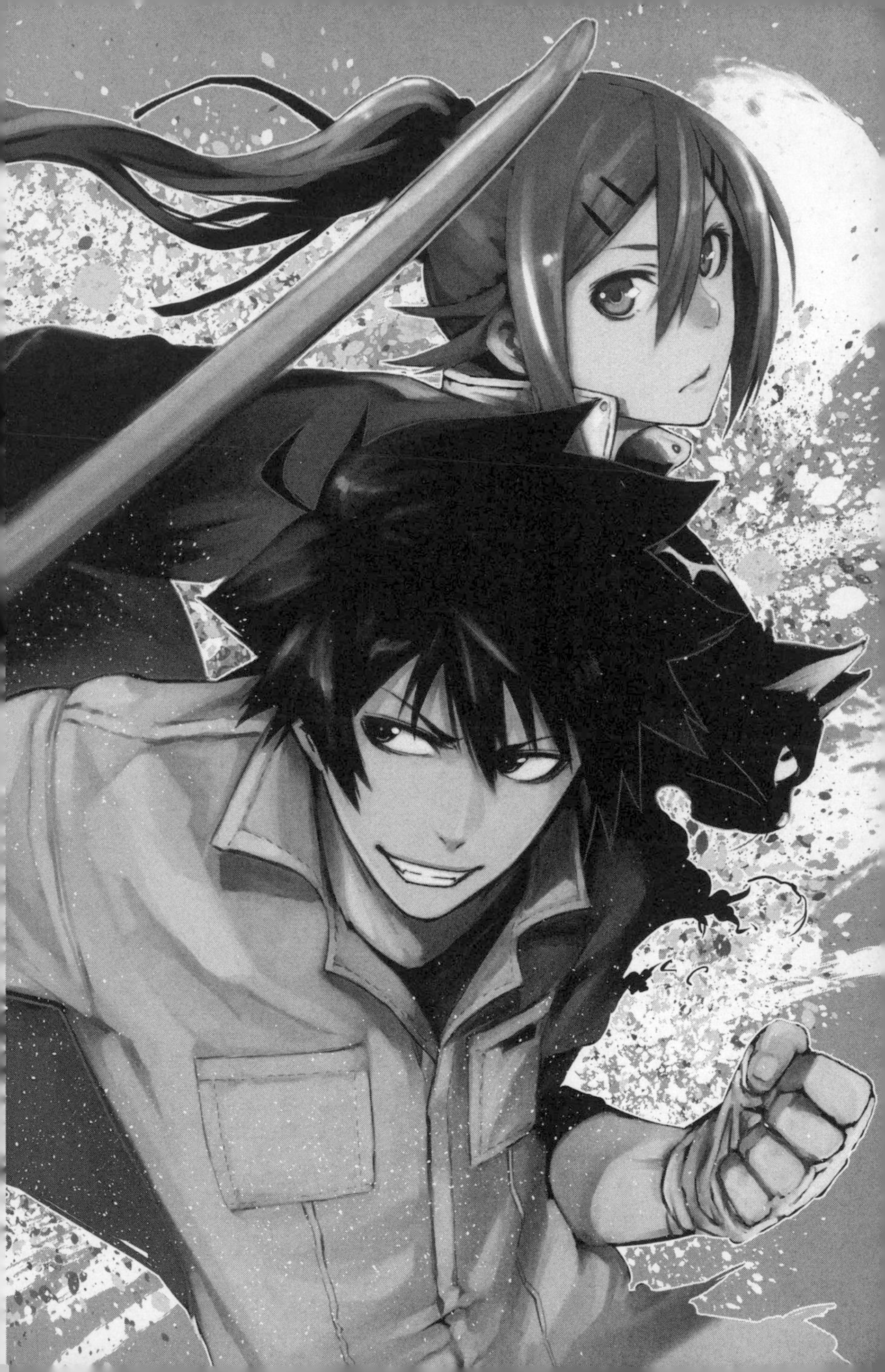

#4 Two Is Not Enough

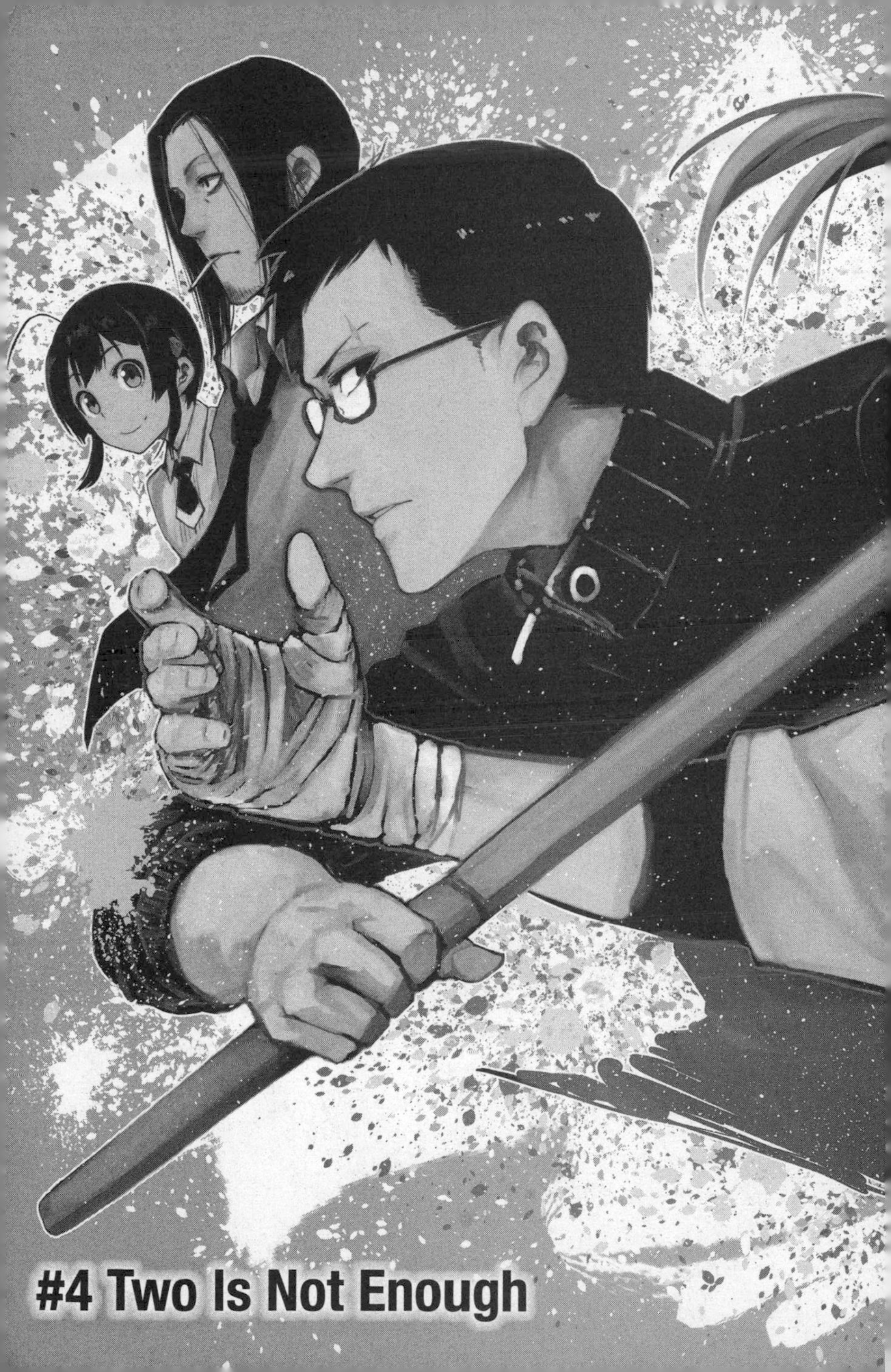

BLACK TORCH

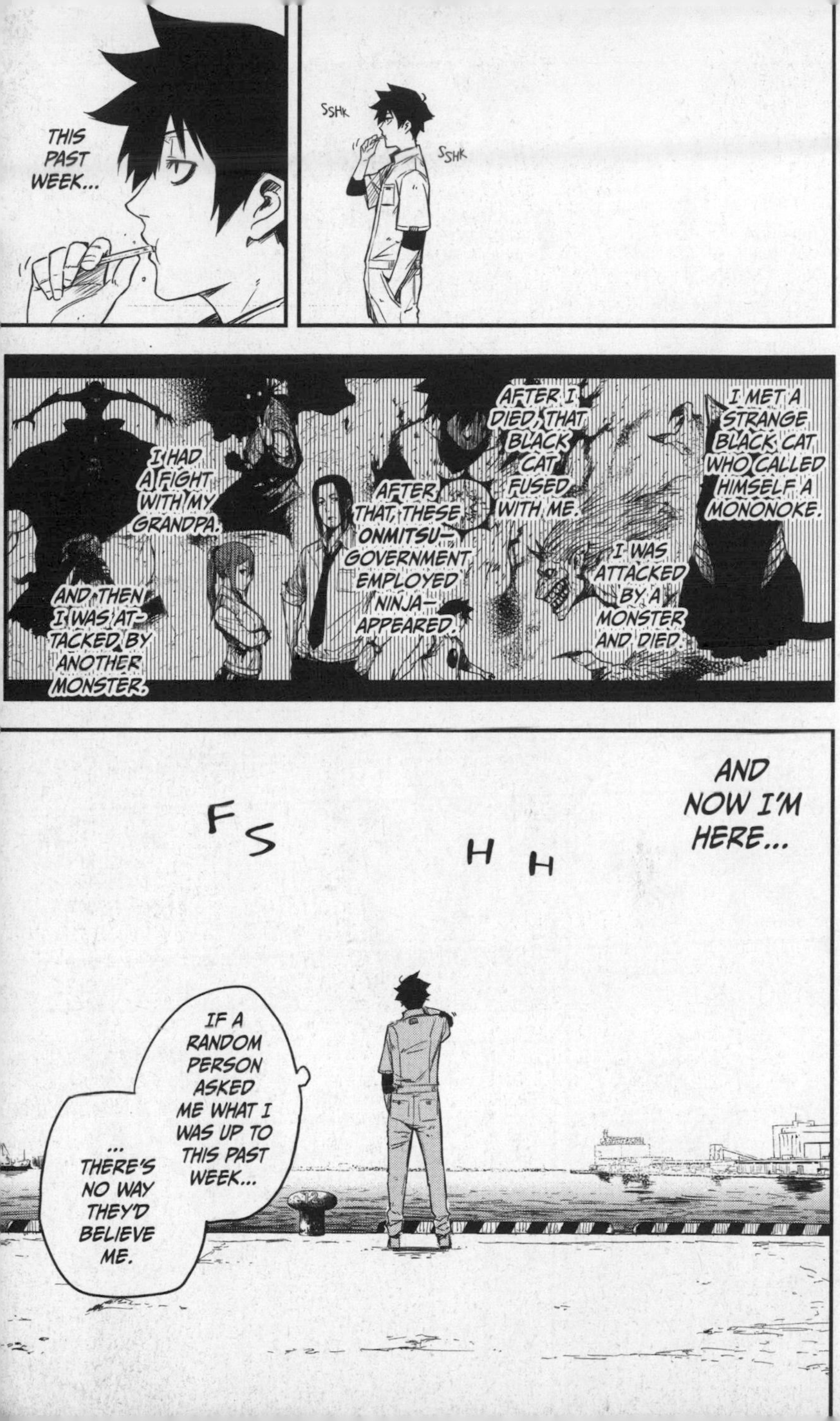
SSHK
SSHK
THIS PAST WEEK...
I MET A STRANGE BLACK CAT WHO CALLED HIMSELF A MONONOKE.
I WAS ATTACKED BY A MONSTER AND DIED.
AFTER I DIED, THAT BLACK CAT FUSED WITH ME.
AFTER THAT, THESE ONMITSU—GOVERNMENT EMPLOYED NINJA—APPEARED.
I HAD A FIGHT WITH MY GRANDPA.
AND THEN I WAS ATTACKED BY ANOTHER MONSTER.
AND NOW I'M HERE...
FSHH
IF A RANDOM PERSON ASKED ME WHAT I WAS UP TO THIS PAST WEEK...
...THERE'S NO WAY THEY'D BELIEVE ME.

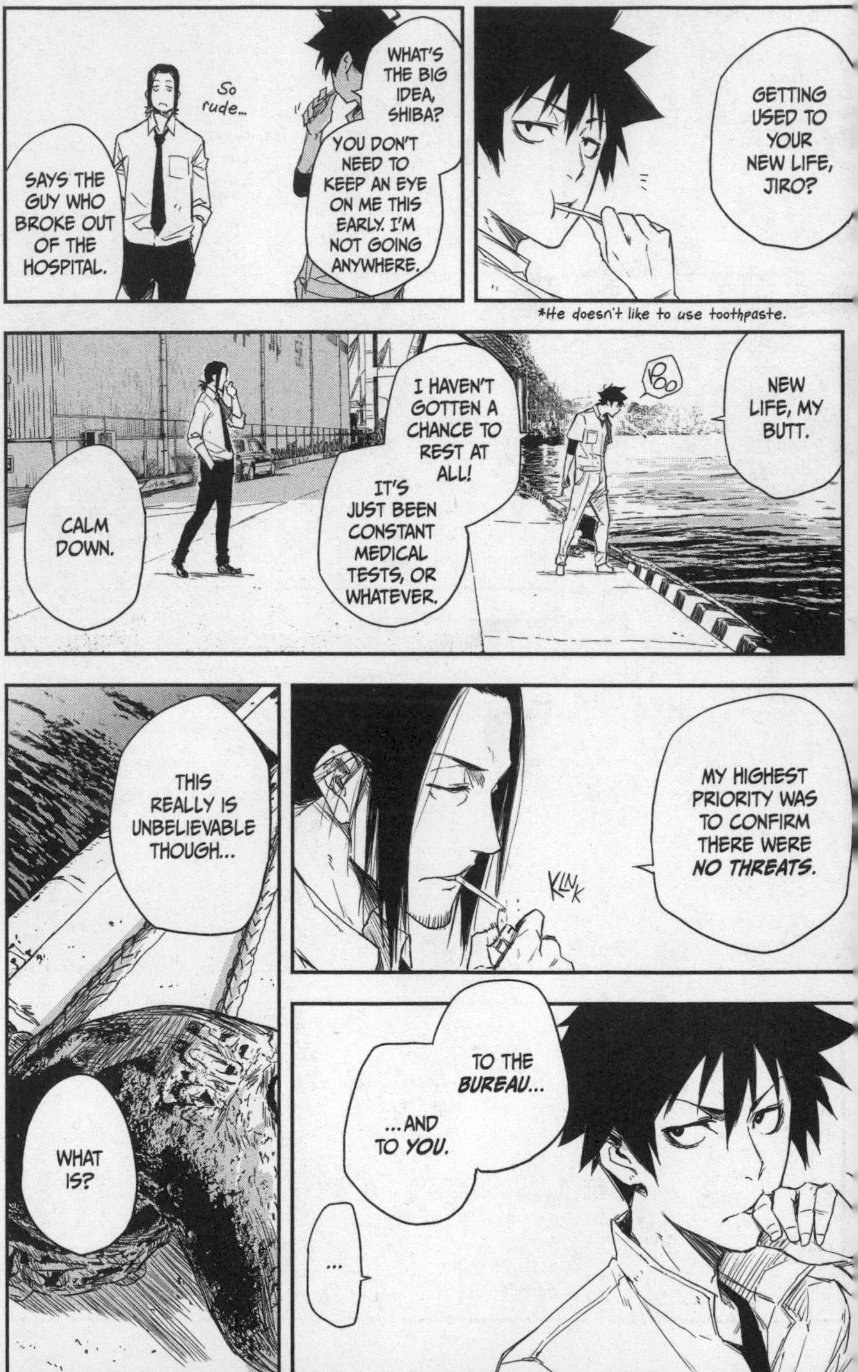
GETTING USED TO YOUR NEW LIFE, JIRO?
*He doesn't like to use toothpaste.
WHAT'S THE BIG IDEA, SHIBA?
YOU DON'T NEED TO KEEP AN EYE ON ME THIS EARLY. I'M NOT GOING ANYWHERE.
So rude...
SAYS THE GUY WHO BROKE OUT OF THE HOSPITAL.
NEW LIFE, MY BUTT.
I HAVEN'T GOTTEN A CHANCE TO REST AT ALL!
IT'S JUST BEEN CONSTANT MEDICAL TESTS, OR WHATEVER.
CALM DOWN.
MY HIGHEST PRIORITY WAS TO CONFIRM THERE WERE NO THREATS.
KLINK
TO THE BUREAU...
...AND TO YOU.
...
THIS REALLY IS UNBELIEVABLE THOUGH...
WHAT IS?

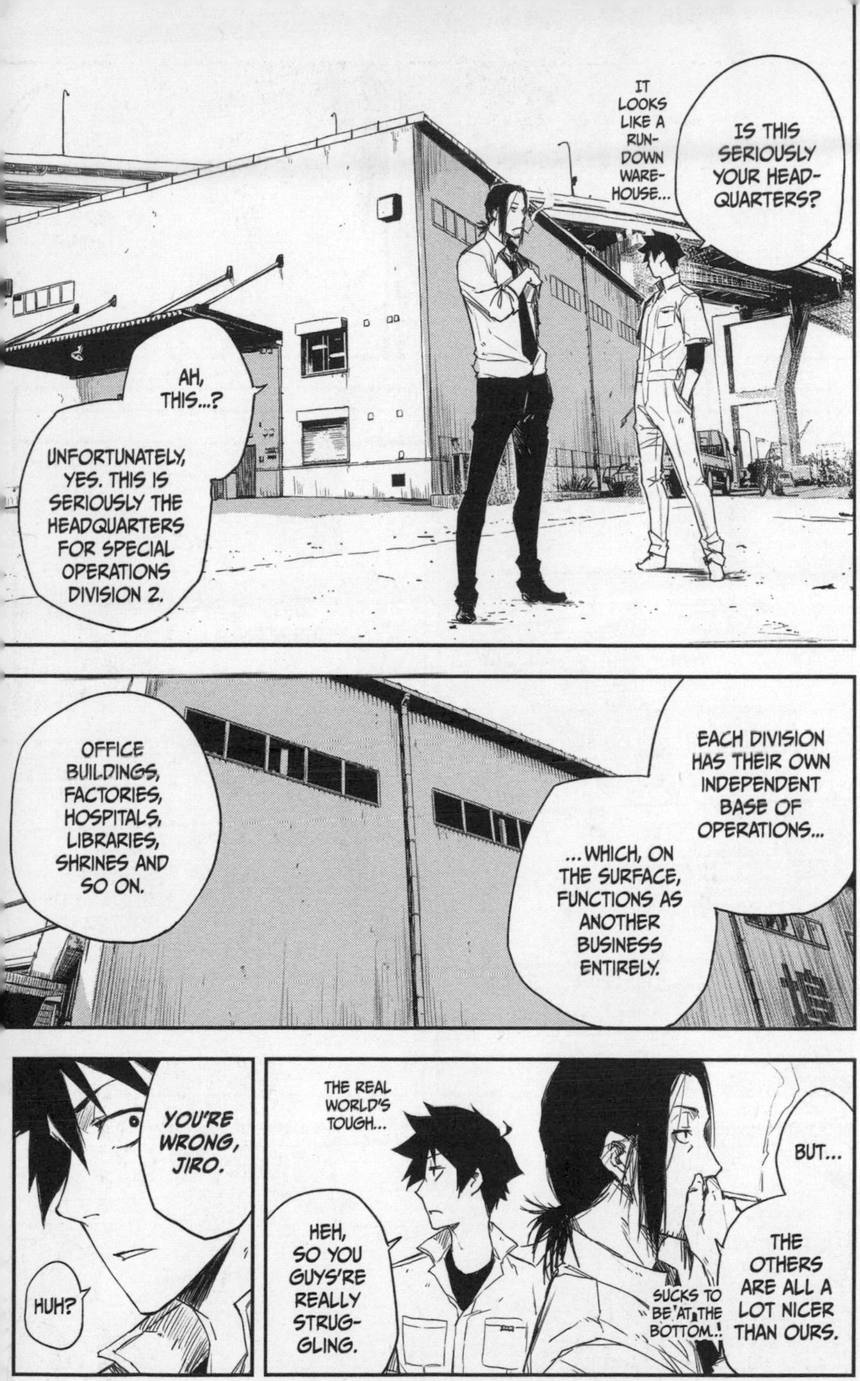
IS THIS SERIOUSLY YOUR HEAD-QUARTERS?
IT LOOKS LIKE A RUN-DOWN WARE-HOUSE...
AH, THIS...?
UNFORTUNATELY, YES. THIS IS SERIOUSLY THE HEADQUARTERS FOR SPECIAL OPERATIONS DIVISION 2.
EACH DIVISION HAS THEIR OWN INDEPENDENT BASE OF OPERATIONS...
...WHICH, ON THE SURFACE, FUNCTIONS AS ANOTHER BUSINESS ENTIRELY.
OFFICE BUILDINGS, FACTORIES, HOSPITALS, LIBRARIES, SHRINES AND SO ON.
HEH, SO YOU GUYS'RE REALLY STRUG-GLING.
THE REAL WORLD'S TOUGH...
BUT...
THE OTHERS ARE ALL A LOT NICER THAN OURS.
SUCKS TO BE AT THE BOTTOM..!
YOU'RE WRONG, JIRO.
HUH?

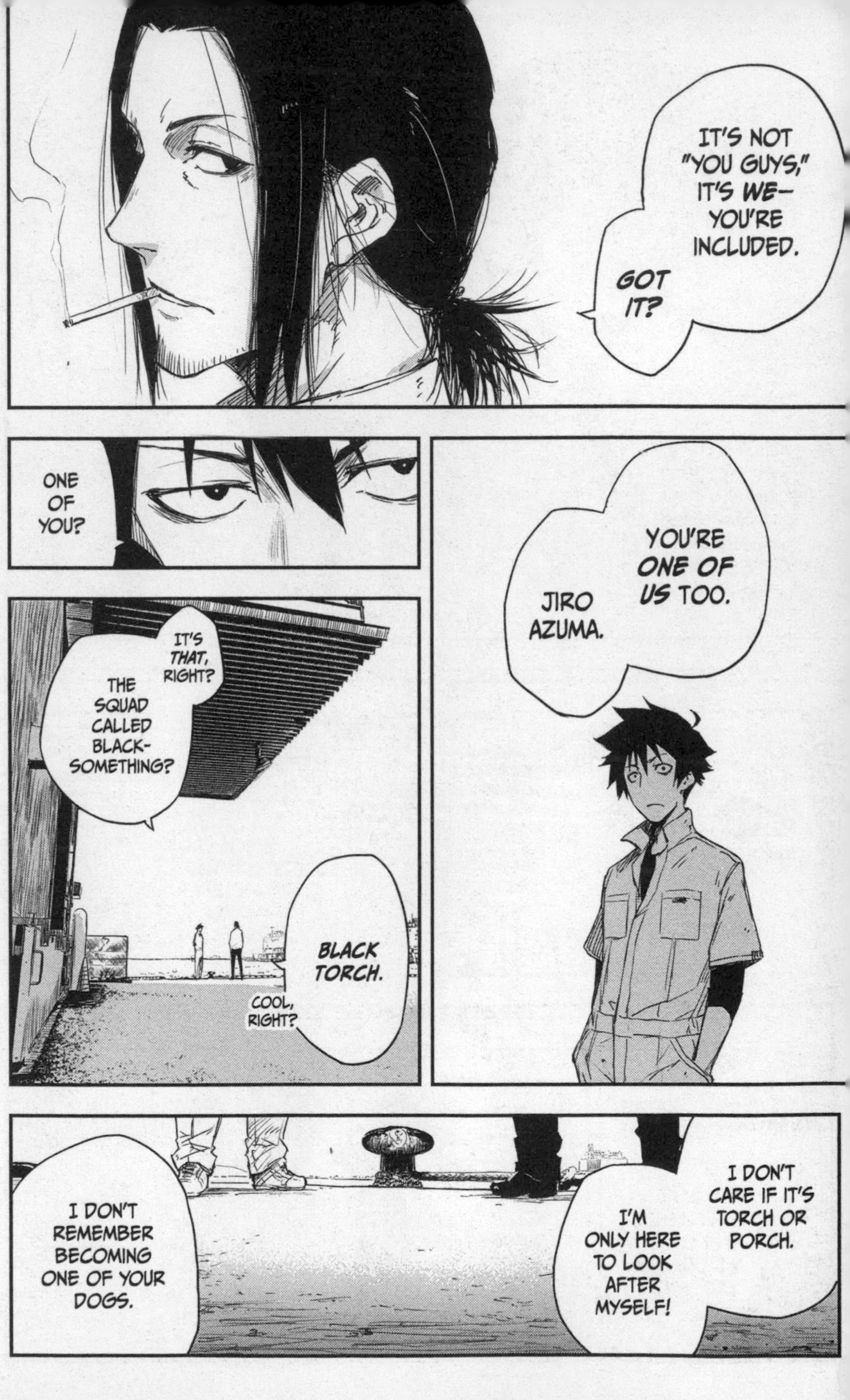
IT'S NOT "YOU GUYS," IT'S *WE*— YOU'RE INCLUDED.
GOT IT?
YOU'RE *ONE OF US* TOO.
JIRO AZUMA.
ONE OF YOU?
IT'S *THAT,* RIGHT?
THE SQUAD CALLED BLACK-SOMETHING?
BLACK TORCH.
COOL, RIGHT?
I DON'T CARE IF IT'S TORCH OR PORCH.
I'M ONLY HERE TO LOOK AFTER MYSELF!
I DON'T REMEMBER BECOMING ONE OF YOUR DOGS.

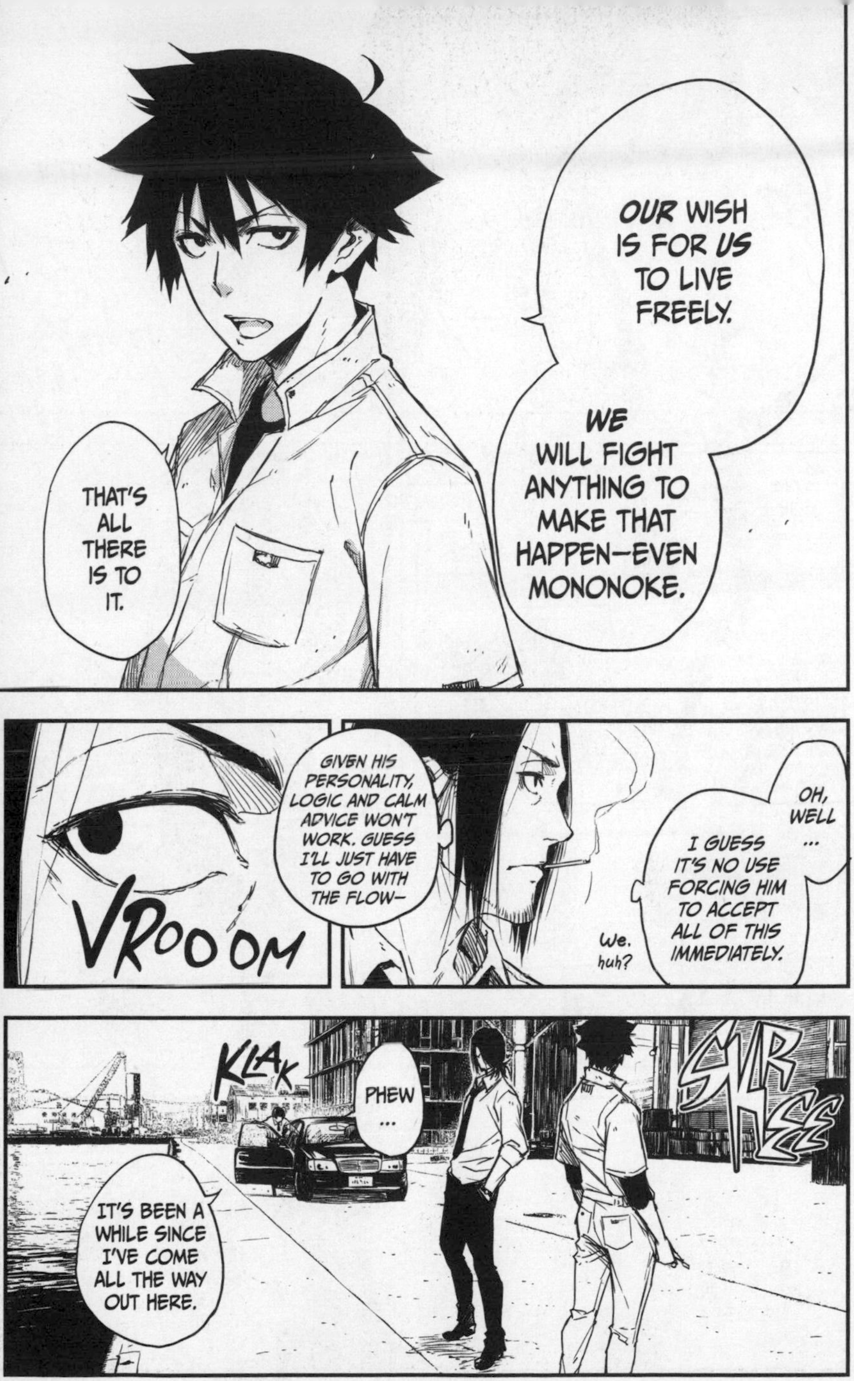
OUR WISH IS FOR US TO LIVE FREELY.
WE WILL FIGHT ANYTHING TO MAKE THAT HAPPEN—EVEN MONONOKE.
THAT'S ALL THERE IS TO IT.
OH, WELL ...
I GUESS IT'S NO USE FORCING HIM TO ACCEPT ALL OF THIS IMMEDIATELY.
We. huh?
GIVEN HIS PERSONALITY, LOGIC AND CALM ADVICE WON'T WORK. GUESS I'LL JUST HAVE TO GO WITH THE FLOW—
VROOOM
SKREE
PHEW ...
KLAK
IT'S BEEN A WHILE SINCE I'VE COME ALL THE WAY OUT HERE.

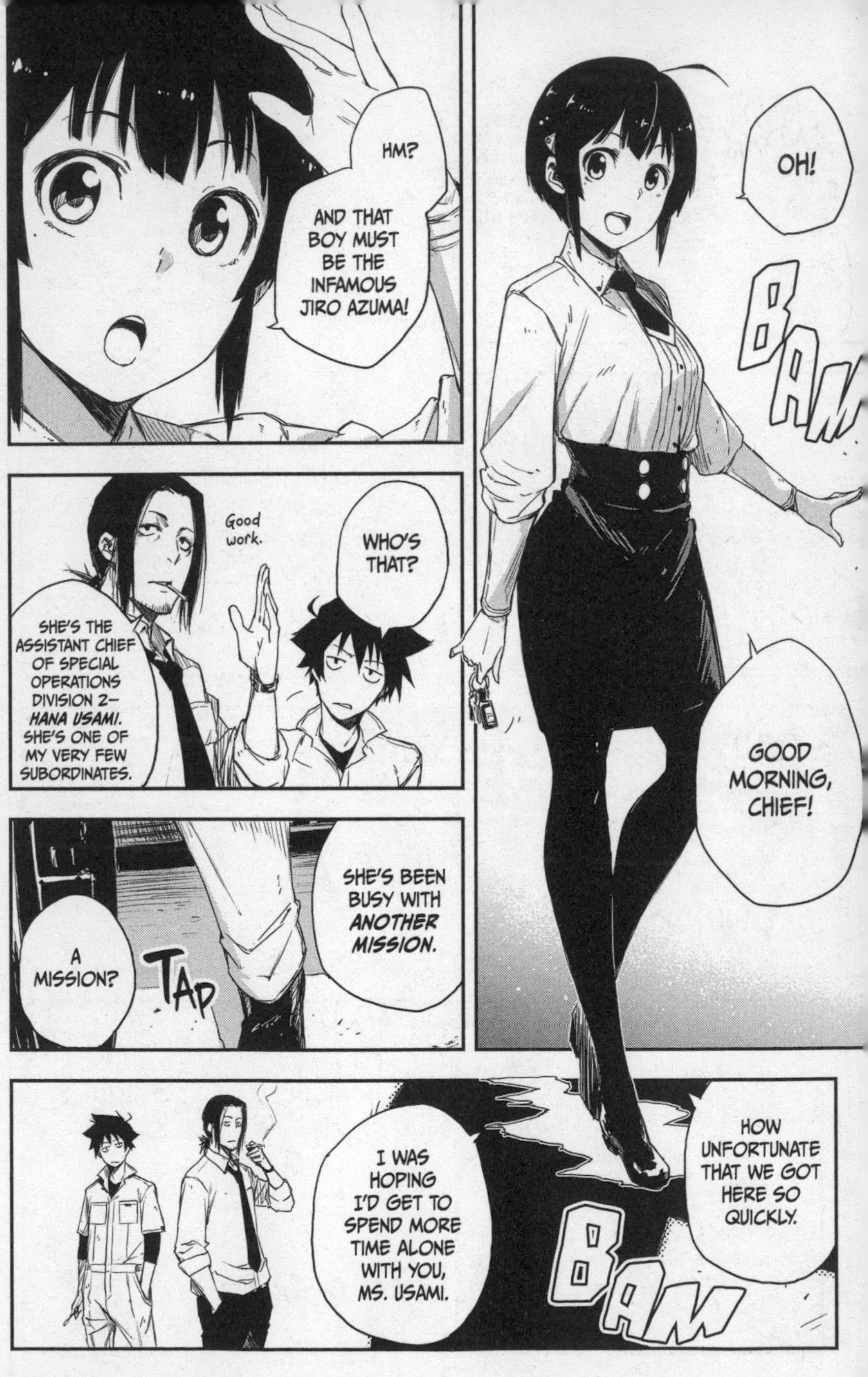
OH!
BAM
GOOD MORNING, CHIEF!
HM?
AND THAT BOY MUST BE THE INFAMOUS JIRO AZUMA!
WHO'S THAT?
Good work.
SHE'S THE ASSISTANT CHIEF OF SPECIAL OPERATIONS DIVISION 2— *HANA USAMI*. SHE'S ONE OF MY VERY FEW SUBORDINATES.
SHE'S BEEN BUSY WITH *ANOTHER MISSION*.
TAP
A MISSION?
HOW UNFORTUNATE THAT WE GOT HERE SO QUICKLY.
BAM
I WAS HOPING I'D GET TO SPEND MORE TIME ALONE WITH YOU, MS. USAMI.

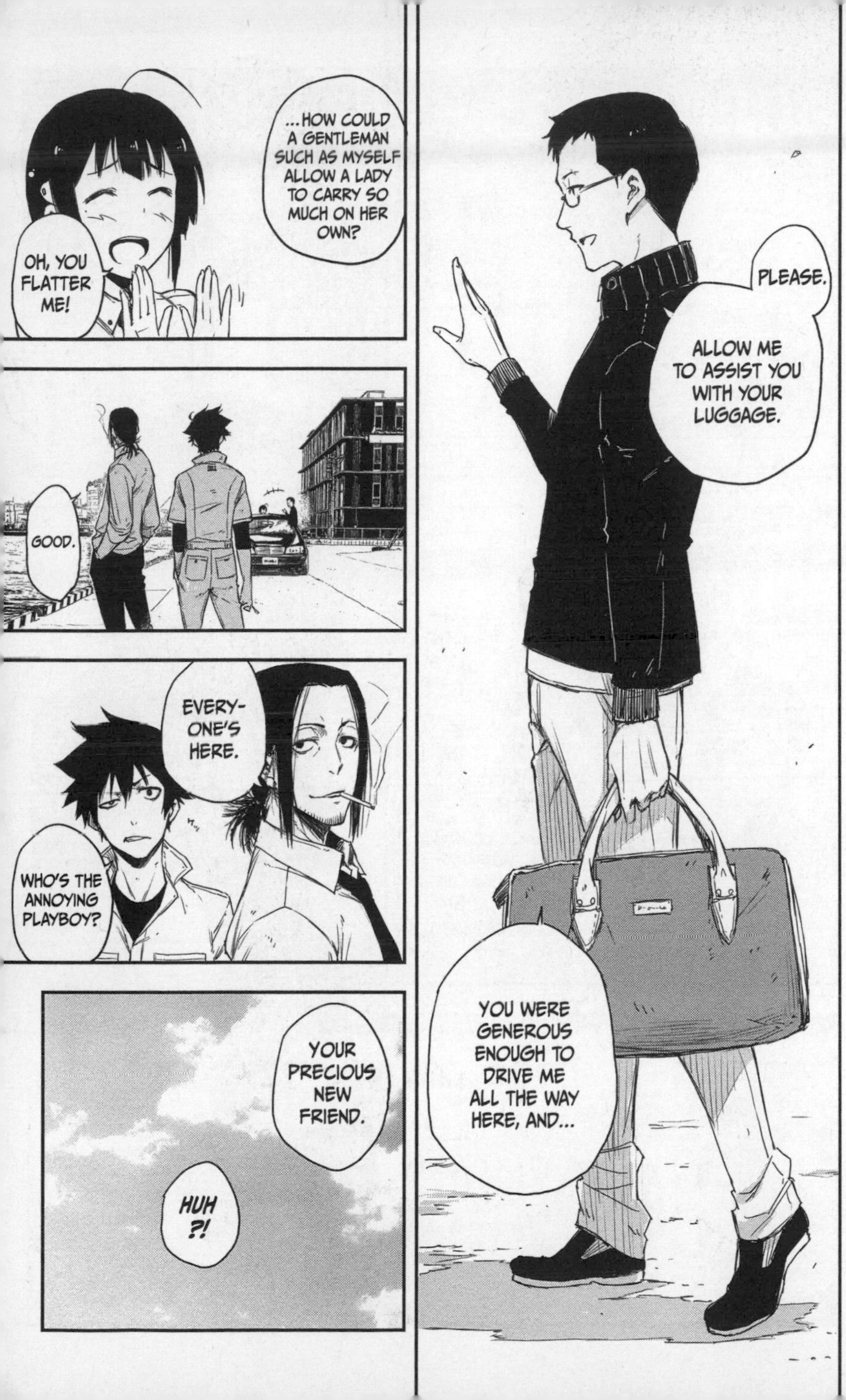
PLEASE.
ALLOW ME TO ASSIST YOU WITH YOUR LUGGAGE.
YOU WERE GENEROUS ENOUGH TO DRIVE ME ALL THE WAY HERE, AND...
...HOW COULD A GENTLEMAN SUCH AS MYSELF ALLOW A LADY TO CARRY SO MUCH ON HER OWN?
OH, YOU FLATTER ME!
GOOD.
EVERY-ONE'S HERE.
WHO'S THE ANNOYING PLAYBOY?
YOUR PRECIOUS NEW FRIEND.
HUH ?!

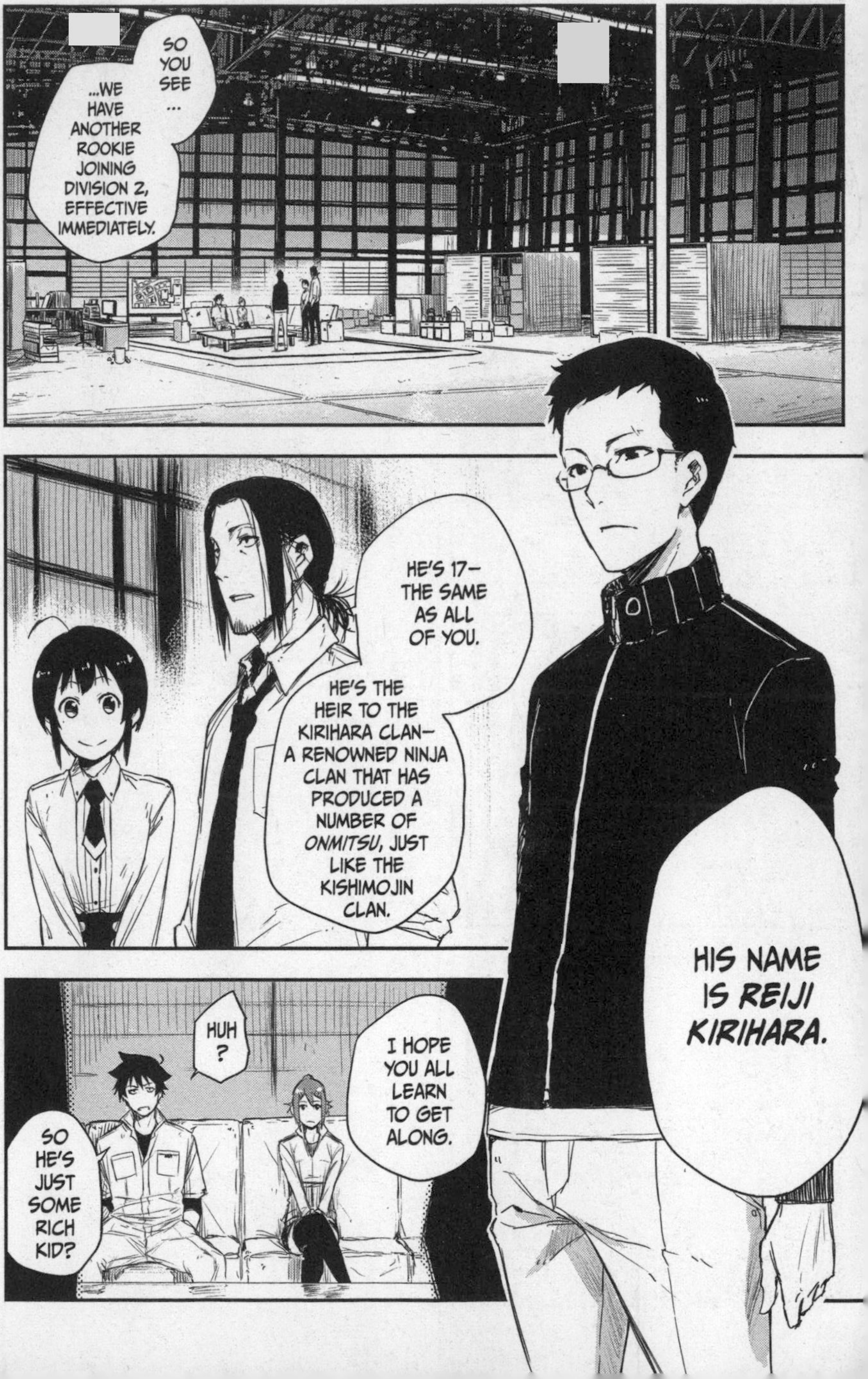
SO YOU SEE ...
...WE HAVE ANOTHER ROOKIE JOINING DIVISION 2, EFFECTIVE IMMEDIATELY.
HE'S 17— THE SAME AS ALL OF YOU.
HE'S THE HEIR TO THE KIRIHARA CLAN— A RENOWNED NINJA CLAN THAT HAS PRODUCED A NUMBER OF *ONMITSU*, JUST LIKE THE KISHIMOJIN CLAN.
HIS NAME IS *REIJI KIRIHARA.*
I HOPE YOU ALL LEARN TO GET ALONG.
HUH?
SO HE'S JUST SOME RICH KID?

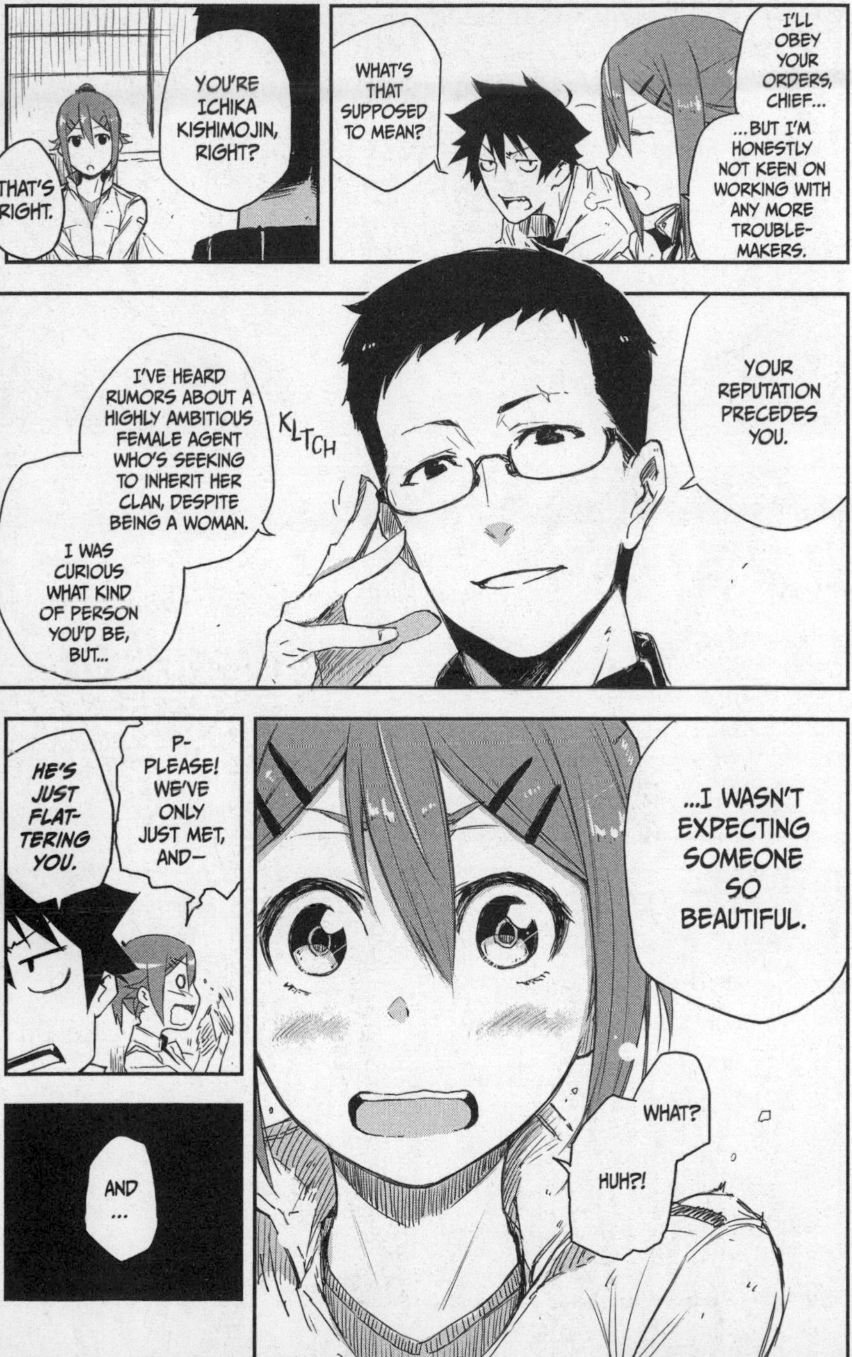
I'LL OBEY YOUR ORDERS, CHIEF...
...BUT I'M HONESTLY NOT KEEN ON WORKING WITH ANY MORE TROUBLE-MAKERS.
WHAT'S THAT SUPPOSED TO MEAN?
YOU'RE ICHIKA KISHIMOJIN, RIGHT?
THAT'S RIGHT.
YOUR REPUTATION PRECEDES YOU.
I'VE HEARD RUMORS ABOUT A HIGHLY AMBITIOUS FEMALE AGENT WHO'S SEEKING TO INHERIT HER CLAN, DESPITE BEING A WOMAN.
KLTCH
I WAS CURIOUS WHAT KIND OF PERSON YOU'D BE, BUT...
...I WASN'T EXPECTING SOMEONE SO BEAUTIFUL.
WHAT?
HUH?!
P-PLEASE! WE'VE ONLY JUST MET, AND—
HE'S JUST FLATTERING YOU.
AND ...

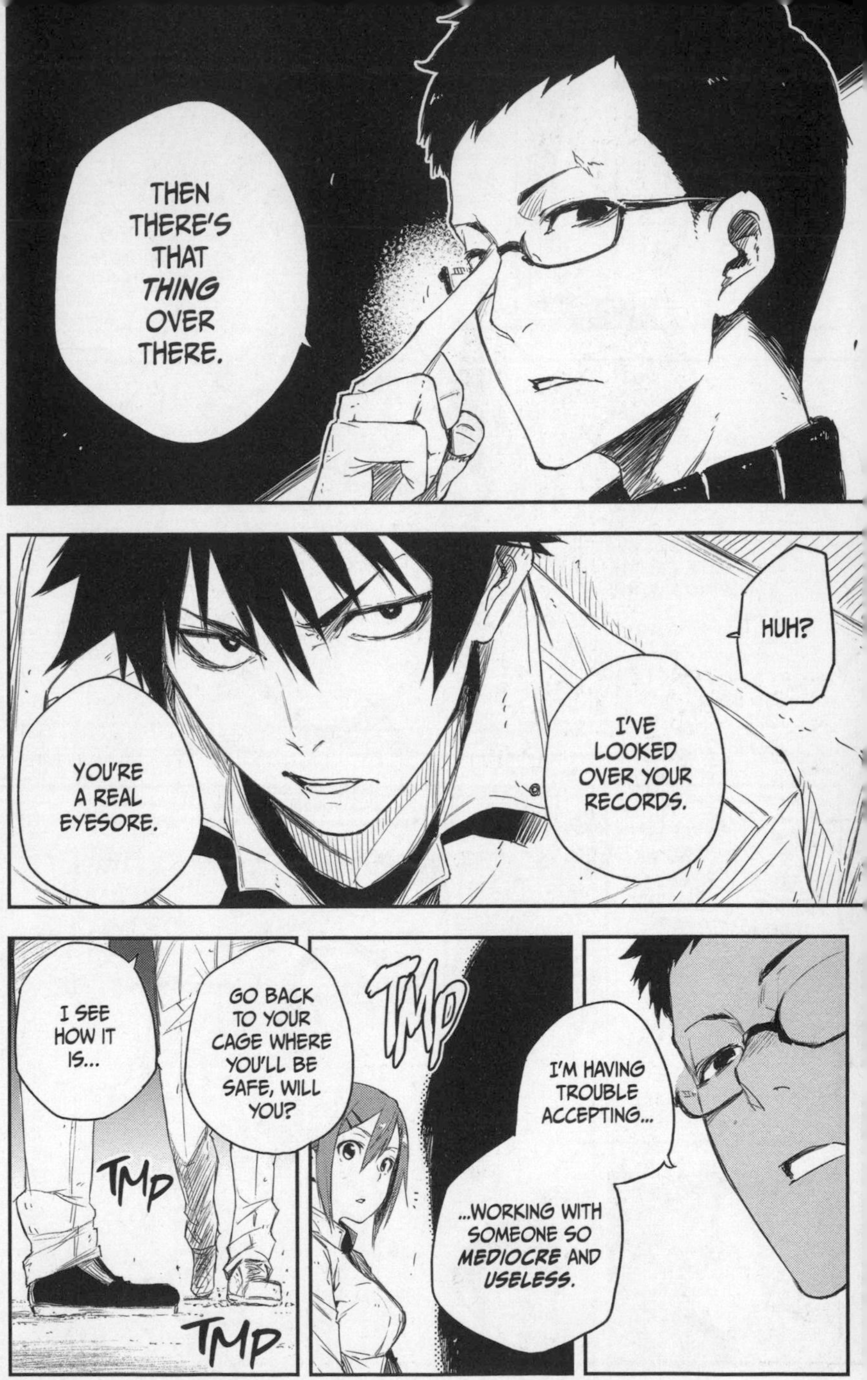
THEN THERE'S THAT *THING* OVER THERE.
HUH?
I'VE LOOKED OVER YOUR RECORDS.
YOU'RE A REAL EYESORE.
I'M HAVING TROUBLE ACCEPTING...
...WORKING WITH SOMEONE SO *MEDIOCRE* AND *USELESS*.
TMP
GO BACK TO YOUR CAGE WHERE YOU'LL BE SAFE, WILL YOU?
I SEE HOW IT IS...
TMP
TMP

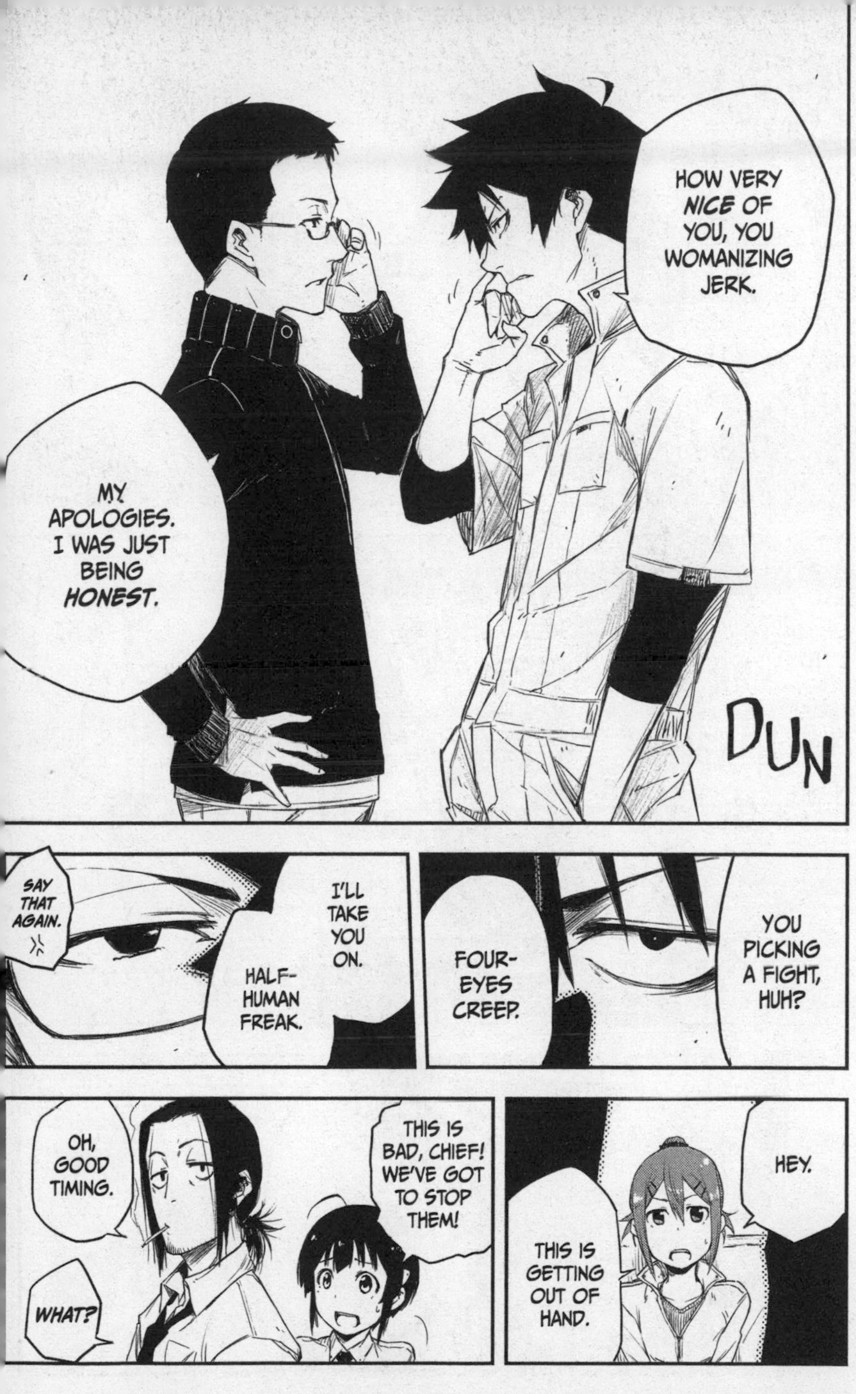
HOW VERY *NICE* OF YOU, YOU WOMANIZING JERK.
MY APOLOGIES. I WAS JUST BEING *HONEST*.
DUN
YOU PICKING A FIGHT, HUH?
FOUR-EYES CREEP.
I'LL TAKE YOU ON.
HALF-HUMAN FREAK.
SAY THAT AGAIN.
HEY.
THIS IS GETTING OUT OF HAND.
THIS IS BAD, CHIEF! WE'VE GOT TO STOP THEM!
OH, GOOD TIMING.
WHAT?

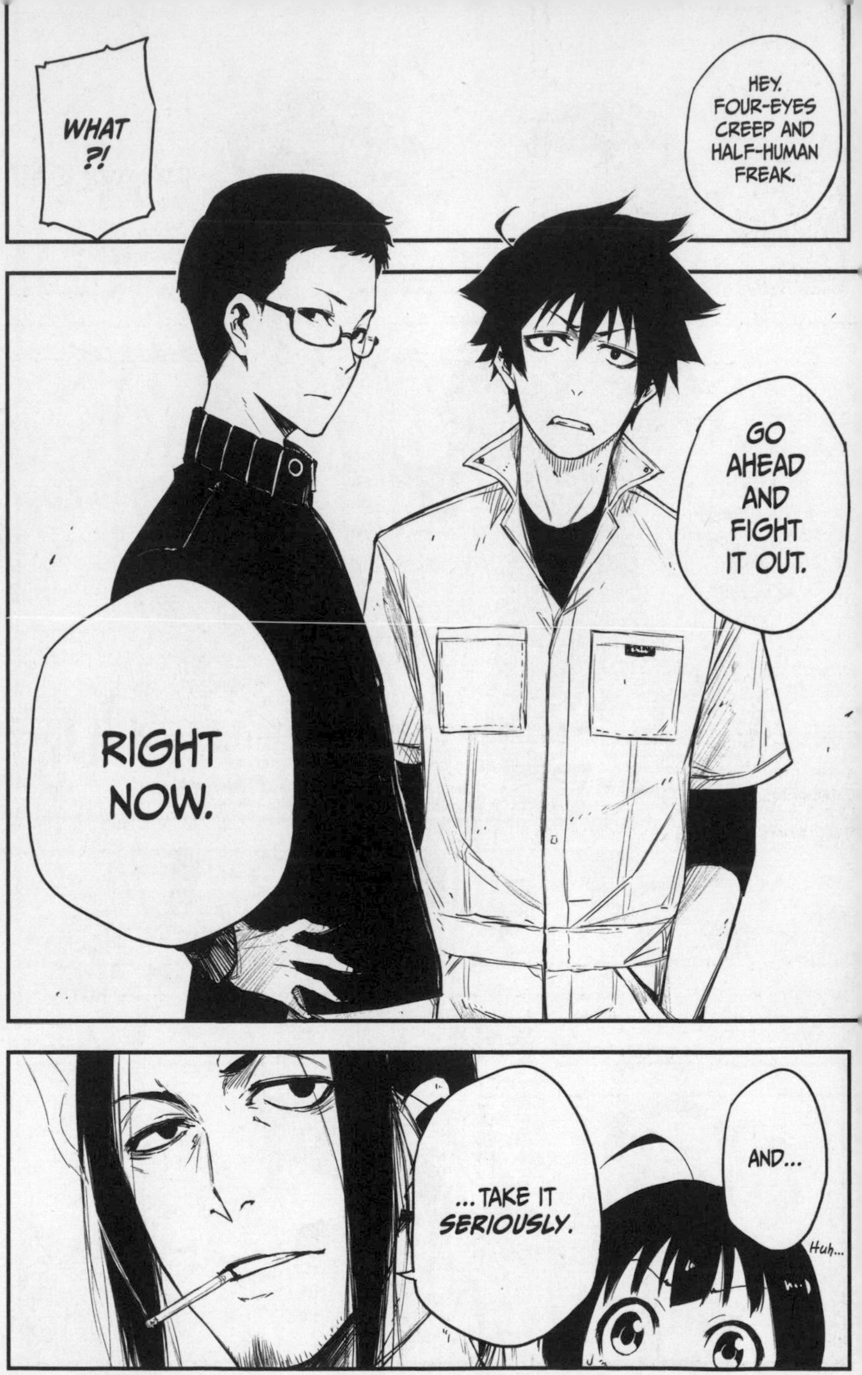
HEY. FOUR-EYES CREEP AND HALF-HUMAN FREAK.
WHAT ?!
GO AHEAD AND FIGHT IT OUT.
RIGHT NOW.
AND...
Huh...
...TAKE IT SERIOUSLY.

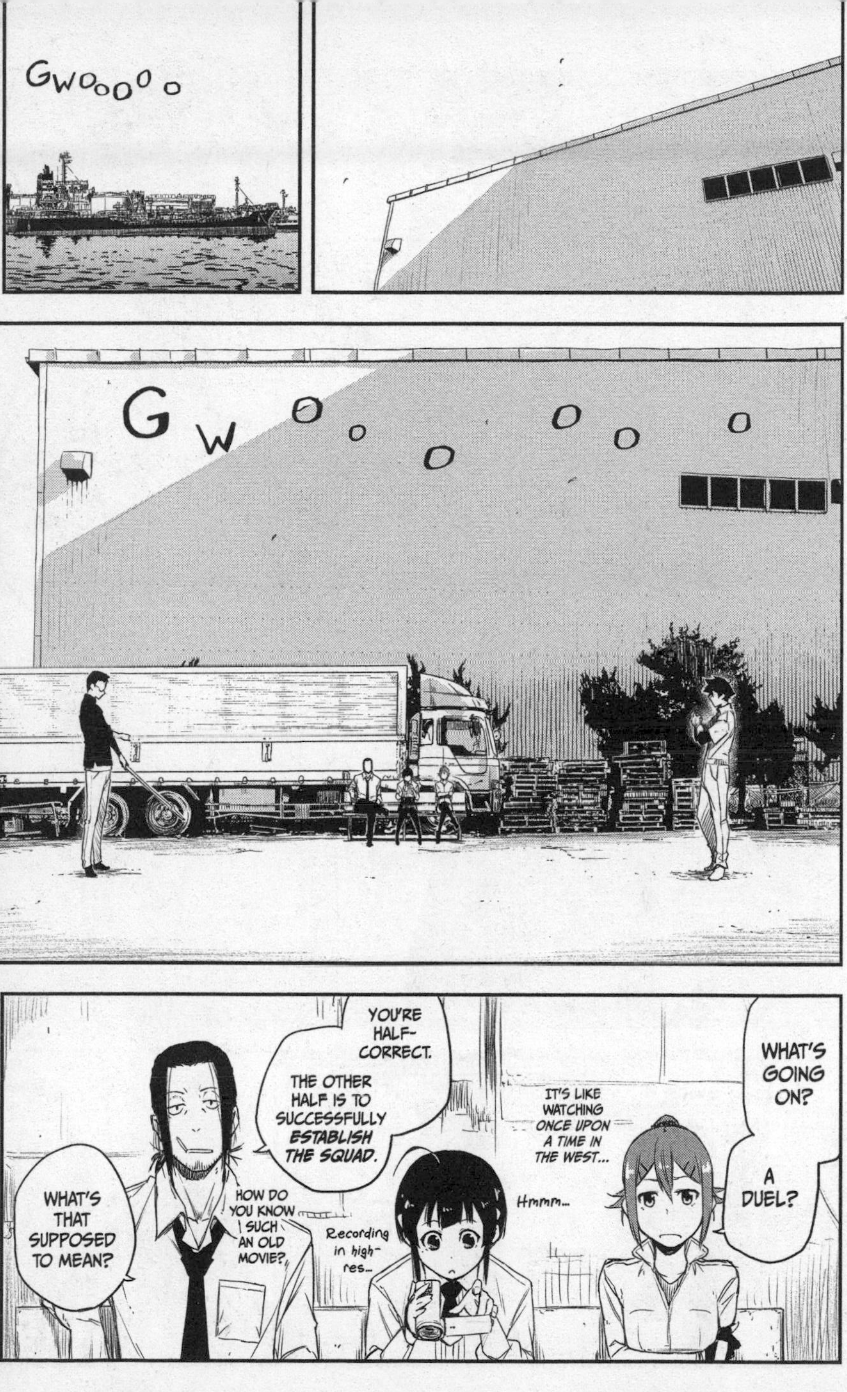
GWOooooo
GWOOOOOO
WHAT'S GOING ON?
A DUEL?
IT'S LIKE WATCHING ONCE UPON A TIME IN THE WEST...
Hmmm...
YOU'RE HALF-CORRECT.
THE OTHER HALF IS TO SUCCESSFULLY ESTABLISH THE SQUAD.
Recording in high-res...
HOW DO YOU KNOW SUCH AN OLD MOVIE?
WHAT'S THAT SUPPOSED TO MEAN?

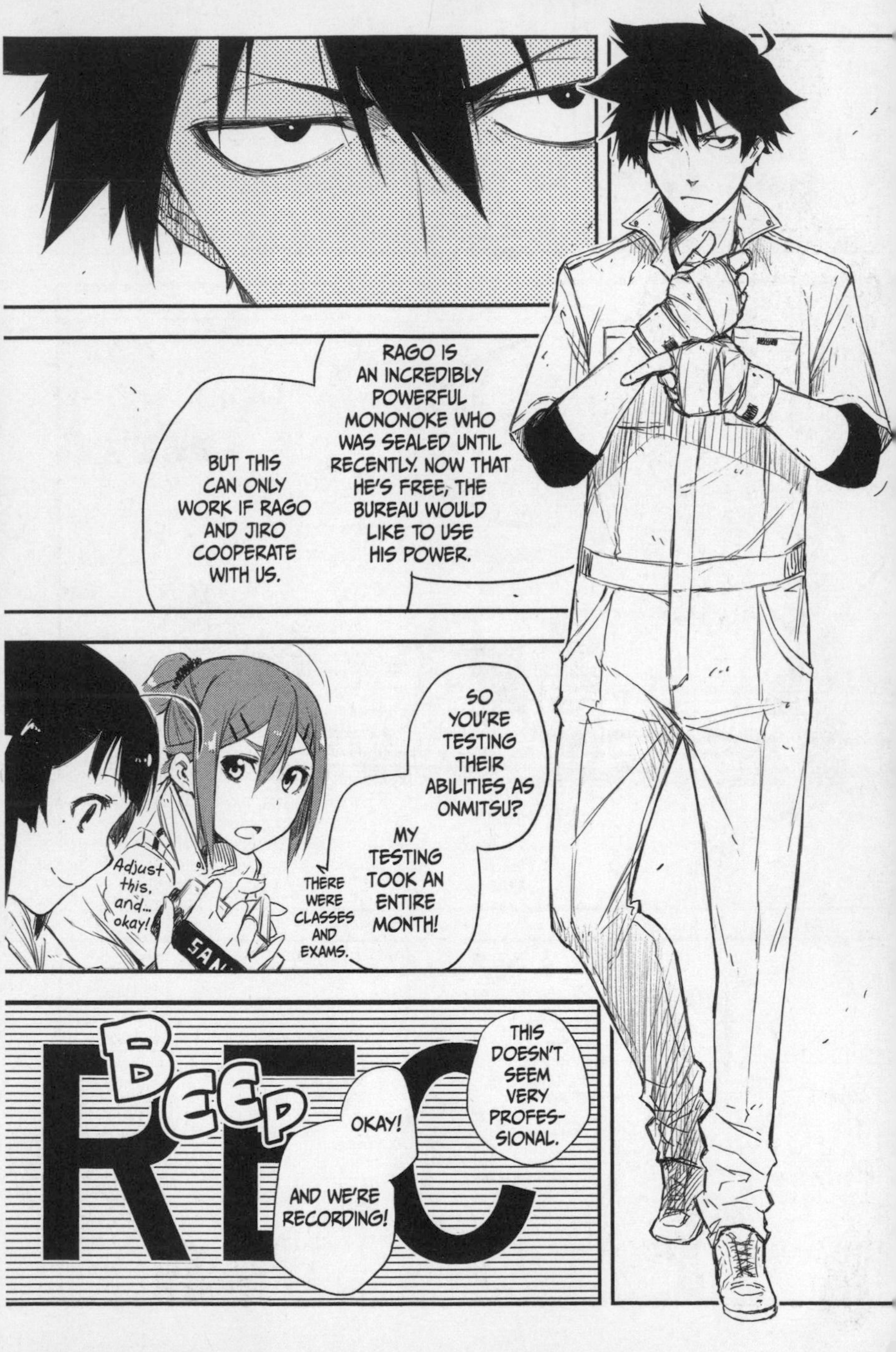
RAGO IS AN INCREDIBLY POWERFUL MONONOKE WHO WAS SEALED UNTIL RECENTLY. NOW THAT HE'S FREE, THE BUREAU WOULD LIKE TO USE HIS POWER.
BUT THIS CAN ONLY WORK IF RAGO AND JIRO COOPERATE WITH US.
SO YOU'RE TESTING THEIR ABILITIES AS ONMITSU?
MY TESTING TOOK AN ENTIRE MONTH!
THERE WERE CLASSES AND EXAMS.
Adjust this, and... okay!
THIS DOESN'T SEEM VERY PROFES-SIONAL.
OKAY!
BEEP
AND WE'RE RECORDING!
REC

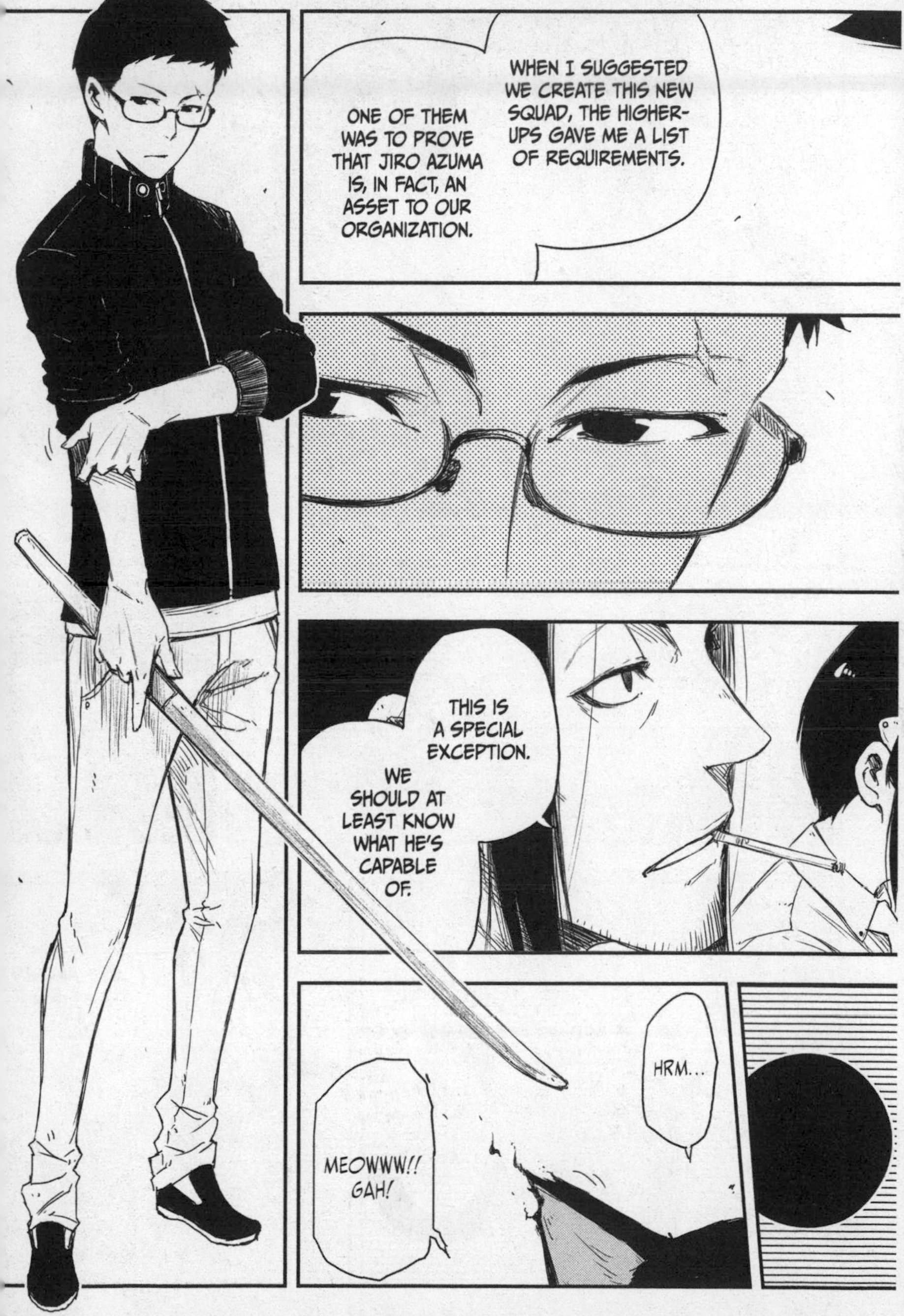
WHEN I SUGGESTED WE CREATE THIS NEW SQUAD, THE HIGHER-UPS GAVE ME A LIST OF REQUIREMENTS.
ONE OF THEM WAS TO PROVE THAT JIRO AZUMA IS, IN FACT, AN ASSET TO OUR ORGANIZATION.
THIS IS A SPECIAL EXCEPTION.
WE SHOULD AT LEAST KNOW WHAT HE'S CAPABLE OF.
HRM...
MEOWWW!! GAH!

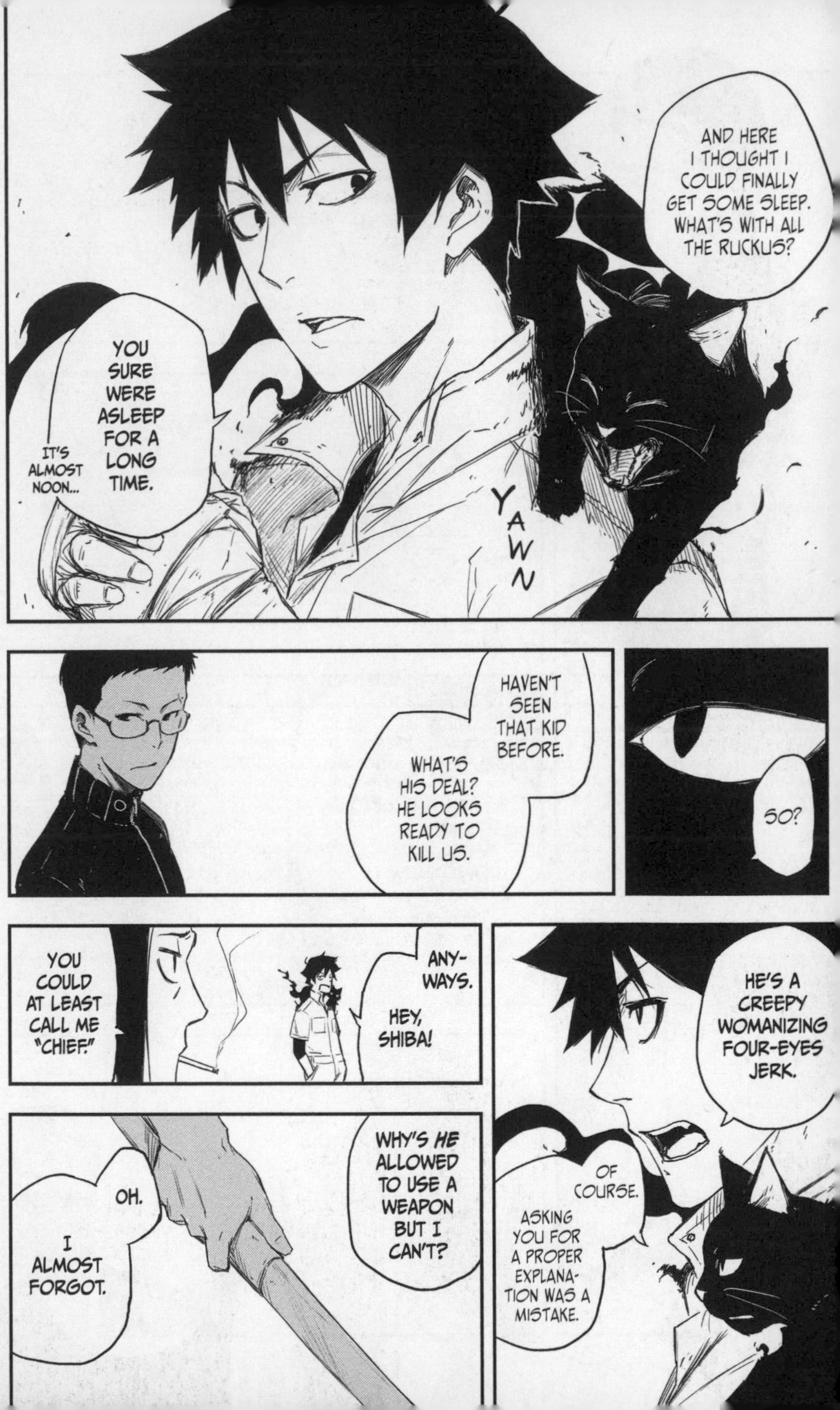
AND HERE I THOUGHT I COULD FINALLY GET SOME SLEEP. WHAT'S WITH ALL THE RUCKUS?
YAWN
YOU SURE WERE ASLEEP FOR A LONG TIME.
IT'S ALMOST NOON...
SO?
HAVEN'T SEEN THAT KID BEFORE.
WHAT'S HIS DEAL? HE LOOKS READY TO KILL US.
HE'S A CREEPY WOMANIZING FOUR-EYES JERK.
OF COURSE.
ASKING YOU FOR A PROPER EXPLANA-TION WAS A MISTAKE.
ANY-WAYS.
HEY, SHIBA!
YOU COULD AT LEAST CALL ME "CHIEF."
WHY'S HE ALLOWED TO USE A WEAPON BUT I CAN'T?
OH.
I ALMOST FORGOT.

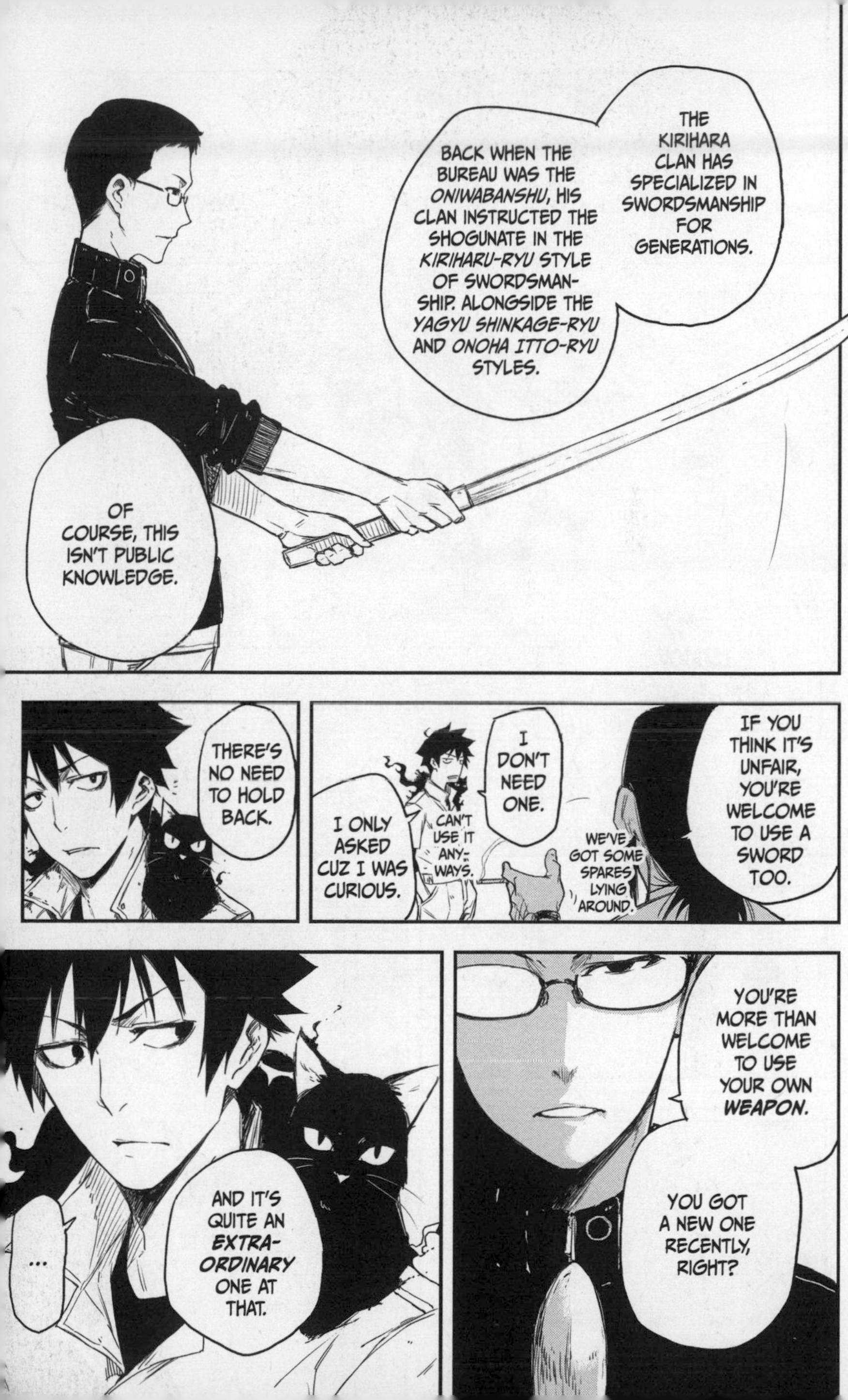
THE KIRIHARA CLAN HAS SPECIALIZED IN SWORDSMANSHIP FOR GENERATIONS.
BACK WHEN THE BUREAU WAS THE *ONIWABANSHU*, HIS CLAN INSTRUCTED THE SHOGUNATE IN THE *KIRIHARU-RYU* STYLE OF SWORDSMANSHIP. ALONGSIDE THE *YAGYU SHINKAGE-RYU* AND *ONOHA ITTO-RYU* STYLES.
OF COURSE, THIS ISN'T PUBLIC KNOWLEDGE.
IF YOU THINK IT'S UNFAIR, YOU'RE WELCOME TO USE A SWORD TOO.
WE'VE GOT SOME SPARES LYING AROUND.
I DON'T NEED ONE.
CAN'T USE IT ANYWAYS.
I ONLY ASKED CUZ I WAS CURIOUS.
THERE'S NO NEED TO HOLD BACK.
YOU'RE MORE THAN WELCOME TO USE YOUR OWN ***WEAPON***.
YOU GOT A NEW ONE RECENTLY, RIGHT?
AND IT'S QUITE AN ***EXTRA-ORDINARY*** ONE AT THAT.
...

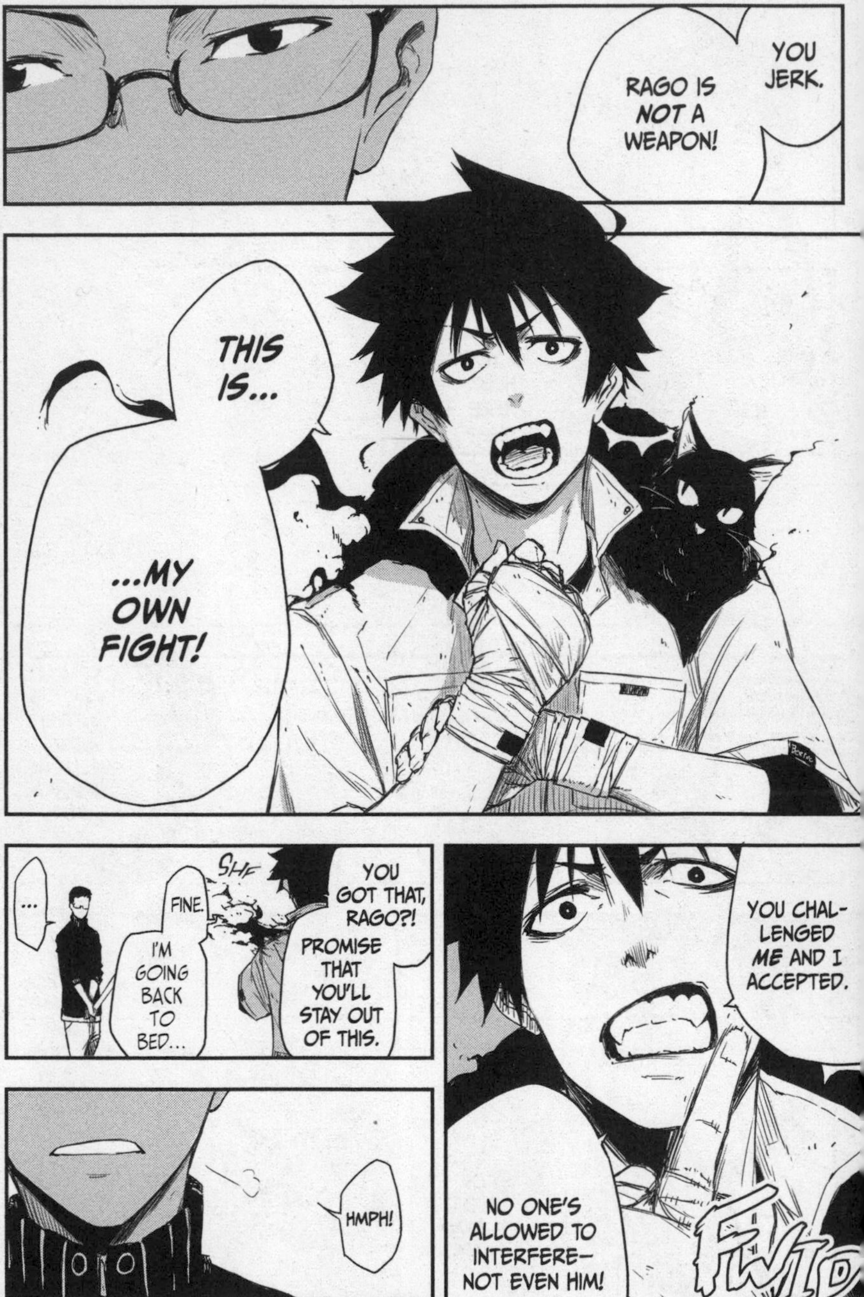
YOU JERK.
RAGO IS NOT A WEAPON!
THIS IS...
...MY OWN FIGHT!
YOU CHALLENGED ME AND I ACCEPTED.
NO ONE'S ALLOWED TO INTERFERE—NOT EVEN HIM!
FWIP
SHF
YOU GOT THAT, RAGO?!
PROMISE THAT YOU'LL STAY OUT OF THIS.
FINE.
I'M GOING BACK TO BED...
...
HMPH!

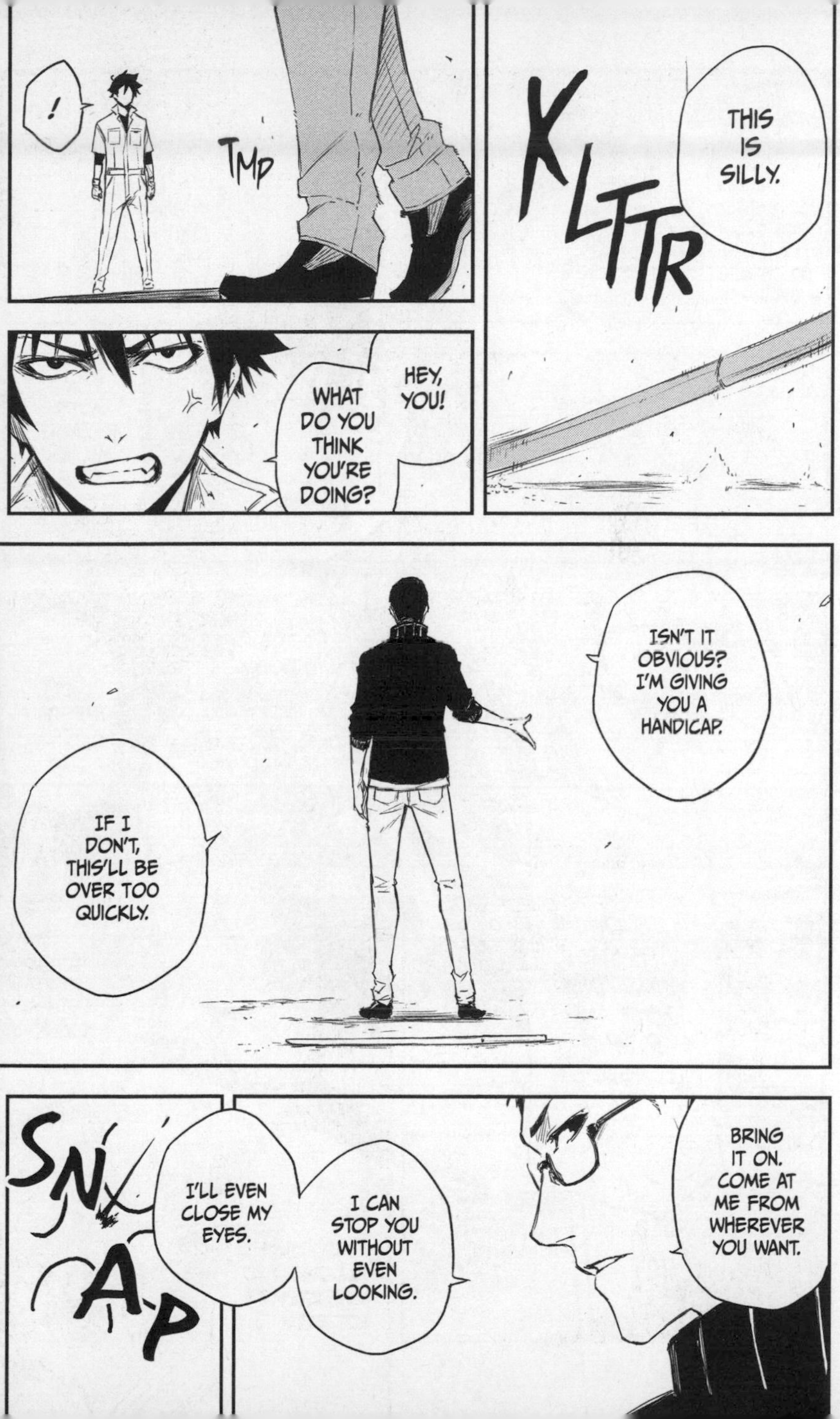
KLTTR
THIS IS SILLY.
TMP
!
HEY, YOU!
WHAT DO YOU THINK YOU'RE DOING?
ISN'T IT OBVIOUS? I'M GIVING YOU A HANDICAP.
IF I DON'T, THIS'LL BE OVER TOO QUICKLY.
BRING IT ON. COME AT ME FROM WHEREVER YOU WANT.
I CAN STOP YOU WITHOUT EVEN LOOKING.
I'LL EVEN CLOSE MY EYES.
SNAP

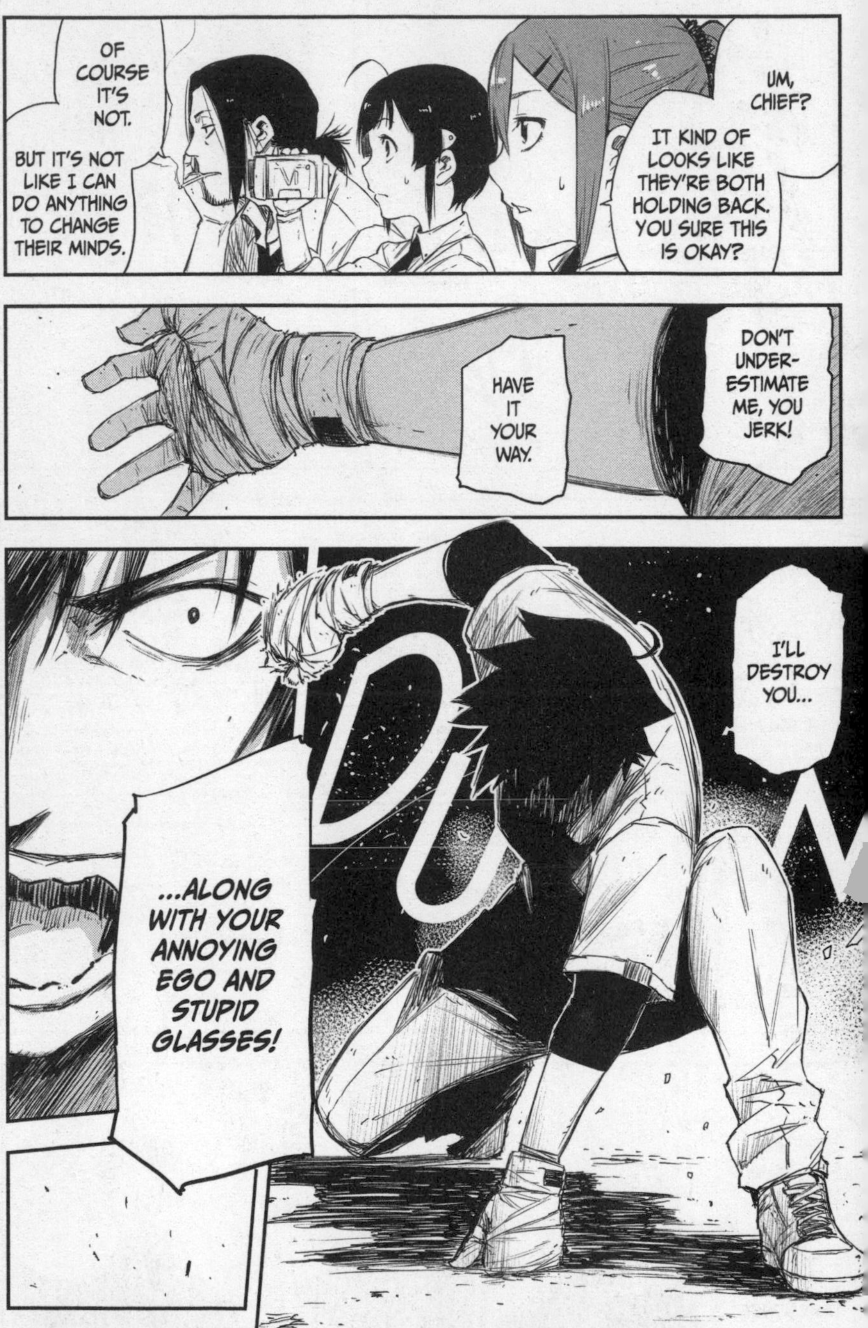
UM, CHIEF?
IT KIND OF LOOKS LIKE THEY'RE BOTH HOLDING BACK. YOU SURE THIS IS OKAY?
OF COURSE IT'S NOT.
BUT IT'S NOT LIKE I CAN DO ANYTHING TO CHANGE THEIR MINDS.
DON'T UNDER-ESTIMATE ME, YOU JERK!
HAVE IT YOUR WAY.
I'LL DESTROY YOU...
...ALONG WITH YOUR ANNOYING EGO AND STUPID GLASSES!

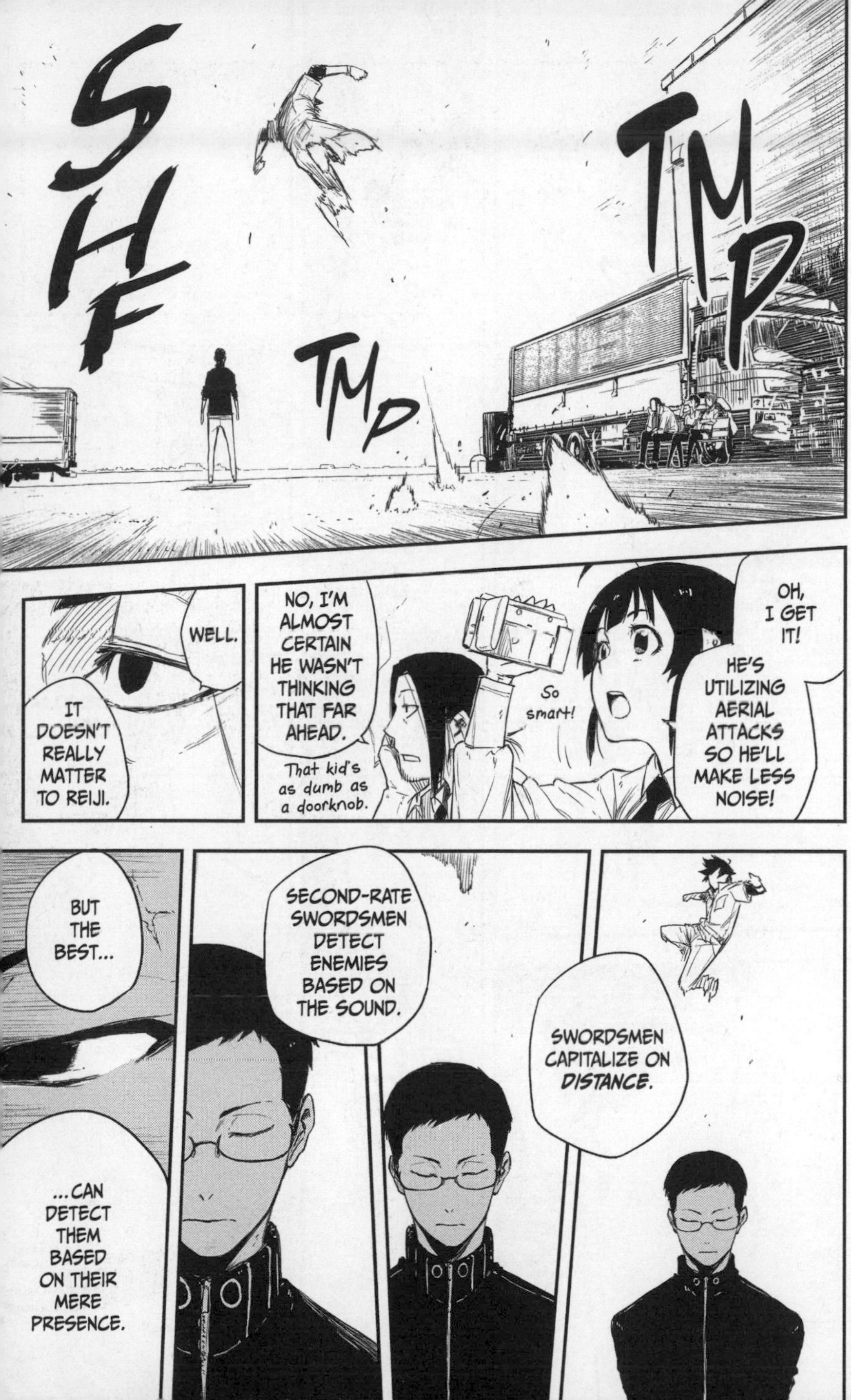
TMP
TMP
SHF
OH, I GET IT!
HE'S UTILIZING AERIAL ATTACKS SO HE'LL MAKE LESS NOISE!
So smart!
NO, I'M ALMOST CERTAIN HE WASN'T THINKING THAT FAR AHEAD.
That kid's as dumb as a doorknob.
WELL.
IT DOESN'T REALLY MATTER TO REIJI.
SWORDSMEN CAPITALIZE ON *DISTANCE*.
SECOND-RATE SWORDSMEN DETECT ENEMIES BASED ON THE SOUND.
BUT THE BEST...
...CAN DETECT THEM BASED ON THEIR MERE PRESENCE.

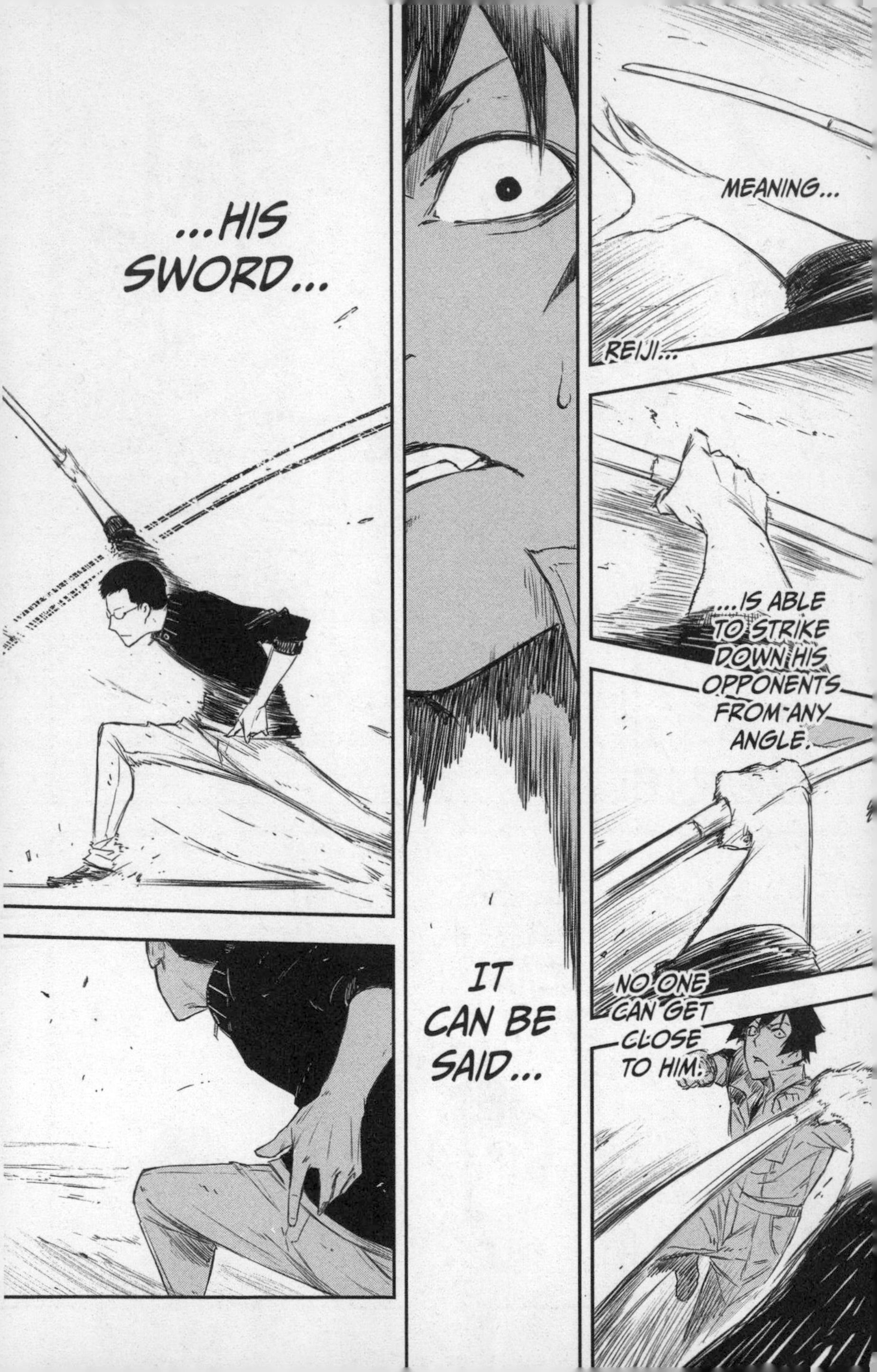
MEANING...
REIJI...
...IS ABLE TO STRIKE DOWN HIS OPPONENTS FROM ANY ANGLE.
NO ONE CAN GET CLOSE TO HIM.
IT CAN BE SAID...
...HIS SWORD...

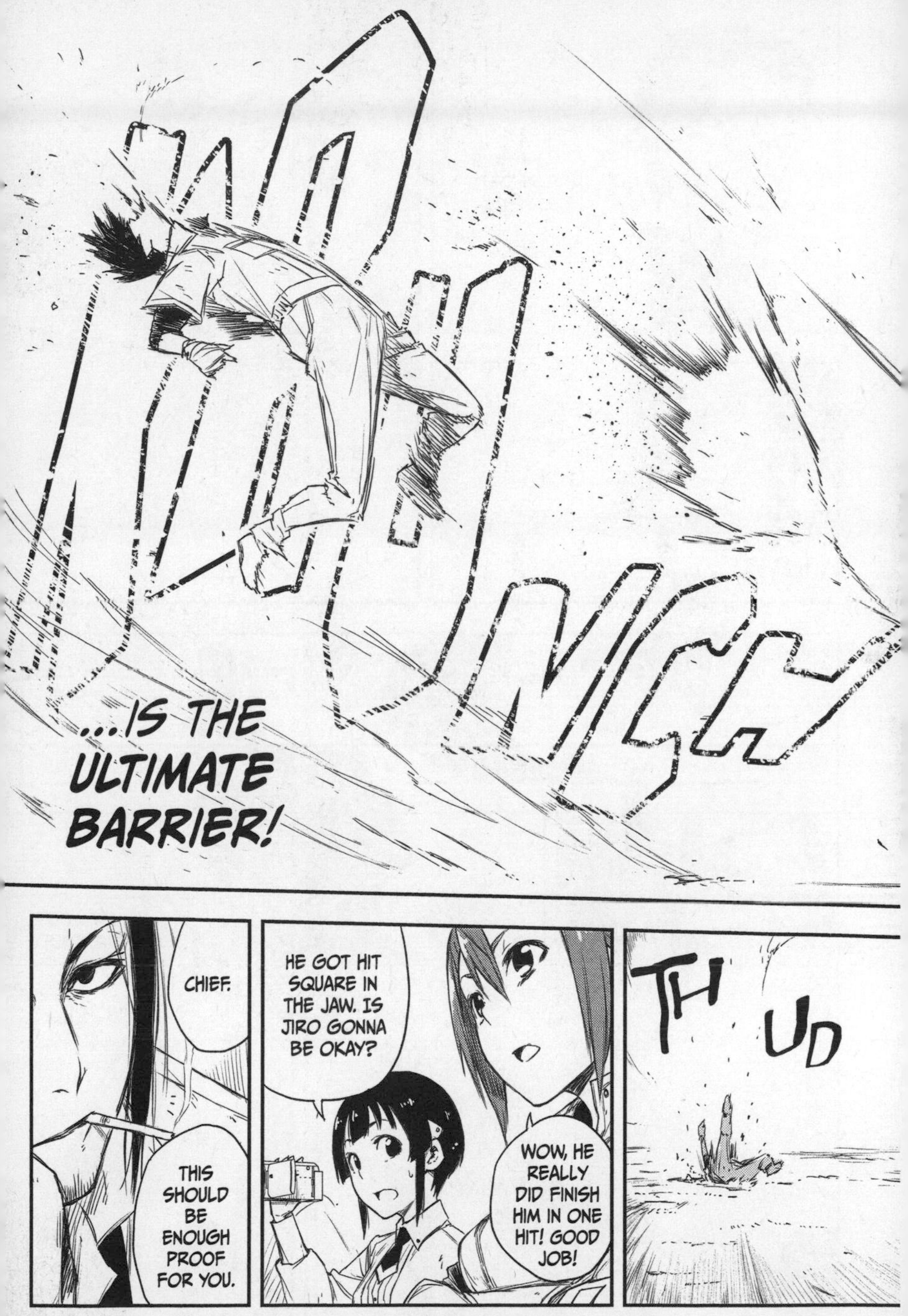
...IS THE ULTIMATE BARRIER!
THUD
HE GOT HIT SQUARE IN THE JAW. IS JIRO GONNA BE OKAY?
WOW, HE REALLY DID FINISH HIM IN ONE HIT! GOOD JOB!
CHIEF.
THIS SHOULD BE ENOUGH PROOF FOR YOU.

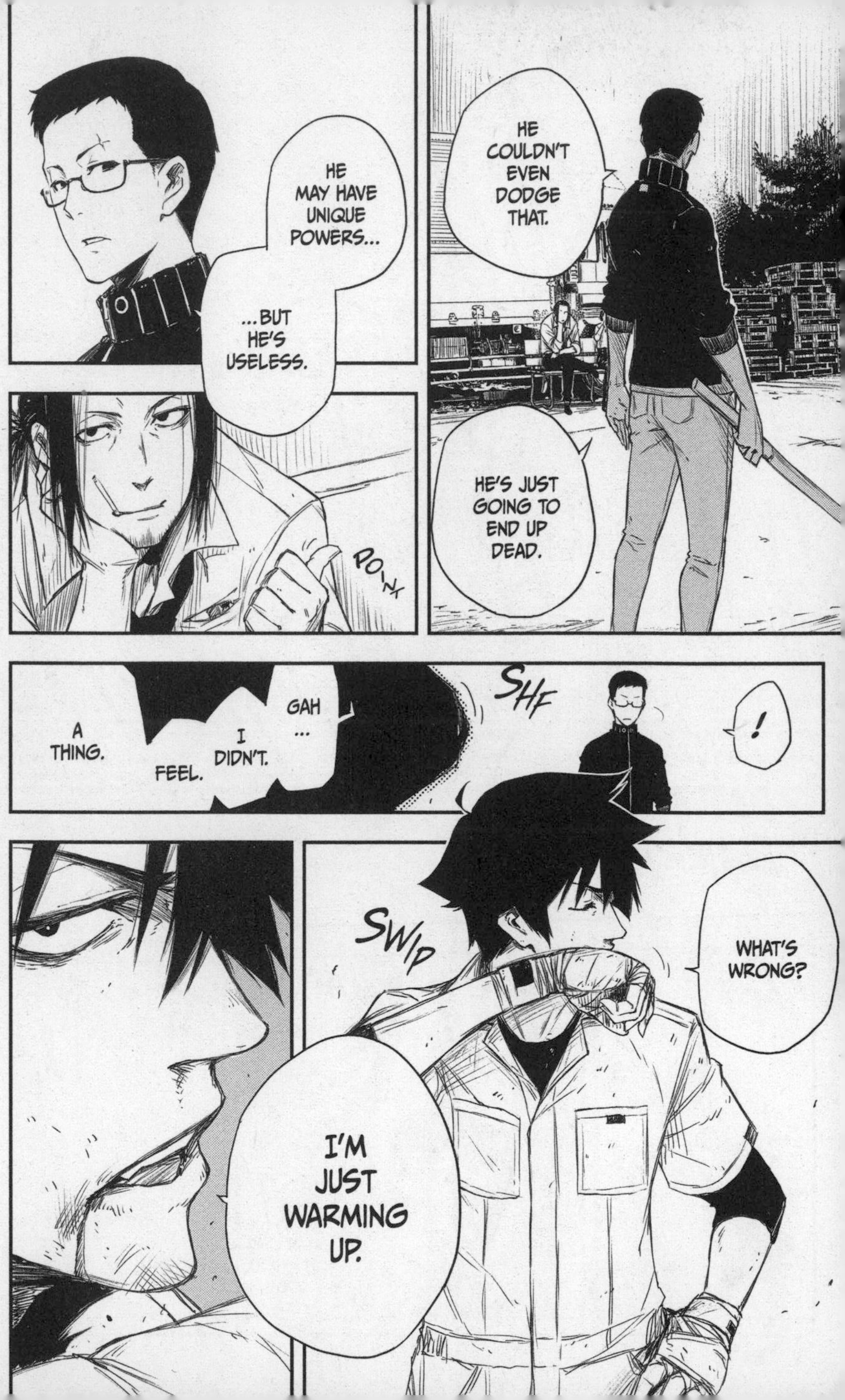
HE COULDN'T EVEN DODGE THAT.
HE'S JUST GOING TO END UP DEAD.
HE MAY HAVE UNIQUE POWERS...
...BUT HE'S USELESS.
POINK
!
SHF
GAH ...
I DIDN'T.
FEEL.
A THING.
WHAT'S WRONG?
SWIP
I'M JUST WARMING UP.

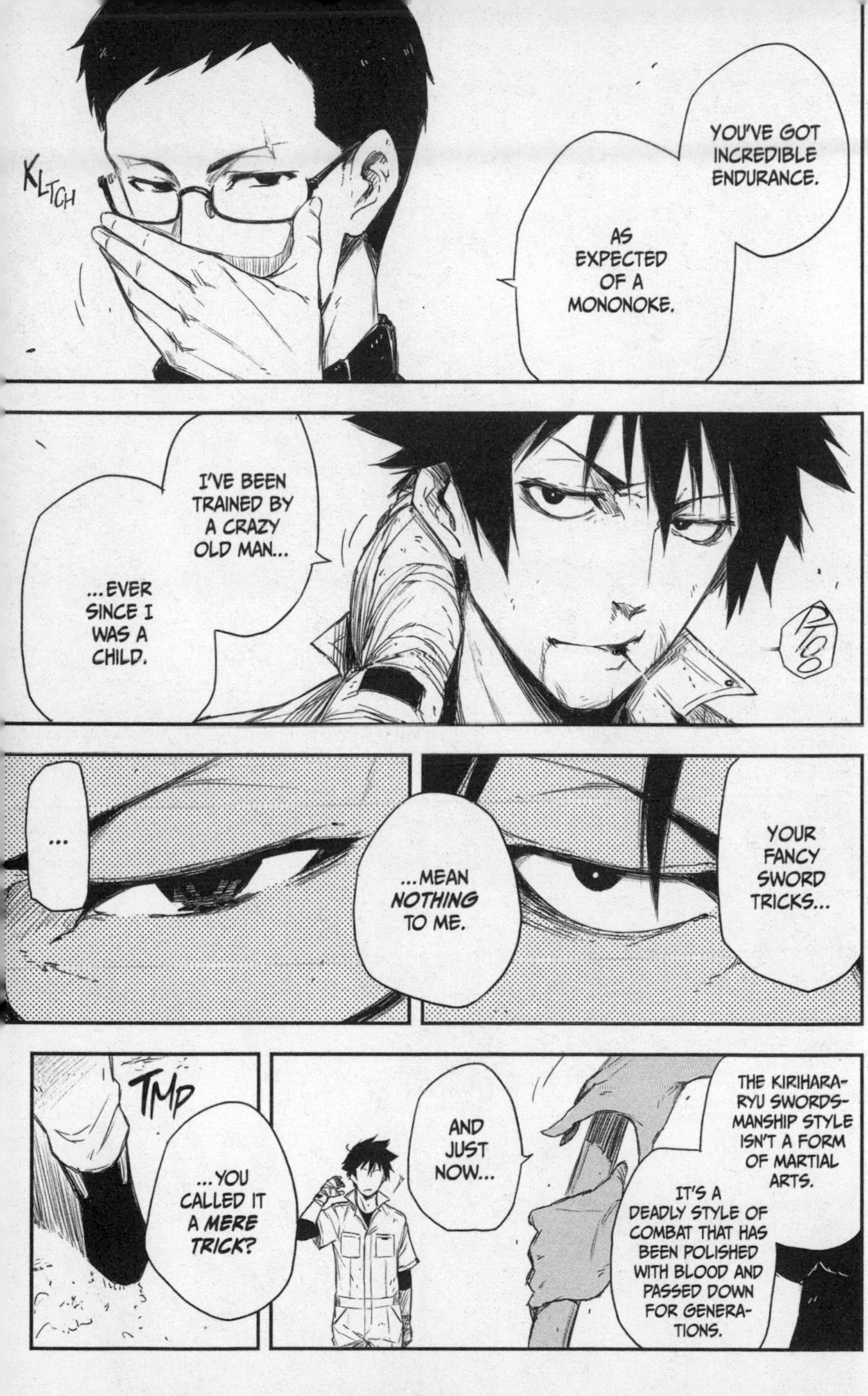
YOU'VE GOT INCREDIBLE ENDURANCE.
AS EXPECTED OF A MONONOKE.
KLTCH
I'VE BEEN TRAINED BY A CRAZY OLD MAN...
...EVER SINCE I WAS A CHILD.
YOUR FANCY SWORD TRICKS...
...MEAN *NOTHING* TO ME.
...
THE KIRIHARA-RYU SWORDS-MANSHIP STYLE ISN'T A FORM OF MARTIAL ARTS.
IT'S A DEADLY STYLE OF COMBAT THAT HAS BEEN POLISHED WITH BLOOD AND PASSED DOWN FOR GENERA-TIONS.
AND JUST NOW...
TMP
...YOU CALLED IT A *MERE* *TRICK*?

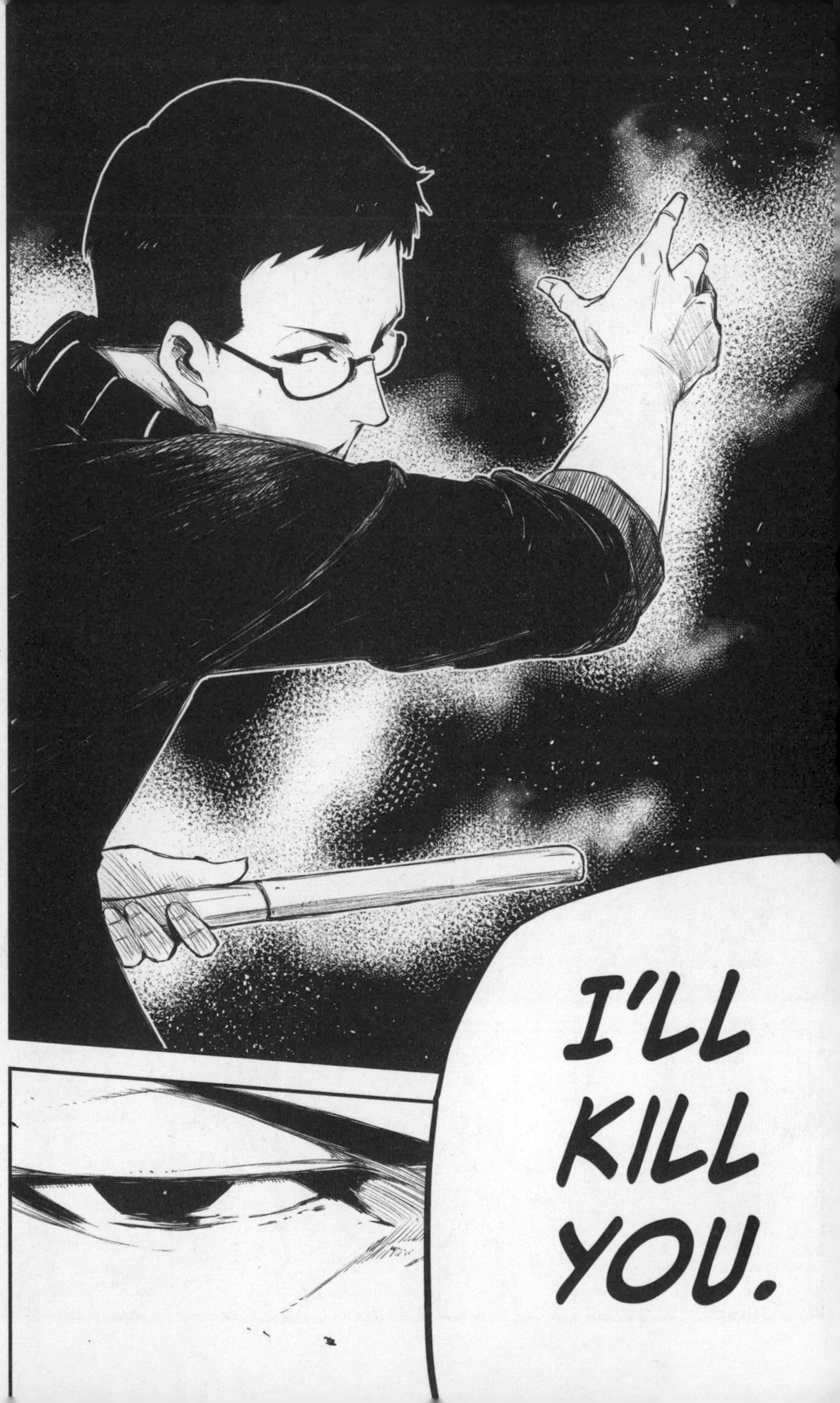
I'LL KILL YOU.

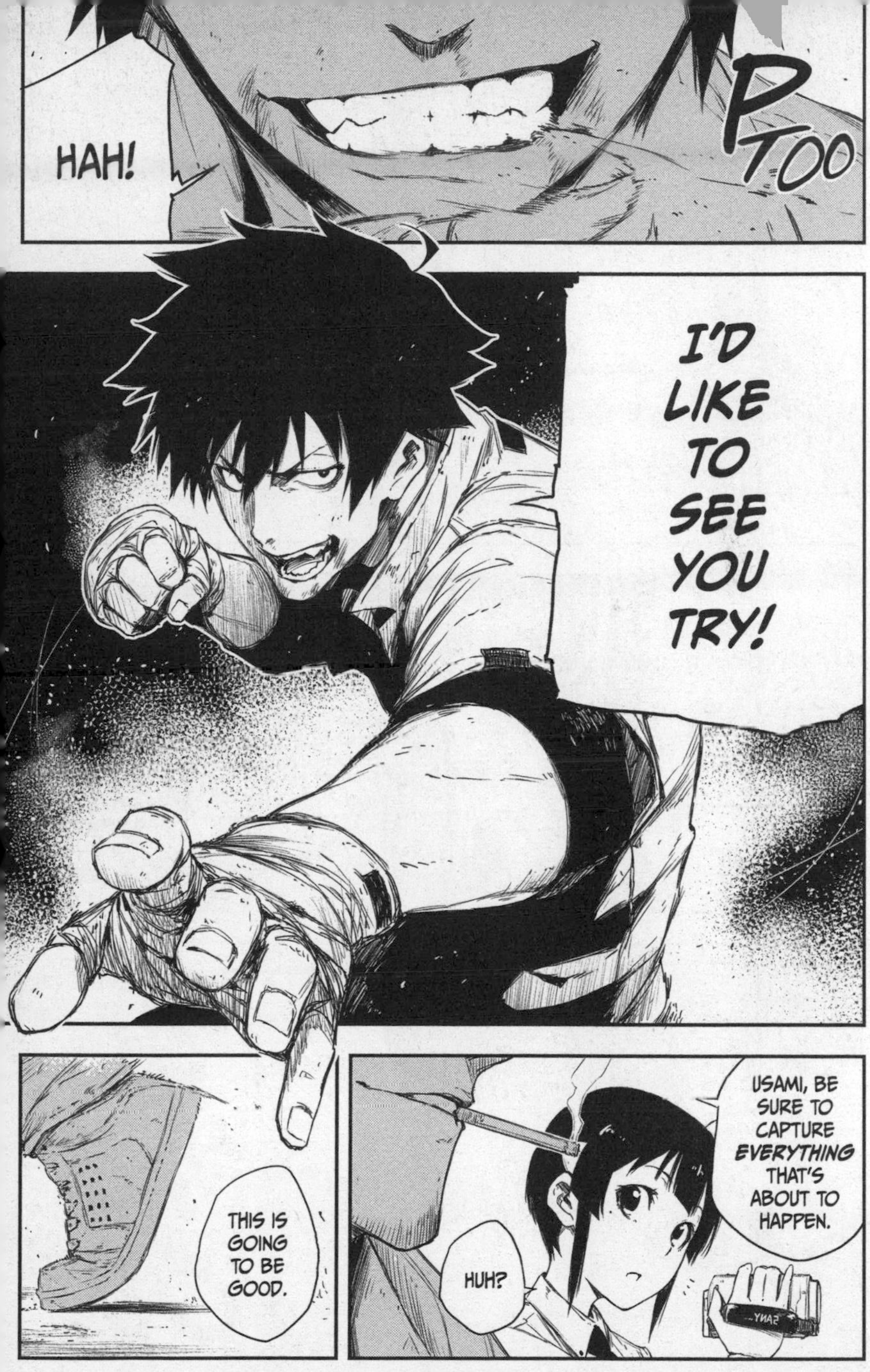
PTOO
HAH!
I'D LIKE TO SEE YOU TRY!
USAMI, BE SURE TO CAPTURE EVERYTHING THAT'S ABOUT TO HAPPEN.
HUH?
THIS IS GOING TO BE GOOD.

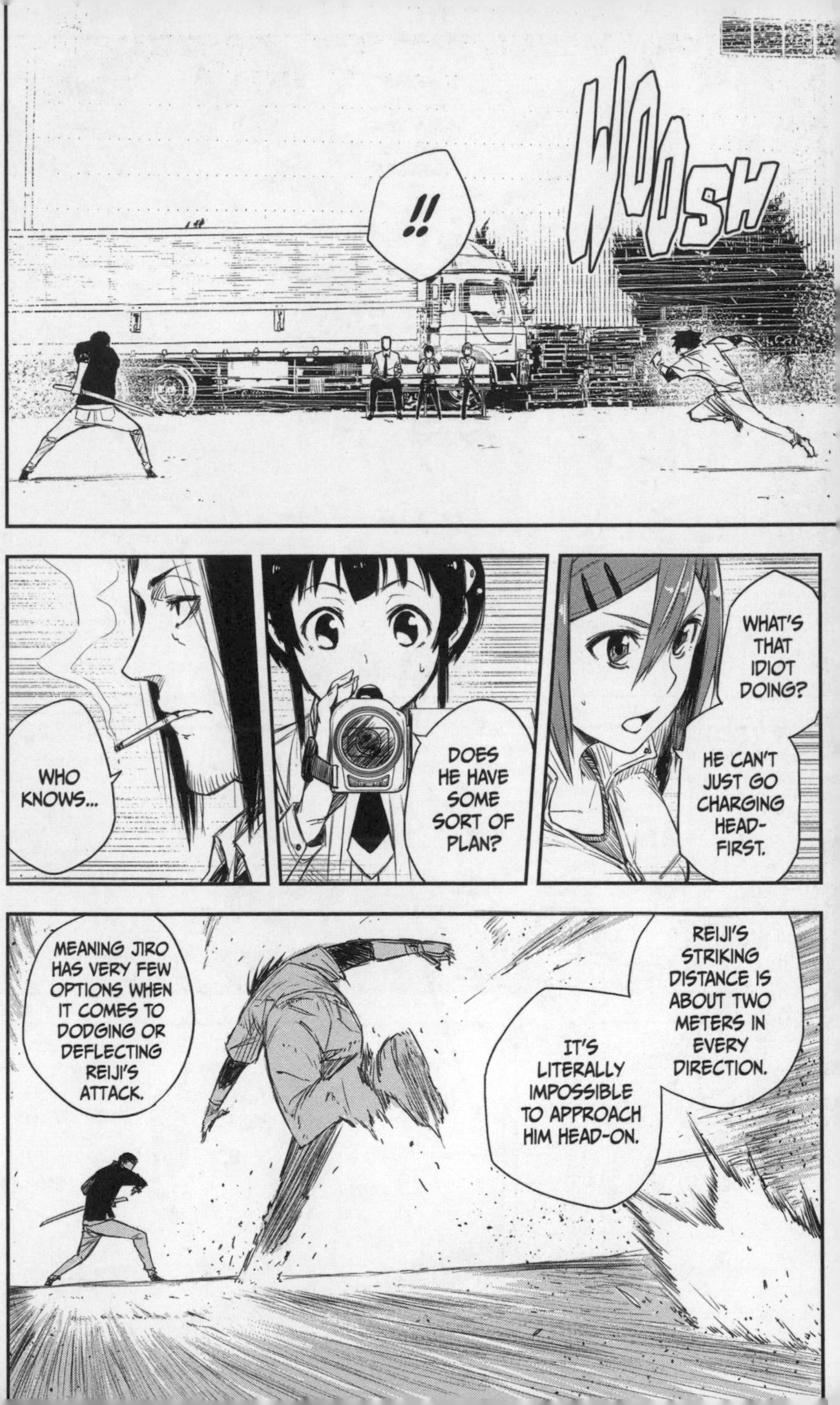
WOOSH
!!
WHAT'S THAT IDIOT DOING?
HE CAN'T JUST GO CHARGING HEAD-FIRST.
DOES HE HAVE SOME SORT OF PLAN?
WHO KNOWS...
REIJI'S STRIKING DISTANCE IS ABOUT TWO METERS IN EVERY DIRECTION.
IT'S LITERALLY IMPOSSIBLE TO APPROACH HIM HEAD-ON.
MEANING JIRO HAS VERY FEW OPTIONS WHEN IT COMES TO DODGING OR DEFLECTING REIJI'S ATTACK.

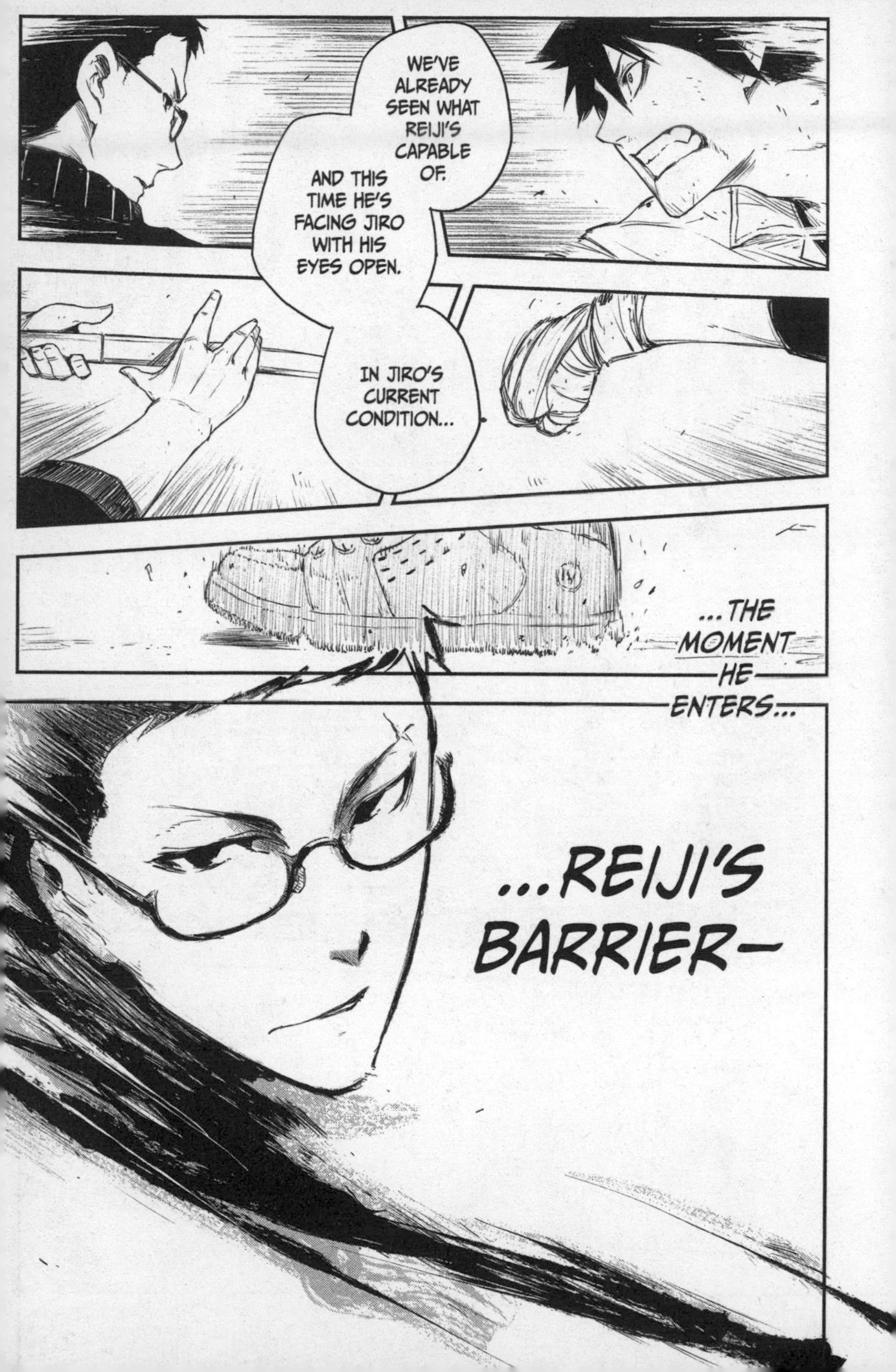

WE'VE ALREADY SEEN WHAT REIJI'S CAPABLE OF.
AND THIS TIME HE'S FACING JIRO WITH HIS EYES OPEN.
IN JIRO'S CURRENT CONDITION...
...THE MOMENT HE ENTERS...
...REIJI'S BARRIER—

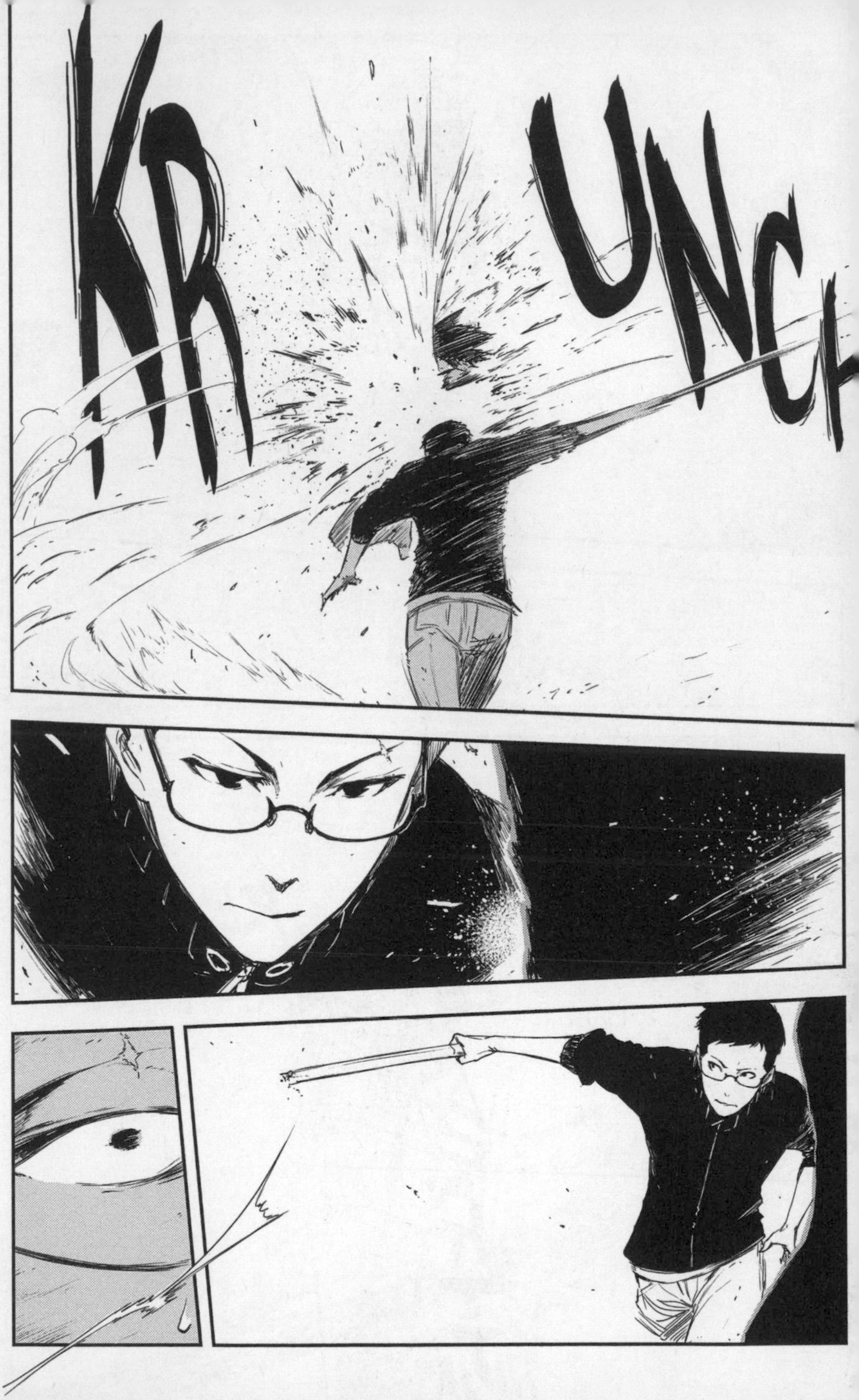
KRUNCH

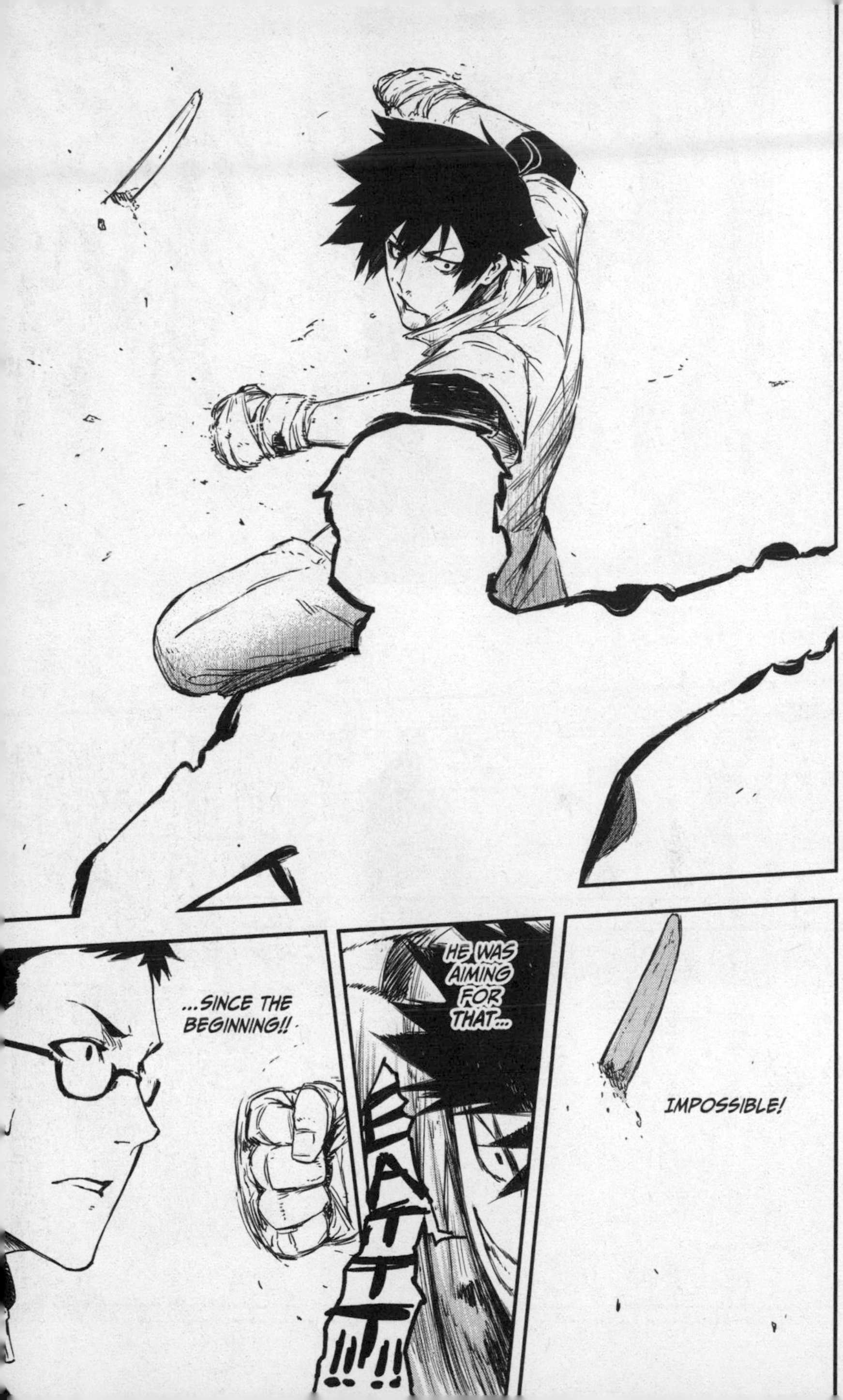
IMPOSSIBLE!
HE WAS AIMING FOR THAT...
EATTT!!!!
...SINCE THE BEGINNING!!

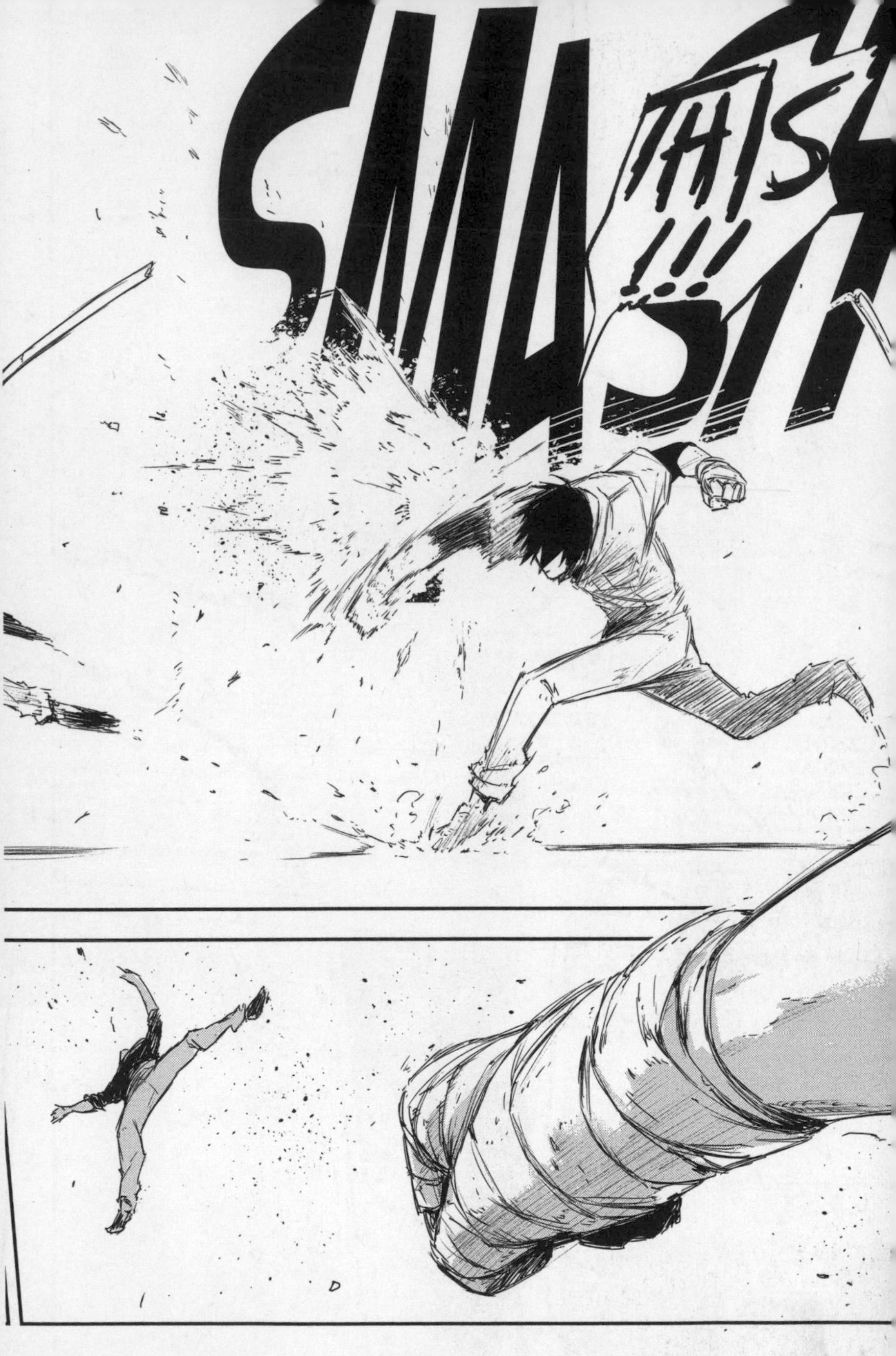
THIS!!!
SMASH

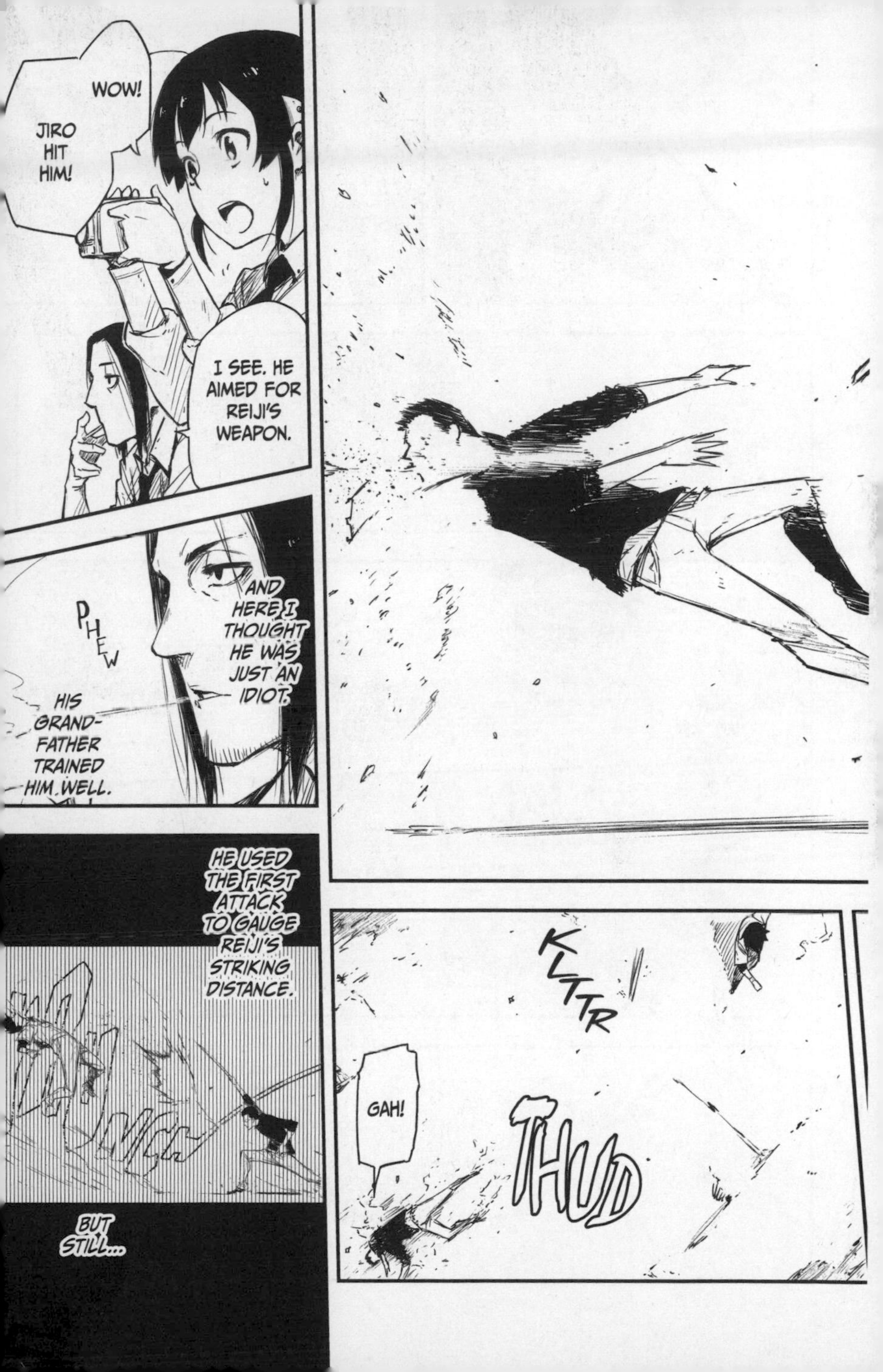
WOW!
JIRO HIT HIM!
I SEE. HE AIMED FOR REIJI'S WEAPON.
PHEW
AND HERE I THOUGHT HE WAS JUST AN IDIOT.
HIS GRAND-FATHER TRAINED HIM WELL.
KLTTR
GAH!
THUD
HE USED THE FIRST ATTACK TO GAUGE REIJI'S STRIKING DISTANCE.
BUT STILL...

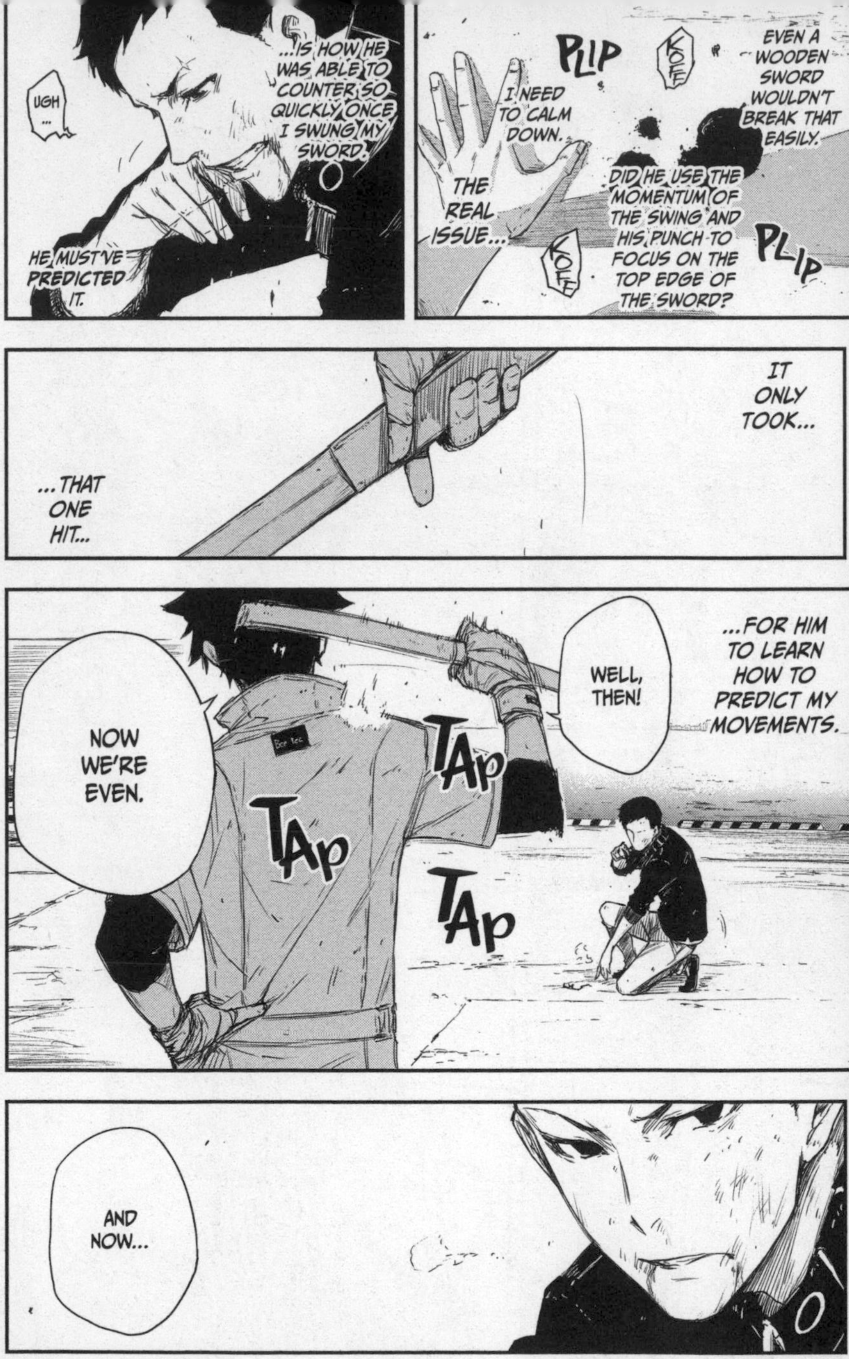

EVEN A WOODEN SWORD WOULDN'T BREAK THAT EASILY.
PLIP
KOFF
I NEED TO CALM DOWN.
DID HE USE THE MOMENTUM OF THE SWING AND HIS PUNCH TO FOCUS ON THE TOP EDGE OF THE SWORD?
PLIP
THE REAL ISSUE...
KOFF
...IS HOW HE WAS ABLE TO COUNTER SO QUICKLY ONCE I SWUNG MY SWORD.
UGH...
HE MUST'VE PREDICTED IT.
IT ONLY TOOK...
...THAT ONE HIT...
...FOR HIM TO LEARN HOW TO PREDICT MY MOVEMENTS.
WELL, THEN!
TAP
TAP
TAP
NOW WE'RE EVEN.
AND NOW...

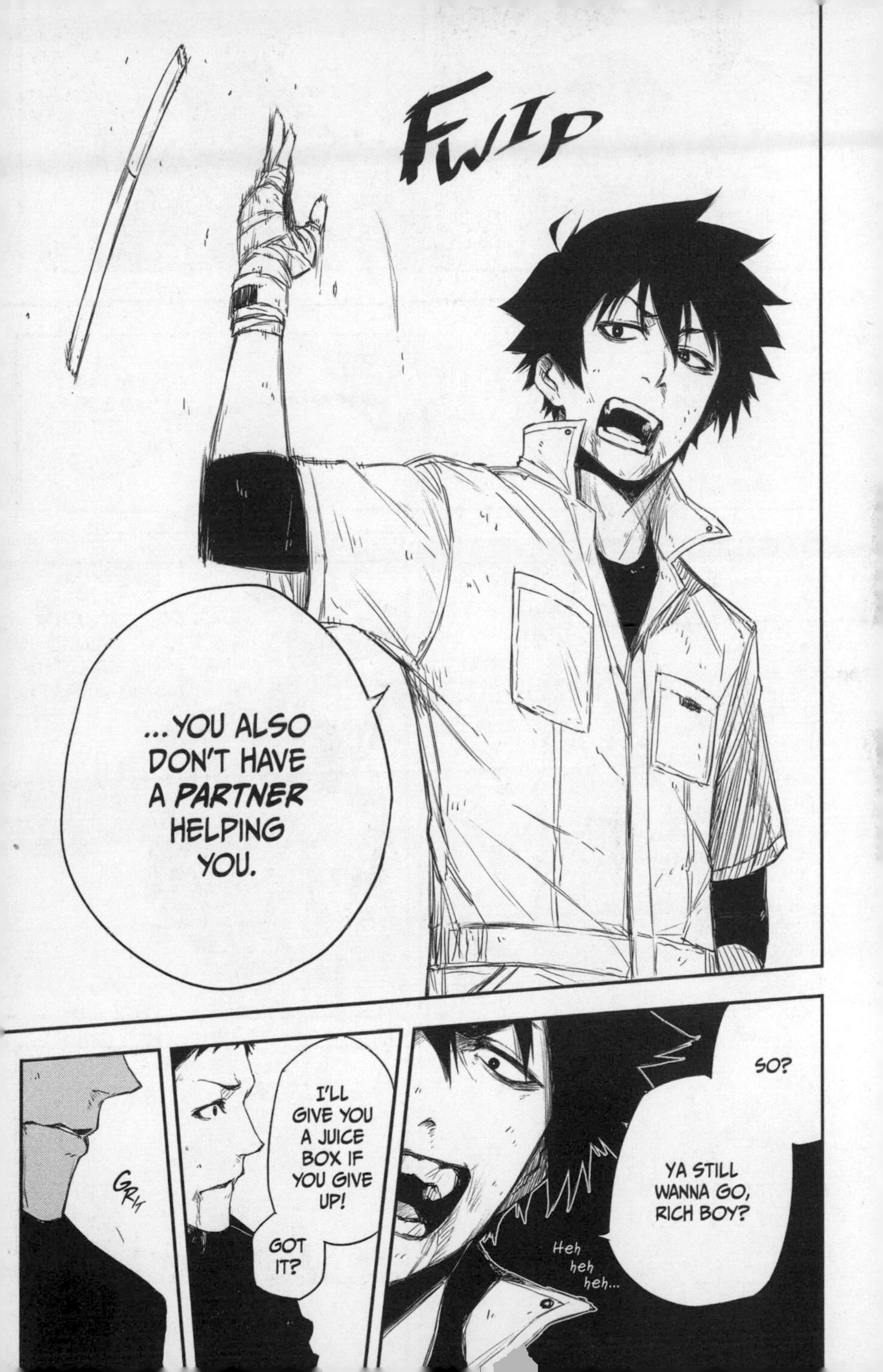
FWIP
...YOU ALSO DON'T HAVE A PARTNER HELPING YOU.
SO?
YA STILL WANNA GO, RICH BOY?
Heh heh heh...
I'LL GIVE YOU A JUICE BOX IF YOU GIVE UP!
GOT IT?
GRK

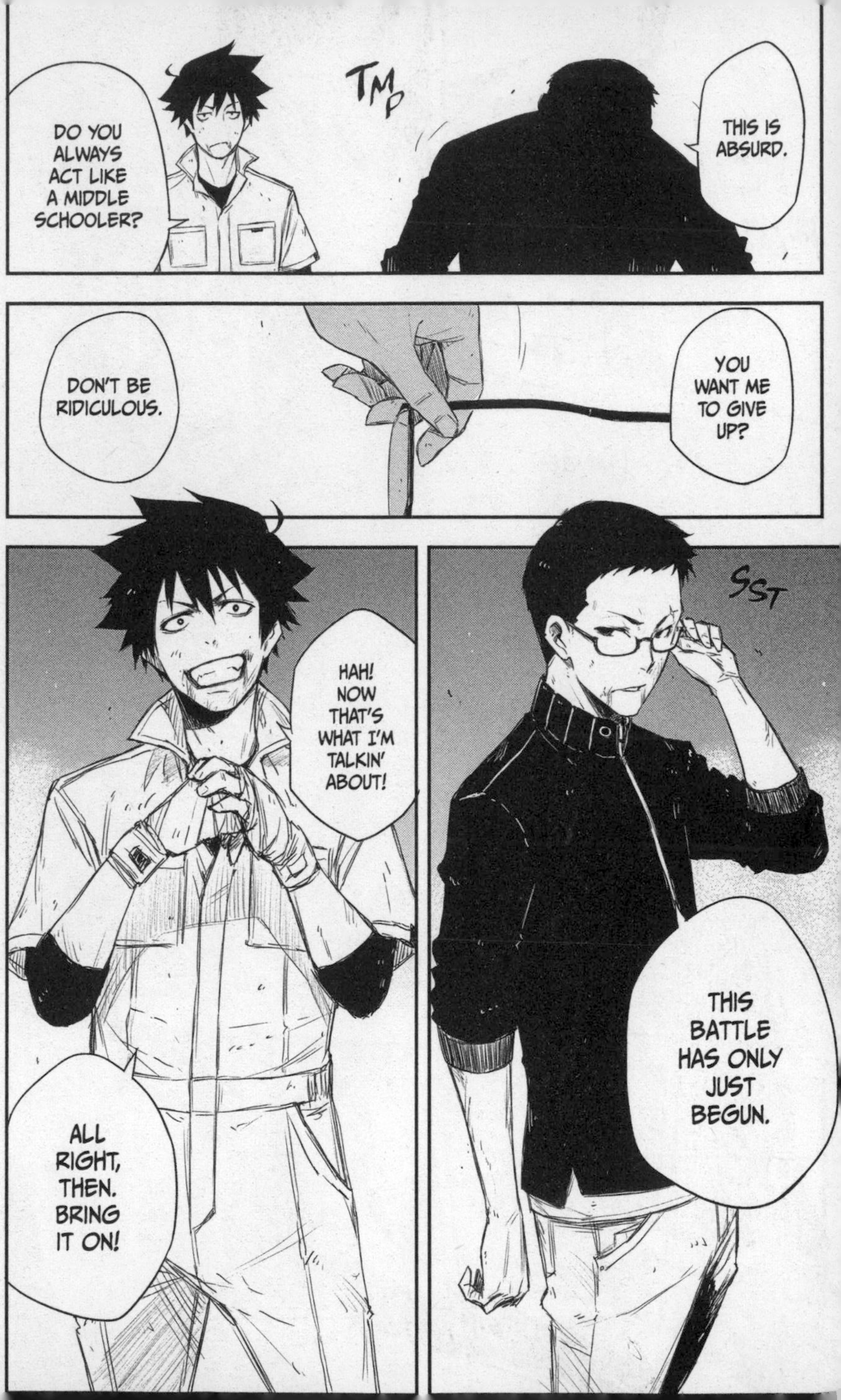
THIS IS ABSURD.
TMP
DO YOU ALWAYS ACT LIKE A MIDDLE SCHOOLER?
YOU WANT ME TO GIVE UP?
DON'T BE RIDICULOUS.
SST
THIS BATTLE HAS ONLY JUST BEGUN.
HAH! NOW THAT'S WHAT I'M TALKIN' ABOUT!
ALL RIGHT, THEN. BRING IT ON!

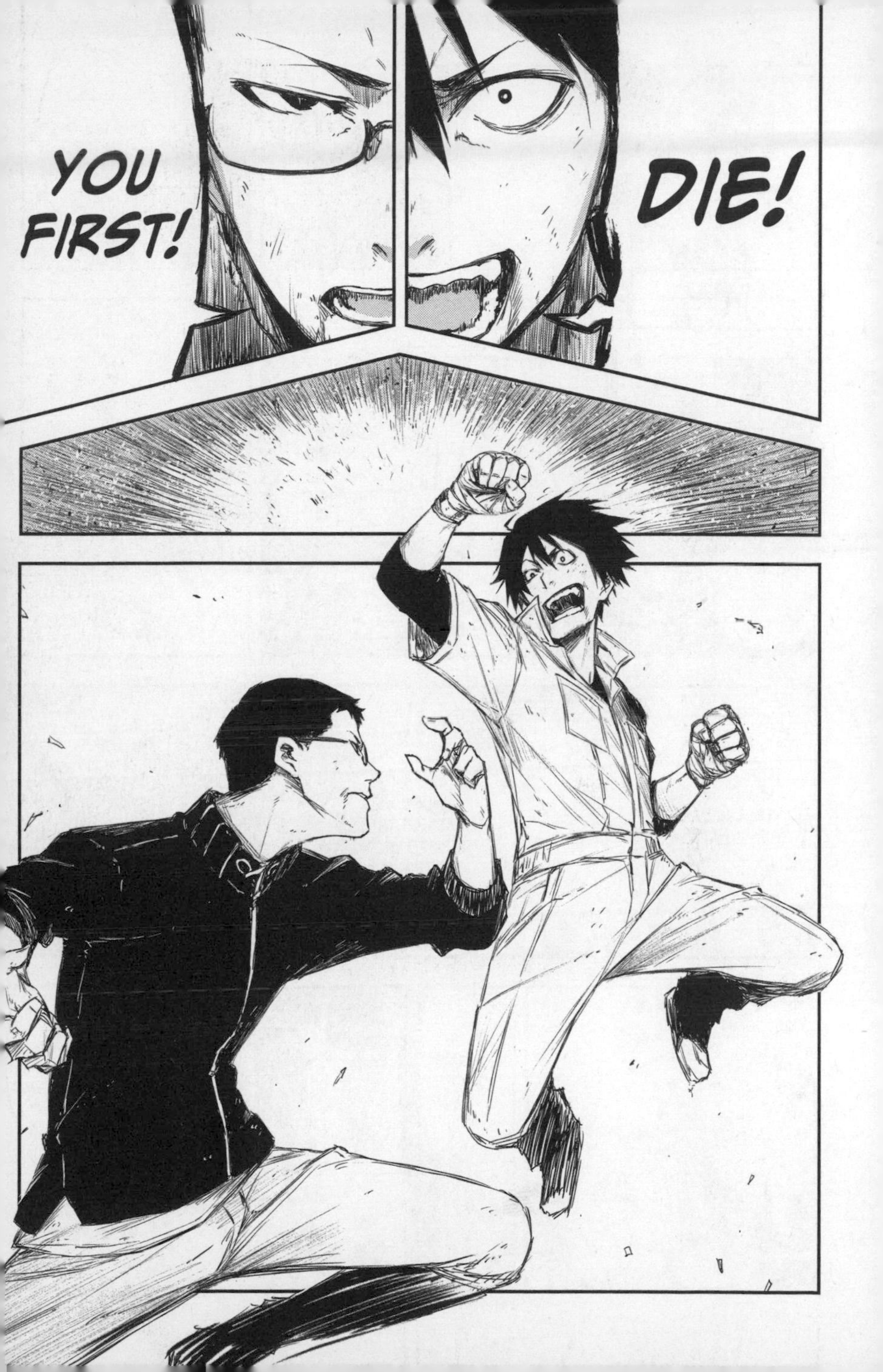
DIE!
YOU FIRST!

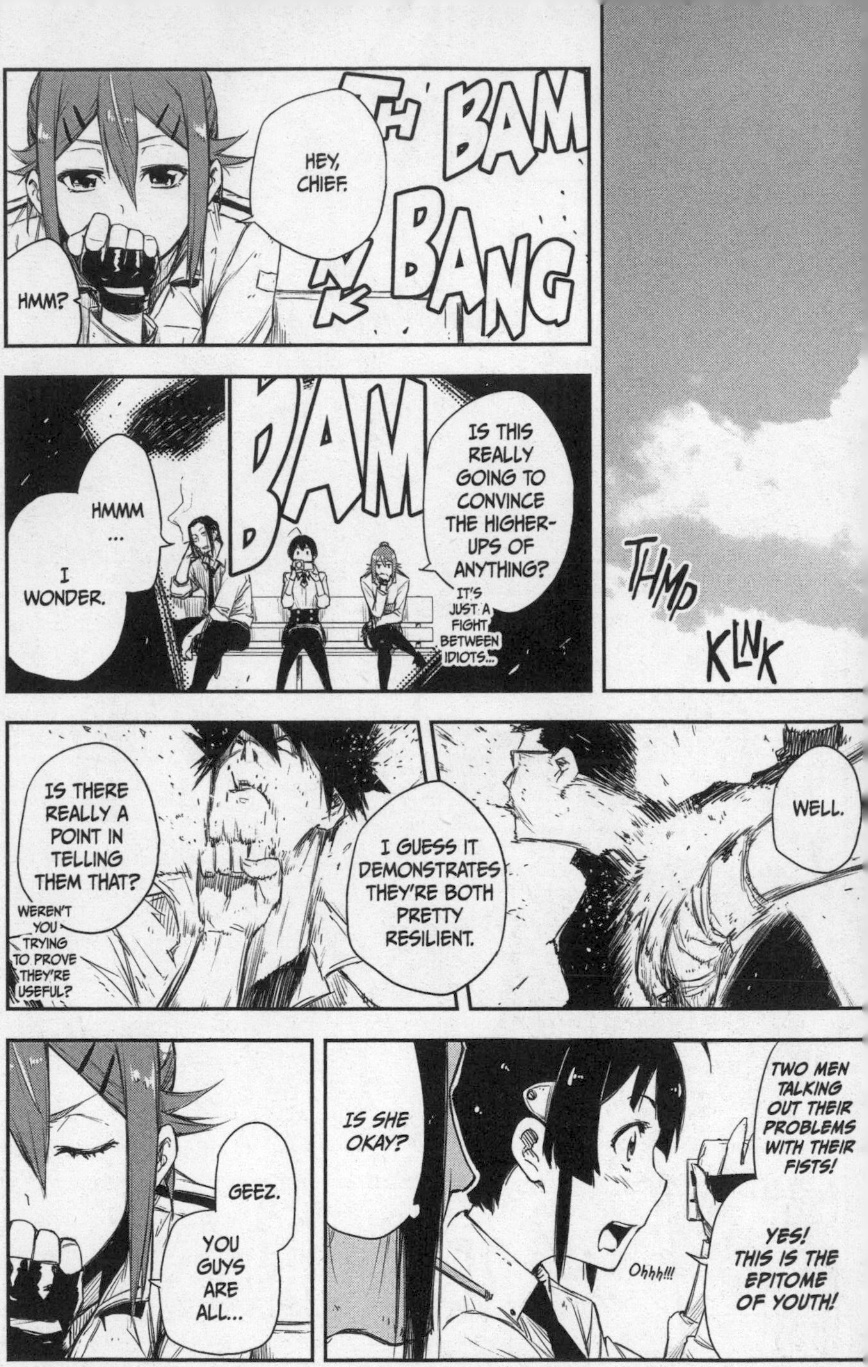
THMP
KLNK
BAM
BANG
HEY, CHIEF.
HMM?
IS THIS REALLY GOING TO CONVINCE THE HIGHER-UPS OF ANYTHING?
IT'S JUST A FIGHT BETWEEN IDIOTS...
BAM
HMMM ... I WONDER.
WELL.
I GUESS IT DEMONSTRATES THEY'RE BOTH PRETTY RESILIENT.
IS THERE REALLY A POINT IN TELLING THEM THAT?
WEREN'T YOU TRYING TO PROVE THEY'RE USEFUL?
TWO MEN TALKING OUT THEIR PROBLEMS WITH THEIR FISTS!
YES! THIS IS THE EPITOME OF YOUTH!
Ohhh!!!
IS SHE OKAY?
GEEZ.
YOU GUYS ARE ALL...

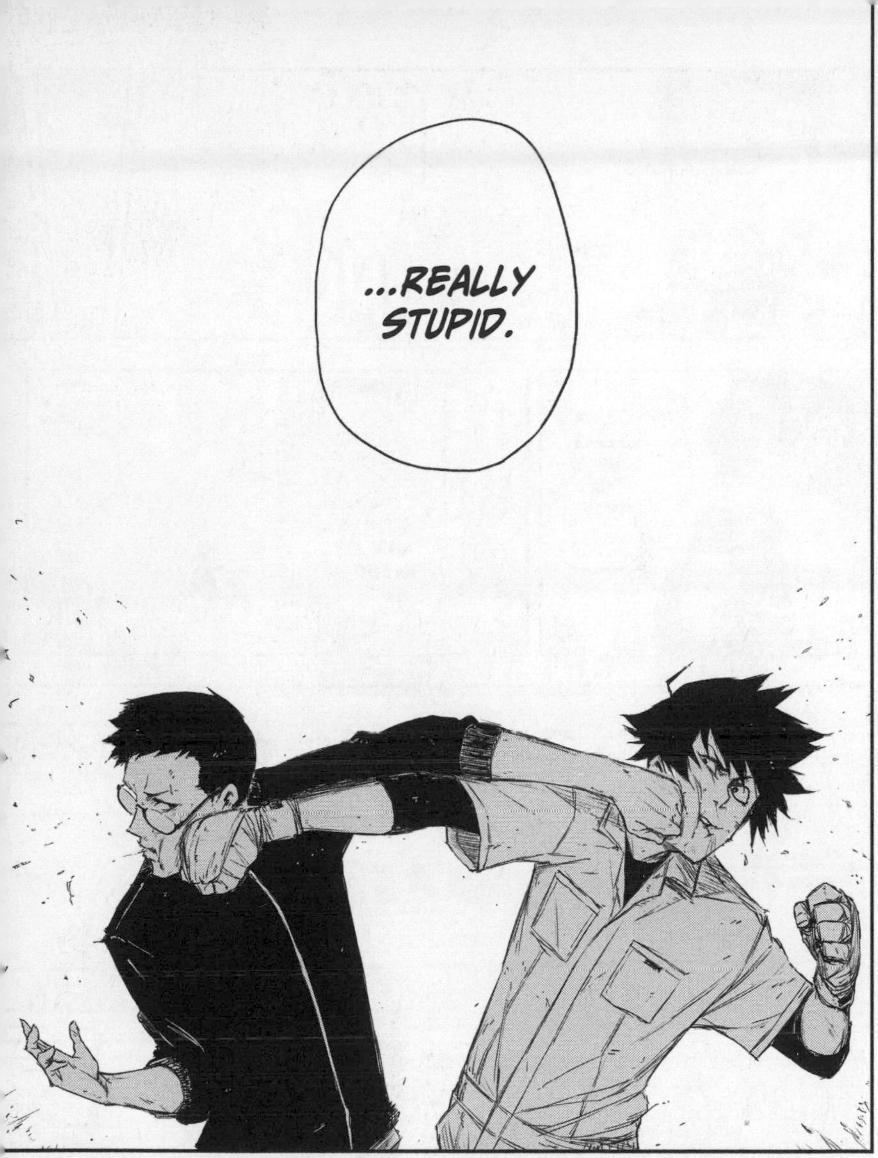
...REALLY STUPID.
RECORDING ST
BEEP

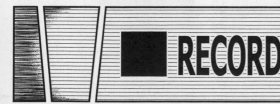

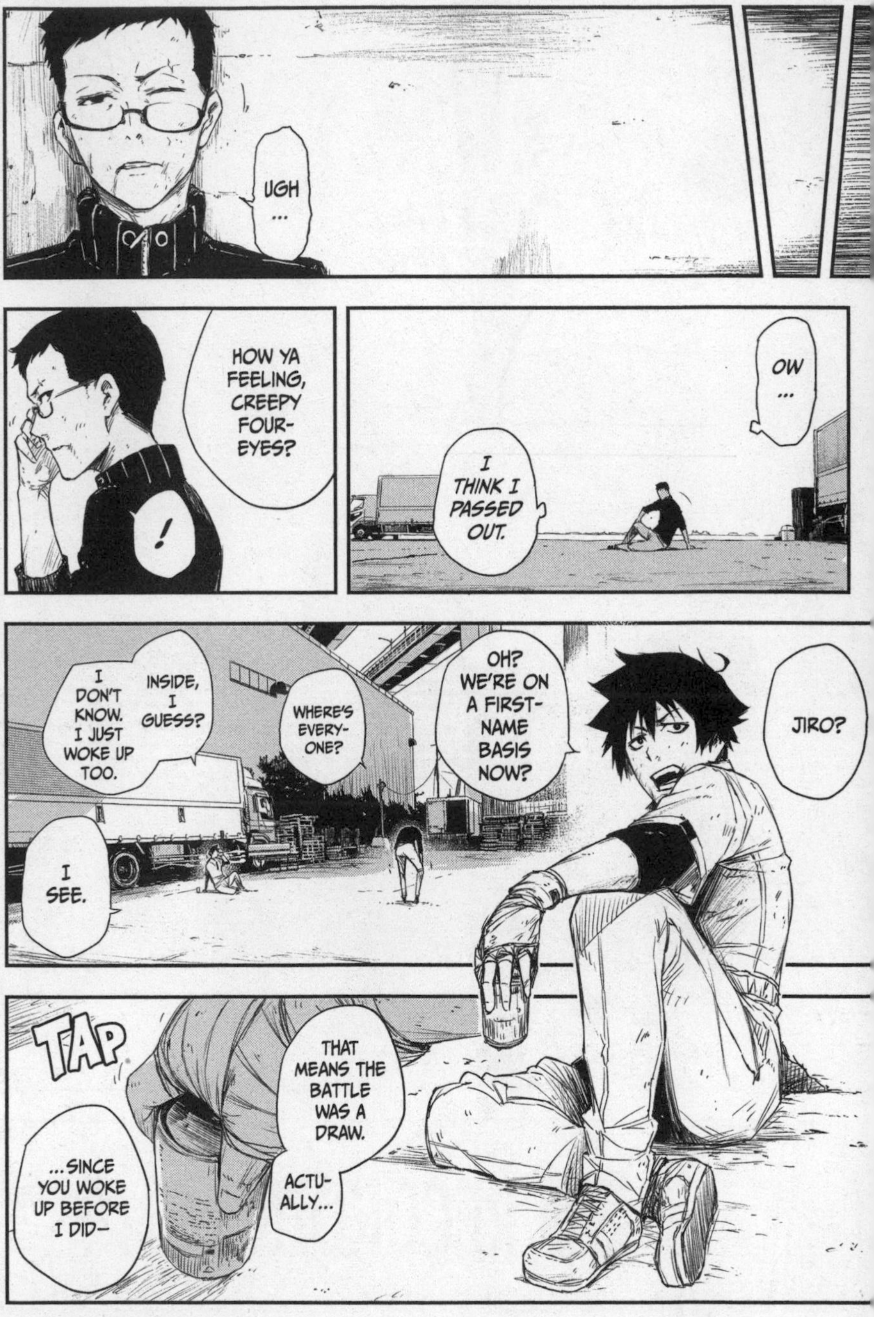
UGH ...
OW ...
I THINK I PASSED OUT.
HOW YA FEELING, CREEPY FOUR-EYES?
!
JIRO?
OH? WE'RE ON A FIRST-NAME BASIS NOW?
WHERE'S EVERYONE?
INSIDE, I GUESS?
I DON'T KNOW. I JUST WOKE UP TOO.
I SEE.
THAT MEANS THE BATTLE WAS A DRAW.
TAP
ACTU-ALLY...
...SINCE YOU WOKE UP BEFORE I DID—

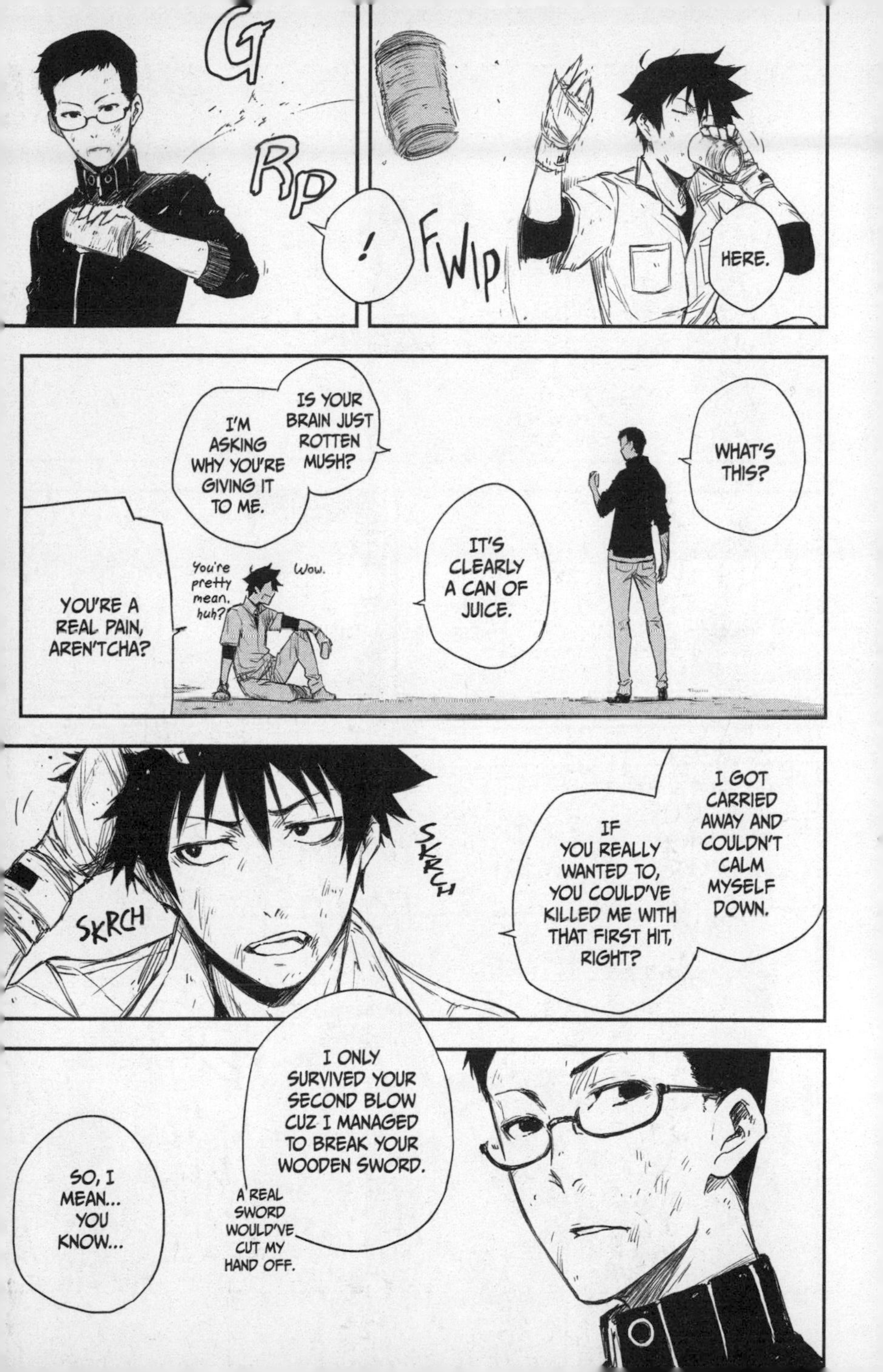
HERE.
FWIP
G
Rp
!
WHAT'S THIS?
IT'S CLEARLY A CAN OF JUICE.
IS YOUR BRAIN JUST ROTTEN MUSH?
I'M ASKING WHY YOU'RE GIVING IT TO ME.
Wow.
You're pretty mean, huh?
YOU'RE A REAL PAIN, AREN'TCHA?
I GOT CARRIED AWAY AND COULDN'T CALM MYSELF DOWN.
IF YOU REALLY WANTED TO, YOU COULD'VE KILLED ME WITH THAT FIRST HIT, RIGHT?
SKRCH
SKRCH
I ONLY SURVIVED YOUR SECOND BLOW CUZ I MANAGED TO BREAK YOUR WOODEN SWORD.
A REAL SWORD WOULD'VE CUT MY HAND OFF.
SO, I MEAN... YOU KNOW...

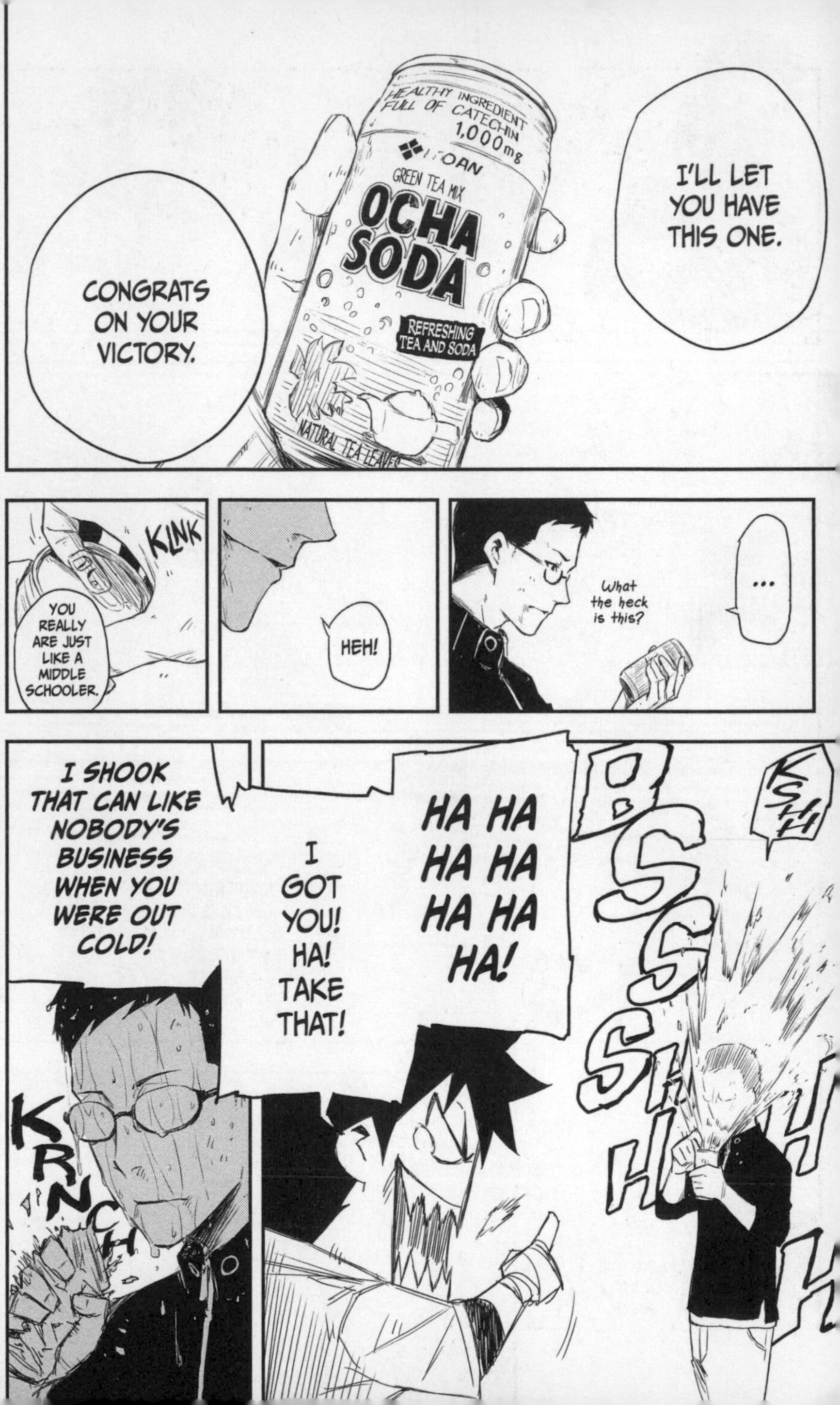
I'LL LET YOU HAVE THIS ONE.
HEALTHY INGREDIENT FULL OF CATECHIN 1,000mg
ITOAN
GREEN TEA MIX
OCHA SODA
REFRESHING TEA AND SODA
NATURAL TEA LEAVES
CONGRATS ON YOUR VICTORY.
...
What the heck is this?
HEH!
KLINK
YOU REALLY ARE JUST LIKE A MIDDLE SCHOOLER.
KSHH
BSSSHHHH
HA HA HA HA HA HA HA!
I GOT YOU! HA! TAKE THAT!
I SHOOK THAT CAN LIKE NOBODY'S BUSINESS WHEN YOU WERE OUT COLD!
KRNCH

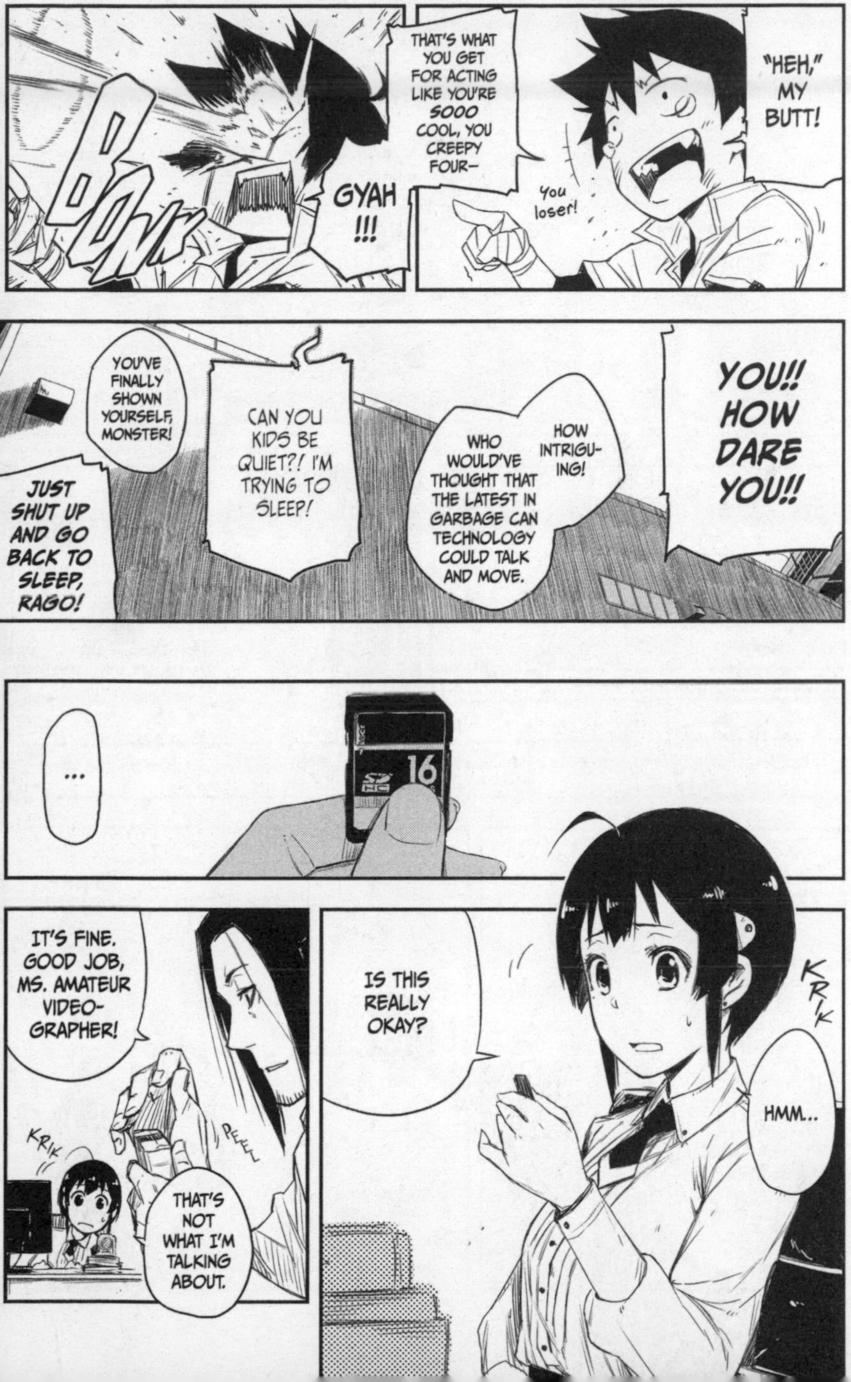
"HEH," MY BUTT!
THAT'S WHAT YOU GET FOR ACTING LIKE YOU'RE SOOO COOL, YOU CREEPY FOUR–
You loser!
GYAH !!!
BONK
YOU!! HOW DARE YOU!!
HOW INTRIGU-ING!
WHO WOULD'VE THOUGHT THAT THE LATEST IN GARBAGE CAN TECHNOLOGY COULD TALK AND MOVE.
CAN YOU KIDS BE QUIET?! I'M TRYING TO SLEEP!
YOU'VE FINALLY SHOWN YOURSELF, MONSTER!
JUST SHUT UP AND GO BACK TO SLEEP, RAGO!
...
KRIK
HMM...
IS THIS REALLY OKAY?
IT'S FINE. GOOD JOB, MS. AMATEUR VIDEO-GRAPHER!
PEEL
KRIK
THAT'S NOT WHAT I'M TALKING ABOUT.

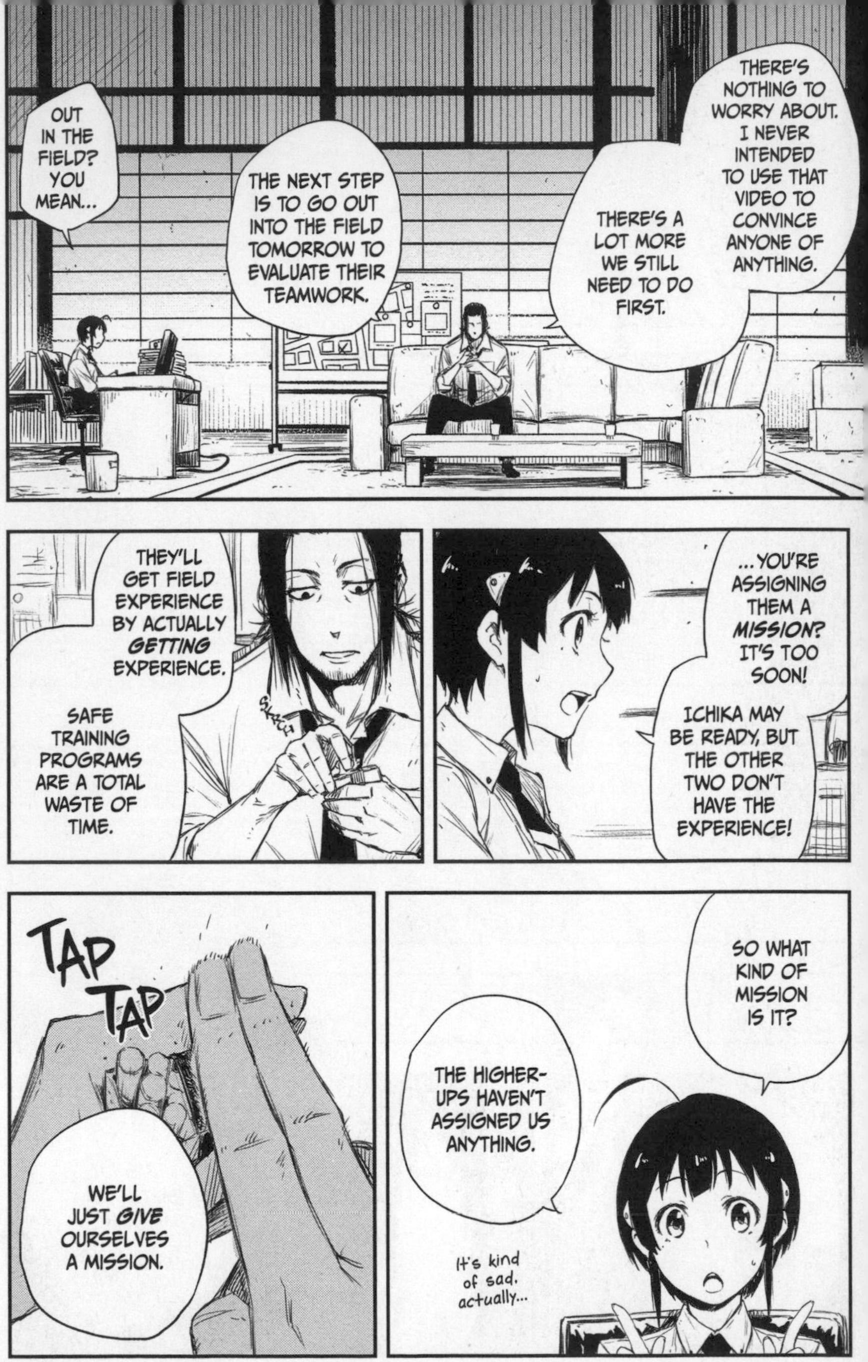
THERE'S NOTHING TO WORRY ABOUT. I NEVER INTENDED TO USE THAT VIDEO TO CONVINCE ANYONE OF ANYTHING.
THERE'S A LOT MORE WE STILL NEED TO DO FIRST.
THE NEXT STEP IS TO GO OUT INTO THE FIELD TOMORROW TO EVALUATE THEIR TEAMWORK.
OUT IN THE FIELD? YOU MEAN...
...YOU'RE ASSIGNING THEM A *MISSION*? IT'S TOO SOON!
ICHIKA MAY BE READY, BUT THE OTHER TWO DON'T HAVE THE EXPERIENCE!
THEY'LL GET FIELD EXPERIENCE BY ACTUALLY *GETTING* EXPERIENCE.
SAFE TRAINING PROGRAMS ARE A TOTAL WASTE OF TIME.
SO WHAT KIND OF MISSION IS IT?
THE HIGHER-UPS HAVEN'T ASSIGNED US ANYTHING.
It's kind of sad, actually...
TAP TAP
WE'LL JUST *GIVE* OURSELVES A MISSION.

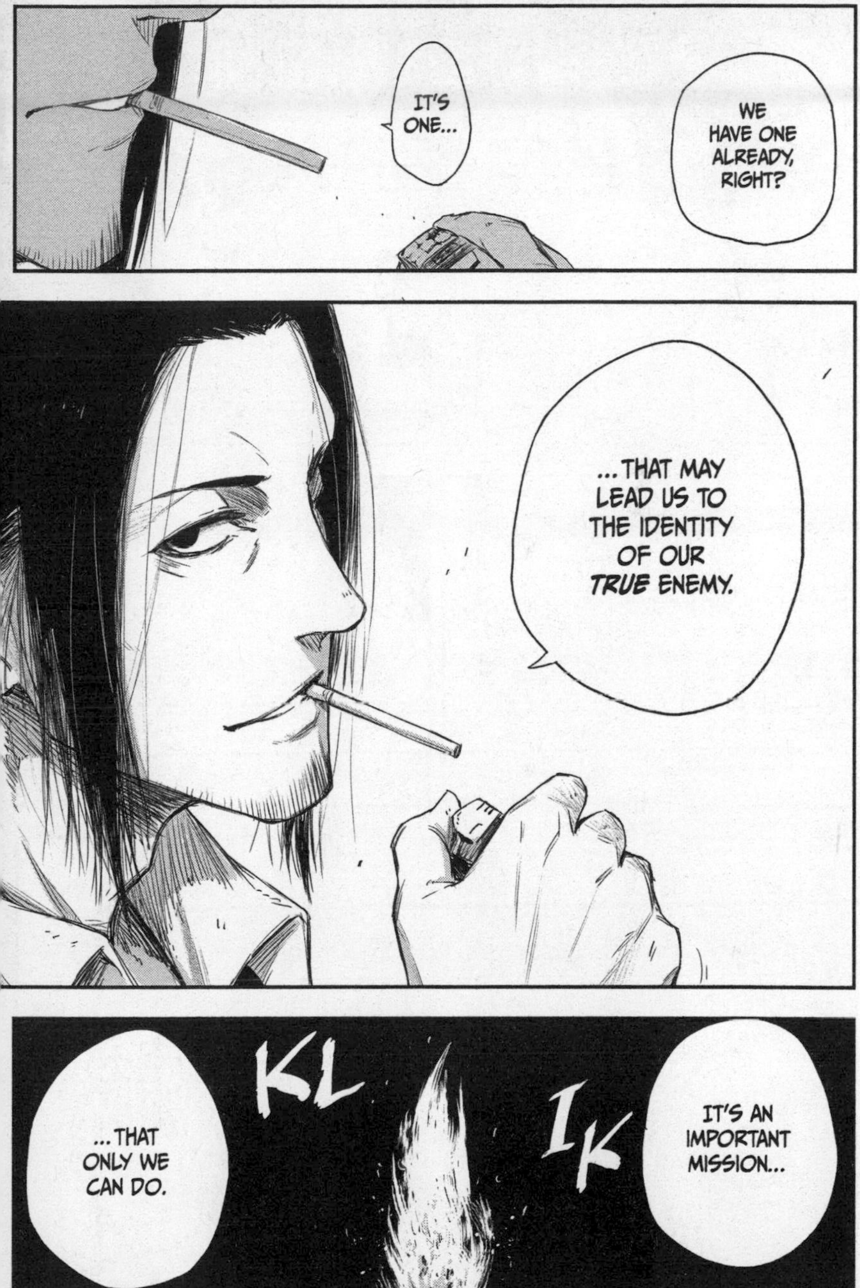
WE HAVE ONE ALREADY, RIGHT?
IT'S ONE...
...THAT MAY LEAD US TO THE IDENTITY OF OUR *TRUE* ENEMY.
IT'S AN IMPORTANT MISSION...
KLIK
...THAT ONLY WE CAN DO.

BLACK TORCH

#5 Testimony

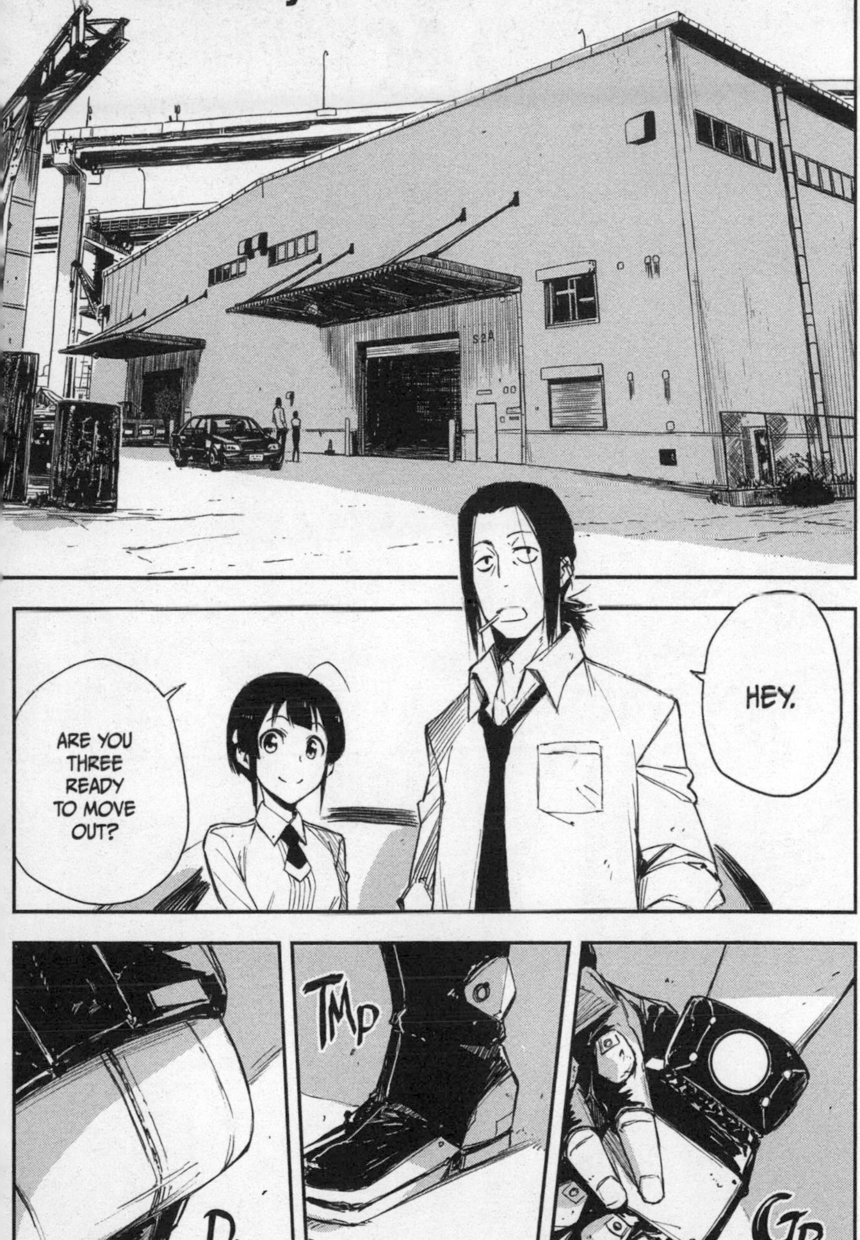
HEY.
ARE YOU THREE READY TO MOVE OUT?
GRP
TMP
DUN

#5 Testimony

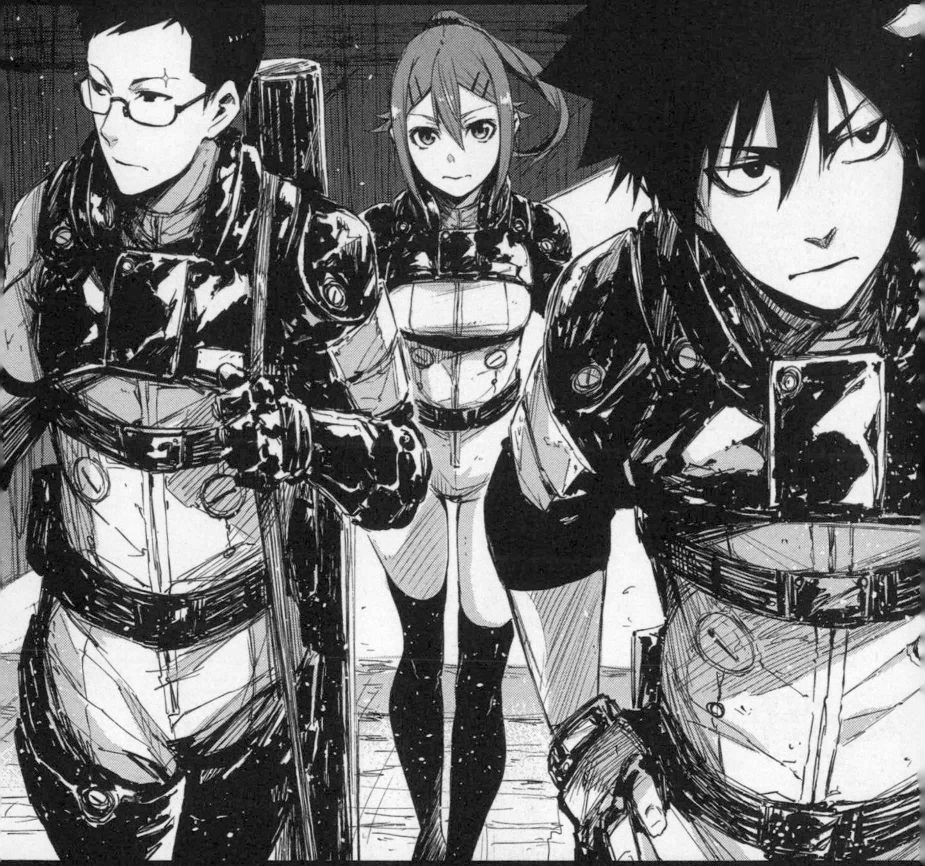

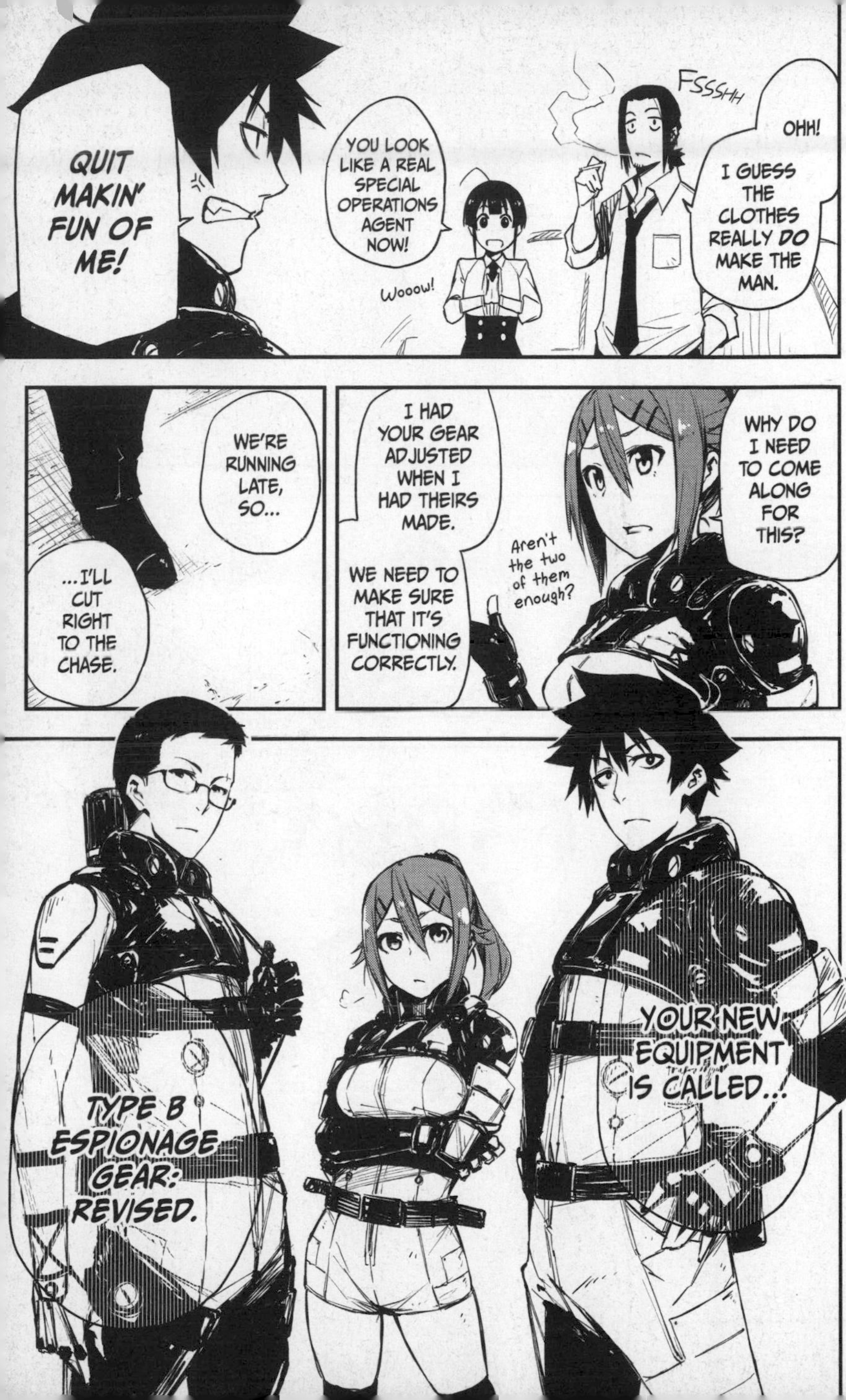
FSSSHH
OHH! I GUESS THE CLOTHES REALLY DO MAKE THE MAN.
YOU LOOK LIKE A REAL SPECIAL OPERATIONS AGENT NOW!
Wooow!
QUIT MAKIN' FUN OF ME!
WHY DO I NEED TO COME ALONG FOR THIS?
Aren't the two of them enough?
I HAD YOUR GEAR ADJUSTED WHEN I HAD THEIRS MADE.
WE NEED TO MAKE SURE THAT IT'S FUNCTIONING CORRECTLY.
WE'RE RUNNING LATE, SO...
...I'LL CUT RIGHT TO THE CHASE.
YOUR NEW EQUIPMENT IS CALLED...
TYPE B ESPIONAGE GEAR: REVISED.

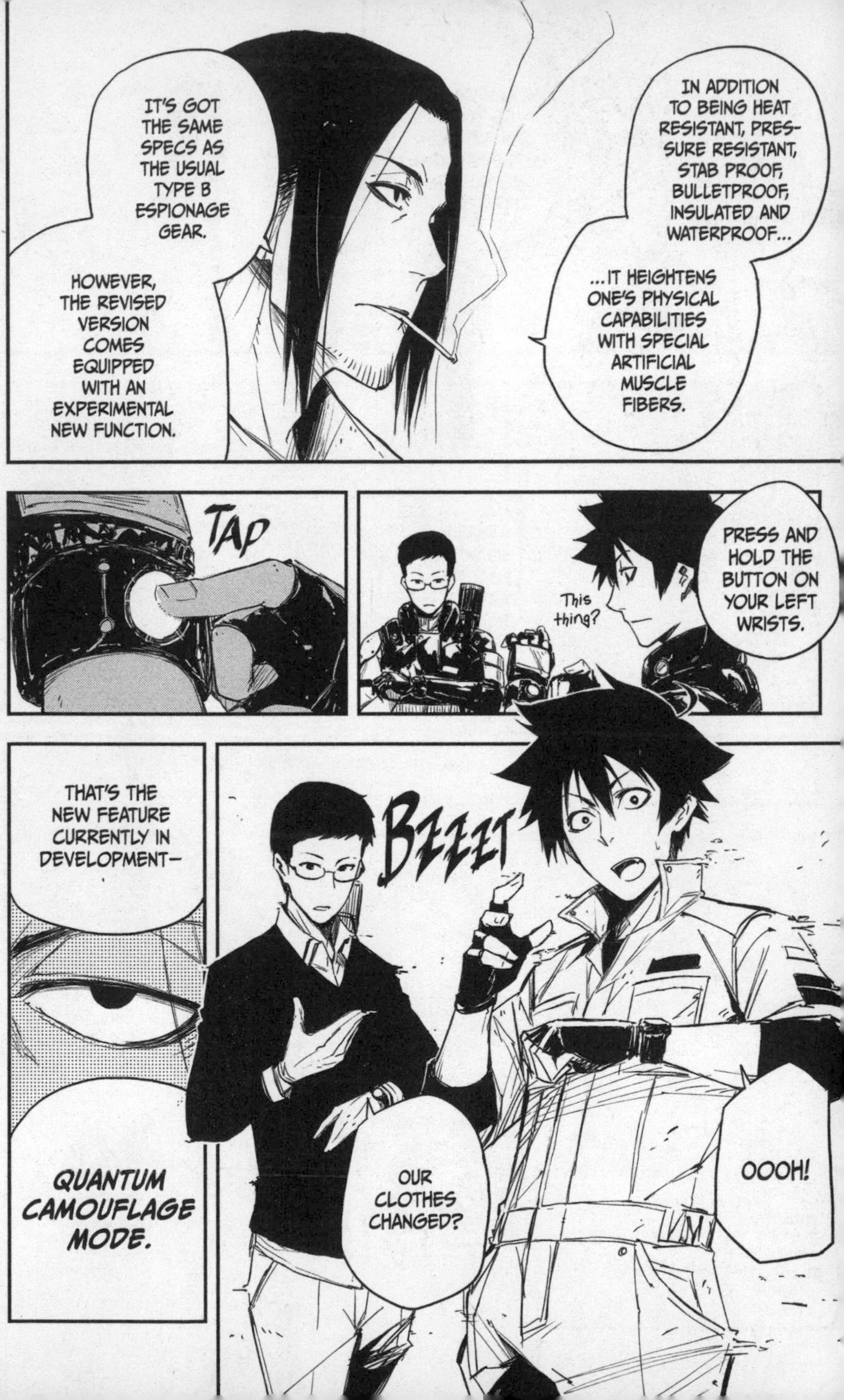
IN ADDITION TO BEING HEAT RESISTANT, PRES-SURE RESISTANT, STAB PROOF, BULLETPROOF, INSULATED AND WATERPROOF...
...IT HEIGHTENS ONE'S PHYSICAL CAPABILITIES WITH SPECIAL ARTIFICIAL MUSCLE FIBERS.
IT'S GOT THE SAME SPECS AS THE USUAL TYPE B ESPIONAGE GEAR.
HOWEVER, THE REVISED VERSION COMES EQUIPPED WITH AN EXPERIMENTAL NEW FUNCTION.
PRESS AND HOLD THE BUTTON ON YOUR LEFT WRISTS.
This thing?
TAP
BZZZT
OOOH!
OUR CLOTHES CHANGED?
THAT'S THE NEW FEATURE CURRENTLY IN DEVELOPMENT—
QUANTUM CAMOUFLAGE MODE.

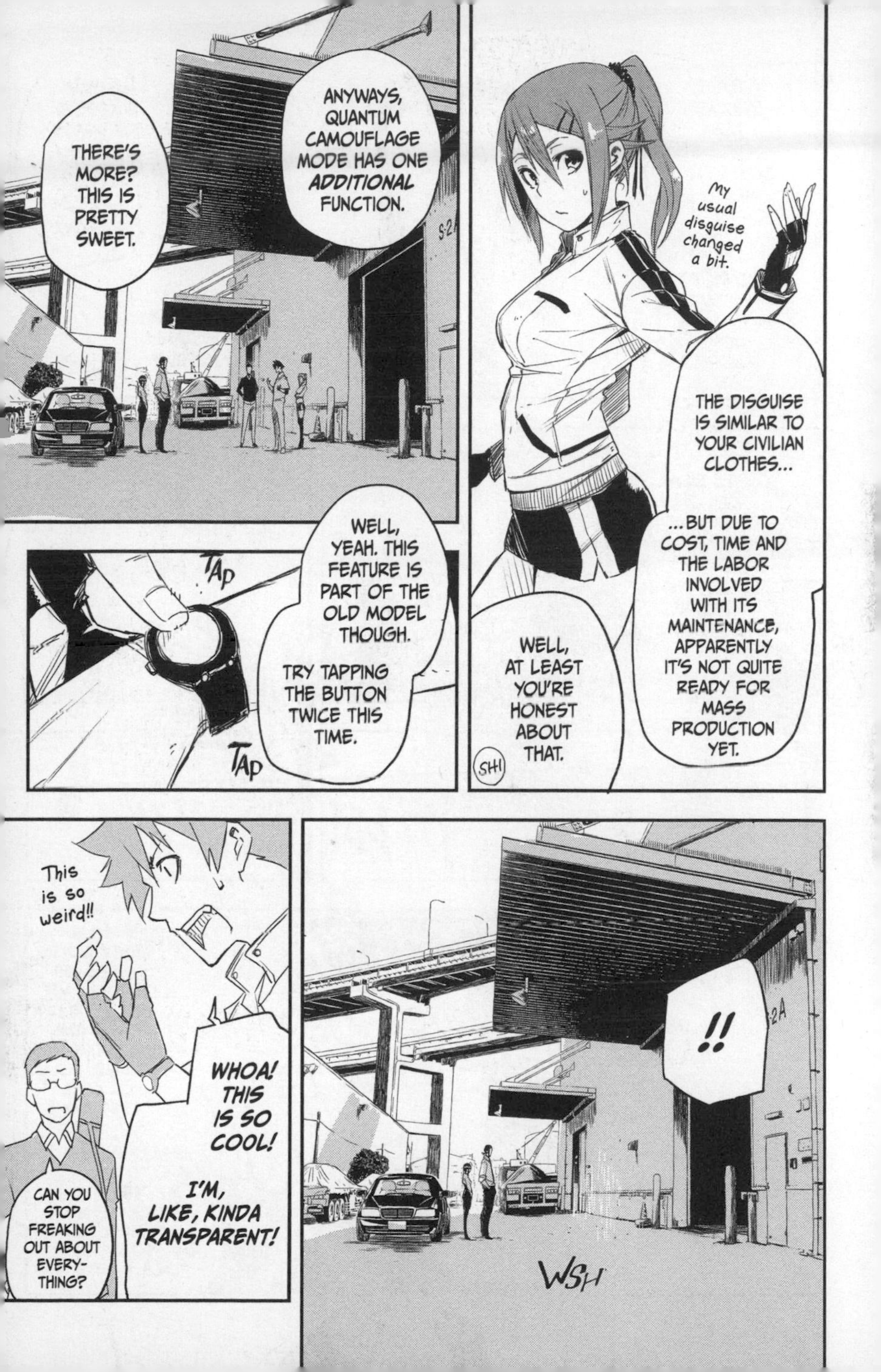
My usual disguise changed a bit.
THE DISGUISE IS SIMILAR TO YOUR CIVILIAN CLOTHES...
...BUT DUE TO COST, TIME AND THE LABOR INVOLVED WITH ITS MAINTENANCE, APPARENTLY IT'S NOT QUITE READY FOR MASS PRODUCTION YET.
WELL, AT LEAST YOU'RE HONEST ABOUT THAT.
SHI
ANYWAYS, QUANTUM CAMOUFLAGE MODE HAS ONE ADDITIONAL FUNCTION.
THERE'S MORE? THIS IS PRETTY SWEET.
WELL, YEAH. THIS FEATURE IS PART OF THE OLD MODEL THOUGH.
TRY TAPPING THE BUTTON TWICE THIS TIME.
TAP
TAP
!!
WSH
This is so weird!!
WHOA! THIS IS SO COOL!
I'M, LIKE, KINDA TRANSPARENT!
CAN YOU STOP FREAKING OUT ABOUT EVERY-THING?

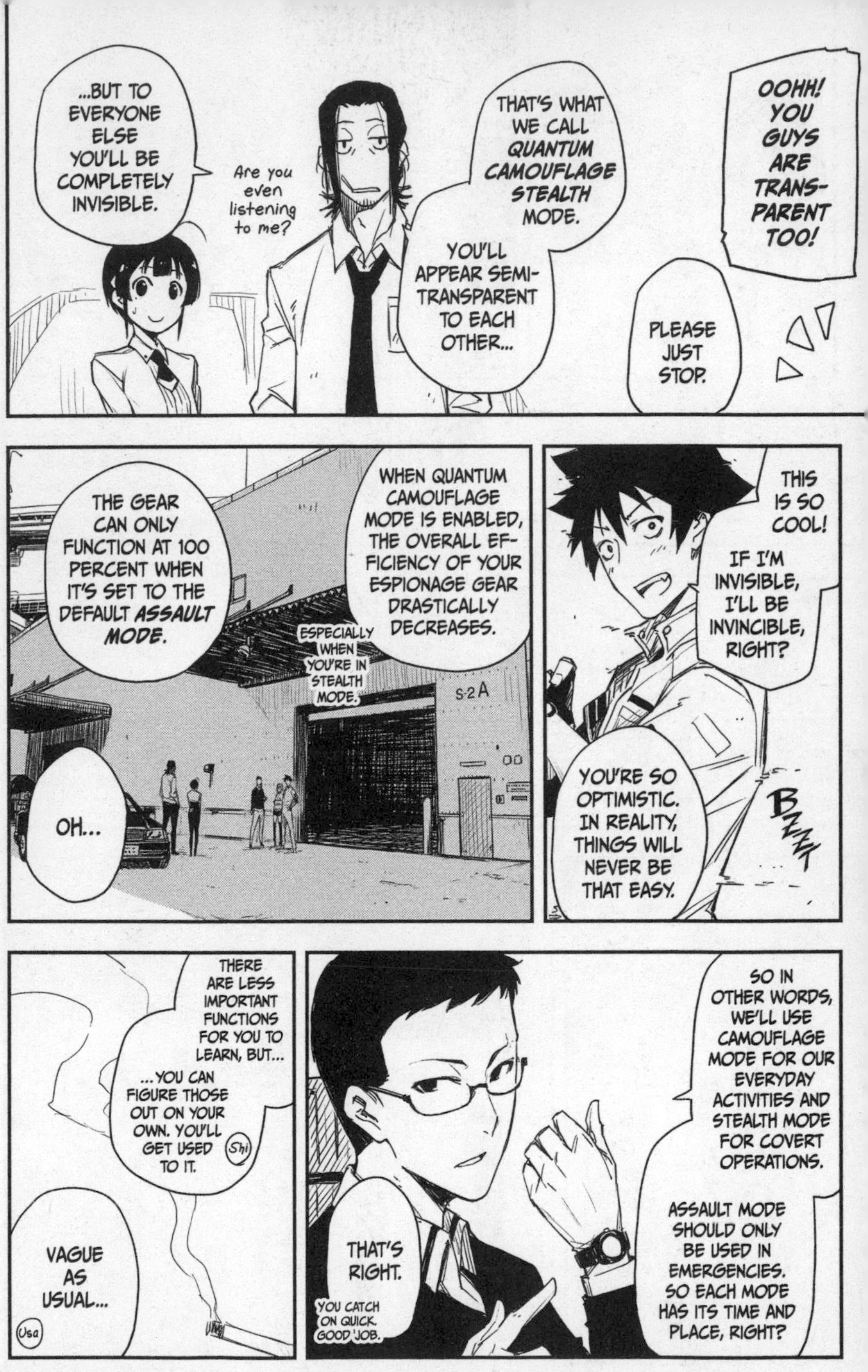
OOHH! YOU GUYS ARE TRANS-PARENT TOO!
PLEASE JUST STOP.
THAT'S WHAT WE CALL *QUANTUM CAMOUFLAGE STEALTH* MODE.
YOU'LL APPEAR SEMI-TRANSPARENT TO EACH OTHER...
Are you even listening to me?
...BUT TO EVERYONE ELSE YOU'LL BE COMPLETELY INVISIBLE.
THIS IS SO COOL!
IF I'M INVISIBLE, I'LL BE INVINCIBLE, RIGHT?
BZZZ
YOU'RE SO OPTIMISTIC. IN REALITY, THINGS WILL NEVER BE THAT EASY.
WHEN QUANTUM CAMOUFLAGE MODE IS ENABLED, THE OVERALL EF-FICIENCY OF YOUR ESPIONAGE GEAR DRASTICALLY DECREASES.
ESPECIALLY WHEN YOU'RE IN STEALTH MODE.
S-2A
THE GEAR CAN ONLY FUNCTION AT 100 PERCENT WHEN IT'S SET TO THE DEFAULT ***ASSAULT MODE***.
OH...
SO IN OTHER WORDS, WE'LL USE CAMOUFLAGE MODE FOR OUR EVERYDAY ACTIVITIES AND STEALTH MODE FOR COVERT OPERATIONS.
ASSAULT MODE SHOULD ONLY BE USED IN EMERGENCIES. SO EACH MODE HAS ITS TIME AND PLACE, RIGHT?
THAT'S RIGHT.
YOU CATCH ON QUICK. GOOD JOB.
THERE ARE LESS IMPORTANT FUNCTIONS FOR YOU TO LEARN, BUT...
...YOU CAN FIGURE THOSE OUT ON YOUR OWN. YOU'LL GET USED TO IT.
Shi
VAGUE AS USUAL...
Usa

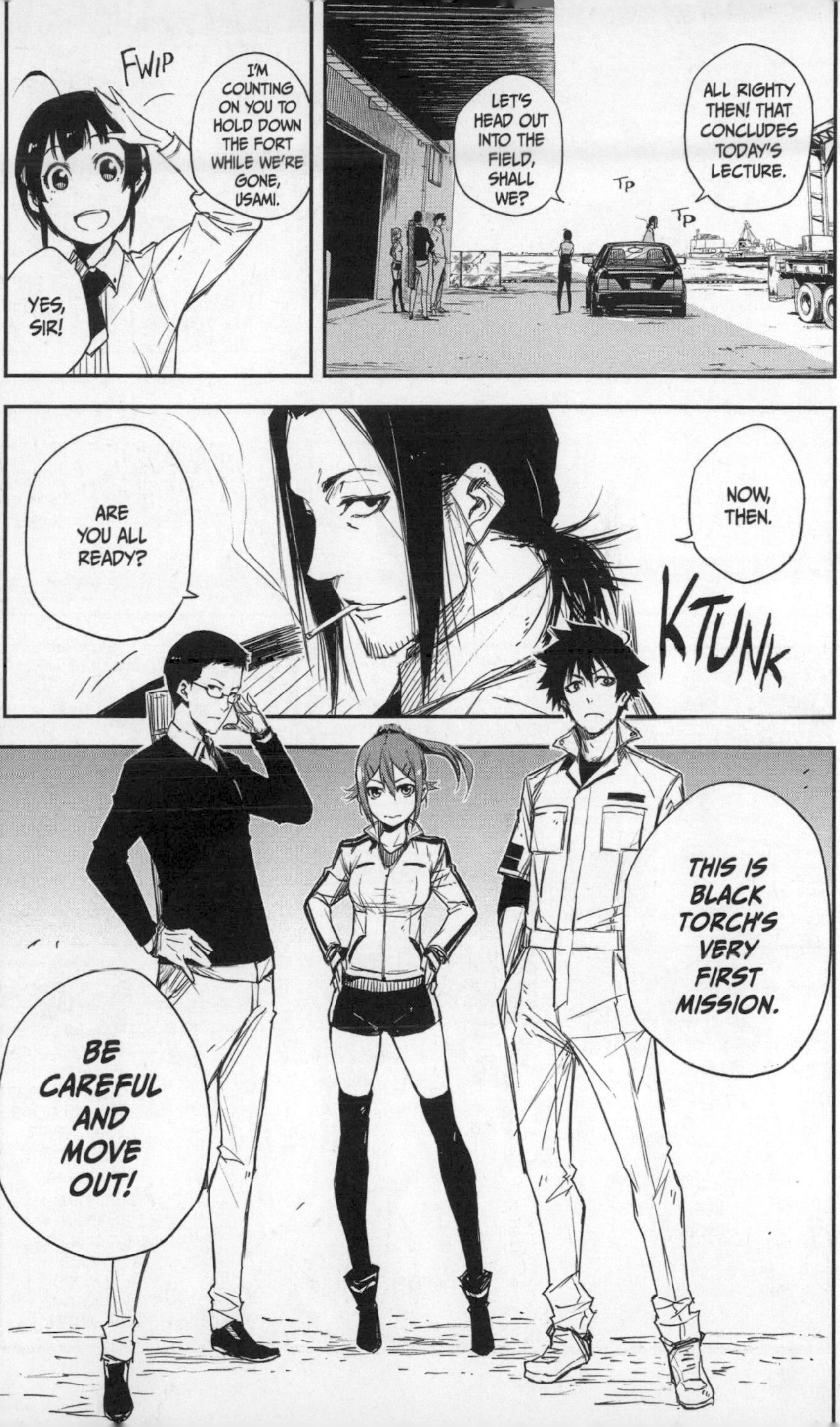
ALL RIGHTY THEN! THAT CONCLUDES TODAY'S LECTURE.
TP
TP
LET'S HEAD OUT INTO THE FIELD, SHALL WE?
I'M COUNTING ON YOU TO HOLD DOWN THE FORT WHILE WE'RE GONE, USAMI.
FWIP
YES, SIR!
NOW, THEN.
KTUNK
ARE YOU ALL READY?
THIS IS BLACK TORCH'S VERY FIRST MISSION.
BE CAREFUL AND MOVE OUT!

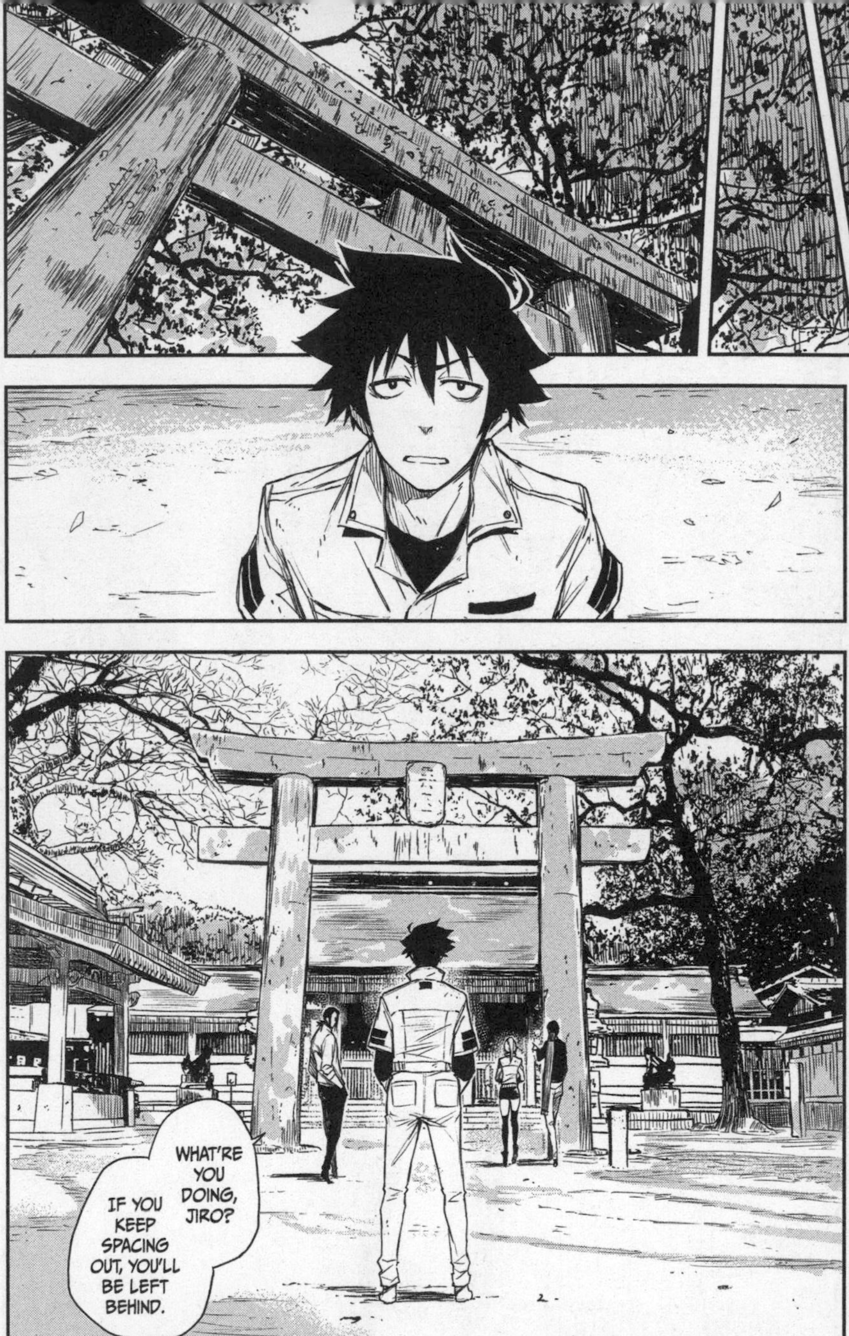
WHAT'RE YOU DOING, JIRO?
IF YOU KEEP SPACING OUT, YOU'LL BE LEFT BEHIND.

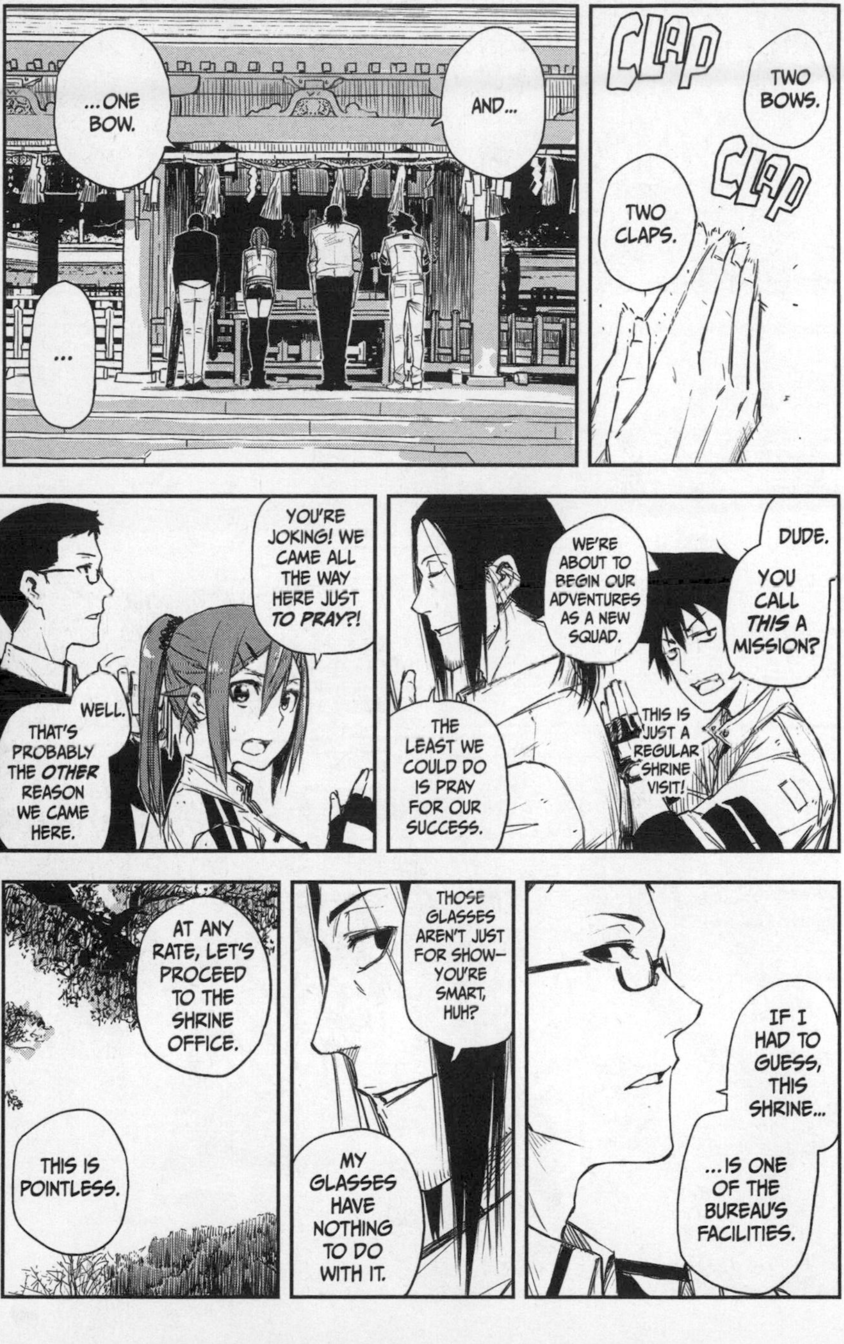
CLAP
TWO BOWS.
CLAP
TWO CLAPS.
AND...
...ONE BOW.
...
DUDE.
YOU CALL THIS A MISSION?
WE'RE ABOUT TO BEGIN OUR ADVENTURES AS A NEW SQUAD.
THIS IS JUST A REGULAR SHRINE VISIT!
THE LEAST WE COULD DO IS PRAY FOR OUR SUCCESS.
YOU'RE JOKING! WE CAME ALL THE WAY HERE JUST *TO PRAY?!*
WELL.
THAT'S PROBABLY THE *OTHER* REASON WE CAME HERE.
IF I HAD TO GUESS, THIS SHRINE...
...IS ONE OF THE BUREAU'S FACILITIES.
THOSE GLASSES AREN'T JUST FOR SHOW—YOU'RE SMART, HUH?
MY GLASSES HAVE NOTHING TO DO WITH IT.
AT ANY RATE, LET'S PROCEED TO THE SHRINE OFFICE.
THIS IS POINTLESS.

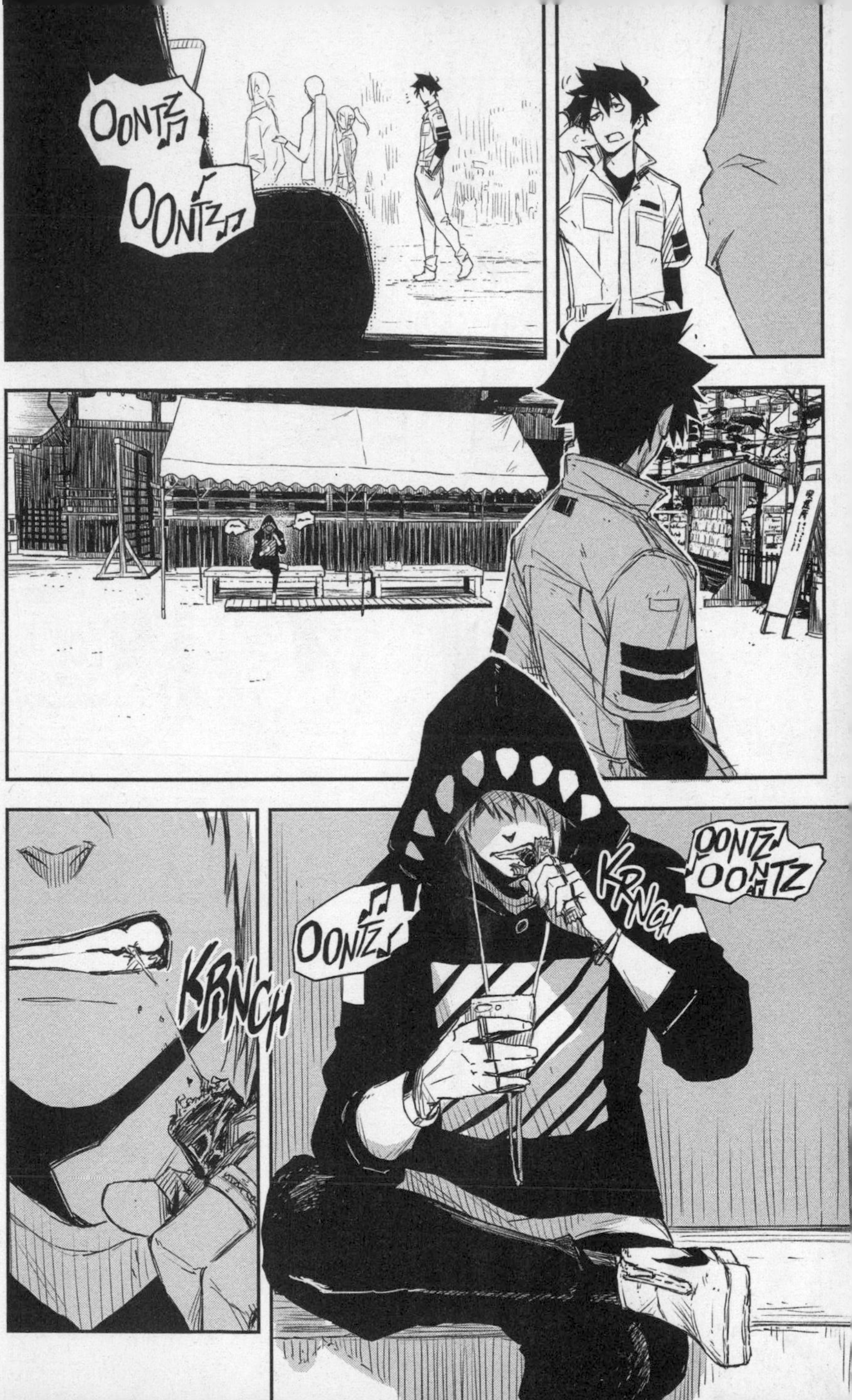
OONTZ
OONTZ
OONTZ OONTZ
KRNCH
OONTZ
KRNCH

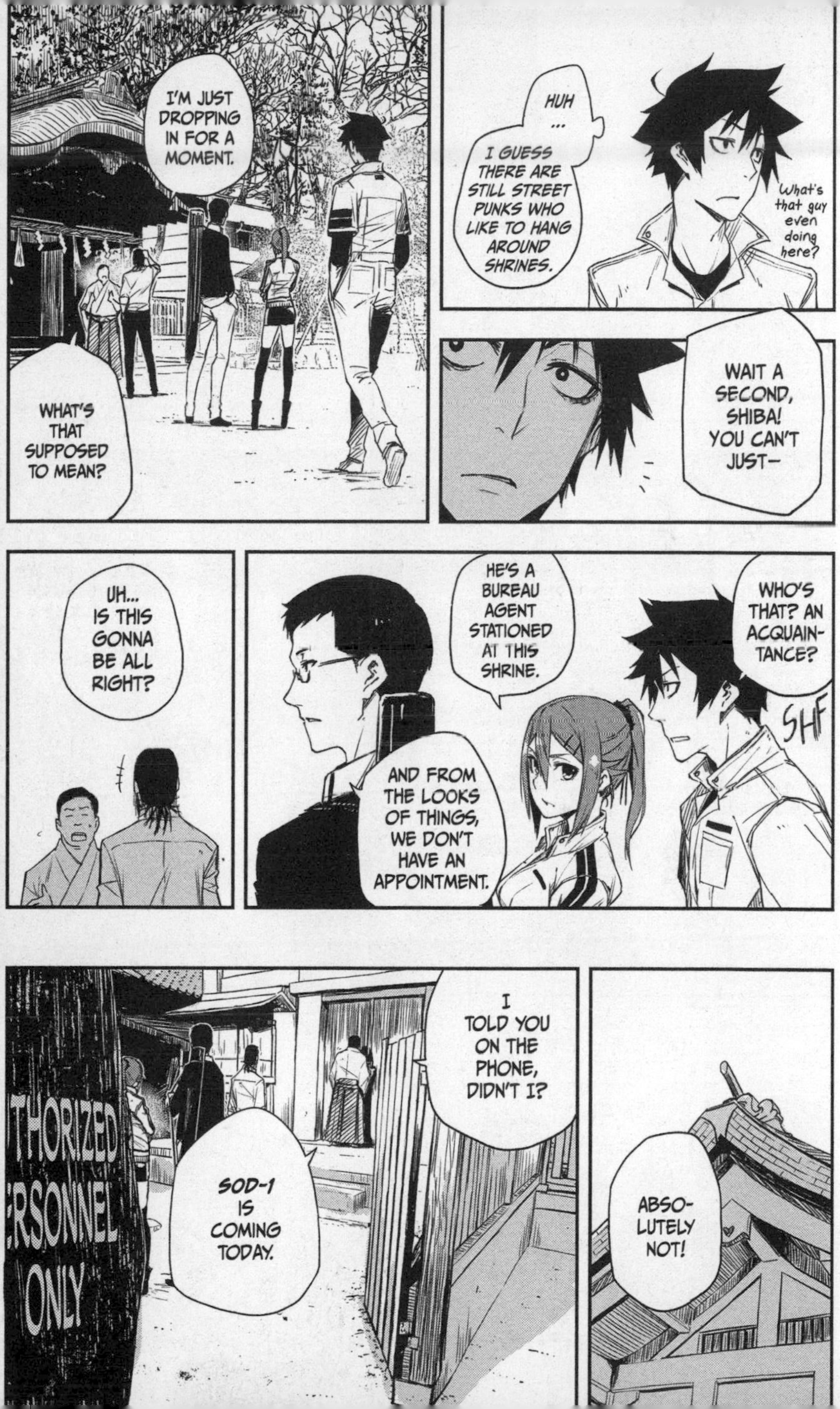
HUH... I GUESS THERE ARE STILL STREET PUNKS WHO LIKE TO HANG AROUND SHRINES.
What's that guy even doing here?
WAIT A SECOND, SHIBA! YOU CAN'T JUST—
I'M JUST DROPPING IN FOR A MOMENT.
WHAT'S THAT SUPPOSED TO MEAN?
WHO'S THAT? AN ACQUAIN-TANCE?
SHF
HE'S A BUREAU AGENT STATIONED AT THIS SHRINE.
AND FROM THE LOOKS OF THINGS, WE DON'T HAVE AN APPOINTMENT.
UH... IS THIS GONNA BE ALL RIGHT?
ABSO-LUTELY NOT!
I TOLD YOU ON THE PHONE, DIDN'T I?
SOD-1 IS COMING TODAY.
THORIZED
ERSONNEL
ONLY

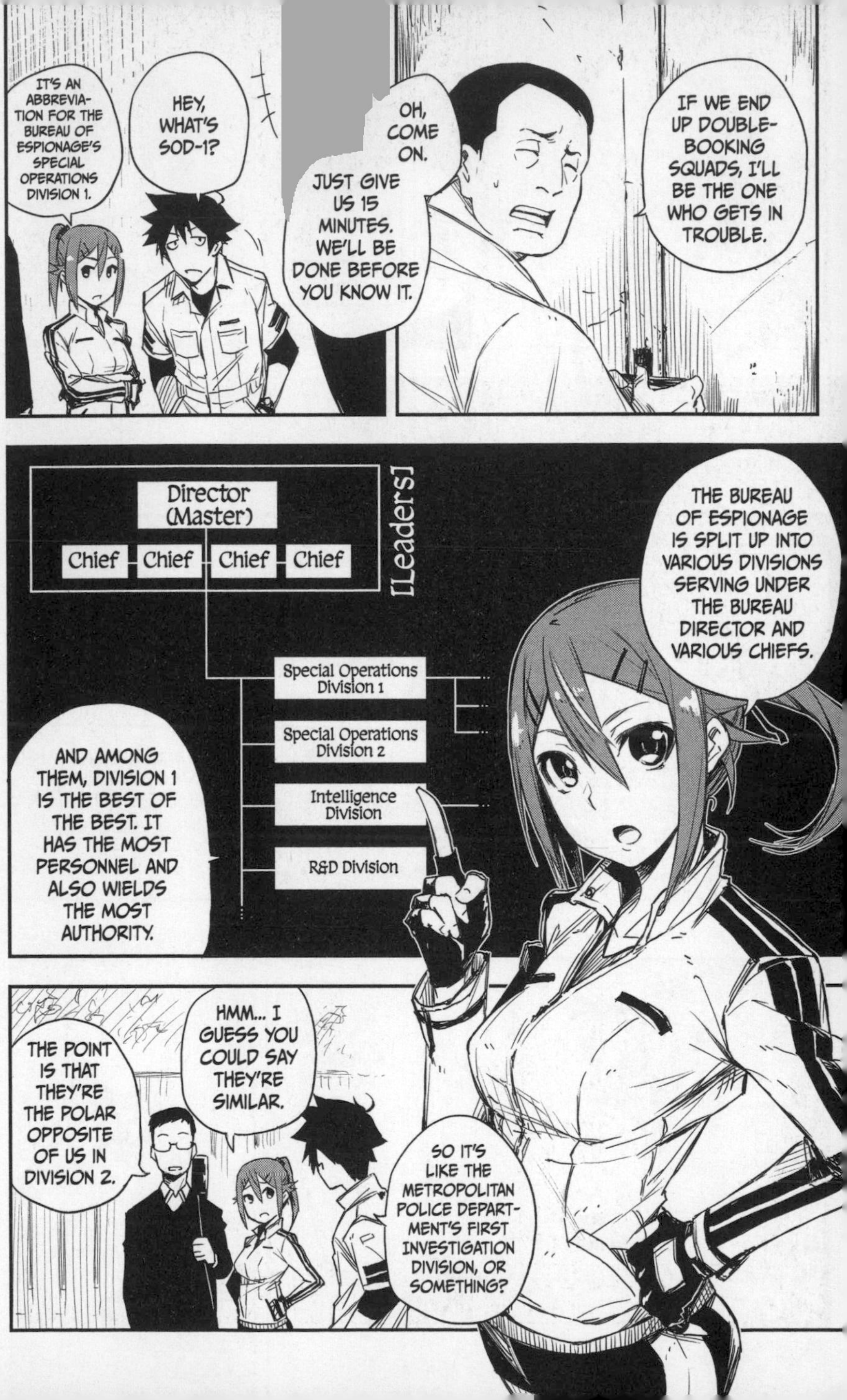
IF WE END UP DOUBLE-BOOKING SQUADS, I'LL BE THE ONE WHO GETS IN TROUBLE.
OH, COME ON.
JUST GIVE US 15 MINUTES. WE'LL BE DONE BEFORE YOU KNOW IT.
HEY, WHAT'S SOD-1?
IT'S AN ABBREVIATION FOR THE BUREAU OF ESPIONAGE'S SPECIAL OPERATIONS DIVISION 1.
THE BUREAU OF ESPIONAGE IS SPLIT UP INTO VARIOUS DIVISIONS SERVING UNDER THE BUREAU DIRECTOR AND VARIOUS CHIEFS.
[Leaders]
Director (Master)
Chief
Chief
Chief
Chief
Special Operations Division 1
Special Operations Division 2
Intelligence Division
R&D Division
AND AMONG THEM, DIVISION 1 IS THE BEST OF THE BEST. IT HAS THE MOST PERSONNEL AND ALSO WIELDS THE MOST AUTHORITY.
SO IT'S LIKE THE METROPOLITAN POLICE DEPARTMENT'S FIRST INVESTIGATION DIVISION, OR SOMETHING?
HMM... I GUESS YOU COULD SAY THEY'RE SIMILAR.
THE POINT IS THAT THEY'RE THE POLAR OPPOSITE OF US IN DIVISION 2.

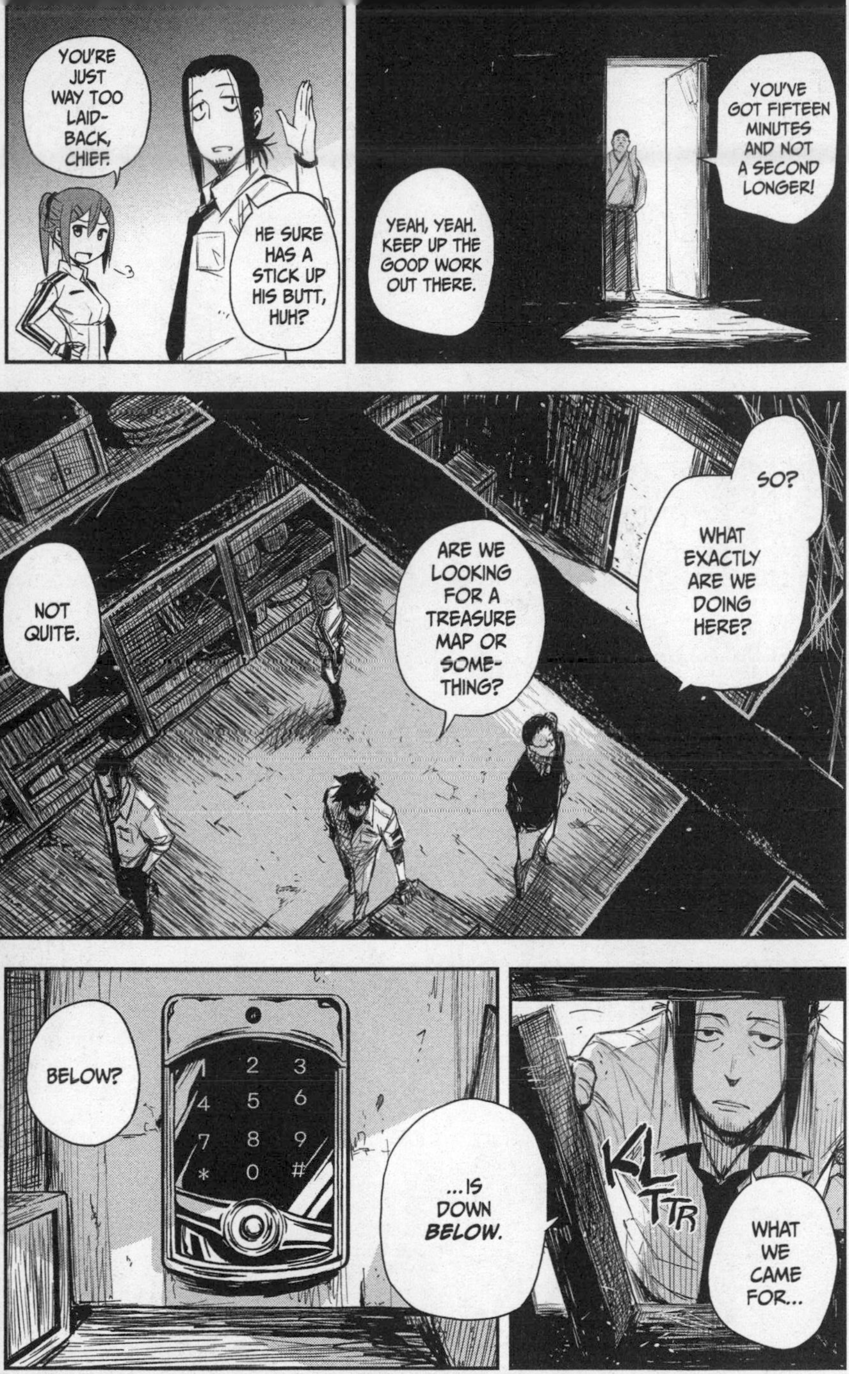
YOU'VE GOT FIFTEEN MINUTES AND NOT A SECOND LONGER!
YEAH, YEAH. KEEP UP THE GOOD WORK OUT THERE.
HE SURE HAS A STICK UP HIS BUTT, HUH?
YOU'RE JUST WAY TOO LAID-BACK, CHIEF.
SO?
WHAT EXACTLY ARE WE DOING HERE?
ARE WE LOOKING FOR A TREASURE MAP OR SOME-THING?
NOT QUITE.
KLTTR
WHAT WE CAME FOR...
...IS DOWN *BELOW*.
BELOW?

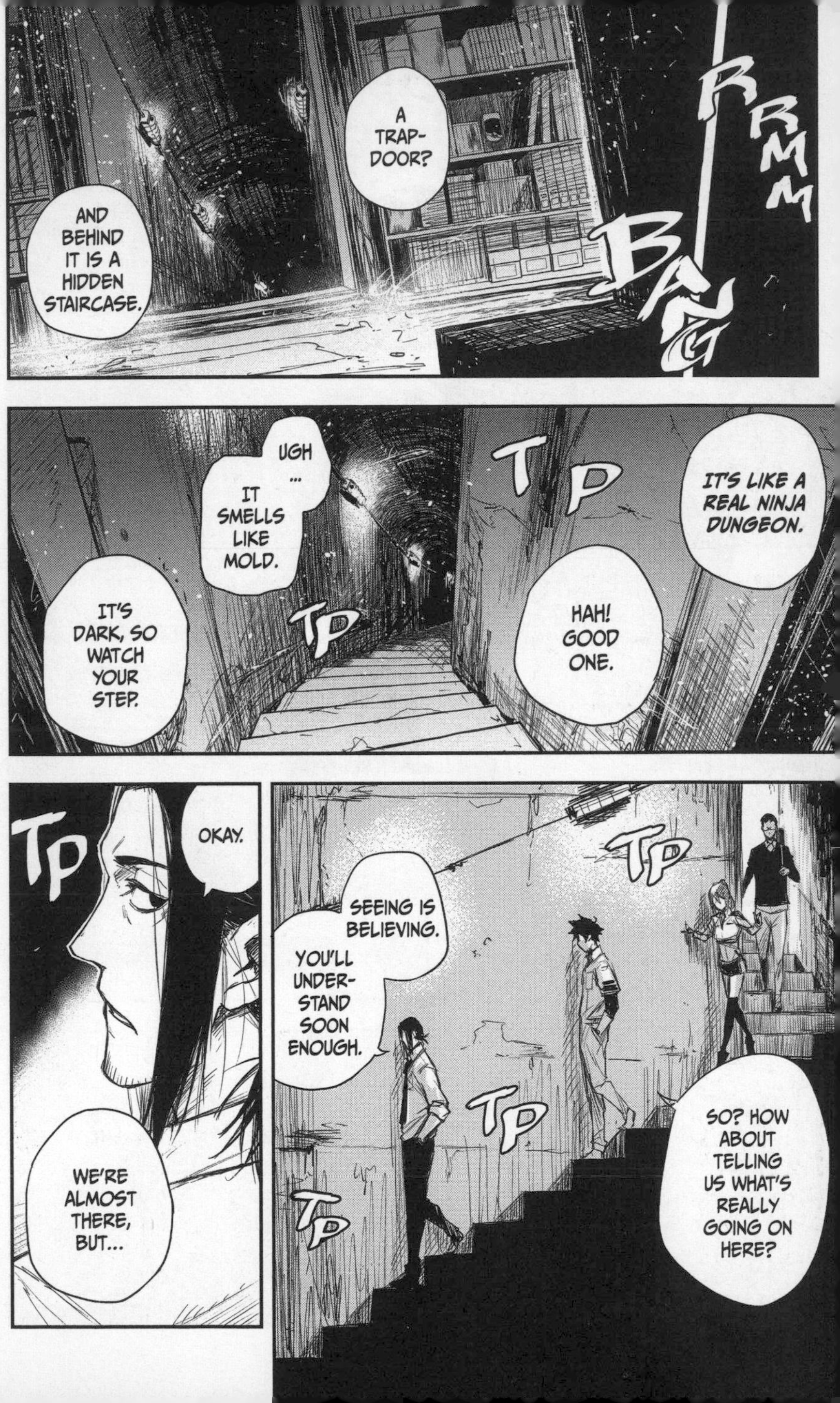
RRMM
BANG
A TRAP-DOOR?
AND BEHIND IT IS A HIDDEN STAIRCASE.
IT'S LIKE A REAL NINJA DUNGEON.
TP
HAH! GOOD ONE.
UGH... IT SMELLS LIKE MOLD.
TP
IT'S DARK, SO WATCH YOUR STEP.
TP
SO? HOW ABOUT TELLING US WHAT'S REALLY GOING ON HERE?
SEEING IS BELIEVING.
YOU'LL UNDER-STAND SOON ENOUGH.
TP
TP
TP
OKAY.
WE'RE ALMOST THERE, BUT...

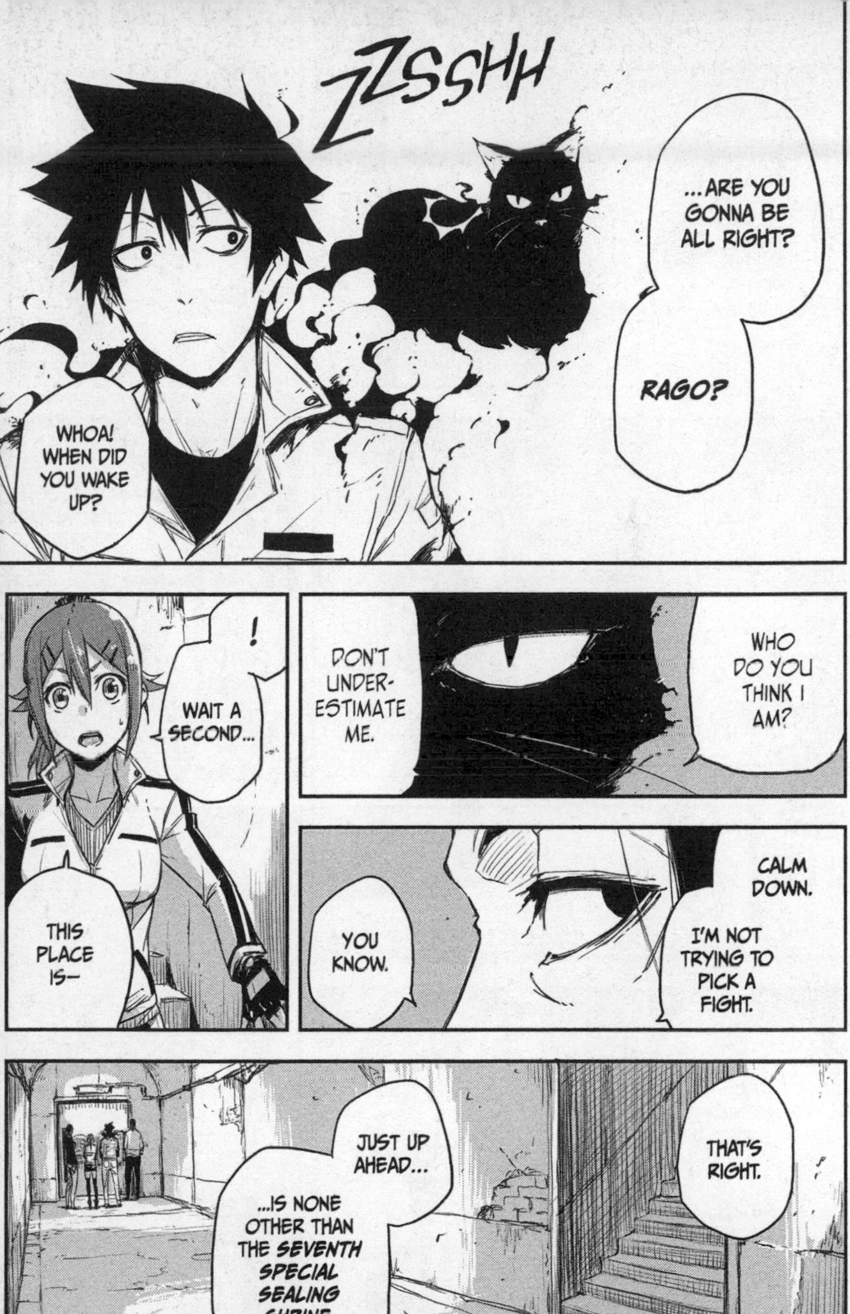
ZZSSHH
...ARE YOU GONNA BE ALL RIGHT?
RAGO?
WHOA! WHEN DID YOU WAKE UP?
WHO DO YOU THINK I AM?
DON'T UNDER-ESTIMATE ME.
CALM DOWN.
I'M NOT TRYING TO PICK A FIGHT.
YOU KNOW.
!
WAIT A SECOND...
THIS PLACE IS—
THAT'S RIGHT.
JUST UP AHEAD...
...IS NONE OTHER THAN THE SEVENTH SPECIAL SEALING SHRINE.

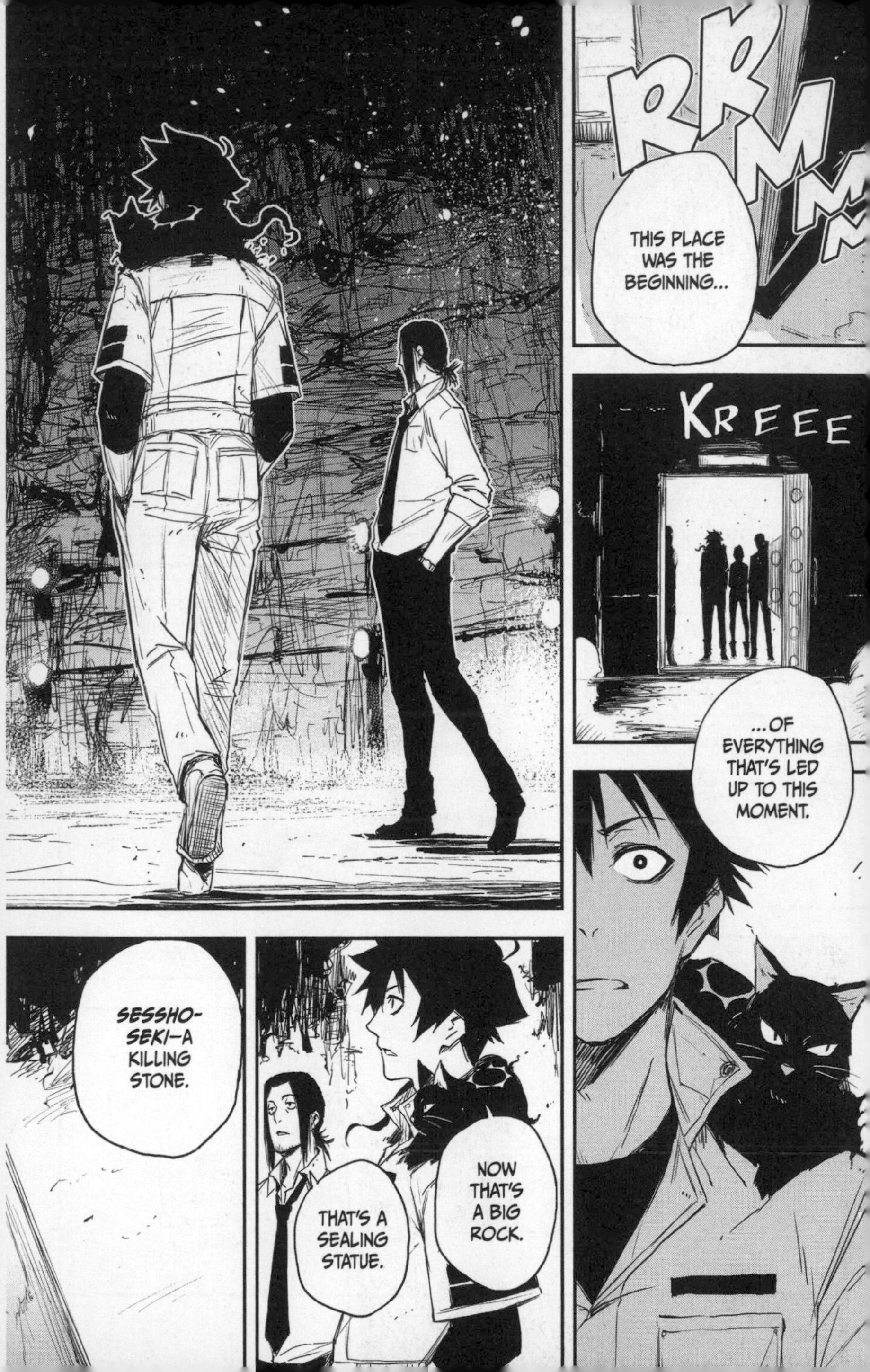
RRMM
THIS PLACE WAS THE BEGINNING...
KREEE
...OF EVERYTHING THAT'S LED UP TO THIS MOMENT.
NOW THAT'S A BIG ROCK.
THAT'S A SEALING STATUE.
SESSHO-SEKI—A KILLING STONE.

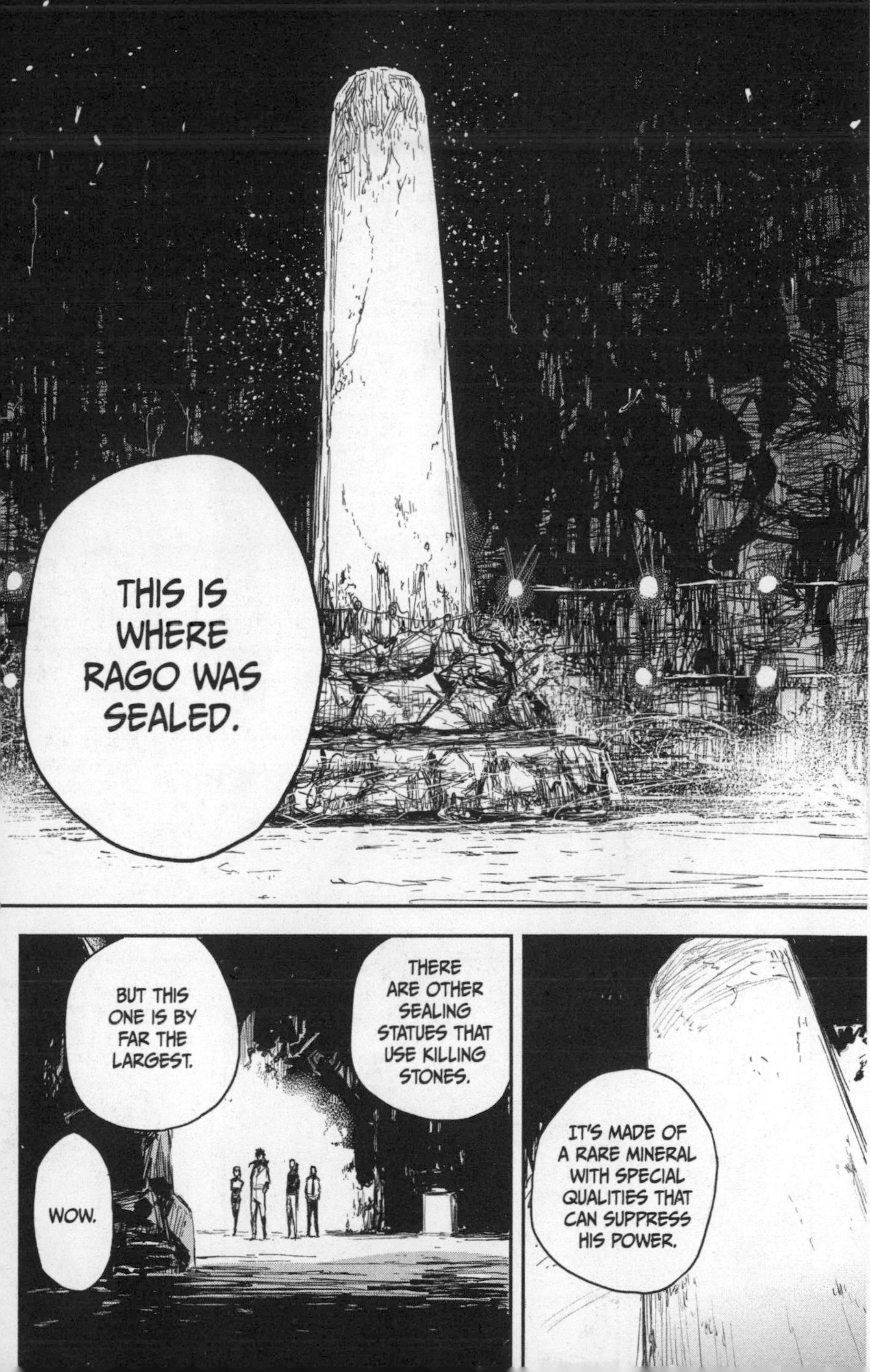
THIS IS WHERE RAGO WAS SEALED.
IT'S MADE OF A RARE MINERAL WITH SPECIAL QUALITIES THAT CAN SUPPRESS HIS POWER.
THERE ARE OTHER SEALING STATUES THAT USE KILLING STONES.
BUT THIS ONE IS BY FAR THE LARGEST.
WOW.

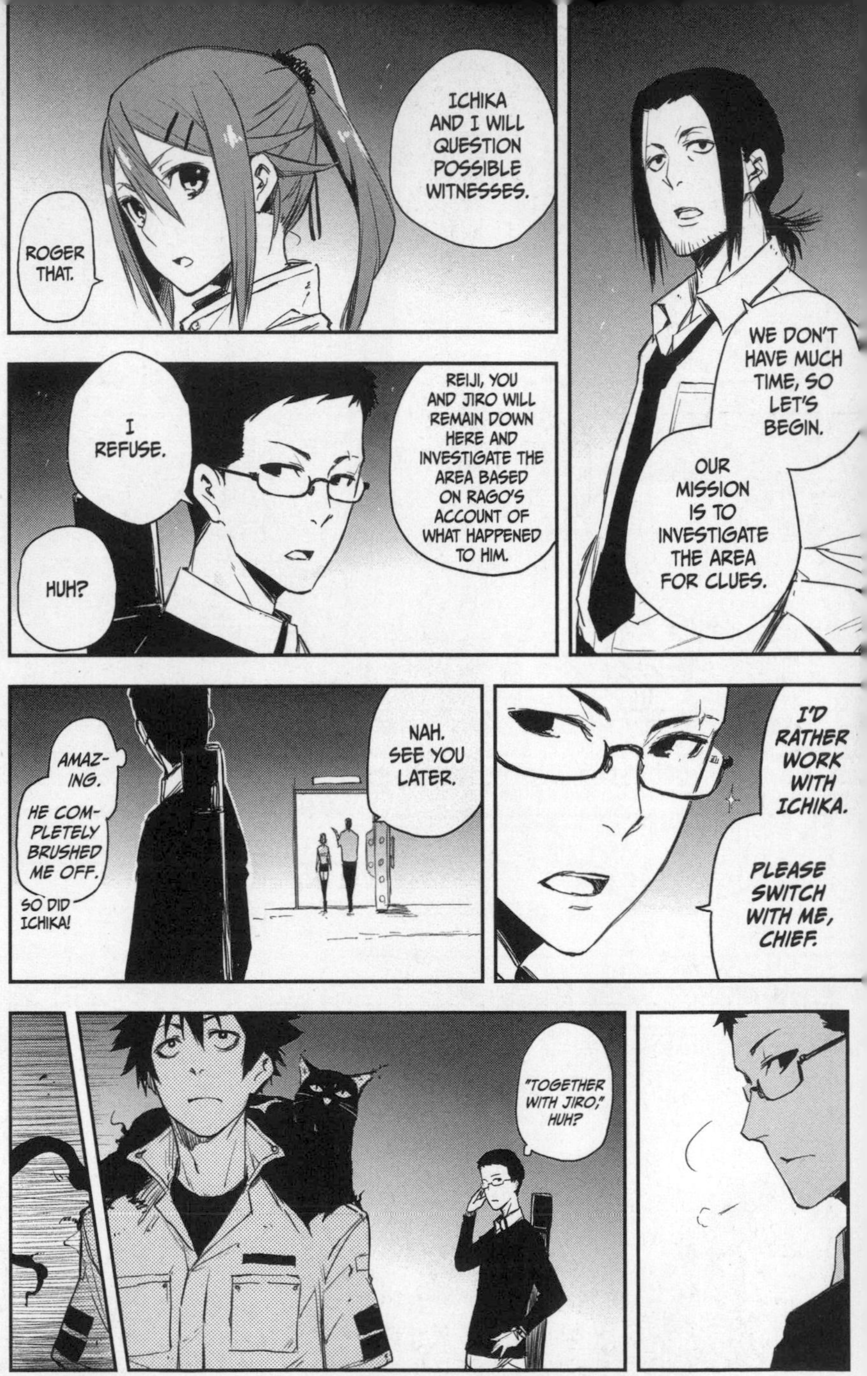
WE DON'T HAVE MUCH TIME, SO LET'S BEGIN.
OUR MISSION IS TO INVESTIGATE THE AREA FOR CLUES.
ICHIKA AND I WILL QUESTION POSSIBLE WITNESSES.
ROGER THAT.
REIJI, YOU AND JIRO WILL REMAIN DOWN HERE AND INVESTIGATE THE AREA BASED ON RAGO'S ACCOUNT OF WHAT HAPPENED TO HIM.
I REFUSE.
HUH?
I'D RATHER WORK WITH ICHIKA.
PLEASE SWITCH WITH ME, CHIEF.
NAH. SEE YOU LATER.
AMAZ-ING.
HE COM-PLETELY BRUSHED ME OFF.
SO DID ICHIKA!
"TOGETHER WITH JIRO," HUH?

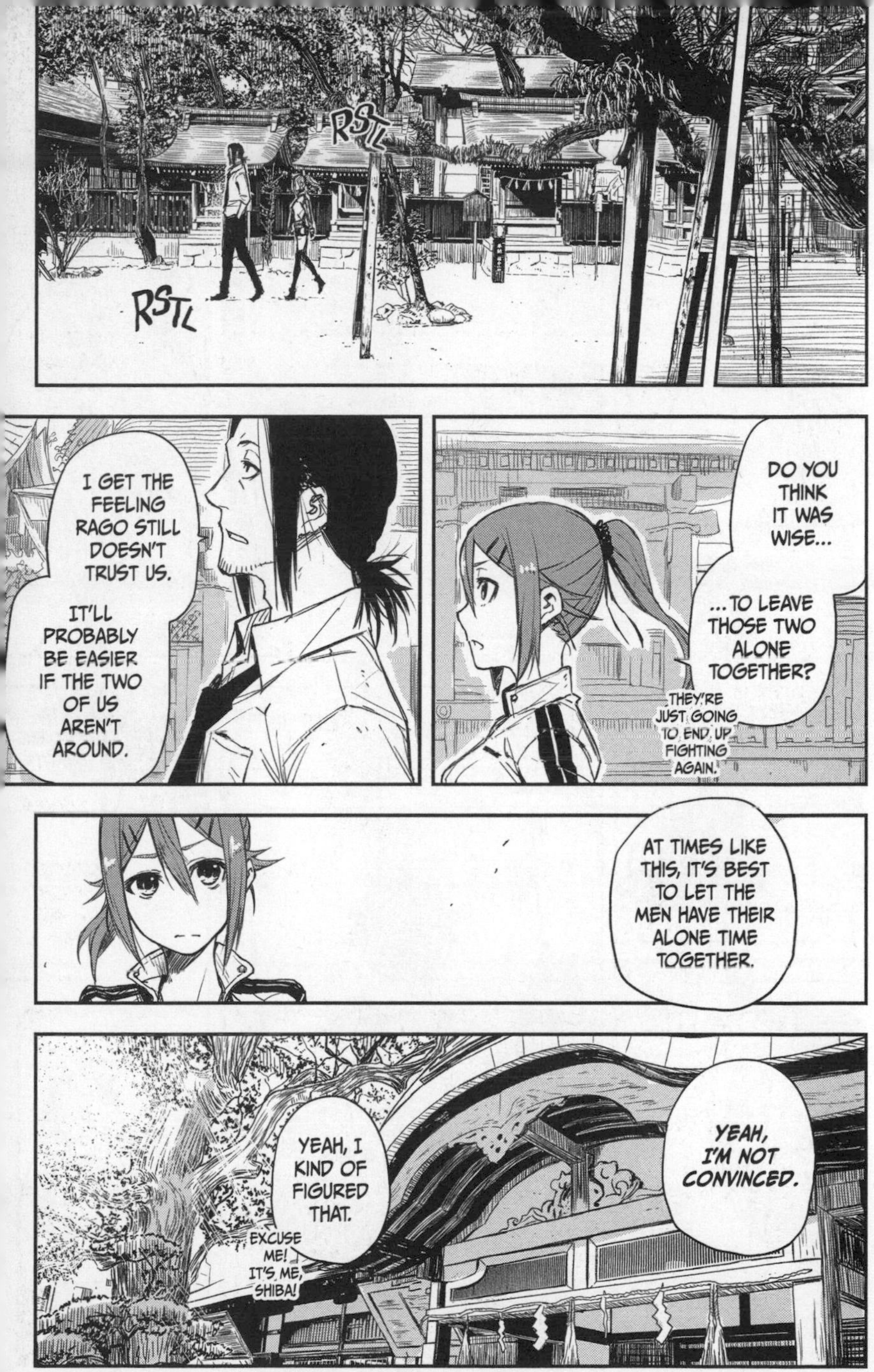
RSTL
RSTL
DO YOU THINK IT WAS WISE...
...TO LEAVE THOSE TWO ALONE TOGETHER?
THEY'RE JUST GOING TO END UP FIGHTING AGAIN.
I GET THE FEELING RAGO STILL DOESN'T TRUST US.
IT'LL PROBABLY BE EASIER IF THE TWO OF US AREN'T AROUND.
AT TIMES LIKE THIS, IT'S BEST TO LET THE MEN HAVE THEIR ALONE TIME TOGETHER.
YEAH, I'M NOT CONVINCED.
YEAH, I KIND OF FIGURED THAT.
EXCUSE ME! IT'S ME, SHIBA!

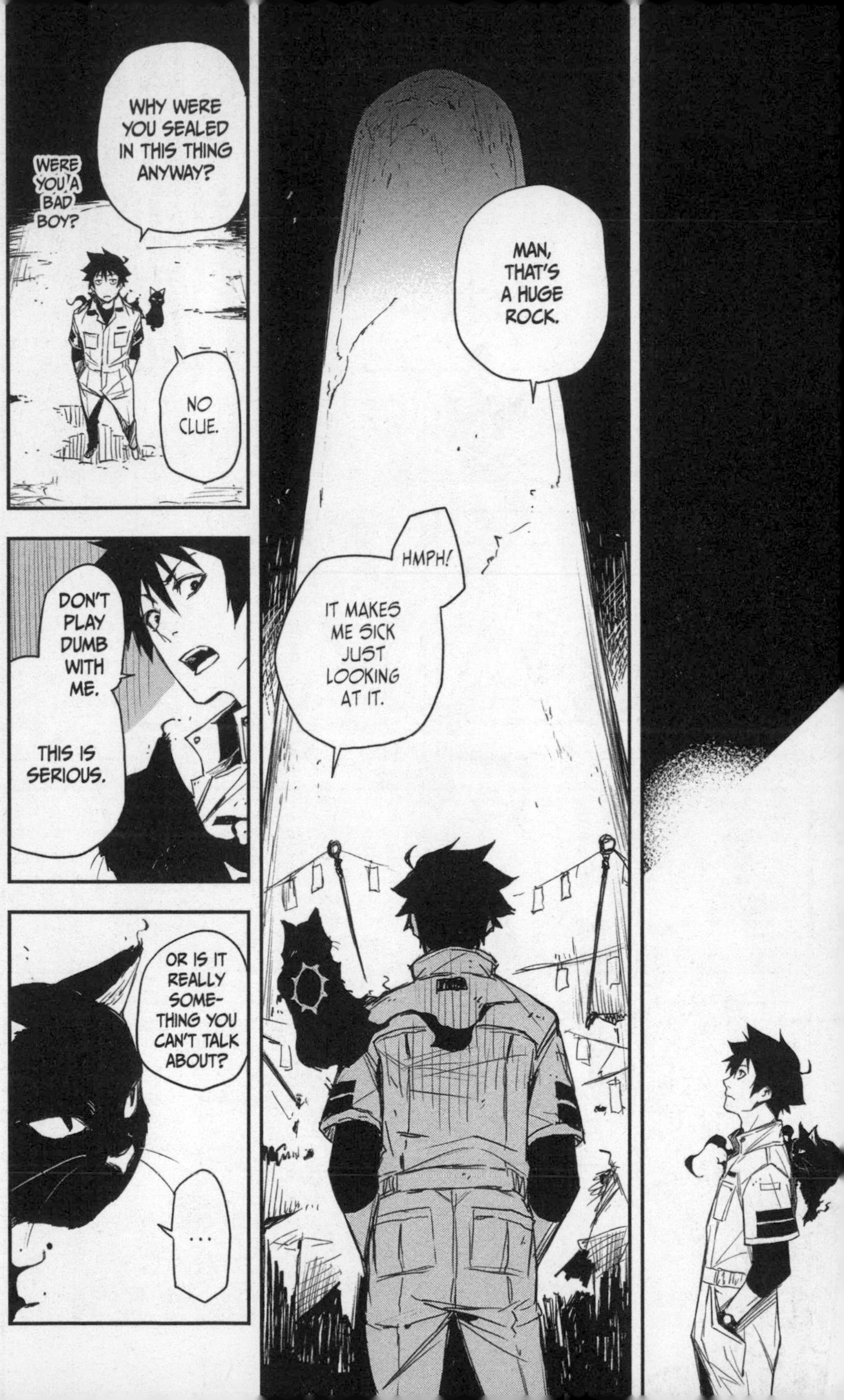
MAN, THAT'S A HUGE ROCK.
HMPH!
IT MAKES ME SICK JUST LOOKING AT IT.
WHY WERE YOU SEALED IN THIS THING ANYWAY?
WERE YOU A BAD BOY?
NO CLUE.
DON'T PLAY DUMB WITH ME.
THIS IS SERIOUS.
OR IS IT REALLY SOME-THING YOU CAN'T TALK ABOUT?
...

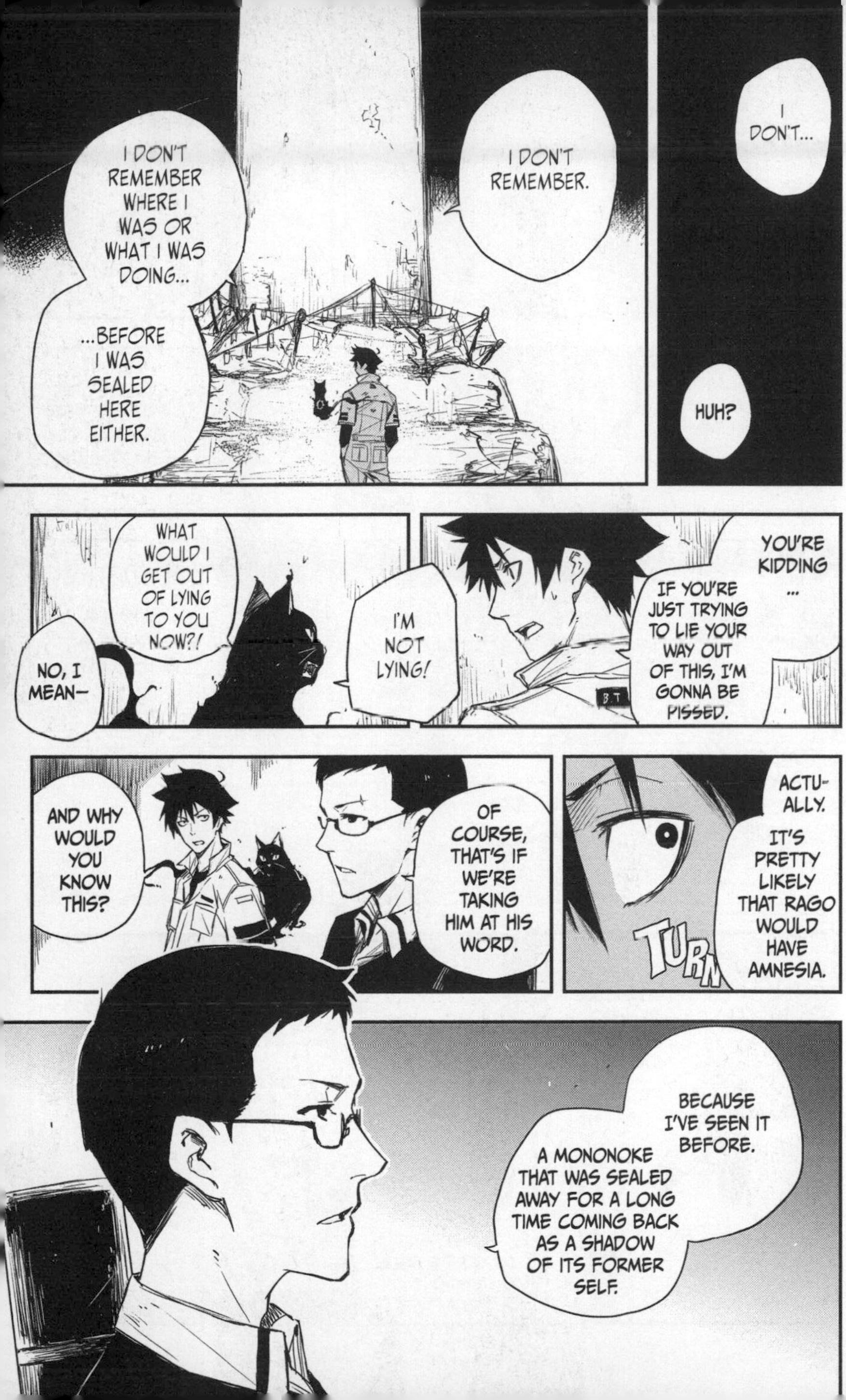
I DON'T...
HUH?
I DON'T REMEMBER.
I DON'T REMEMBER WHERE I WAS OR WHAT I WAS DOING...
...BEFORE I WAS SEALED HERE EITHER.
YOU'RE KIDDING ...
IF YOU'RE JUST TRYING TO LIE YOUR WAY OUT OF THIS, I'M GONNA BE PISSED.
I'M NOT LYING!
WHAT WOULD I GET OUT OF LYING TO YOU NOW?!
NO, I MEAN—
ACTU-ALLY.
IT'S PRETTY LIKELY THAT RAGO WOULD HAVE AMNESIA.
TURN
OF COURSE, THAT'S IF WE'RE TAKING HIM AT HIS WORD.
AND WHY WOULD YOU KNOW THIS?
BECAUSE I'VE SEEN IT BEFORE.
A MONONOKE THAT WAS SEALED AWAY FOR A LONG TIME COMING BACK AS A SHADOW OF ITS FORMER SELF.

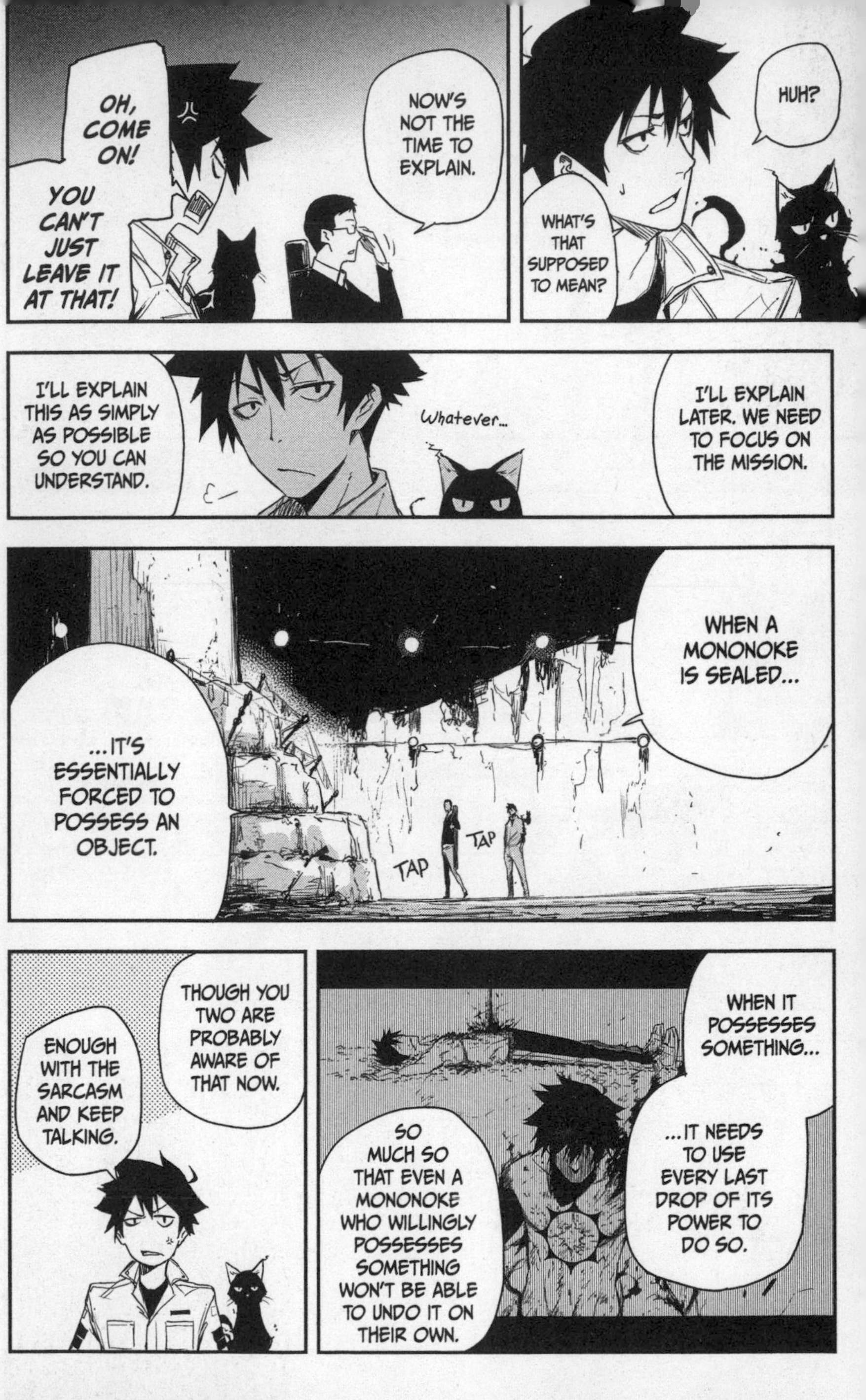
HUH?
WHAT'S THAT SUPPOSED TO MEAN?
NOW'S NOT THE TIME TO EXPLAIN.
OH, COME ON!
YOU CAN'T JUST LEAVE IT AT THAT!
I'LL EXPLAIN LATER. WE NEED TO FOCUS ON THE MISSION.
Whatever...
I'LL EXPLAIN THIS AS SIMPLY AS POSSIBLE SO YOU CAN UNDERSTAND.
WHEN A MONONOKE IS SEALED...
TAP
TAP
...IT'S ESSENTIALLY FORCED TO POSSESS AN OBJECT.
WHEN IT POSSESSES SOMETHING...
...IT NEEDS TO USE EVERY LAST DROP OF ITS POWER TO DO SO.
SO MUCH SO THAT EVEN A MONONOKE WHO WILLINGLY POSSESSES SOMETHING WON'T BE ABLE TO UNDO IT ON THEIR OWN.
THOUGH YOU TWO ARE PROBABLY AWARE OF THAT NOW.
ENOUGH WITH THE SARCASM AND KEEP TALKING.

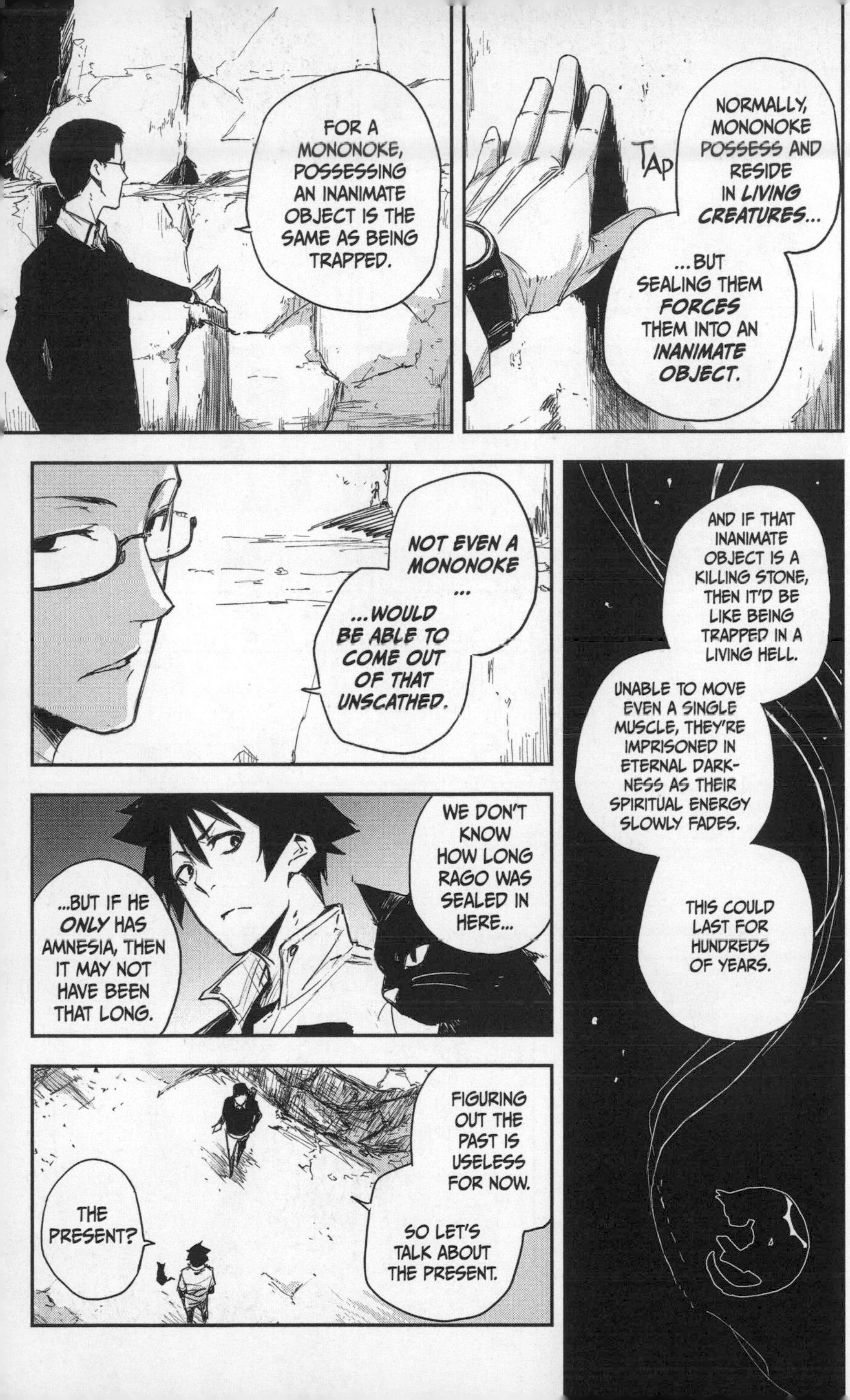
NORMALLY, MONONOKE POSSESS AND RESIDE IN *LIVING CREATURES*...
TAP
...BUT SEALING THEM *FORCES* THEM INTO AN *INANIMATE OBJECT*.
FOR A MONONOKE, POSSESSING AN INANIMATE OBJECT IS THE SAME AS BEING TRAPPED.
AND IF THAT INANIMATE OBJECT IS A KILLING STONE, THEN IT'D BE LIKE BEING TRAPPED IN A LIVING HELL.
UNABLE TO MOVE EVEN A SINGLE MUSCLE, THEY'RE IMPRISONED IN ETERNAL DARK-NESS AS THEIR SPIRITUAL ENERGY SLOWLY FADES.
THIS COULD LAST FOR HUNDREDS OF YEARS.
NOT EVEN A MONONOKE ...
...WOULD BE ABLE TO COME OUT OF THAT UNSCATHED.
WE DON'T KNOW HOW LONG RAGO WAS SEALED IN HERE...
...BUT IF HE *ONLY* HAS AMNESIA, THEN IT MAY NOT HAVE BEEN THAT LONG.
FIGURING OUT THE PAST IS USELESS FOR NOW.
SO LET'S TALK ABOUT THE PRESENT.
THE PRESENT?

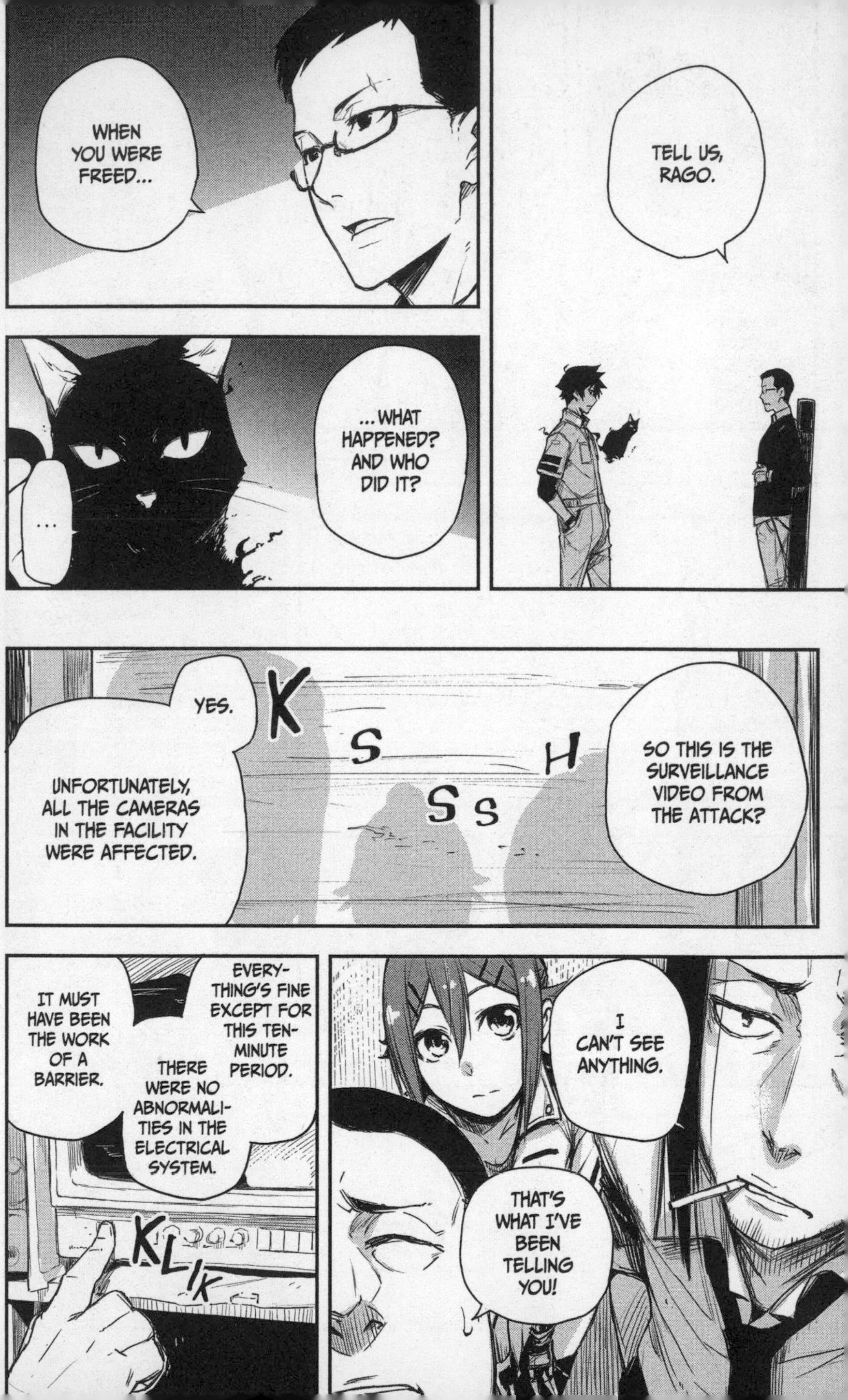
TELL US, RAGO.
WHEN YOU WERE FREED...
...WHAT HAPPENED? AND WHO DID IT?
...
SO THIS IS THE SURVEILLANCE VIDEO FROM THE ATTACK?
KSHSS
YES.
UNFORTUNATELY, ALL THE CAMERAS IN THE FACILITY WERE AFFECTED.
I CAN'T SEE ANYTHING.
THAT'S WHAT I'VE BEEN TELLING YOU!
EVERYTHING'S FINE EXCEPT FOR THIS TEN-MINUTE PERIOD.
THERE WERE NO ABNORMALITIES IN THE ELECTRICAL SYSTEM.
IT MUST HAVE BEEN THE WORK OF A BARRIER.
KLIK

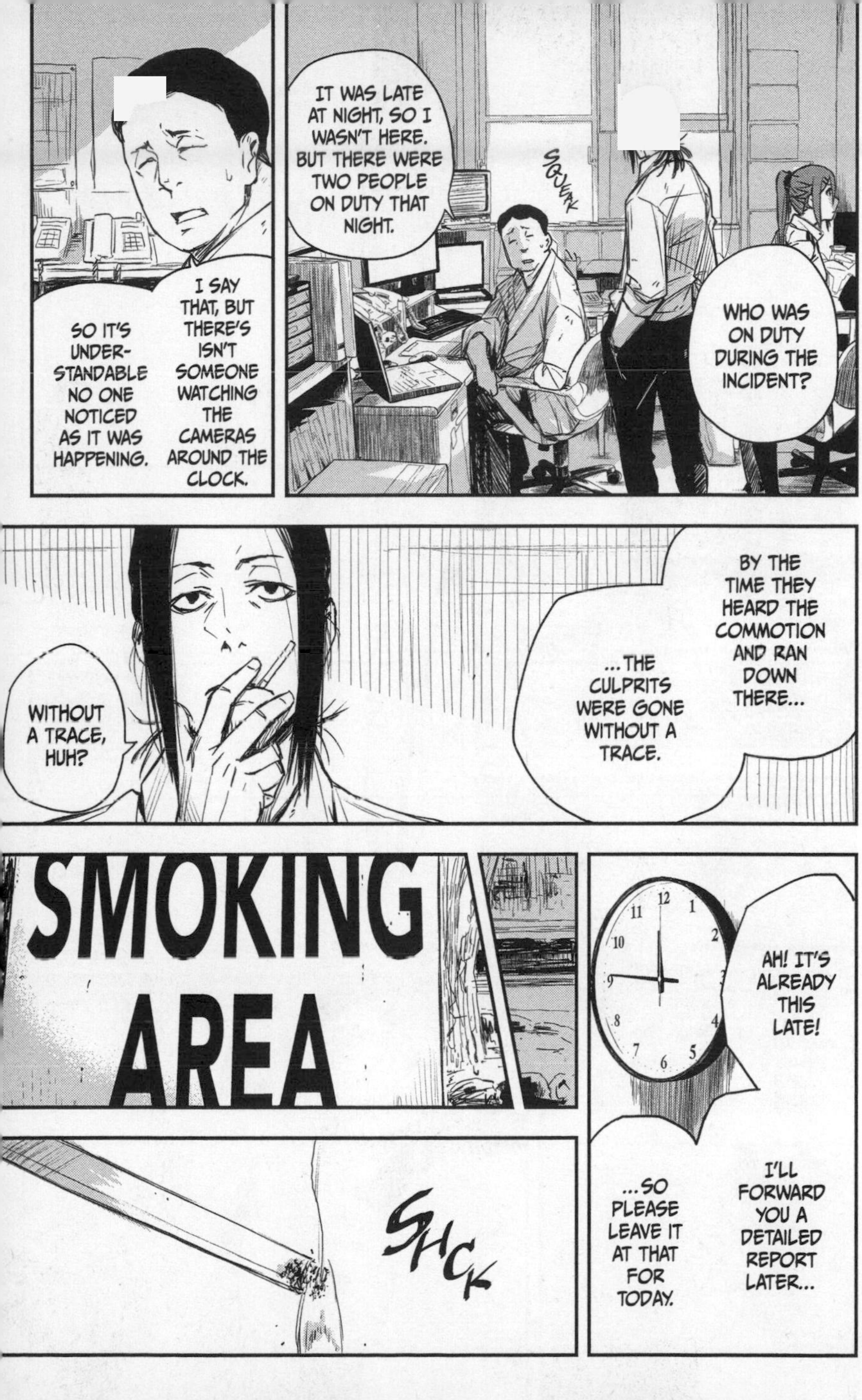
WHO WAS ON DUTY DURING THE INCIDENT?
SQUEAK
IT WAS LATE AT NIGHT, SO I WASN'T HERE. BUT THERE WERE TWO PEOPLE ON DUTY THAT NIGHT.
I SAY THAT, BUT THERE'S ISN'T SOMEONE WATCHING THE CAMERAS AROUND THE CLOCK.
SO IT'S UNDER-STANDABLE NO ONE NOTICED AS IT WAS HAPPENING.
BY THE TIME THEY HEARD THE COMMOTION AND RAN DOWN THERE...
...THE CULPRITS WERE GONE WITHOUT A TRACE.
WITHOUT A TRACE, HUH?
AH! IT'S ALREADY THIS LATE!
I'LL FORWARD YOU A DETAILED REPORT LATER...
...SO PLEASE LEAVE IT AT THAT FOR TODAY.
SMOKING AREA
SHCK

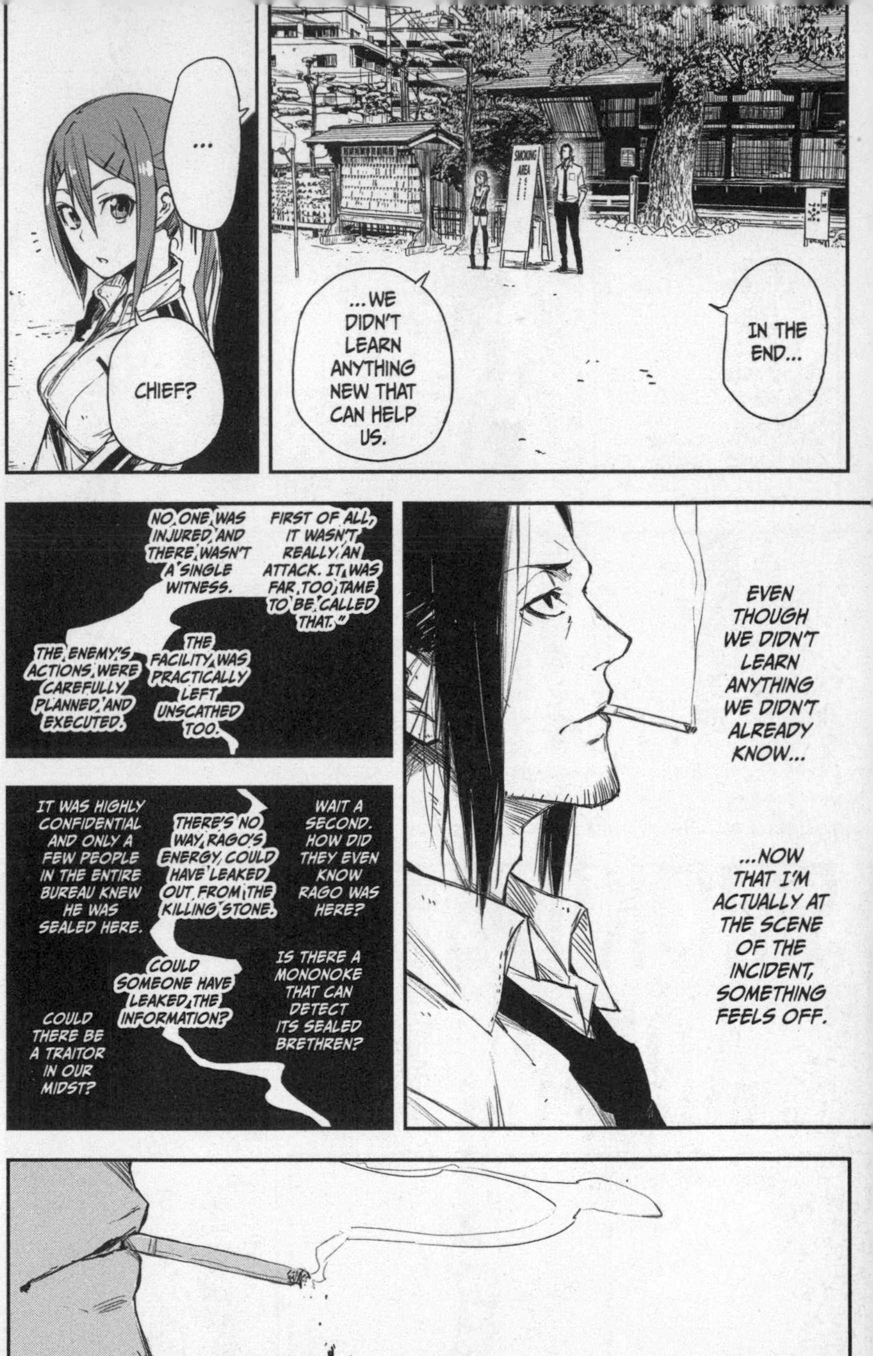
SMOKING AREA
IN THE END...
...WE DIDN'T LEARN ANYTHING NEW THAT CAN HELP US.
...
CHIEF?
EVEN THOUGH WE DIDN'T LEARN ANYTHING WE DIDN'T ALREADY KNOW...
...NOW THAT I'M ACTUALLY AT THE SCENE OF THE INCIDENT, SOMETHING FEELS OFF.
FIRST OF ALL, IT WASN'T REALLY AN ATTACK. IT WAS FAR TOO TAME TO BE CALLED THAT."
NO ONE WAS INJURED, AND THERE WASN'T A SINGLE WITNESS.
THE FACILITY WAS PRACTICALLY LEFT UNSCATHED TOO.
THE ENEMY'S ACTIONS WERE CAREFULLY PLANNED AND EXECUTED.
WAIT A SECOND. HOW DID THEY EVEN KNOW RAGO WAS HERE?
THERE'S NO WAY RAGO'S ENERGY COULD HAVE LEAKED OUT FROM THE KILLING STONE.
IT WAS HIGHLY CONFIDENTIAL AND ONLY A FEW PEOPLE IN THE ENTIRE BUREAU KNEW HE WAS SEALED HERE.
IS THERE A MONONOKE THAT CAN DETECT ITS SEALED BRETHREN?
COULD SOMEONE HAVE LEAKED THE INFORMATION?
COULD THERE BE A TRAITOR IN OUR MIDST?

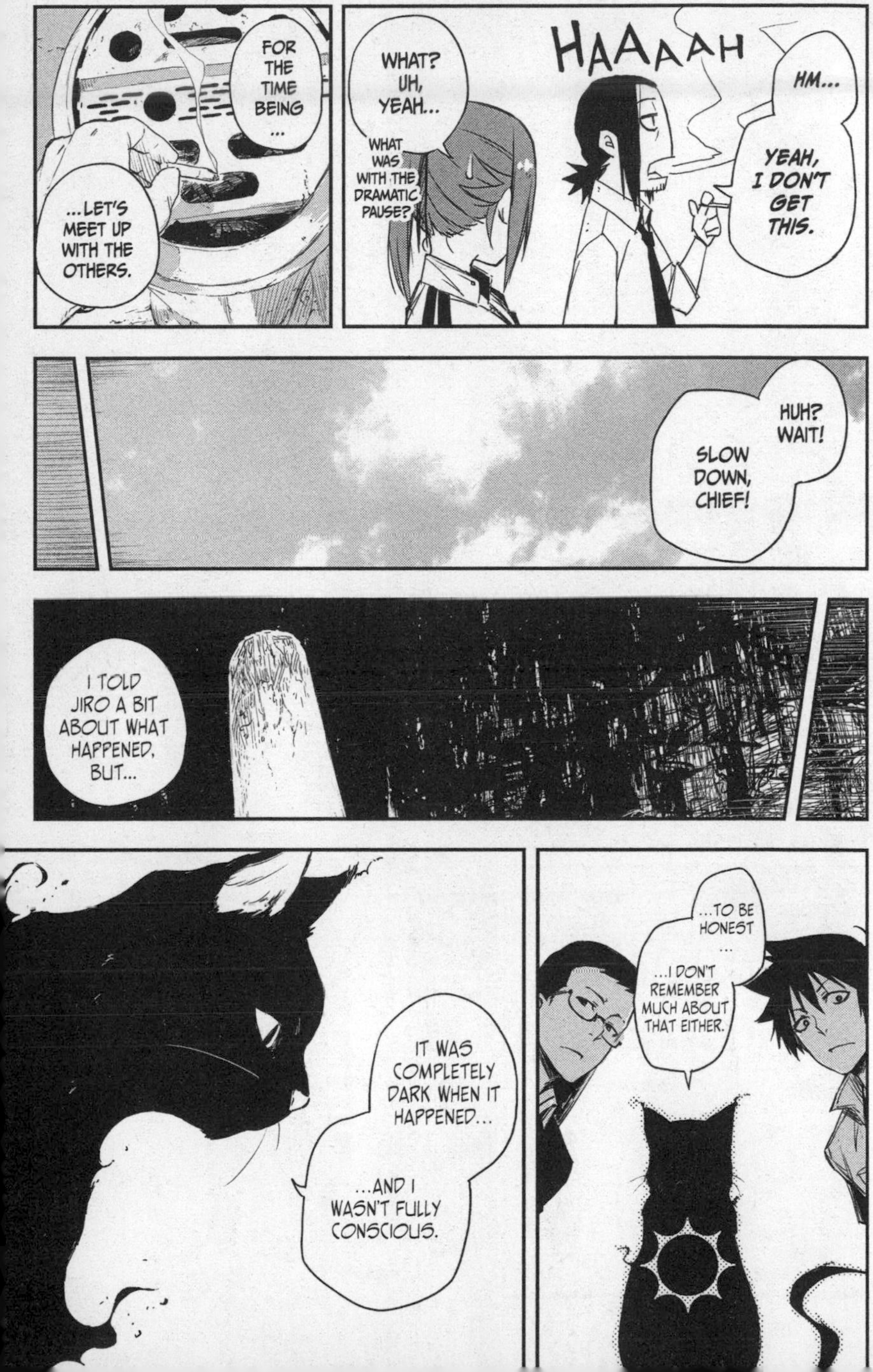
HAAAAH
HM...
YEAH, I DON'T GET THIS.
WHAT? UH, YEAH...
WHAT WAS WITH THE DRAMATIC PAUSE?
FOR THE TIME BEING ...
...LET'S MEET UP WITH THE OTHERS.
HUH? WAIT!
SLOW DOWN, CHIEF!
I TOLD JIRO A BIT ABOUT WHAT HAPPENED, BUT...
...TO BE HONEST ...
...I DON'T REMEMBER MUCH ABOUT THAT EITHER.
IT WAS COMPLETELY DARK WHEN IT HAPPENED...
...AND I WASN'T FULLY CONSCIOUS.

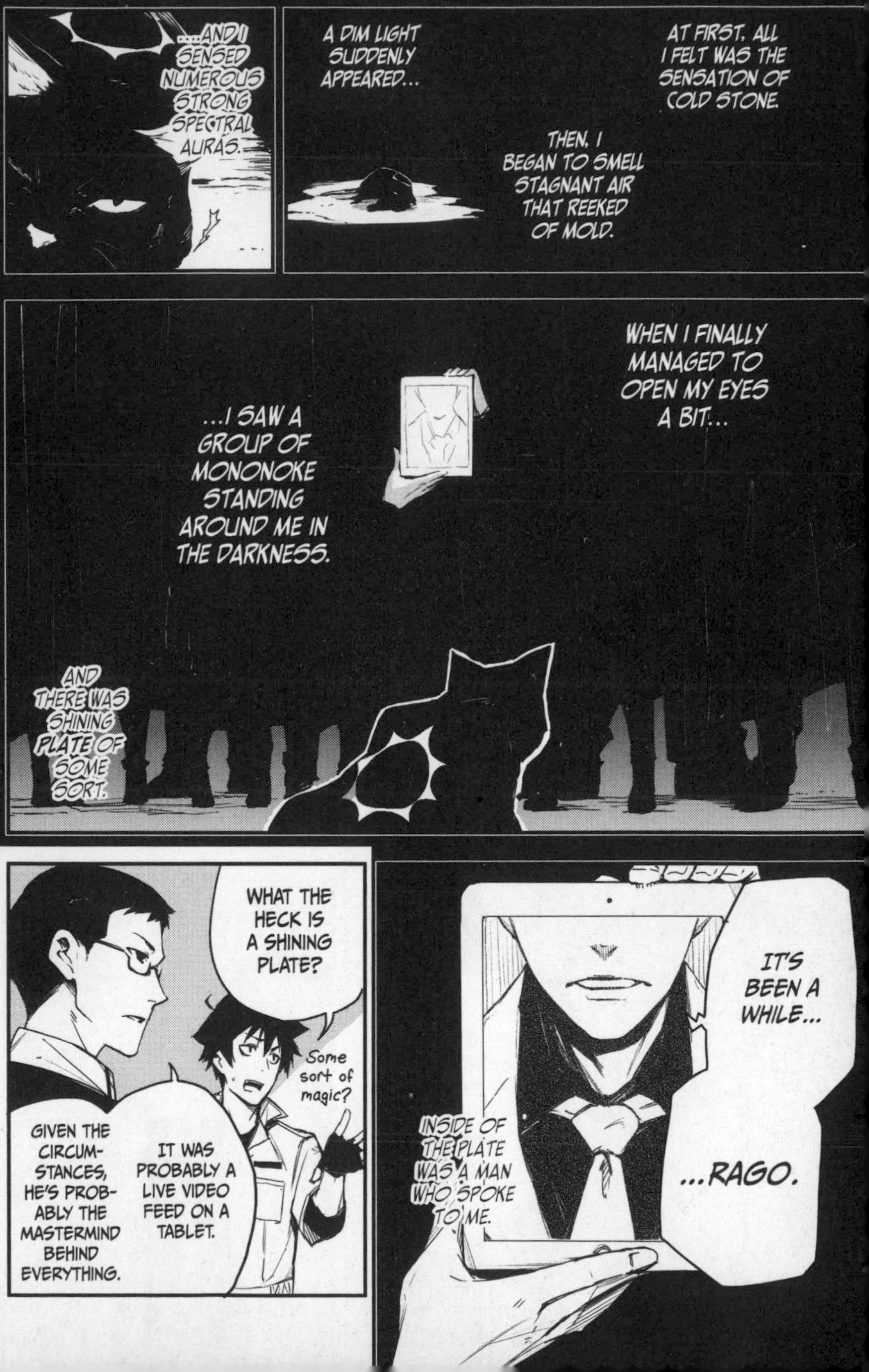

AT FIRST, ALL I FELT WAS THE SENSATION OF COLD STONE.
A DIM LIGHT SUDDENLY APPEARED...
THEN, I BEGAN TO SMELL STAGNANT AIR THAT REEKED OF MOLD.
...AND I SENSED NUMEROUS STRONG SPECTRAL AURAS.
WHEN I FINALLY MANAGED TO OPEN MY EYES A BIT...
...I SAW A GROUP OF MONONOKE STANDING AROUND ME IN THE DARKNESS.
AND THERE WAS SHINING PLATE OF SOME SORT.
IT'S BEEN A WHILE...
...RAGO.
INSIDE OF THE PLATE WAS A MAN WHO SPOKE TO ME.
WHAT THE HECK IS A SHINING PLATE?
Some sort of magic?
IT WAS PROBABLY A LIVE VIDEO FEED ON A TABLET.
GIVEN THE CIRCUM-STANCES, HE'S PROB-ABLY THE MASTERMIND BEHIND EVERYTHING.

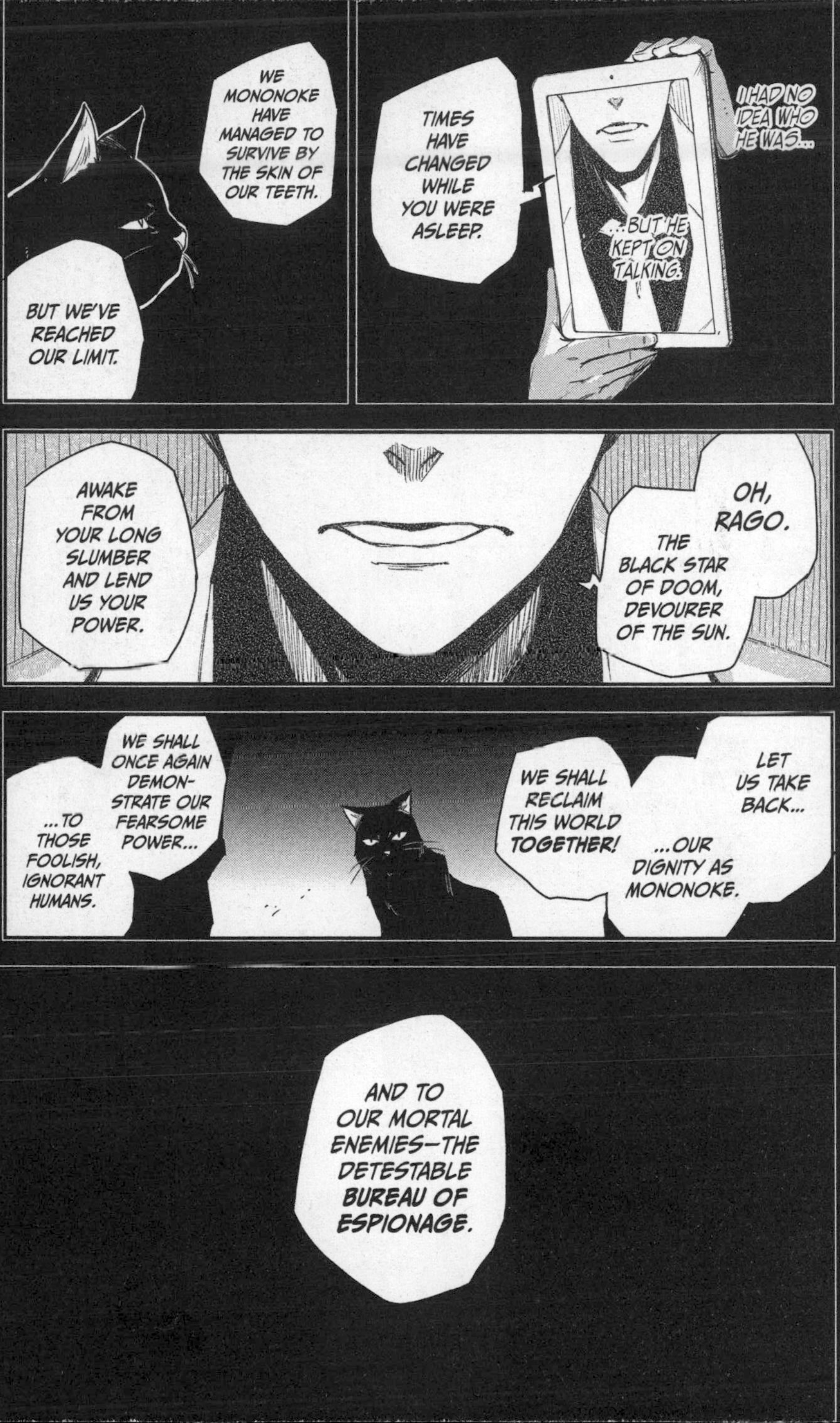
I HAD NO IDEA WHO HE WAS...
TIMES HAVE CHANGED WHILE YOU WERE ASLEEP.
...BUT HE KEPT ON TALKING.
WE MONONOKE HAVE MANAGED TO SURVIVE BY THE SKIN OF OUR TEETH.
BUT WE'VE REACHED OUR LIMIT.
OH, RAGO.
THE BLACK STAR OF DOOM, DEVOURER OF THE SUN.
AWAKE FROM YOUR LONG SLUMBER AND LEND US YOUR POWER.
LET US TAKE BACK...
...OUR DIGNITY AS MONONOKE.
WE SHALL RECLAIM THIS WORLD TOGETHER!
WE SHALL ONCE AGAIN DEMON-STRATE OUR FEARSOME POWER...
...TO THOSE FOOLISH, IGNORANT HUMANS.
AND TO OUR MORTAL ENEMIES—THE DETESTABLE BUREAU OF ESPIONAGE.

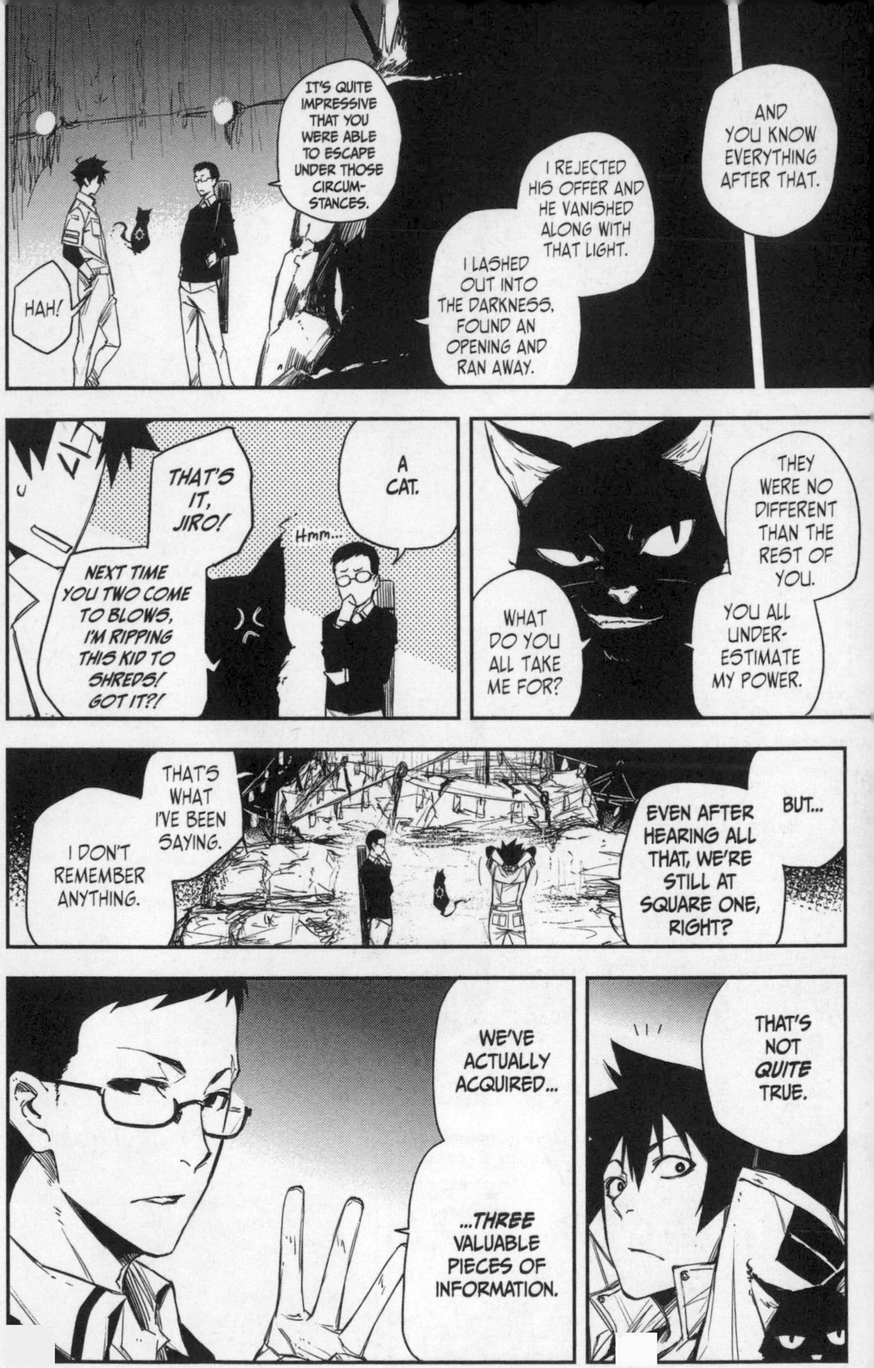
AND YOU KNOW EVERYTHING AFTER THAT.
I REJECTED HIS OFFER AND HE VANISHED ALONG WITH THAT LIGHT.
I LASHED OUT INTO THE DARKNESS, FOUND AN OPENING AND RAN AWAY.
IT'S QUITE IMPRESSIVE THAT YOU WERE ABLE TO ESCAPE UNDER THOSE CIRCUMSTANCES.
HAH!
THEY WERE NO DIFFERENT THAN THE REST OF YOU.
YOU ALL UNDERESTIMATE MY POWER.
WHAT DO YOU ALL TAKE ME FOR?
A CAT.
Hmm...
THAT'S IT, JIRO!
NEXT TIME YOU TWO COME TO BLOWS, I'M RIPPING THIS KID TO SHREDS! GOT IT?!
BUT...
EVEN AFTER HEARING ALL THAT, WE'RE STILL AT SQUARE ONE, RIGHT?
THAT'S WHAT I'VE BEEN SAYING.
I DON'T REMEMBER ANYTHING.
THAT'S NOT QUITE TRUE.
WE'VE ACTUALLY ACQUIRED...
...THREE VALUABLE PIECES OF INFORMATION.

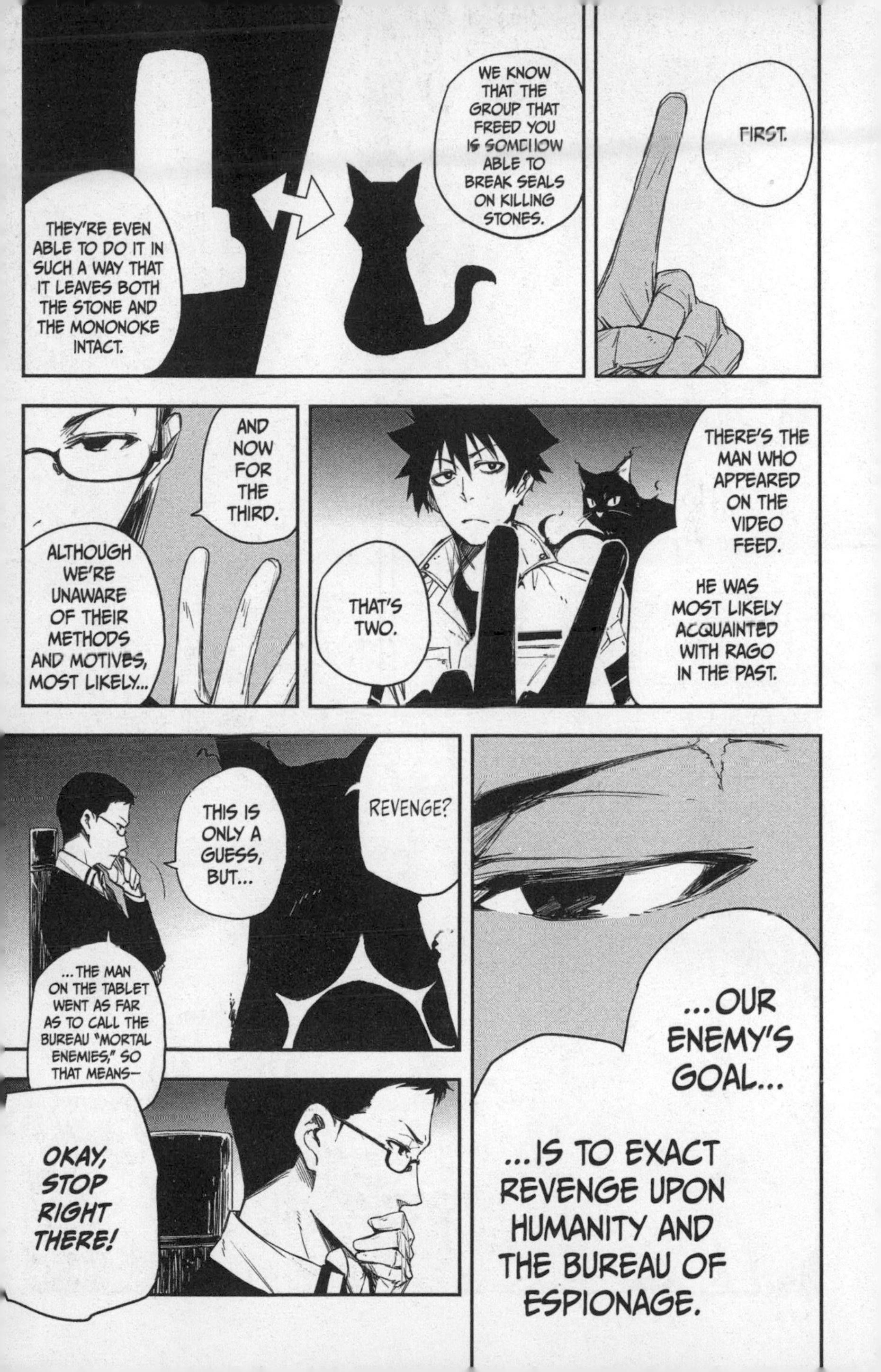
FIRST.
WE KNOW THAT THE GROUP THAT FREED YOU IS SOMEHOW ABLE TO BREAK SEALS ON KILLING STONES.
THEY'RE EVEN ABLE TO DO IT IN SUCH A WAY THAT IT LEAVES BOTH THE STONE AND THE MONONOKE INTACT.
THERE'S THE MAN WHO APPEARED ON THE VIDEO FEED.
HE WAS MOST LIKELY ACQUAINTED WITH RAGO IN THE PAST.
THAT'S TWO.
AND NOW FOR THE THIRD.
ALTHOUGH WE'RE UNAWARE OF THEIR METHODS AND MOTIVES, MOST LIKELY...
...OUR ENEMY'S GOAL...
...IS TO EXACT REVENGE UPON HUMANITY AND THE BUREAU OF ESPIONAGE.
REVENGE?
THIS IS ONLY A GUESS, BUT...
...THE MAN ON THE TABLET WENT AS FAR AS TO CALL THE BUREAU "MORTAL ENEMIES," SO THAT MEANS—
OKAY, STOP RIGHT THERE!

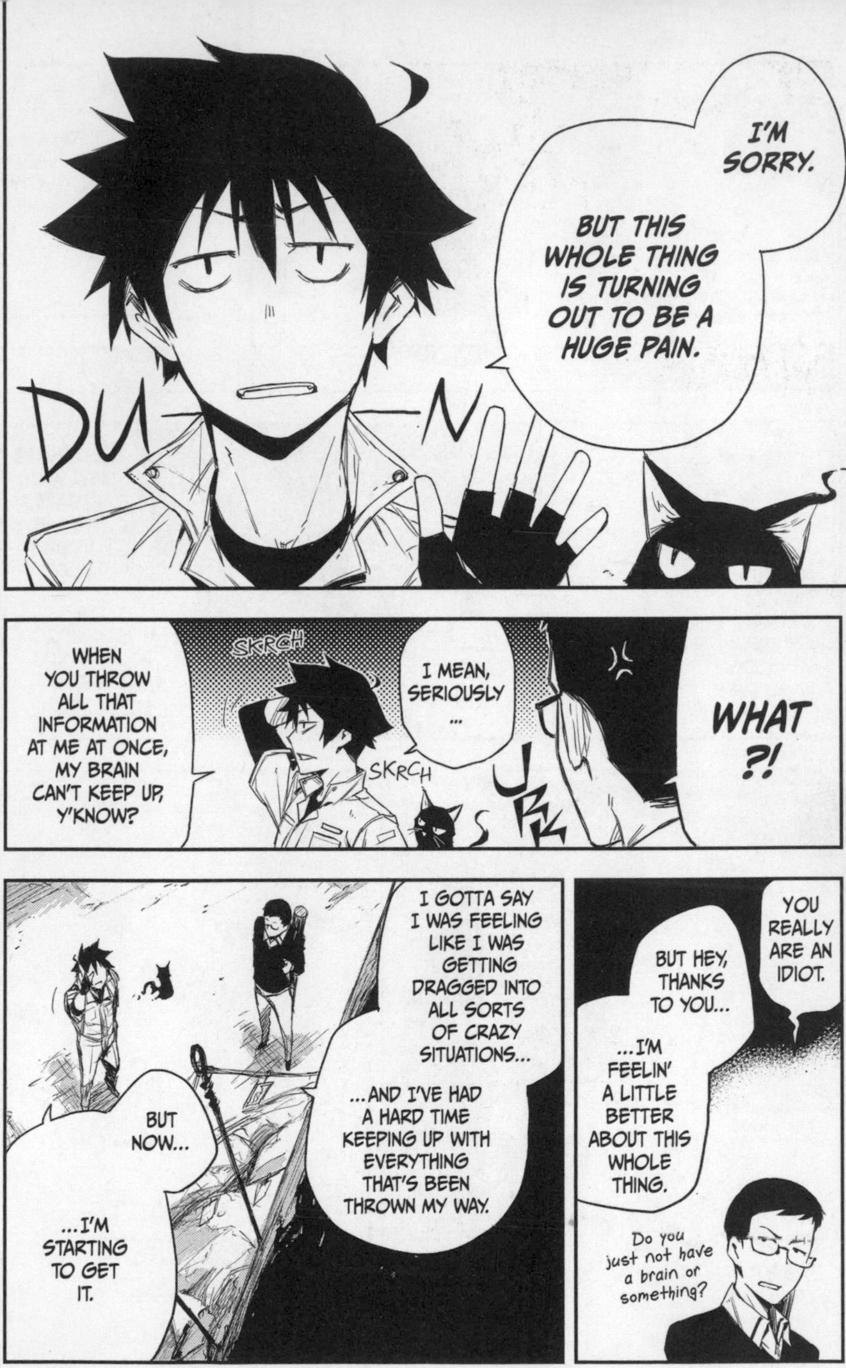
I'M SORRY.
BUT THIS WHOLE THING IS TURNING OUT TO BE A HUGE PAIN.
DU—N
WHAT?!
JRK
I MEAN, SERIOUSLY ...
SKRCH
SKRCH
WHEN YOU THROW ALL THAT INFORMATION AT ME AT ONCE, MY BRAIN CAN'T KEEP UP, Y'KNOW?
YOU REALLY ARE AN IDIOT.
BUT HEY, THANKS TO YOU...
...I'M FEELIN' A LITTLE BETTER ABOUT THIS WHOLE THING.
Do you just not have a brain or something?
I GOTTA SAY I WAS FEELING LIKE I WAS GETTING DRAGGED INTO ALL SORTS OF CRAZY SITUATIONS...
...AND I'VE HAD A HARD TIME KEEPING UP WITH EVERYTHING THAT'S BEEN THROWN MY WAY.
BUT NOW...
...I'M STARTING TO GET IT.

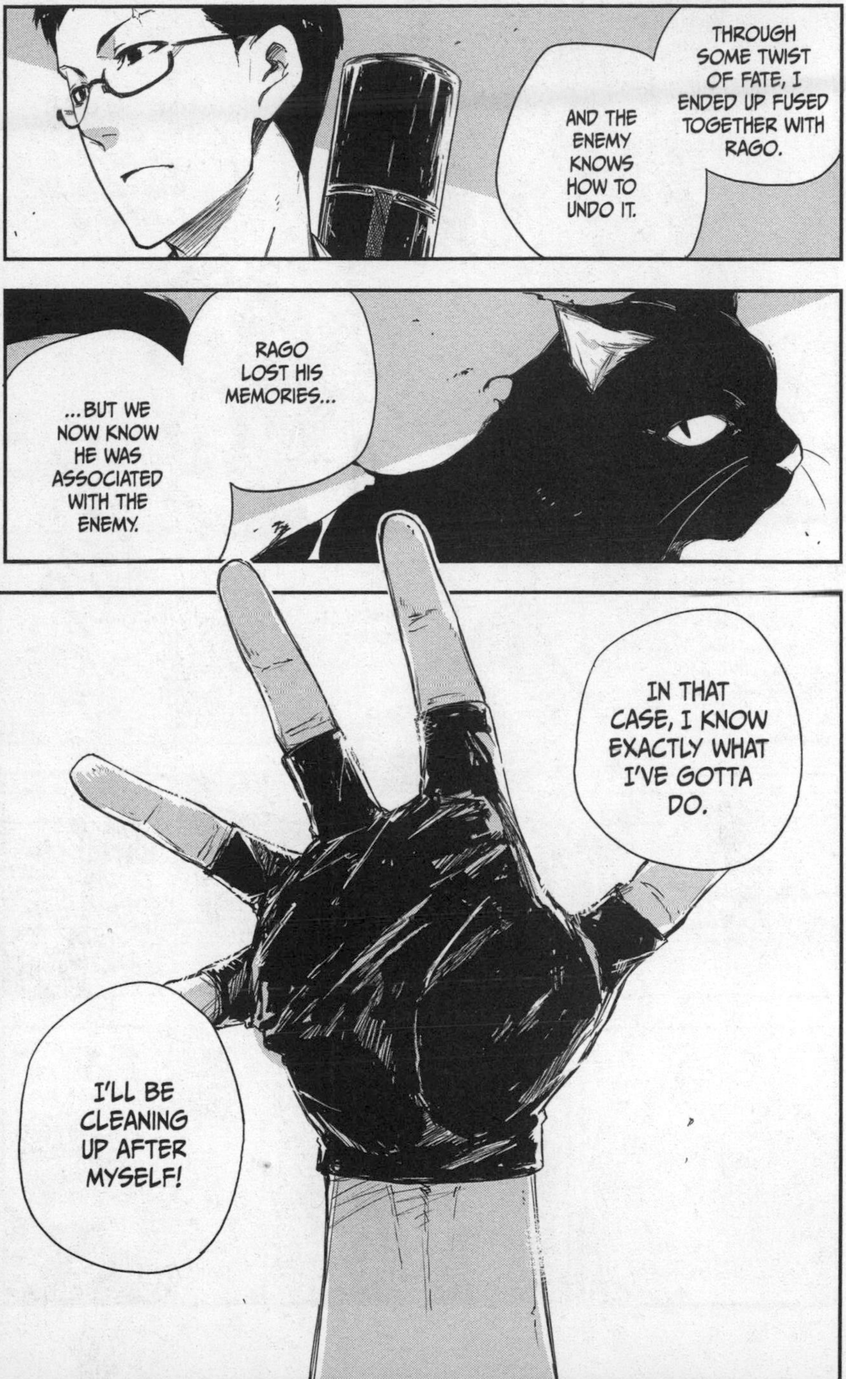
THROUGH SOME TWIST OF FATE, I ENDED UP FUSED TOGETHER WITH RAGO.
AND THE ENEMY KNOWS HOW TO UNDO IT.
RAGO LOST HIS MEMORIES...
...BUT WE NOW KNOW HE WAS ASSOCIATED WITH THE ENEMY.
IN THAT CASE, I KNOW EXACTLY WHAT I'VE GOTTA DO.
I'LL BE CLEANING UP AFTER MYSELF!

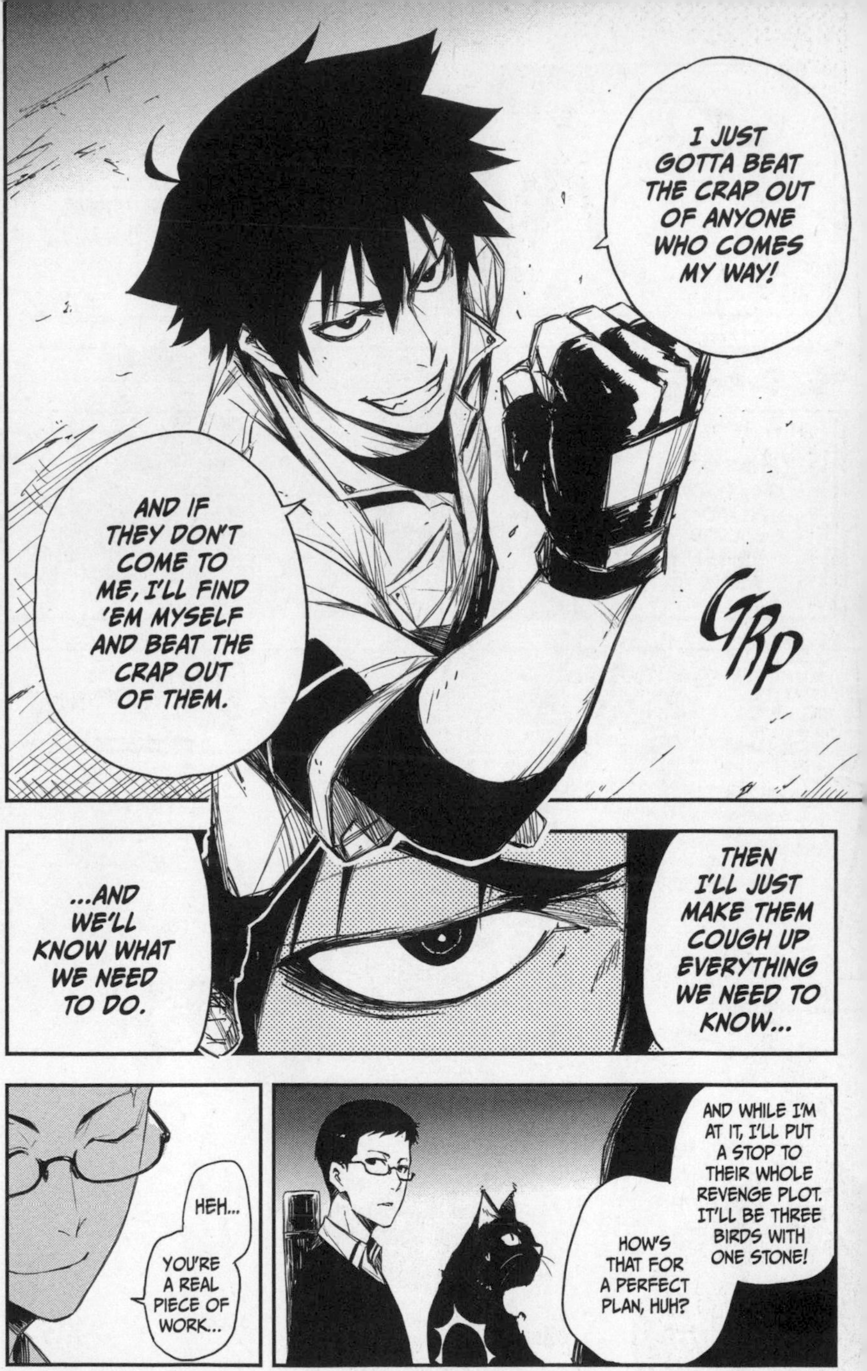
I JUST GOTTA BEAT THE CRAP OUT OF ANYONE WHO COMES MY WAY!
AND IF THEY DON'T COME TO ME, I'LL FIND 'EM MYSELF AND BEAT THE CRAP OUT OF THEM.
GRP
THEN I'LL JUST MAKE THEM COUGH UP EVERYTHING WE NEED TO KNOW...
...AND WE'LL KNOW WHAT WE NEED TO DO.
AND WHILE I'M AT IT, I'LL PUT A STOP TO THEIR WHOLE REVENGE PLOT. IT'LL BE THREE BIRDS WITH ONE STONE!
HOW'S THAT FOR A PERFECT PLAN, HUH?
HEH...
YOU'RE A REAL PIECE OF WORK...

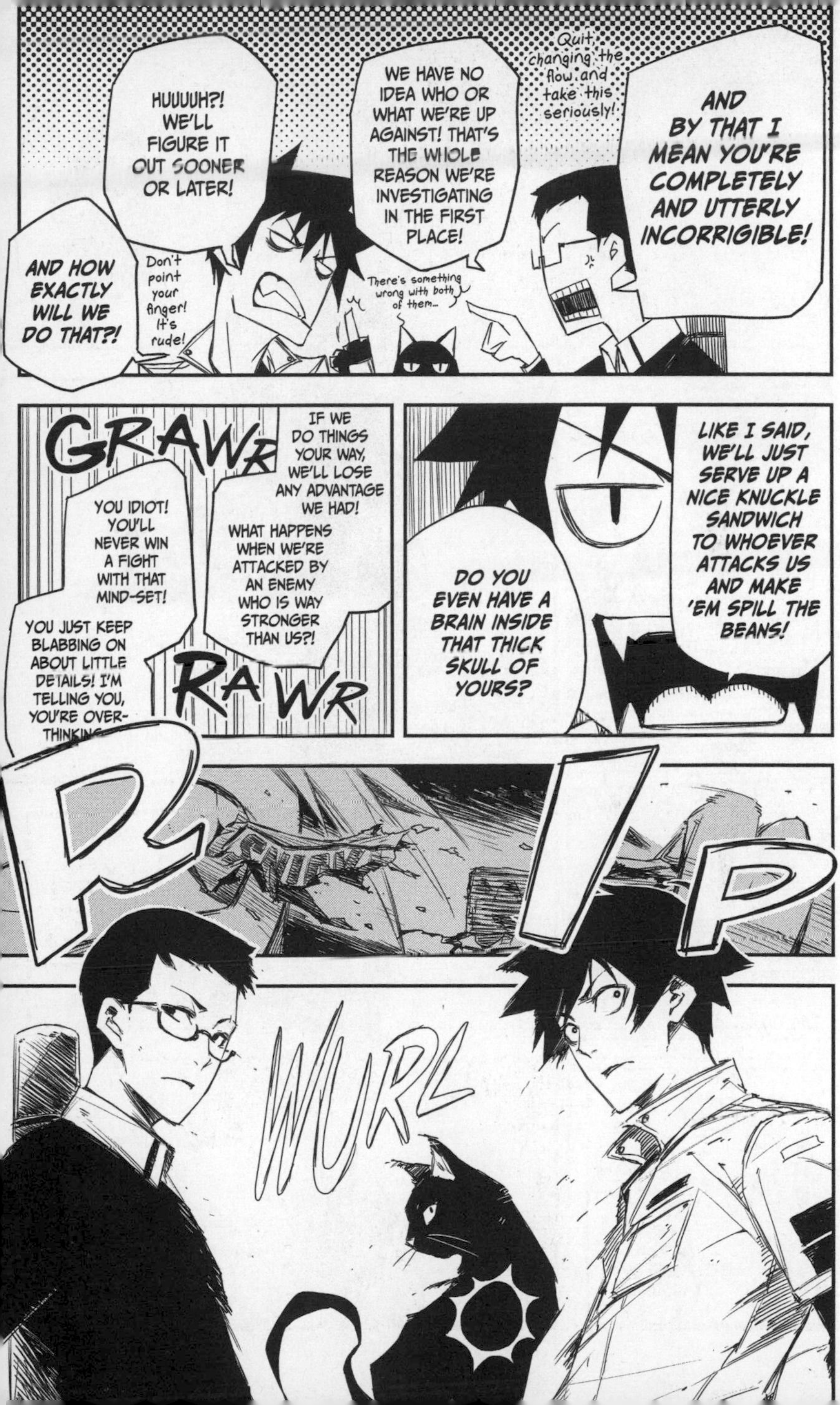
AND BY THAT I MEAN YOU'RE COMPLETELY AND UTTERLY INCORRIGIBLE!
Quit changing the flow and take this seriously!
WE HAVE NO IDEA WHO OR WHAT WE'RE UP AGAINST! THAT'S THE WHOLE REASON WE'RE INVESTIGATING IN THE FIRST PLACE!
HUUUUH?! WE'LL FIGURE IT OUT SOONER OR LATER!
There's something wrong with both of them...
Don't point your finger! It's rude!
AND HOW EXACTLY WILL WE DO THAT?!
LIKE I SAID, WE'LL JUST SERVE UP A NICE KNUCKLE SANDWICH TO WHOEVER ATTACKS US AND MAKE 'EM SPILL THE BEANS!
DO YOU EVEN HAVE A BRAIN INSIDE THAT THICK SKULL OF YOURS?
IF WE DO THINGS YOUR WAY, WE'LL LOSE ANY ADVANTAGE WE HAD!
GRAWR
WHAT HAPPENS WHEN WE'RE ATTACKED BY AN ENEMY WHO IS WAY STRONGER THAN US?!
YOU IDIOT! YOU'LL NEVER WIN A FIGHT WITH THAT MIND-SET!
RAWR
YOU JUST KEEP BLABBING ON ABOUT LITTLE DETAILS! I'M TELLING YOU, YOU'RE OVER-THINKING
RIP
WURL

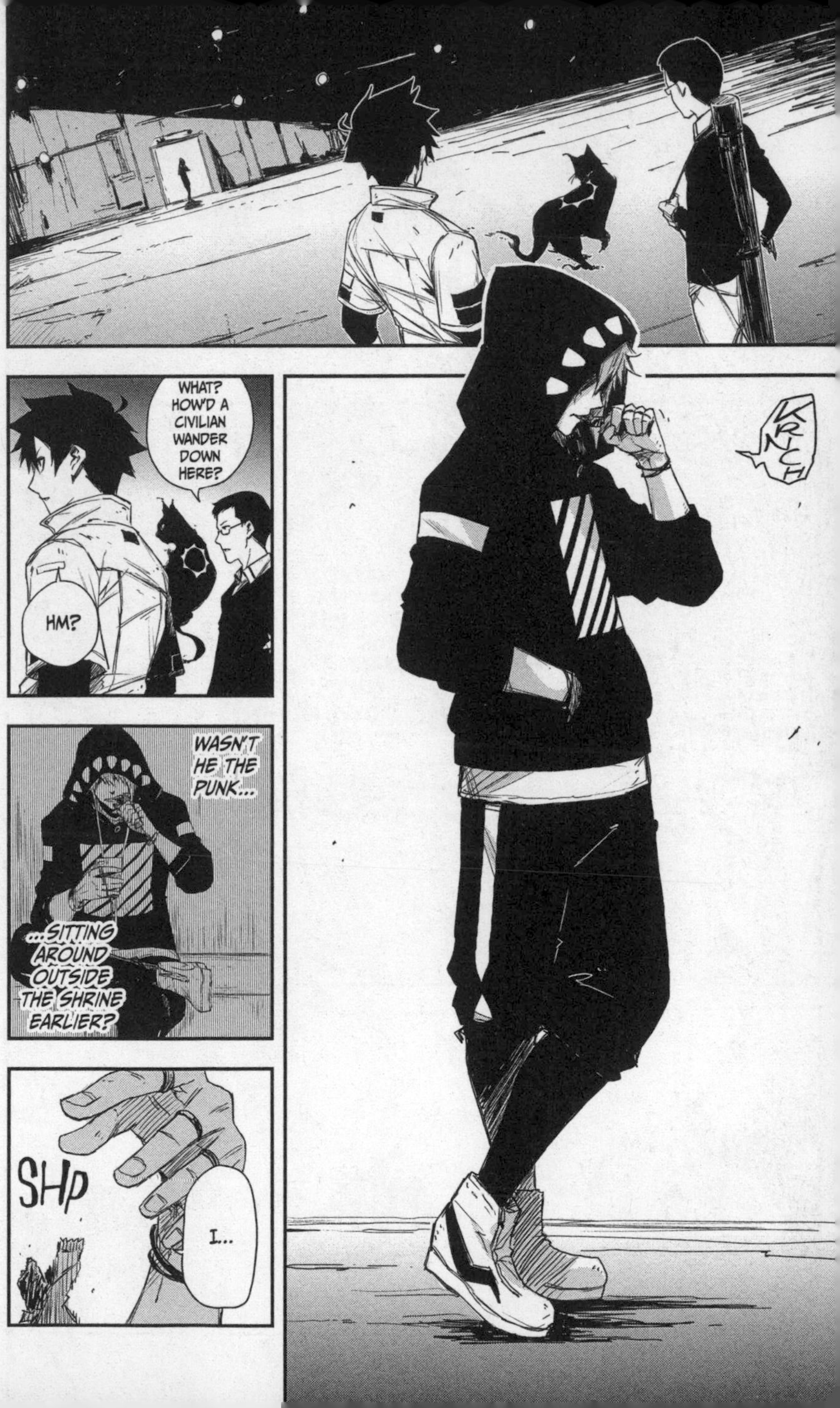
KRNCH
WHAT? HOW'D A CIVILIAN WANDER DOWN HERE?
HM?
WASN'T HE THE PUNK...
...SITTING AROUND OUTSIDE THE SHRINE EARLIER?
SHP
I...

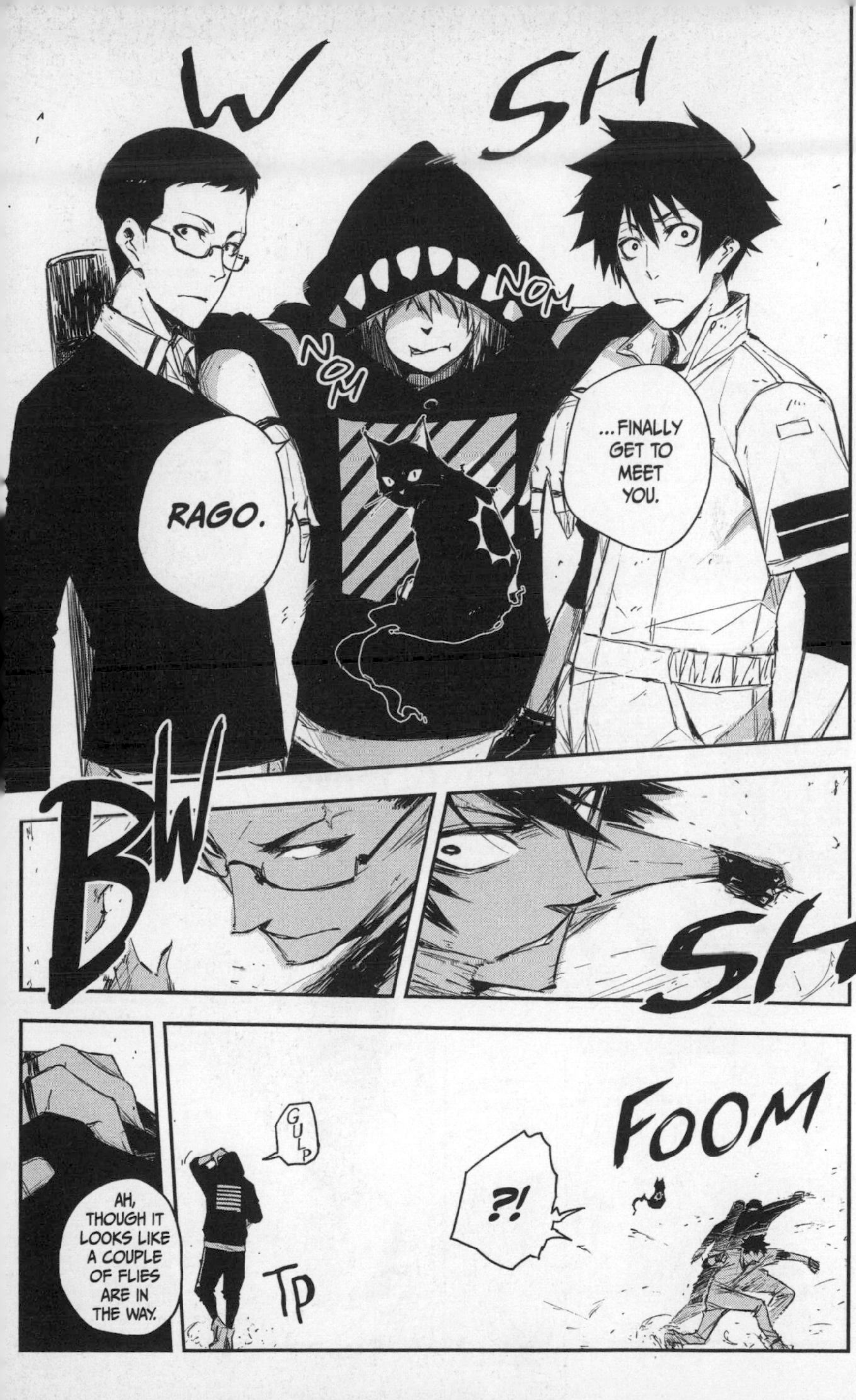
W SH
NOM NOM
...FINALLY GET TO MEET YOU.
RAGO.
BWSH
FOOM
?!
GULP
TP
AH, THOUGH IT LOOKS LIKE A COUPLE OF FLIES ARE IN THE WAY.

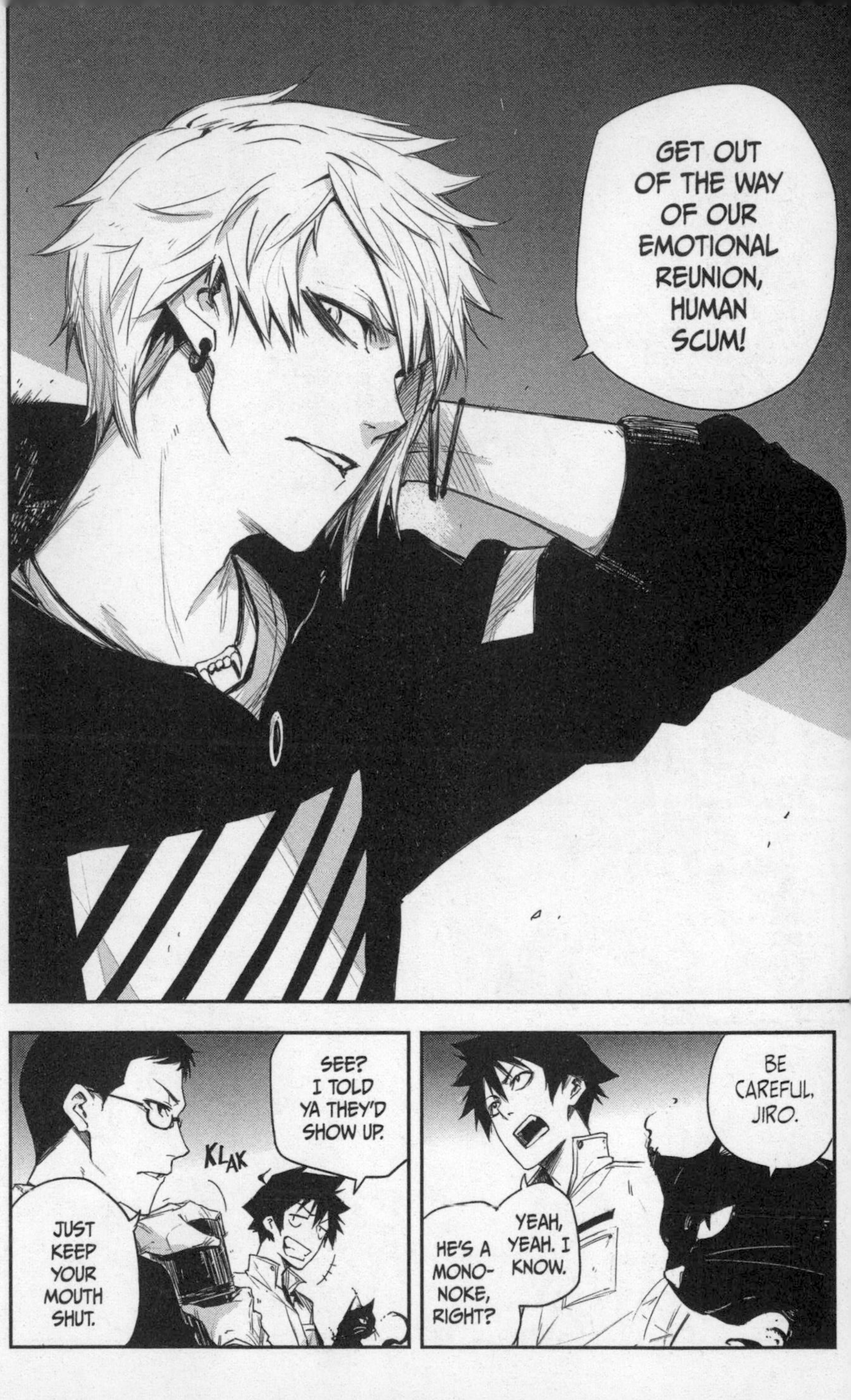
GET OUT OF THE WAY OF OUR EMOTIONAL REUNION, HUMAN SCUM!
BE CAREFUL, JIRO.
YEAH, YEAH. I KNOW.
HE'S A MONO-NOKE, RIGHT?
SEE? I TOLD YA THEY'D SHOW UP.
KLAK
JUST KEEP YOUR MOUTH SHUT.

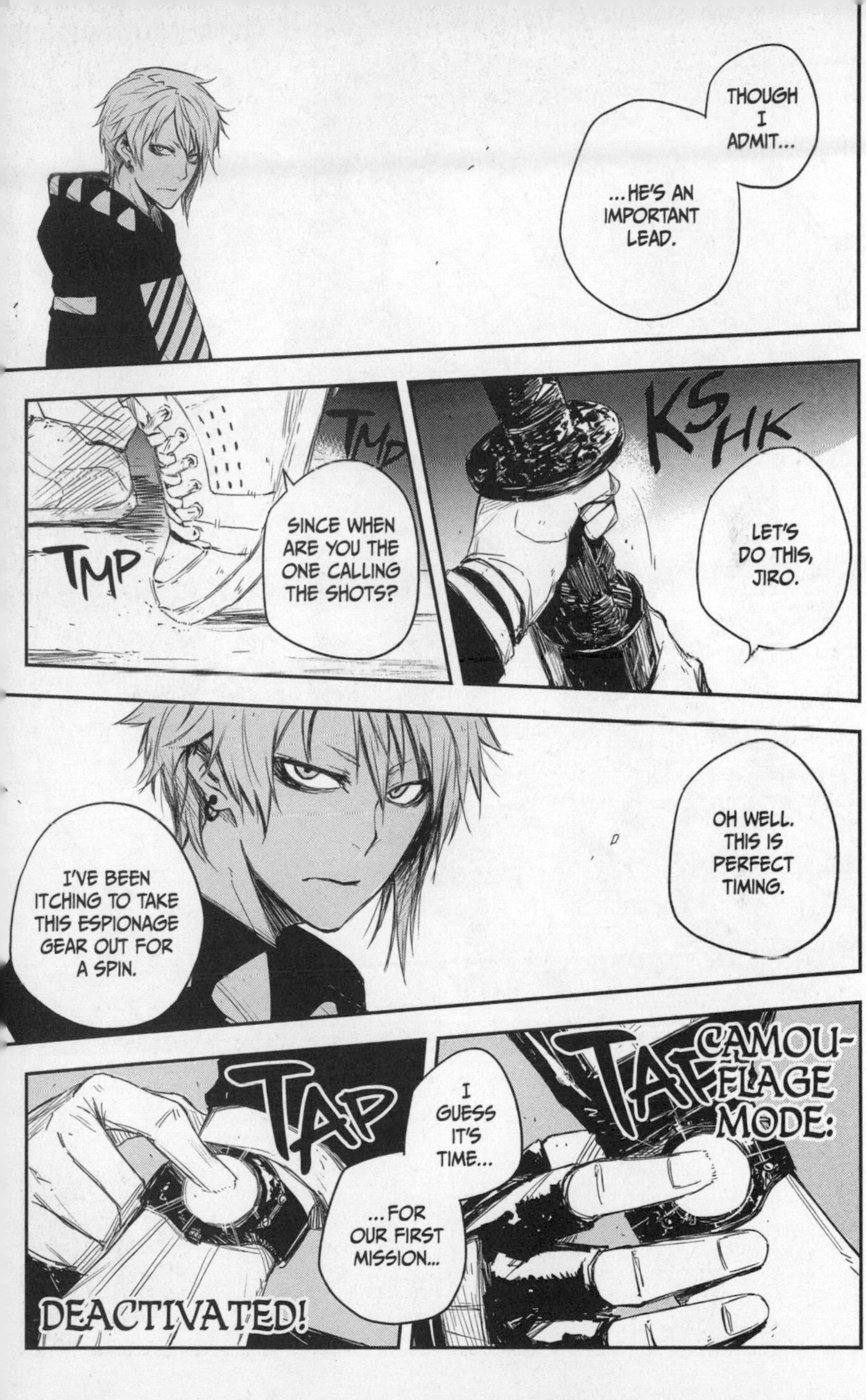
THOUGH I ADMIT...
...HE'S AN IMPORTANT LEAD.
KSHK
LET'S DO THIS, JIRO.
TMP
SINCE WHEN ARE YOU THE ONE CALLING THE SHOTS?
TMP
OH WELL. THIS IS PERFECT TIMING.
I'VE BEEN ITCHING TO TAKE THIS ESPIONAGE GEAR OUT FOR A SPIN.
TAP
CAMOU-FLAGE MODE:
I GUESS IT'S TIME...
TAP
...FOR OUR FIRST MISSION...
DEACTIVATED!

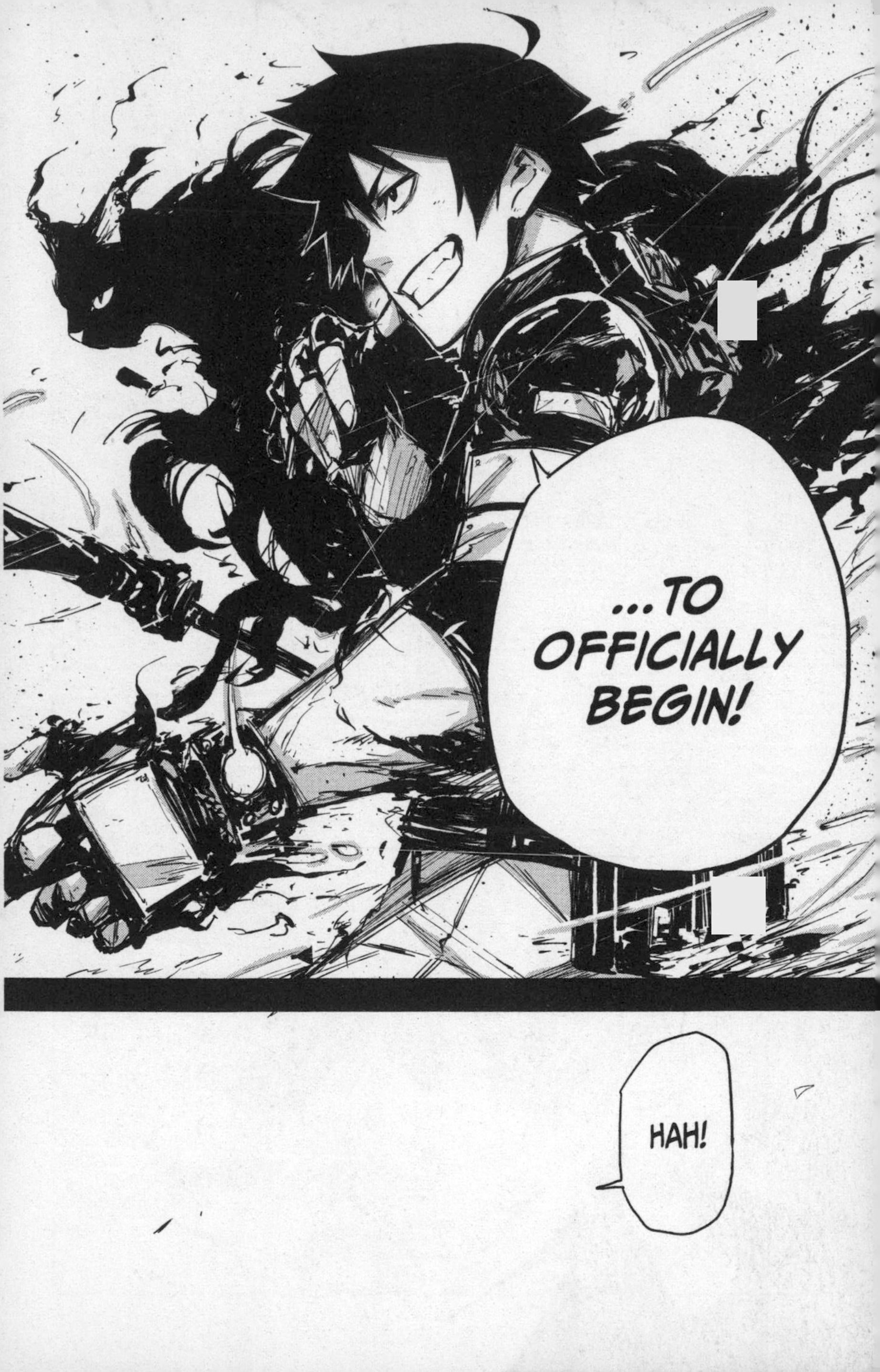
...TO OFFICIALLY BEGIN!
HAH!

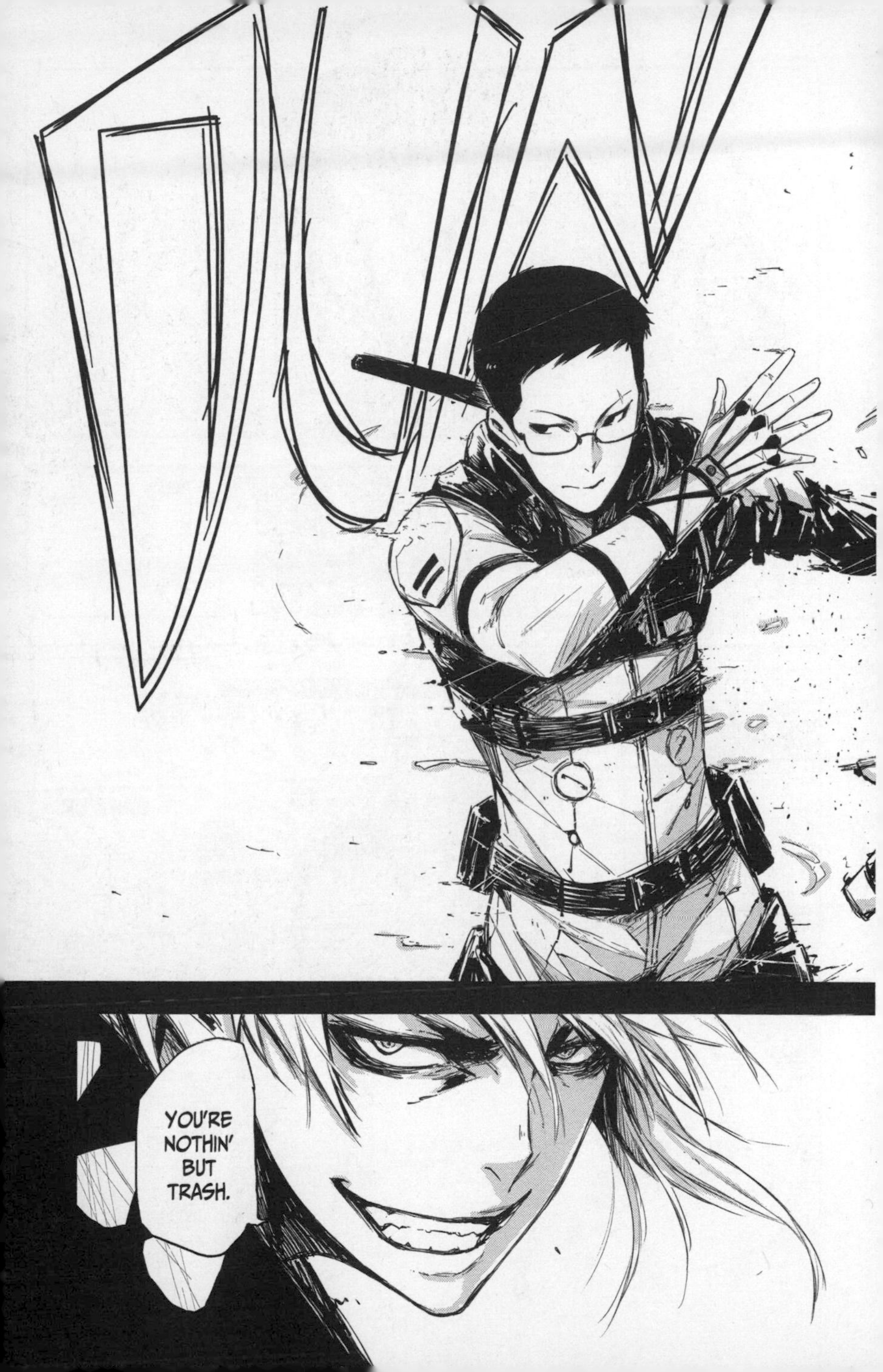
YOU'RE NOTHIN' BUT TRASH.

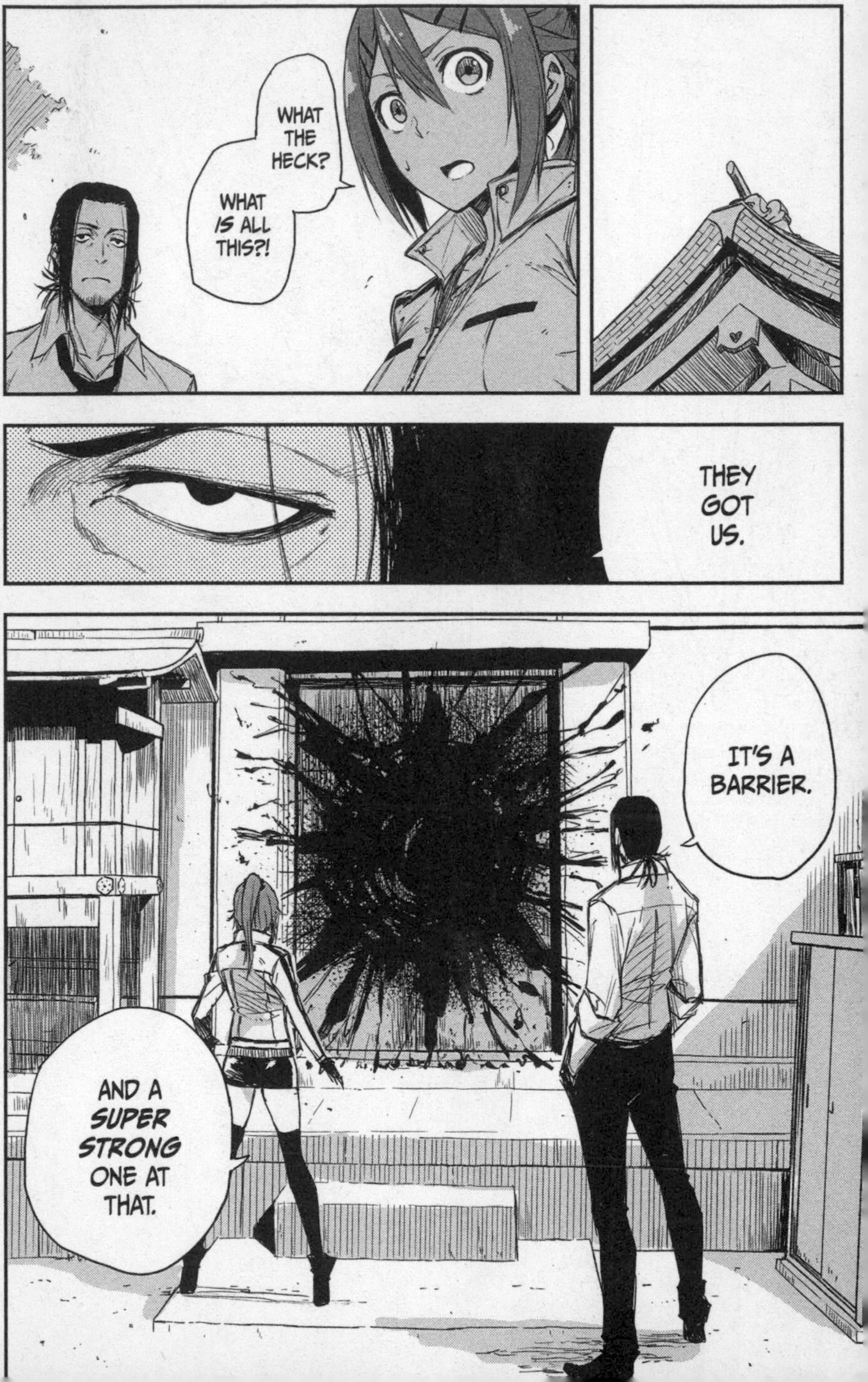
WHAT THE HECK?
WHAT IS ALL THIS?!
THEY GOT US.
IT'S A BARRIER.
AND A SUPER STRONG ONE AT THAT.

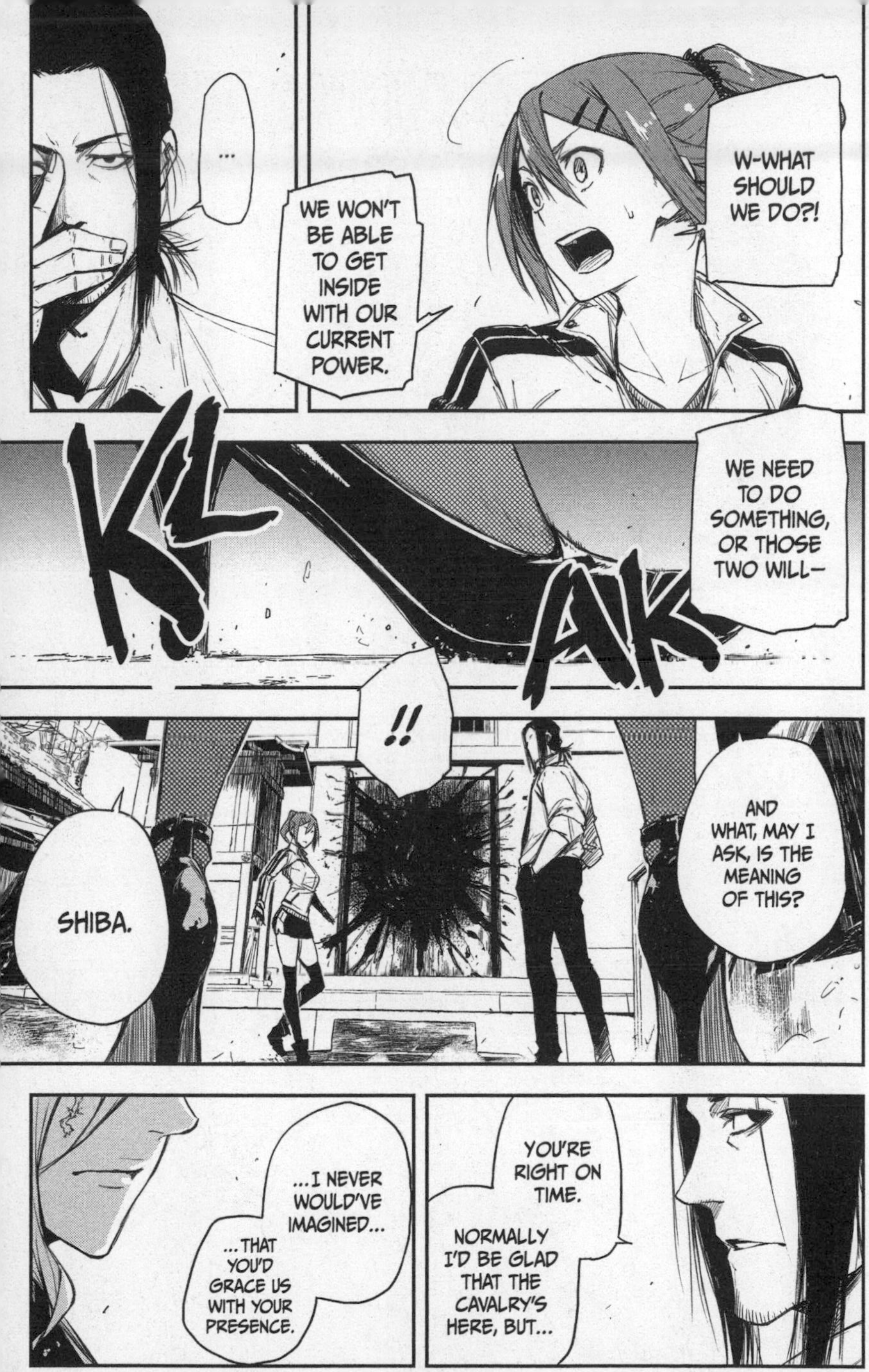
W-WHAT SHOULD WE DO?!
WE WON'T BE ABLE TO GET INSIDE WITH OUR CURRENT POWER.
...
WE NEED TO DO SOMETHING, OR THOSE TWO WILL—
KRAK
!!
AND WHAT, MAY I ASK, IS THE MEANING OF THIS?
SHIBA.
YOU'RE RIGHT ON TIME.
NORMALLY I'D BE GLAD THAT THE CAVALRY'S HERE, BUT...
...I NEVER WOULD'VE IMAGINED...
...THAT YOU'D GRACE US WITH YOUR PRESENCE.

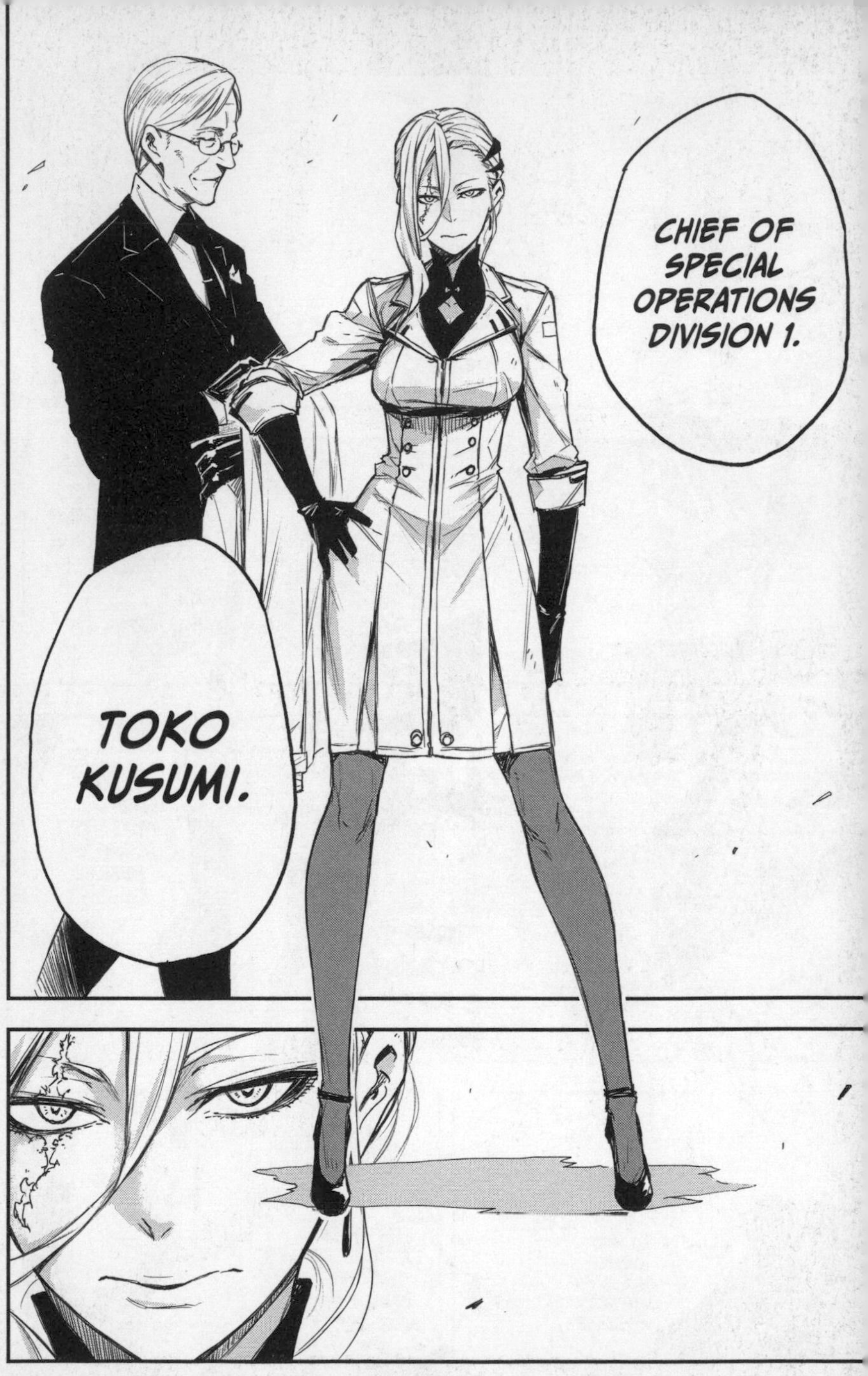
CHIEF OF SPECIAL OPERATIONS DIVISION 1.
TOKO KUSUMI.

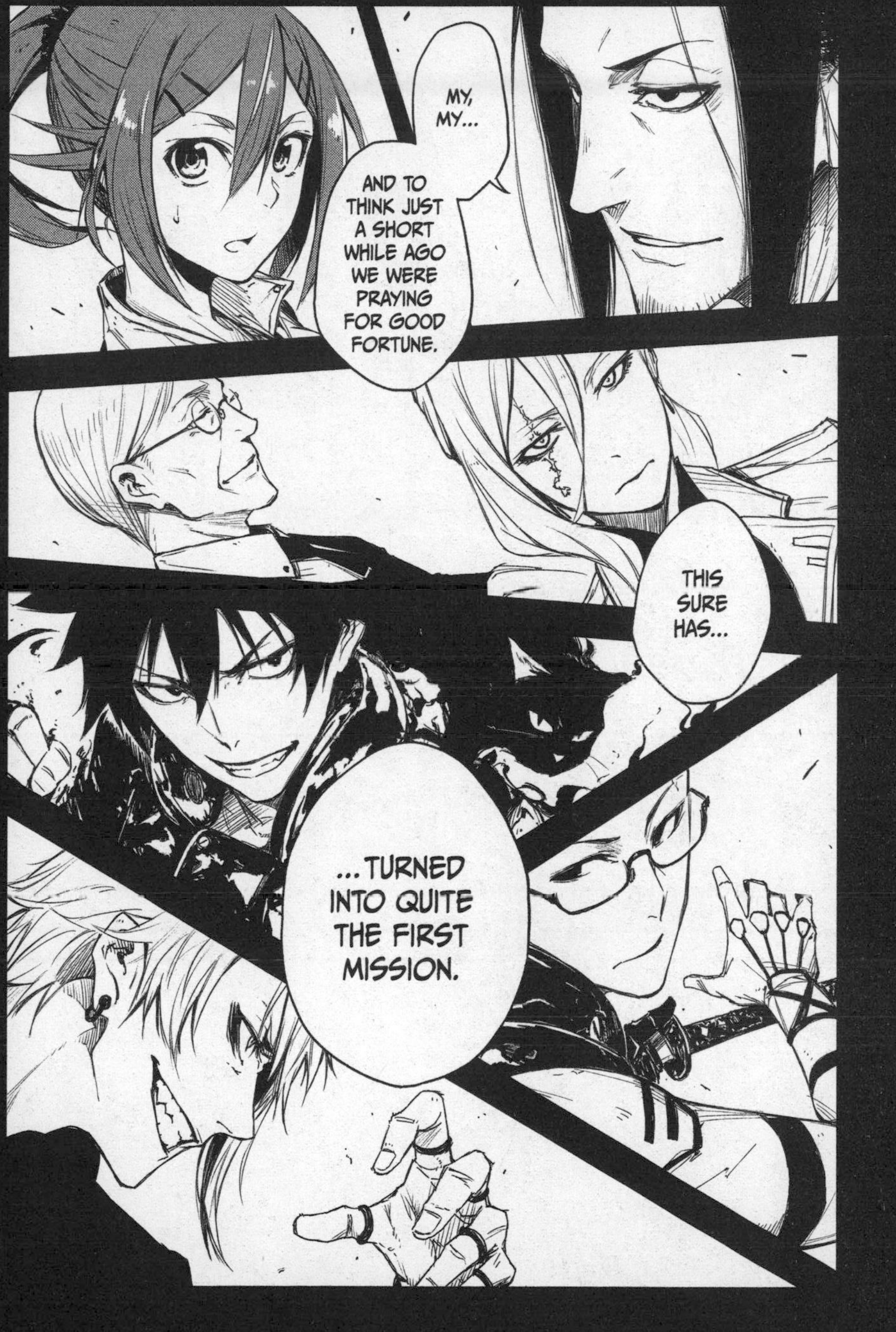
MY, MY...
AND TO THINK JUST A SHORT WHILE AGO WE WERE PRAYING FOR GOOD FORTUNE.
THIS SURE HAS...
...TURNED INTO QUITE THE FIRST MISSION.

BLACK TORCH

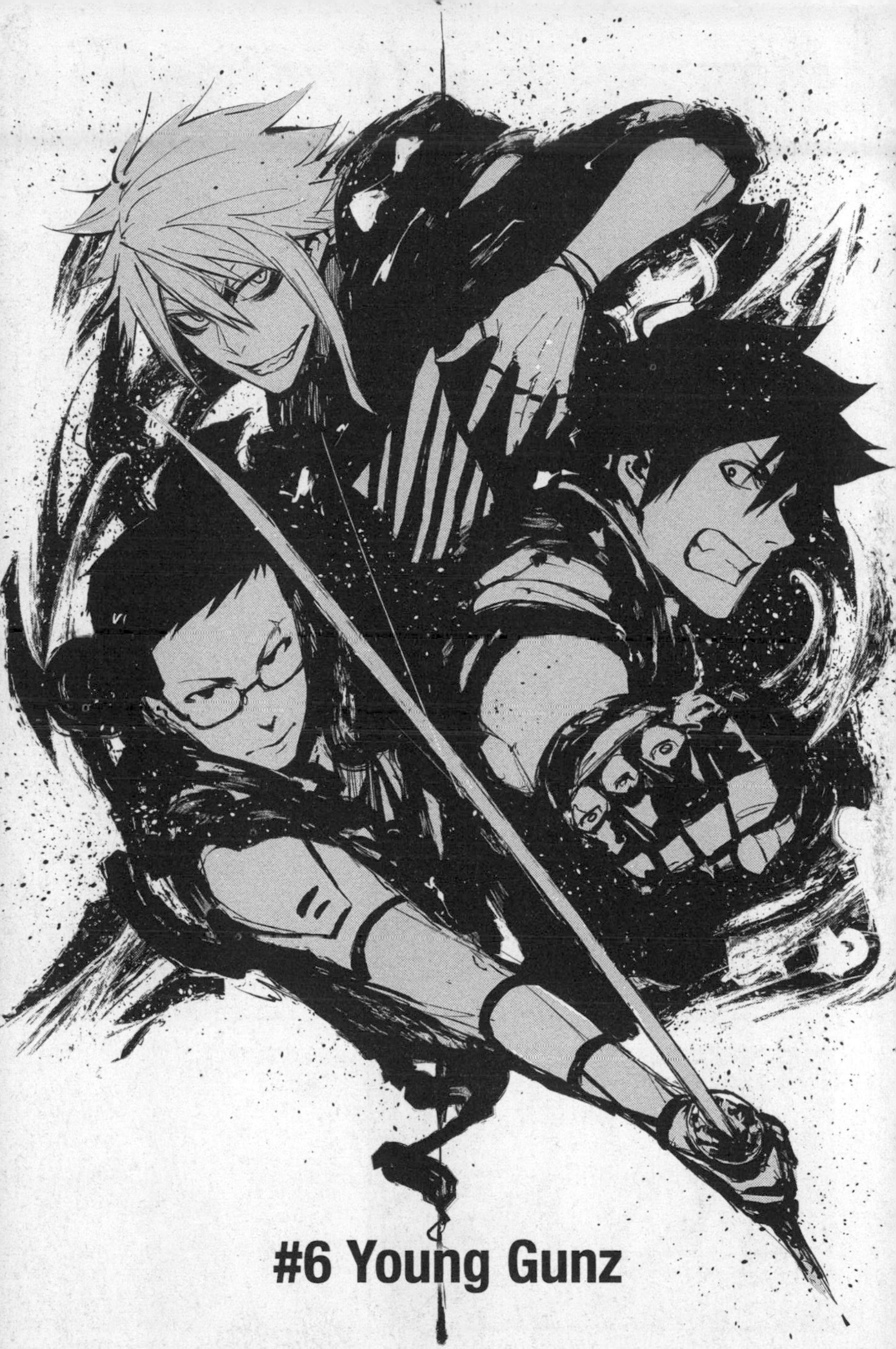

#6 Young Gunz

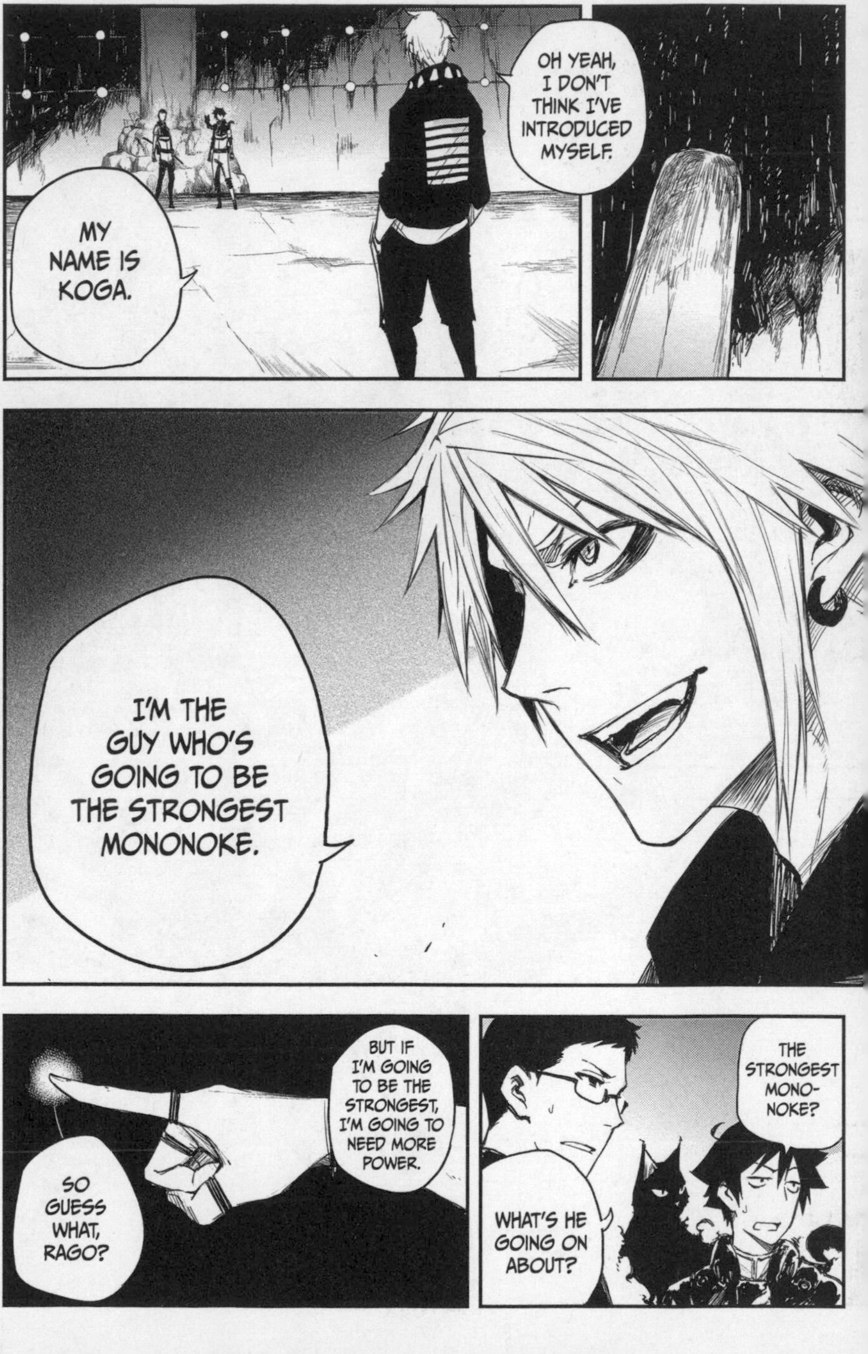
OH YEAH, I DON'T THINK I'VE INTRODUCED MYSELF.
MY NAME IS KOGA.
I'M THE GUY WHO'S GOING TO BE THE STRONGEST MONONOKE.
THE STRONGEST MONO-NOKE?
WHAT'S HE GOING ON ABOUT?
BUT IF I'M GOING TO BE THE STRONGEST, I'M GOING TO NEED MORE POWER.
SO GUESS WHAT, RAGO?

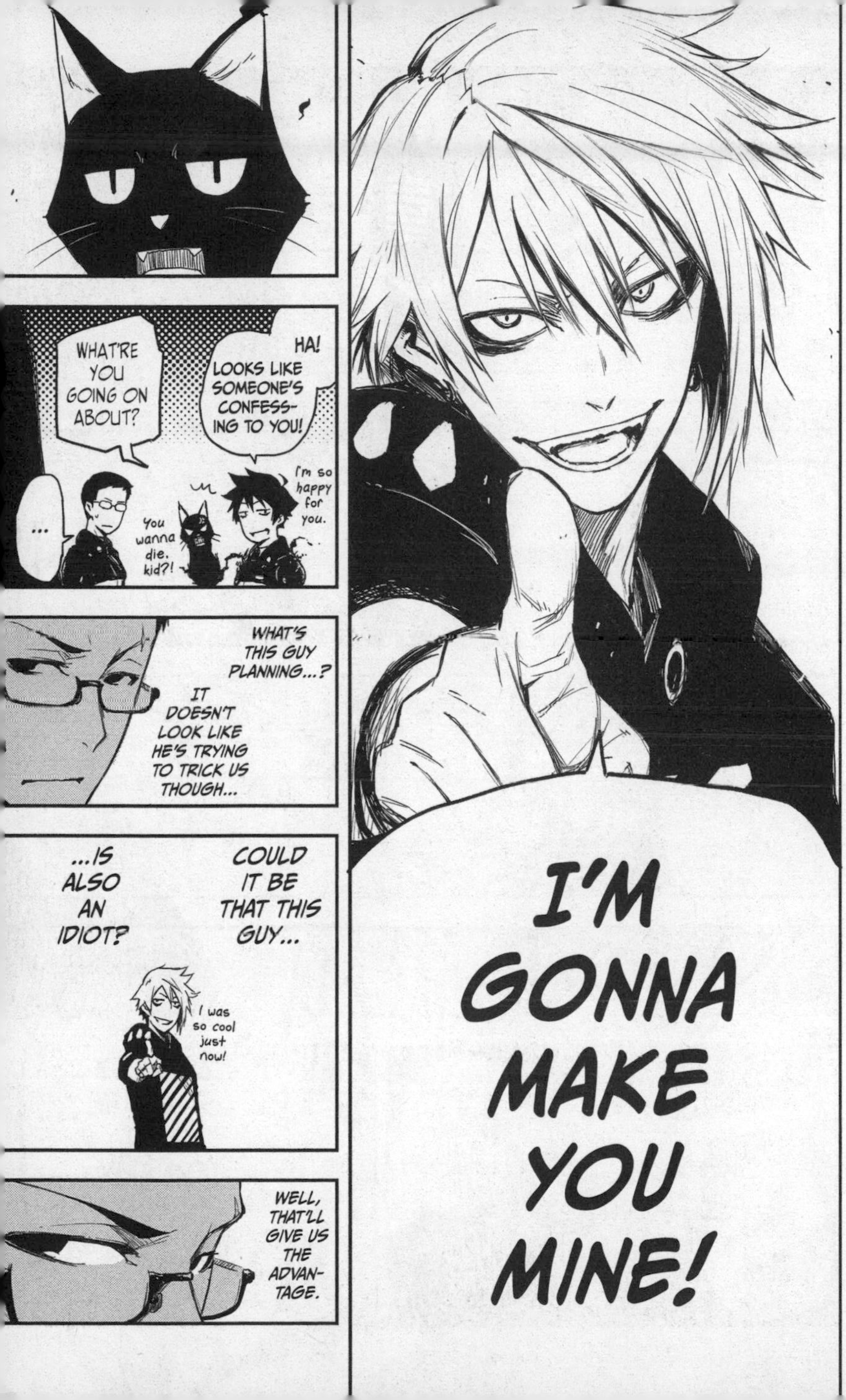
I'M GONNA MAKE YOU MINE!
HA! LOOKS LIKE SOMEONE'S CONFESSING TO YOU!
WHAT'RE YOU GOING ON ABOUT?
I'm so happy for you.
You wanna die, kid?!
...
WHAT'S THIS GUY PLANNING...?
IT DOESN'T LOOK LIKE HE'S TRYING TO TRICK US THOUGH...
COULD IT BE THAT THIS GUY...
...IS ALSO AN IDIOT?
I was so cool just now!
WELL, THAT'LL GIVE US THE ADVANTAGE.

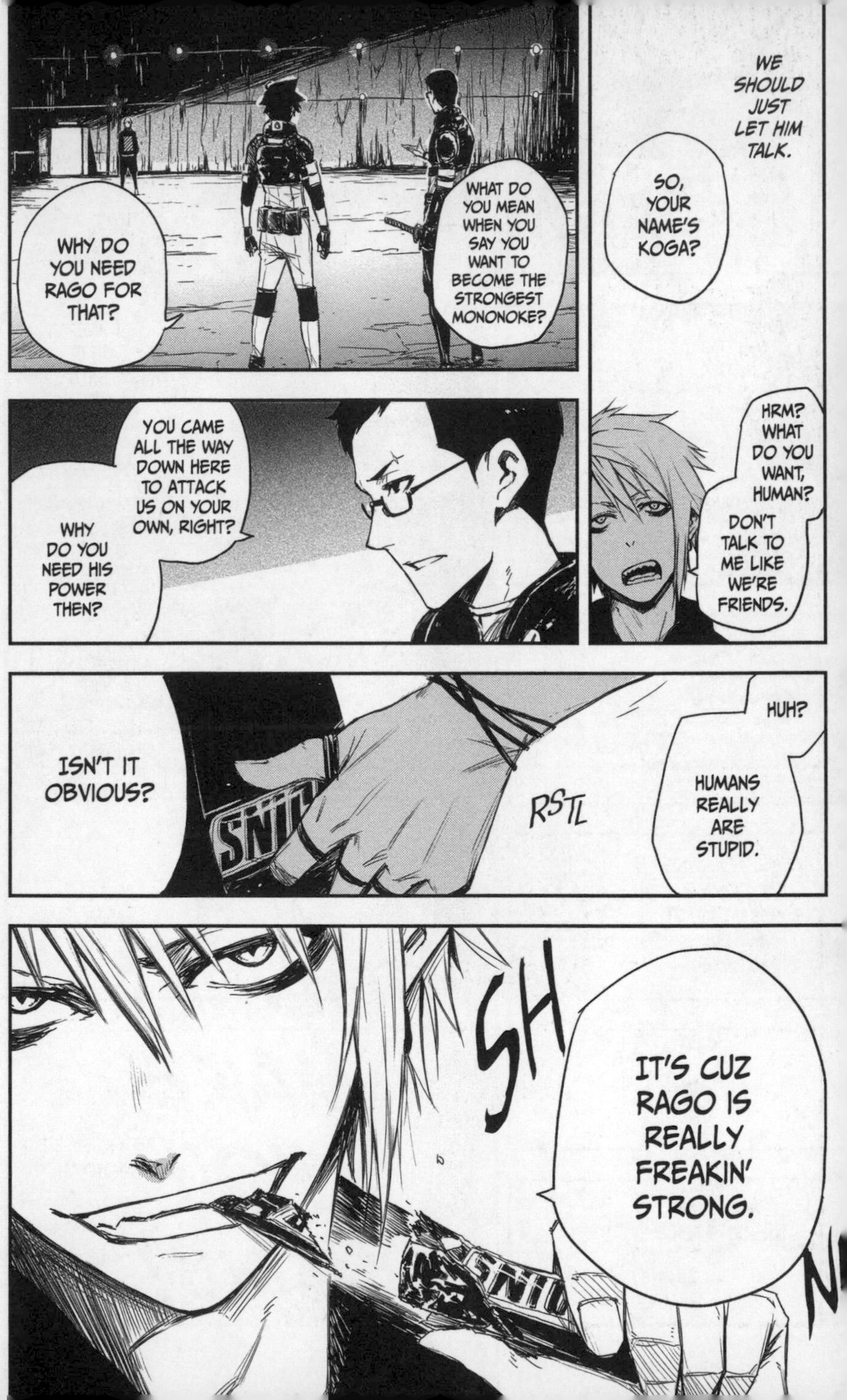
WE SHOULD JUST LET HIM TALK.
SO, YOUR NAME'S KOGA?
HRM? WHAT DO YOU WANT, HUMAN?
DON'T TALK TO ME LIKE WE'RE FRIENDS.
WHAT DO YOU MEAN WHEN YOU SAY YOU WANT TO BECOME THE STRONGEST MONONOKE?
WHY DO YOU NEED RAGO FOR THAT?
YOU CAME ALL THE WAY DOWN HERE TO ATTACK US ON YOUR OWN, RIGHT?
WHY DO YOU NEED HIS POWER THEN?
HUH?
HUMANS REALLY ARE STUPID.
RSTL
ISN'T IT OBVIOUS?
SH
IT'S CUZ RAGO IS REALLY FREAKIN' STRONG.

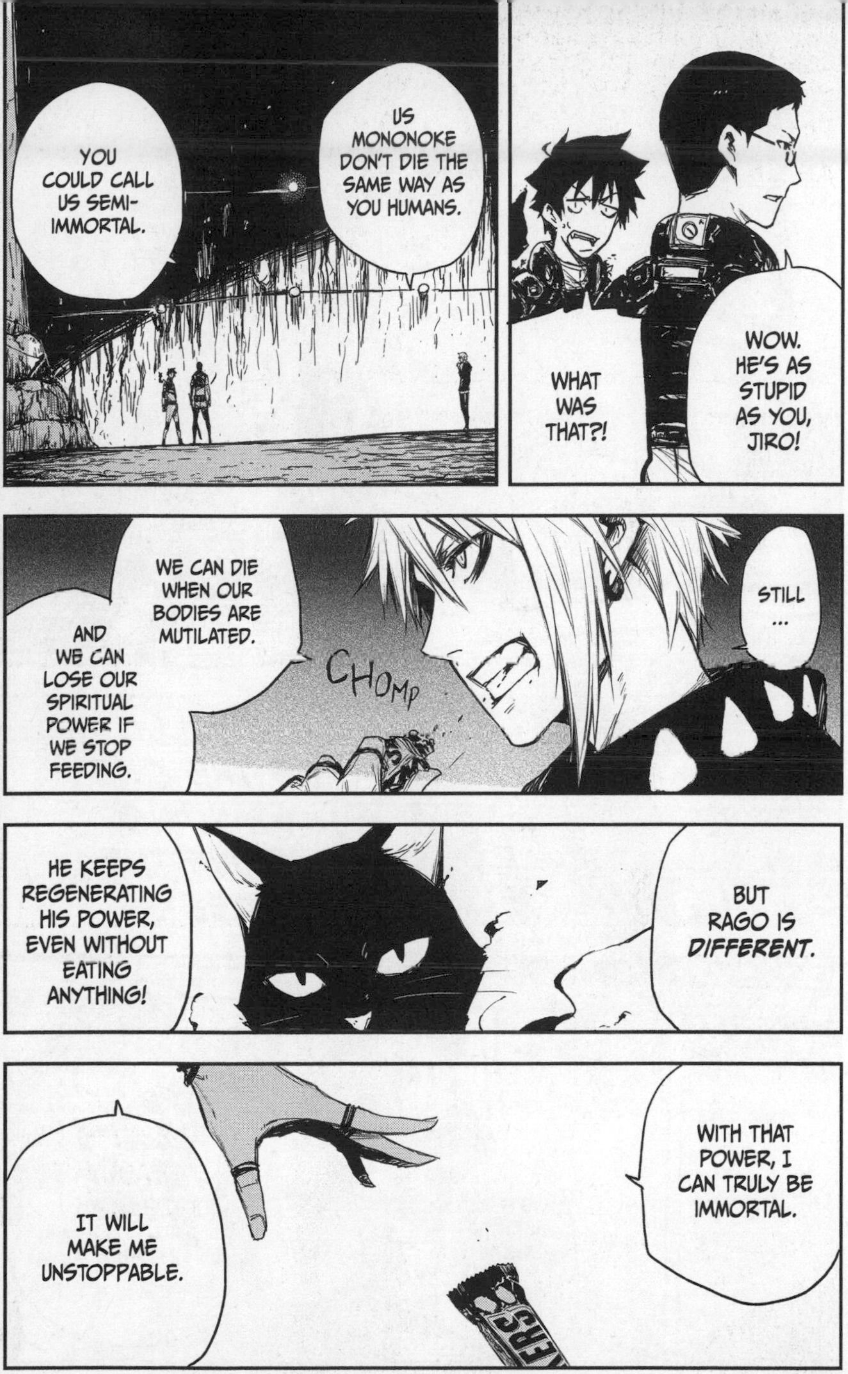
WOW. HE'S AS STUPID AS YOU, JIRO!
WHAT WAS THAT?!
US MONONOKE DON'T DIE THE SAME WAY AS YOU HUMANS.
YOU COULD CALL US SEMI-IMMORTAL.
STILL ...
WE CAN DIE WHEN OUR BODIES ARE MUTILATED.
AND WE CAN LOSE OUR SPIRITUAL POWER IF WE STOP FEEDING.
CHOMP
BUT RAGO IS *DIFFERENT.*
HE KEEPS REGENERATING HIS POWER, EVEN WITHOUT EATING ANYTHING!
WITH THAT POWER, I CAN TRULY BE IMMORTAL.
IT WILL MAKE ME UNSTOPPABLE.

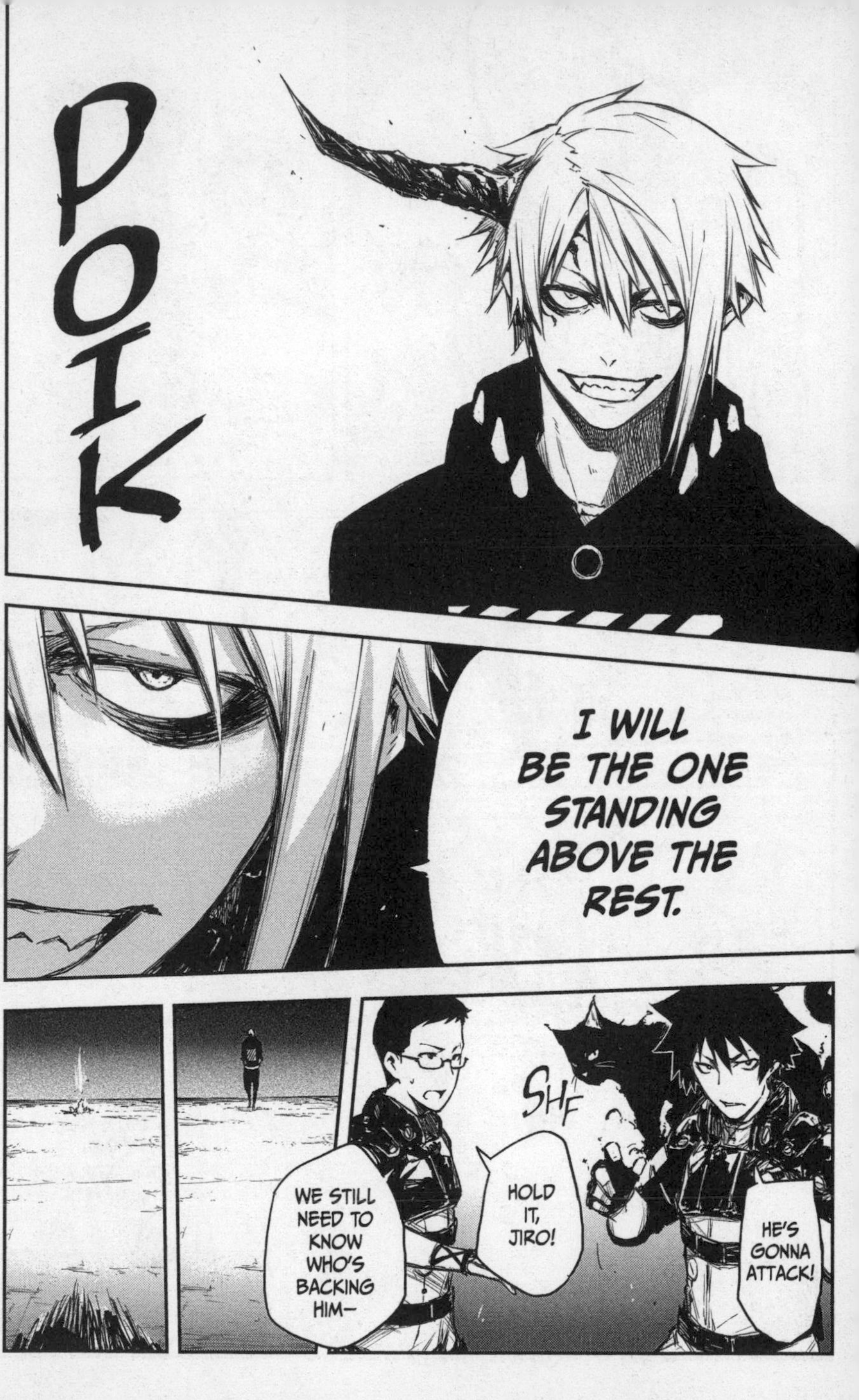
POIK
I WILL BE THE ONE STANDING ABOVE THE REST.
HE'S GONNA ATTACK!
SHF
HOLD IT, JIRO!
WE STILL NEED TO KNOW WHO'S BACKING HIM—

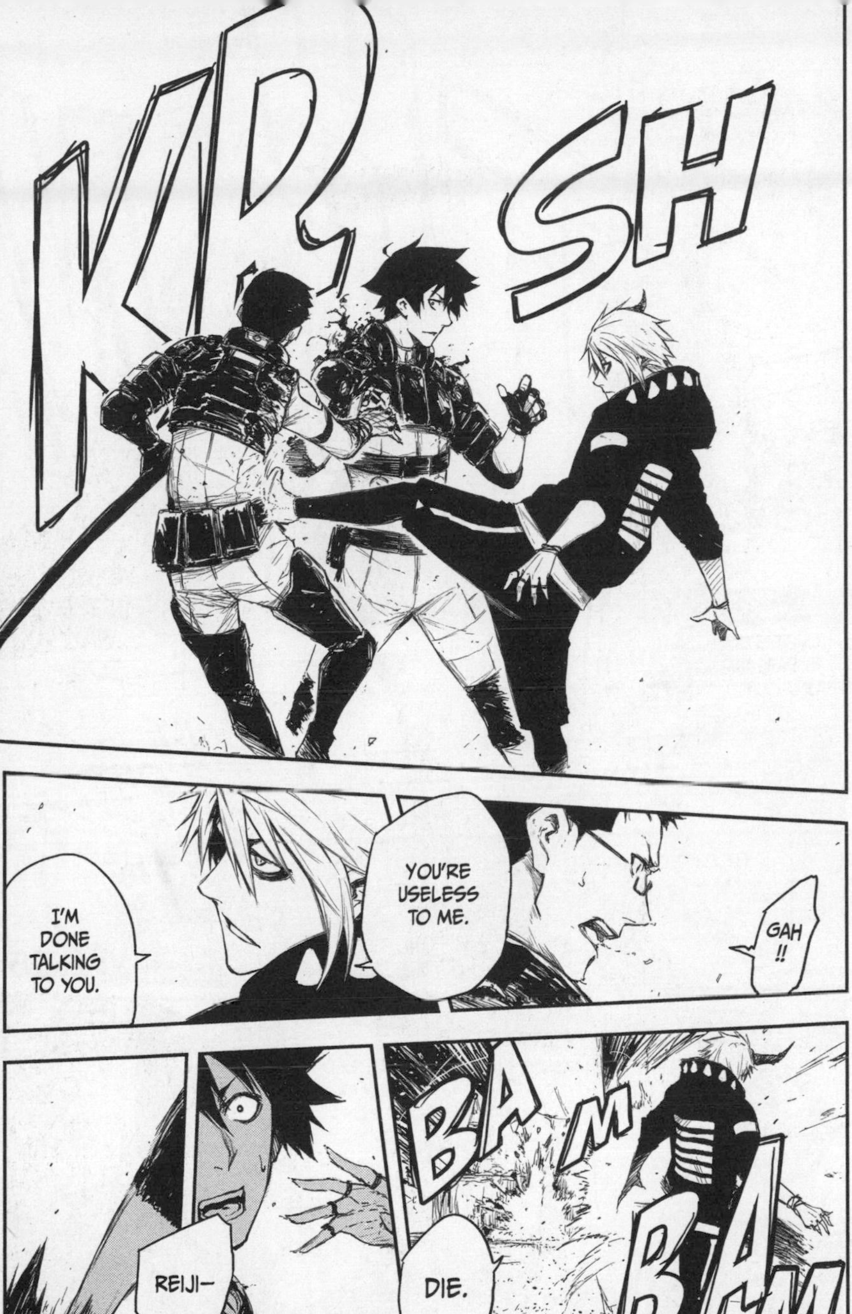
KRSH
GAH !!
YOU'RE USELESS TO ME.
I'M DONE TALKING TO YOU.
BAM
DIE.
BAM
REIJI—

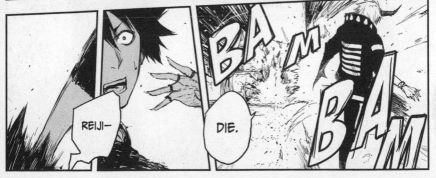

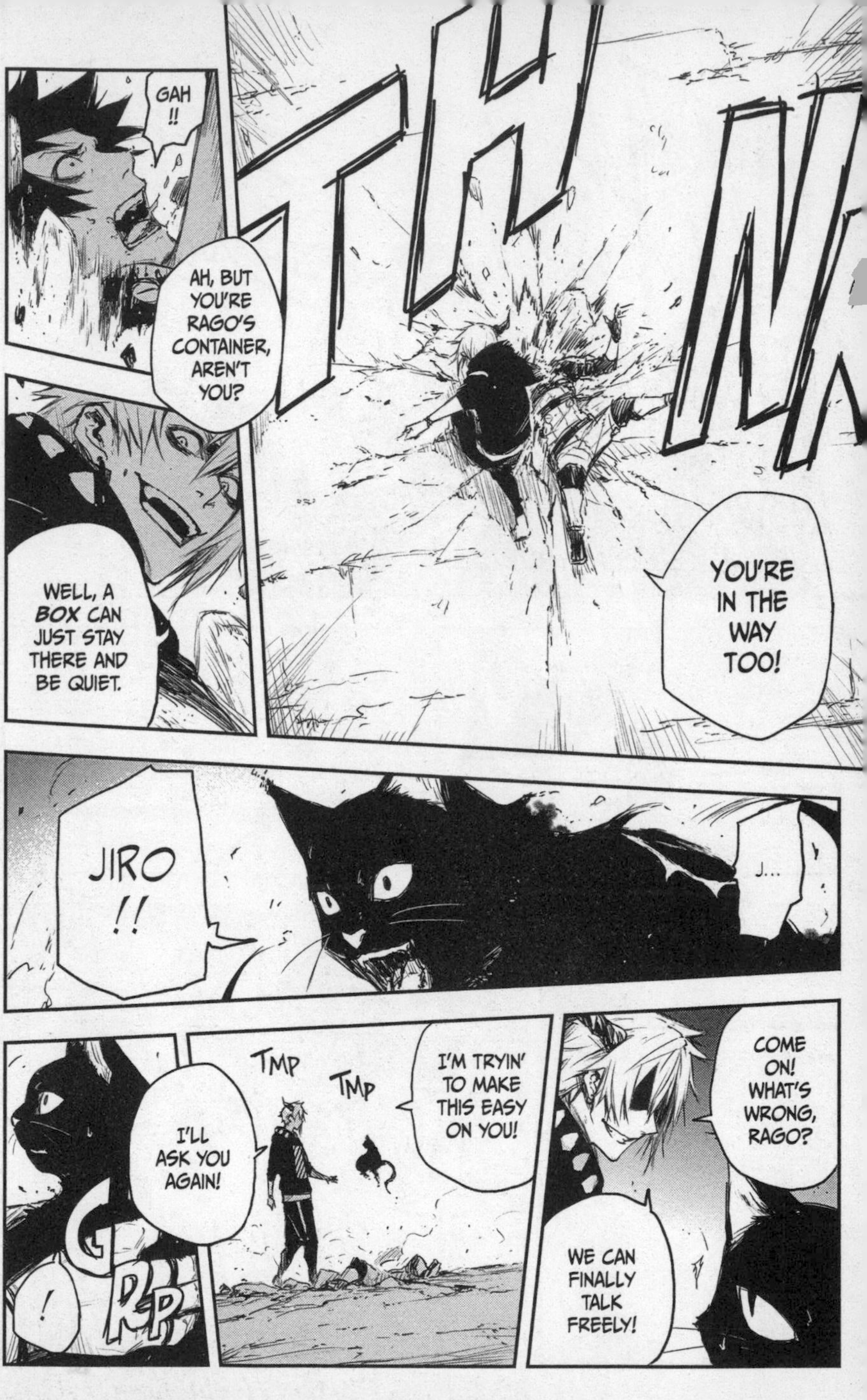
THNK
YOU'RE IN THE WAY TOO!
GAH !!
AH, BUT YOU'RE RAGO'S CONTAINER, AREN'T YOU?
WELL, A BOX CAN JUST STAY THERE AND BE QUIET.
J...
JIRO !!
COME ON! WHAT'S WRONG, RAGO?
WE CAN FINALLY TALK FREELY!
I'M TRYIN' TO MAKE THIS EASY ON YOU!
TMP
TMP
I'LL ASK YOU AGAIN!
GRP
!

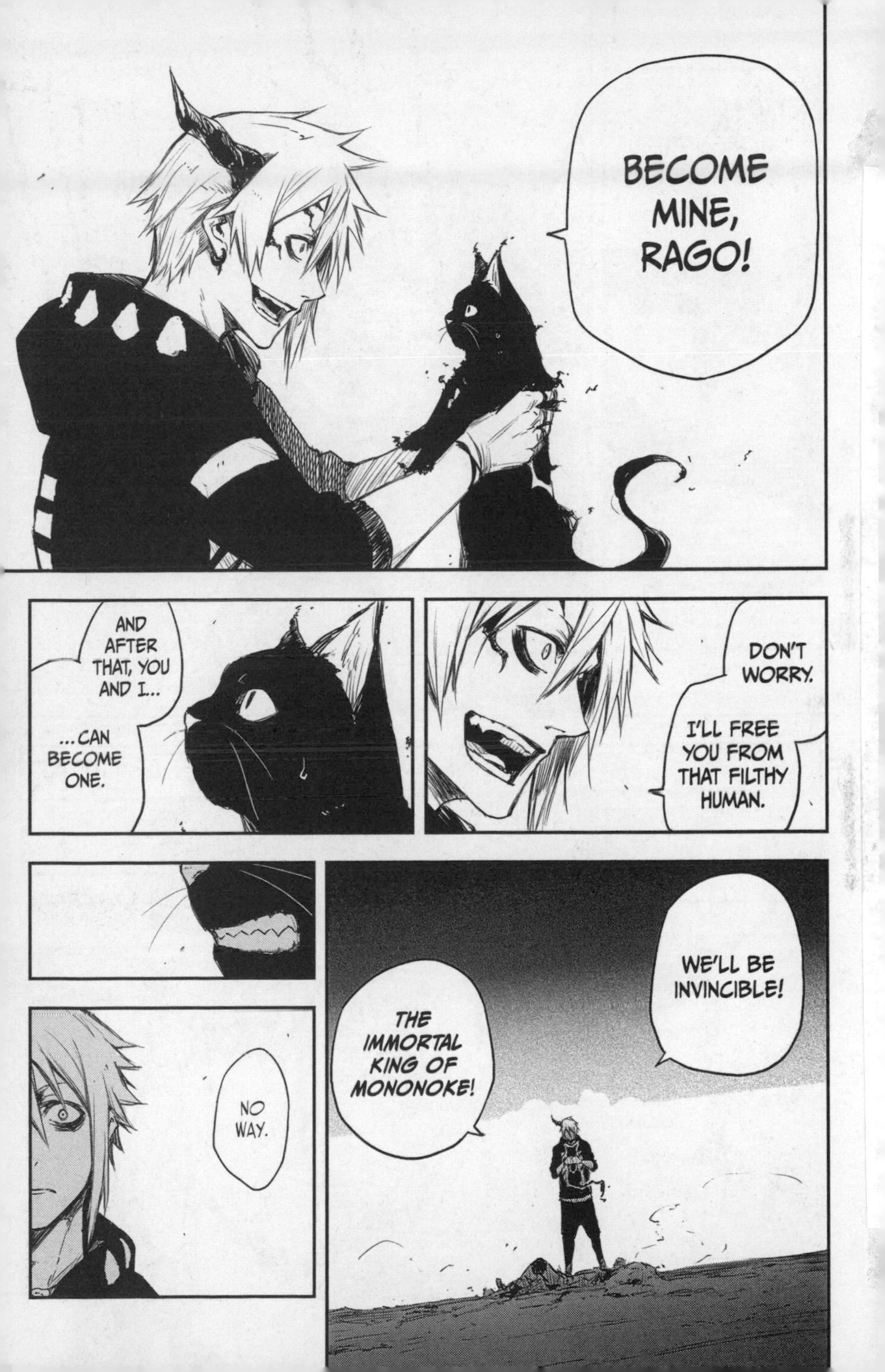
BECOME MINE, RAGO!
DON'T WORRY.
I'LL FREE YOU FROM THAT FILTHY HUMAN.
AND AFTER THAT, YOU AND I...
...CAN BECOME ONE.
WE'LL BE INVINCIBLE!
THE IMMORTAL KING OF MONONOKE!
NO WAY.

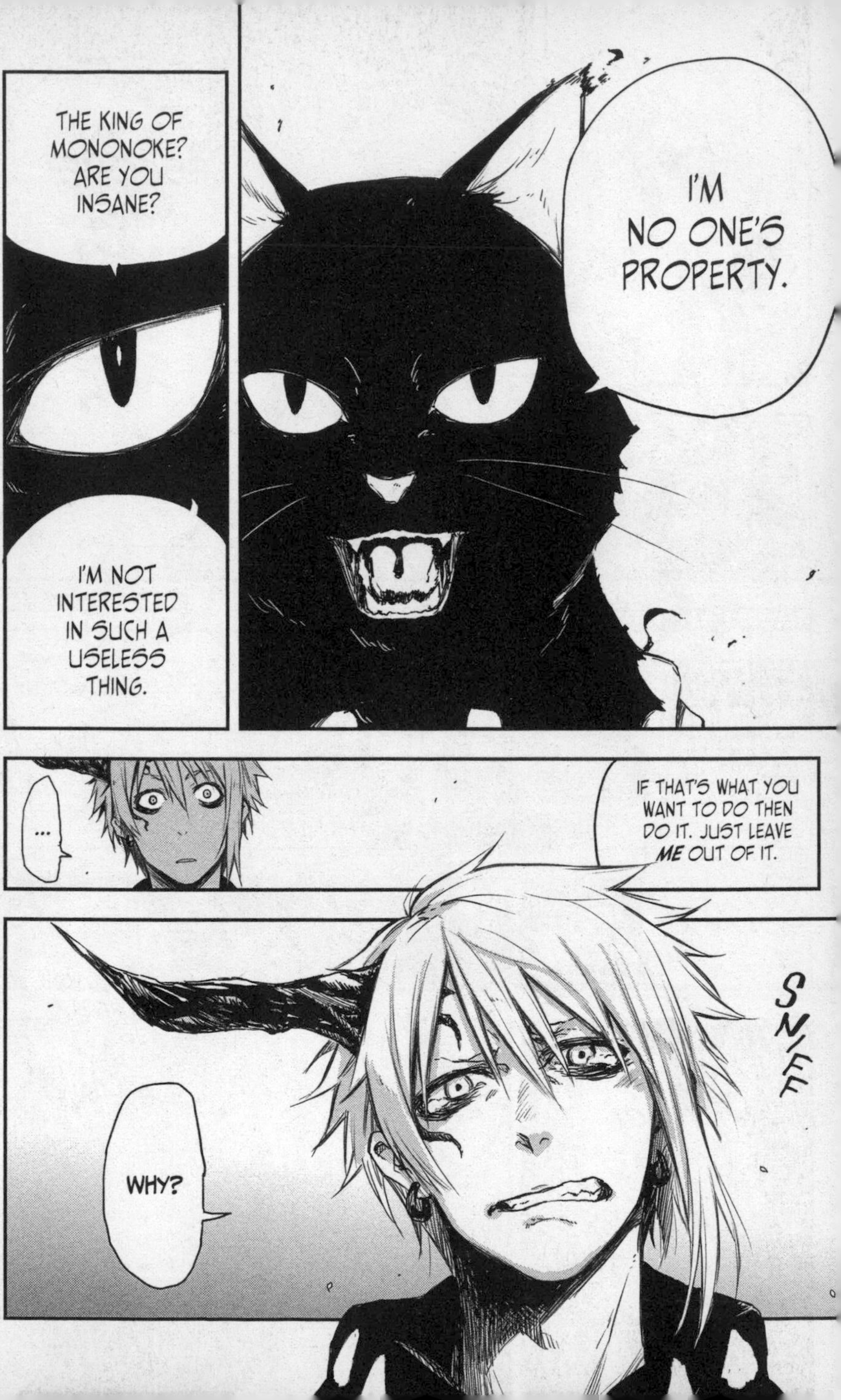
I'M NO ONE'S PROPERTY.
THE KING OF MONONOKE? ARE YOU INSANE?
I'M NOT INTERESTED IN SUCH A USELESS THING.
IF THAT'S WHAT YOU WANT TO DO THEN DO IT. JUST LEAVE ME OUT OF IT.
...
SNIFF
WHY?

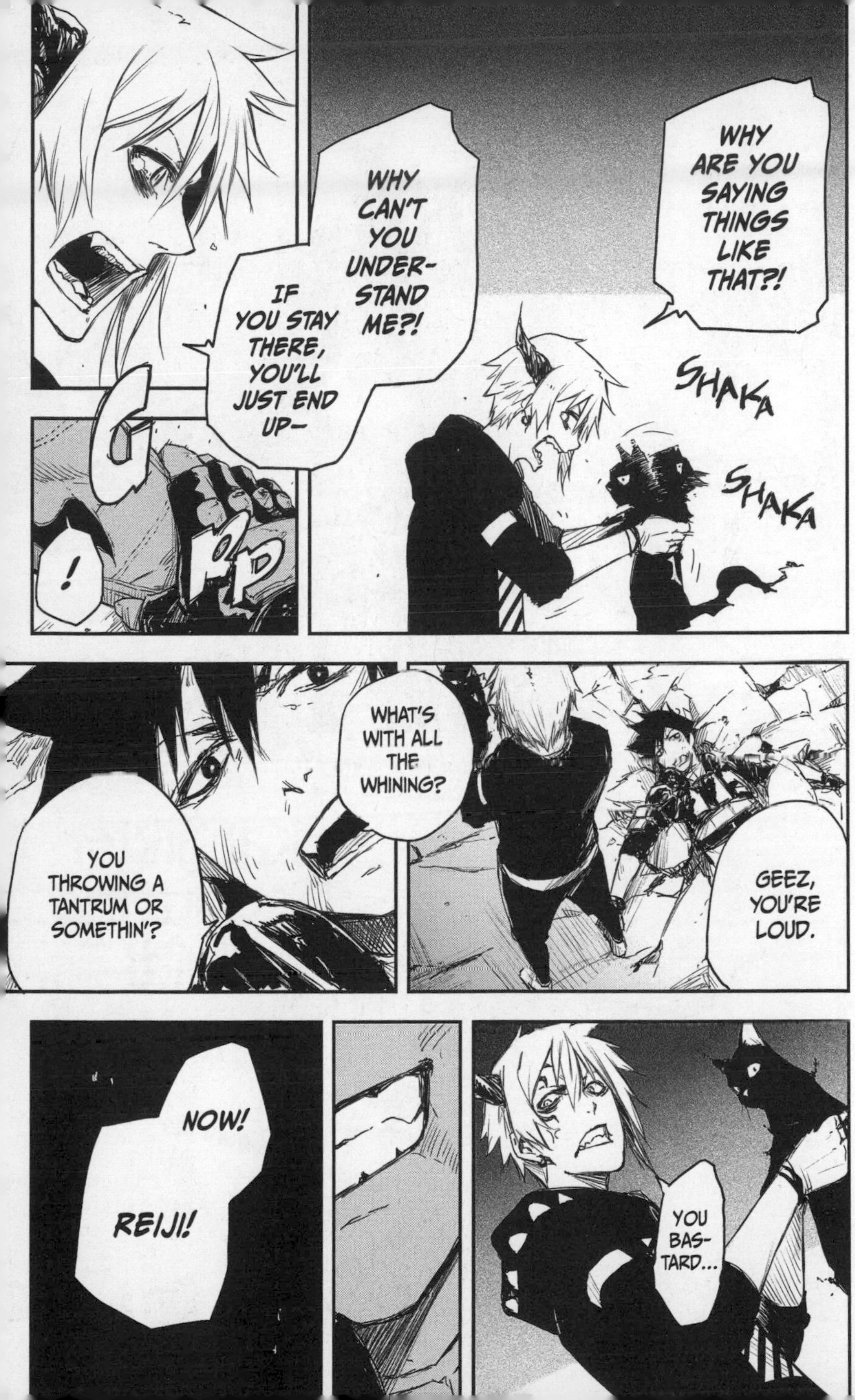
WHY ARE YOU SAYING THINGS LIKE THAT?!
SHAKA
SHAKA
WHY CAN'T YOU UNDER-STAND ME?!
IF YOU STAY THERE, YOU'LL JUST END UP—
!
GEEZ, YOU'RE LOUD.
WHAT'S WITH ALL THE WHINING?
YOU THROWING A TANTRUM OR SOMETHIN'?
YOU BAS-TARD...
NOW!
REIJI!

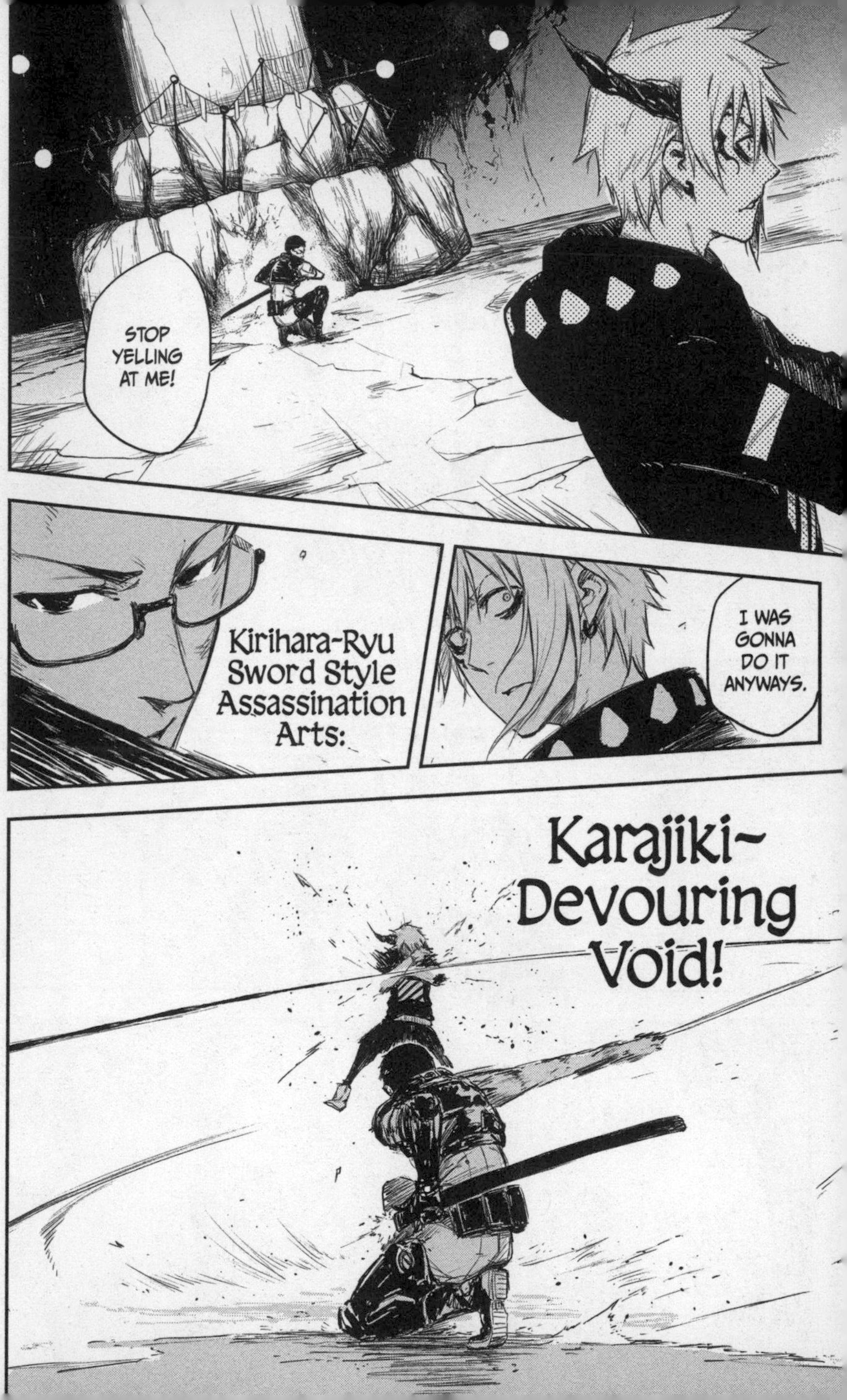
STOP YELLING AT ME!
I WAS GONNA DO IT ANYWAYS.
Kirihara-Ryu Sword Style Assassination Arts:
Karajiki- Devouring Void!

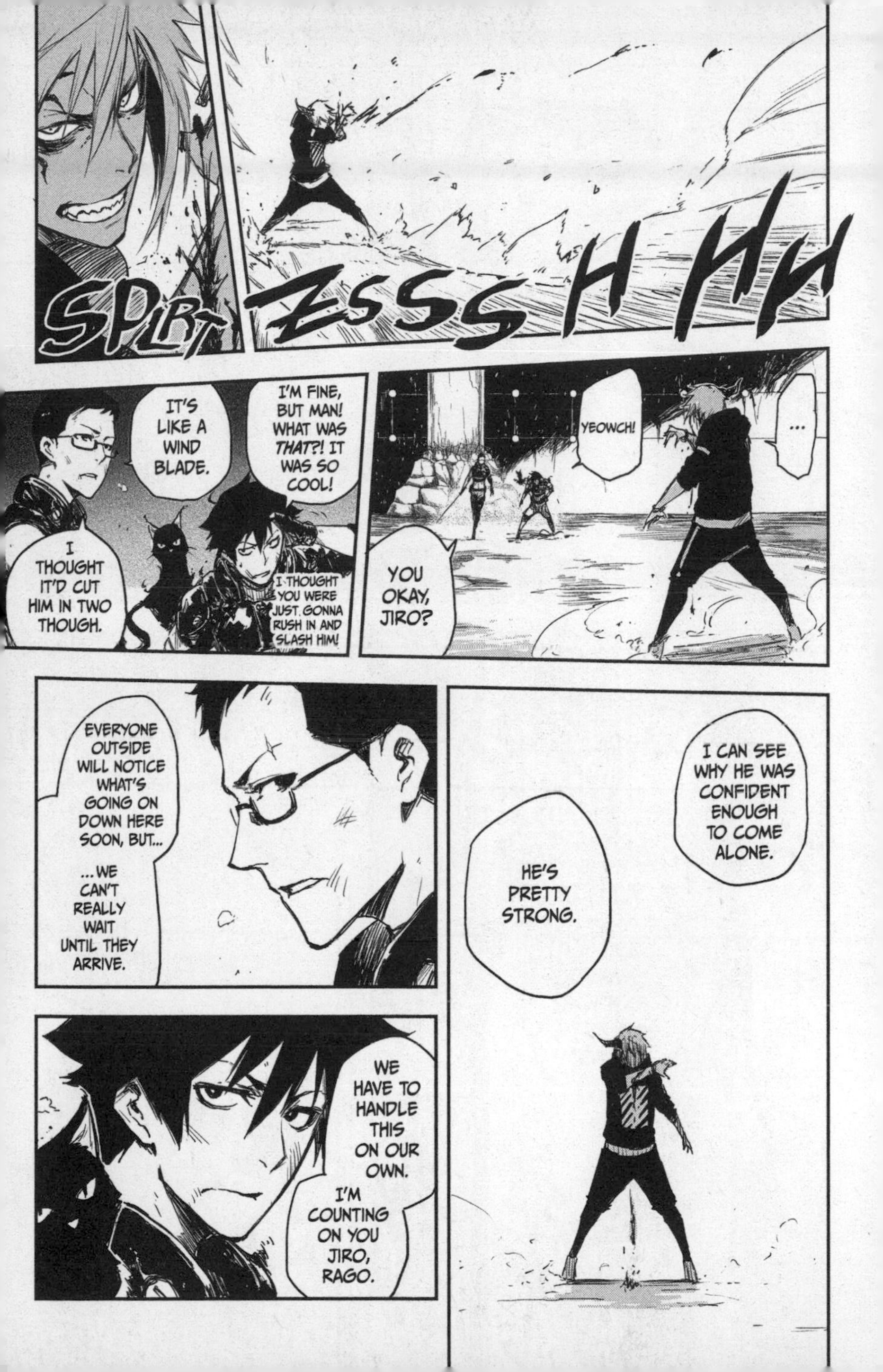
ZSSSHHHH
SPLRT
...
YEOWCH!
YOU OKAY, JIRO?
I'M FINE, BUT MAN! WHAT WAS *THAT*?! IT WAS SO COOL!
IT'S LIKE A WIND BLADE.
I THOUGHT YOU WERE JUST GONNA RUSH IN AND SLASH HIM!
I THOUGHT IT'D CUT HIM IN TWO THOUGH.
I CAN SEE WHY HE WAS CONFIDENT ENOUGH TO COME ALONE.
HE'S PRETTY STRONG.
EVERYONE OUTSIDE WILL NOTICE WHAT'S GOING ON DOWN HERE SOON, BUT...
...WE CAN'T REALLY WAIT UNTIL THEY ARRIVE.
WE HAVE TO HANDLE THIS ON OUR OWN.
I'M COUNTING ON YOU JIRO, RAGO.

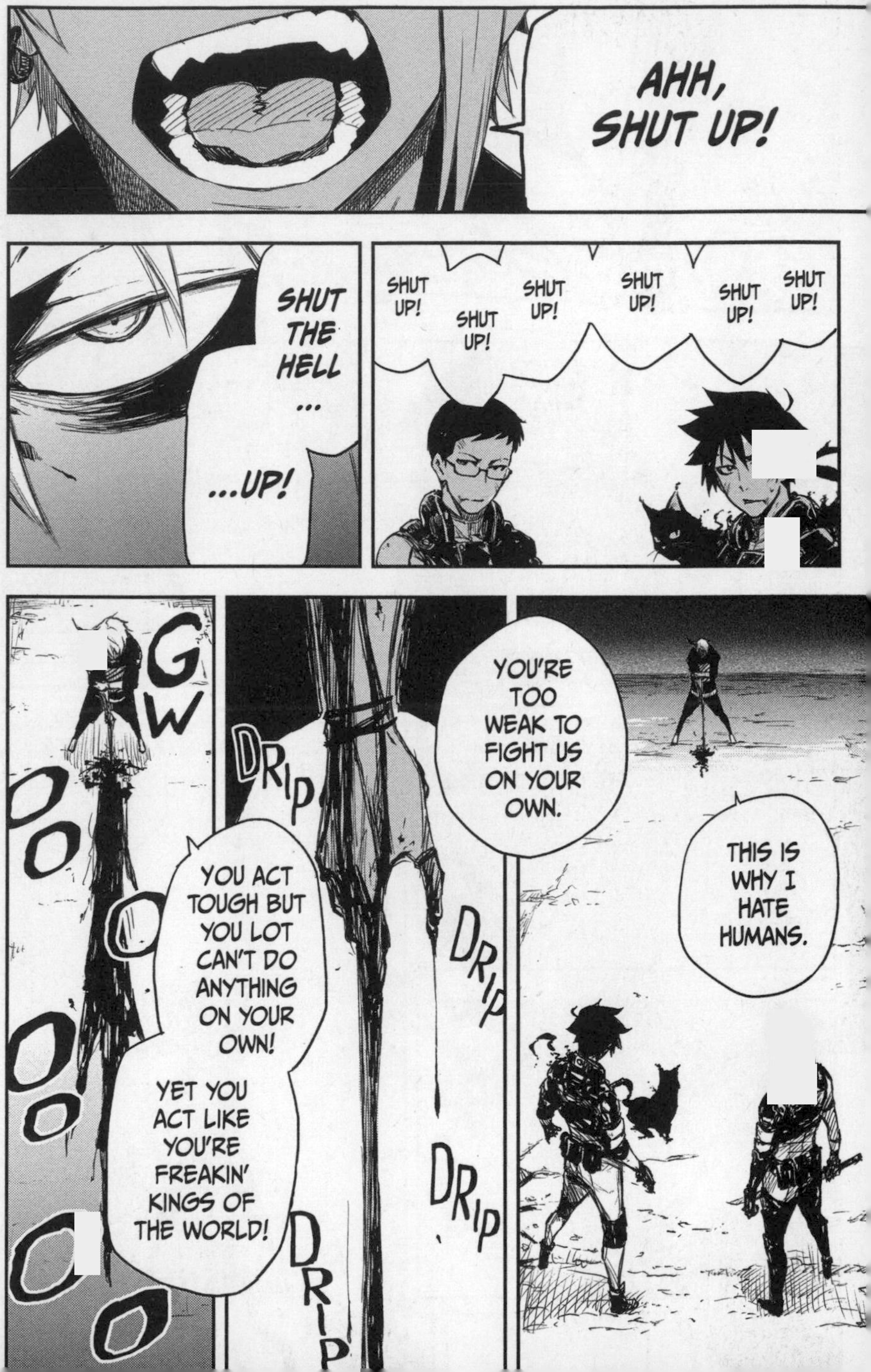

AHH, SHUT UP!
SHUT UP!
SHUT UP!
SHUT UP!
SHUT UP!
SHUT UP!
SHUT UP!
SHUT THE HELL...
...UP!
THIS IS WHY I HATE HUMANS.
YOU'RE TOO WEAK TO FIGHT US ON YOUR OWN.
DRIP
DRIP
DRIP
DRIP
YOU ACT TOUGH BUT YOU LOT CAN'T DO ANYTHING ON YOUR OWN!
YET YOU ACT LIKE YOU'RE FREAKIN' KINGS OF THE WORLD!
GWOOOOOOO

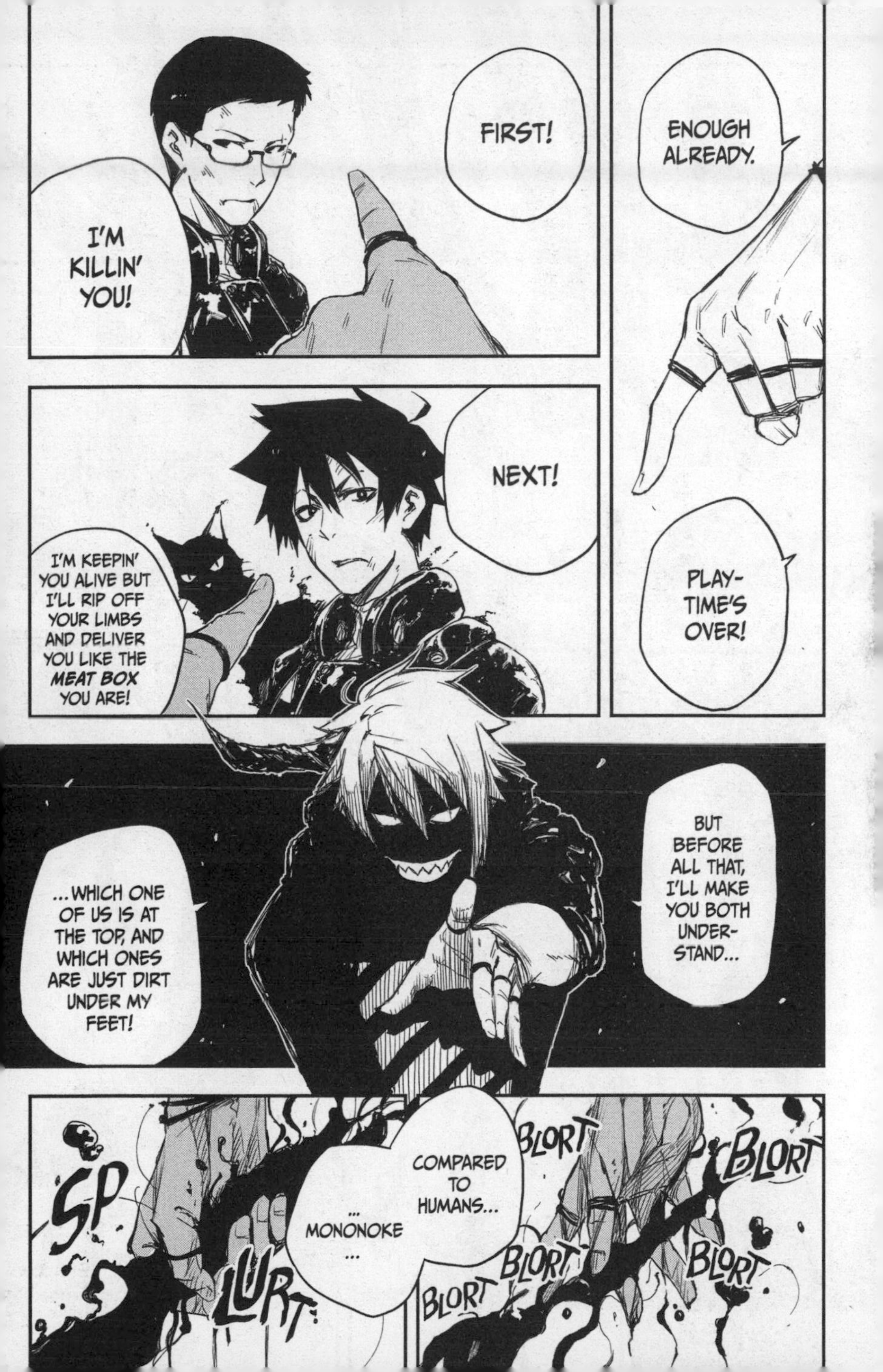
ENOUGH ALREADY.
PLAY-TIME'S OVER!
FIRST!
I'M KILLIN' YOU!
NEXT!
I'M KEEPIN' YOU ALIVE BUT I'LL RIP OFF YOUR LIMBS AND DELIVER YOU LIKE THE *MEAT BOX* YOU ARE!
BUT BEFORE ALL THAT, I'LL MAKE YOU BOTH UNDER-STAND...
...WHICH ONE OF US IS AT THE TOP, AND WHICH ONES ARE JUST DIRT UNDER MY FEET!
BLORT
BLORT
BLORT
BLORT
COMPARED TO HUMANS...
...MONONOKE...
BLORT
BLORT
SP
LURT

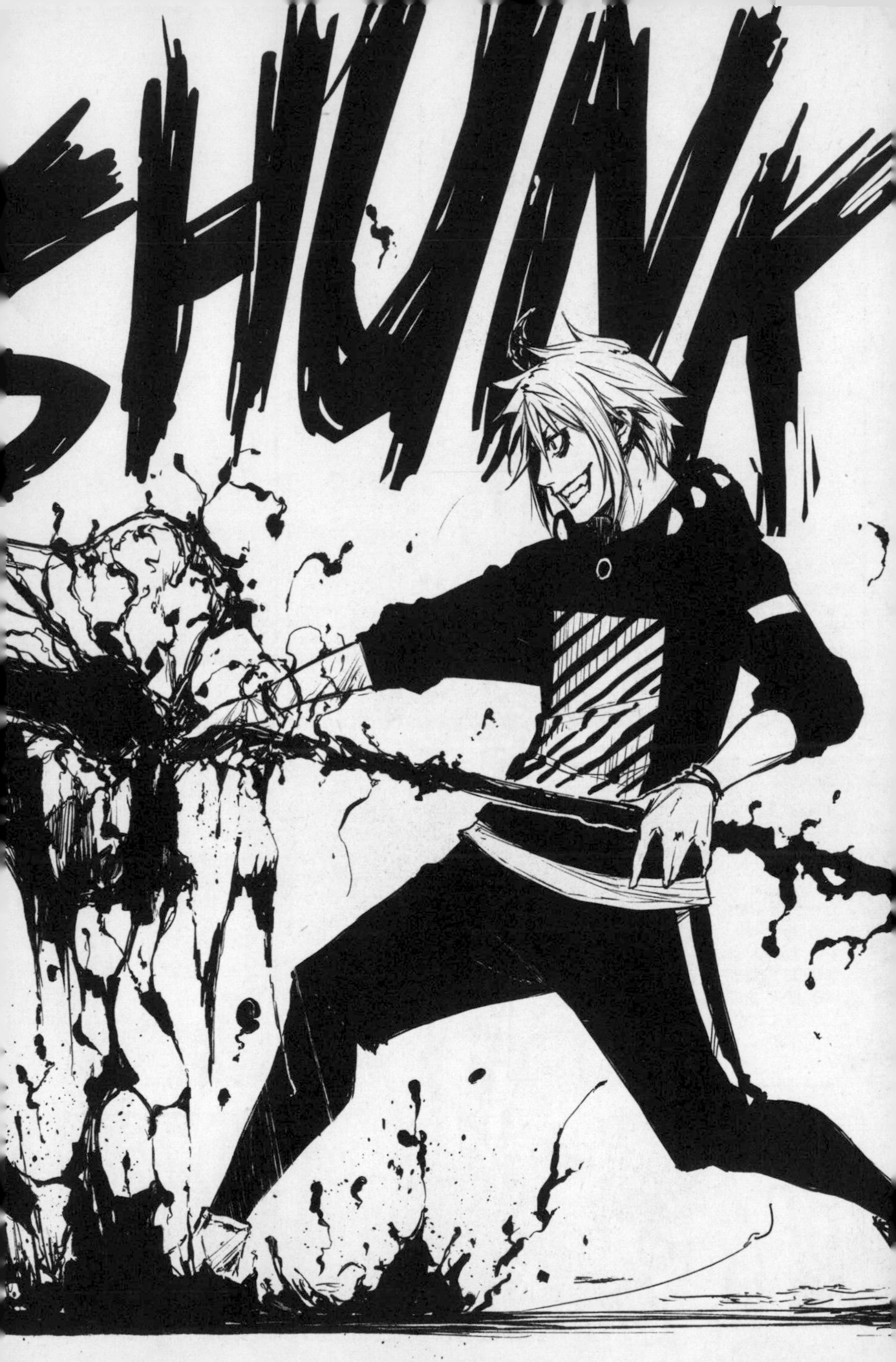
SHUNK

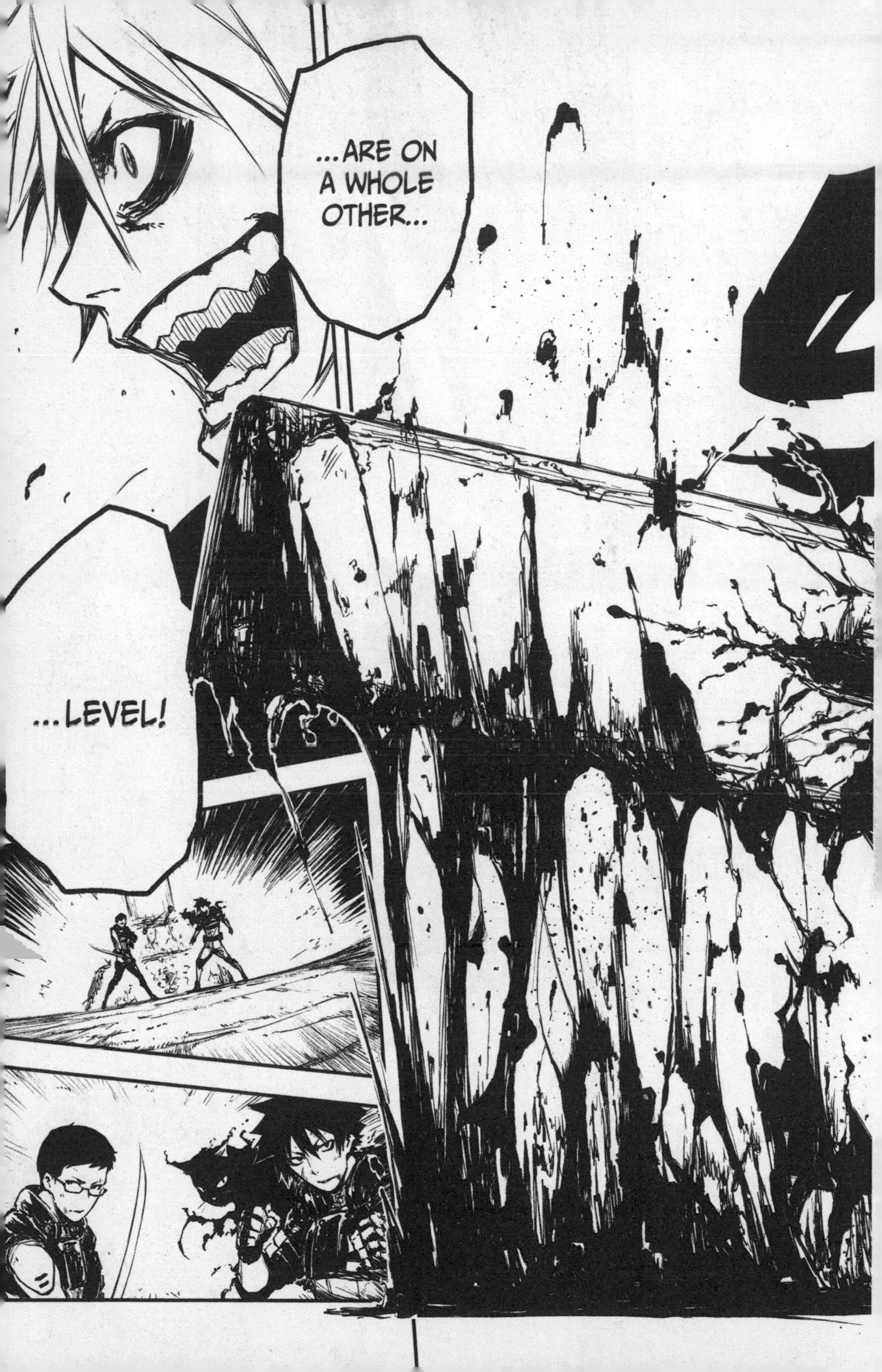
...ARE ON A WHOLE OTHER...
...LEVEL!

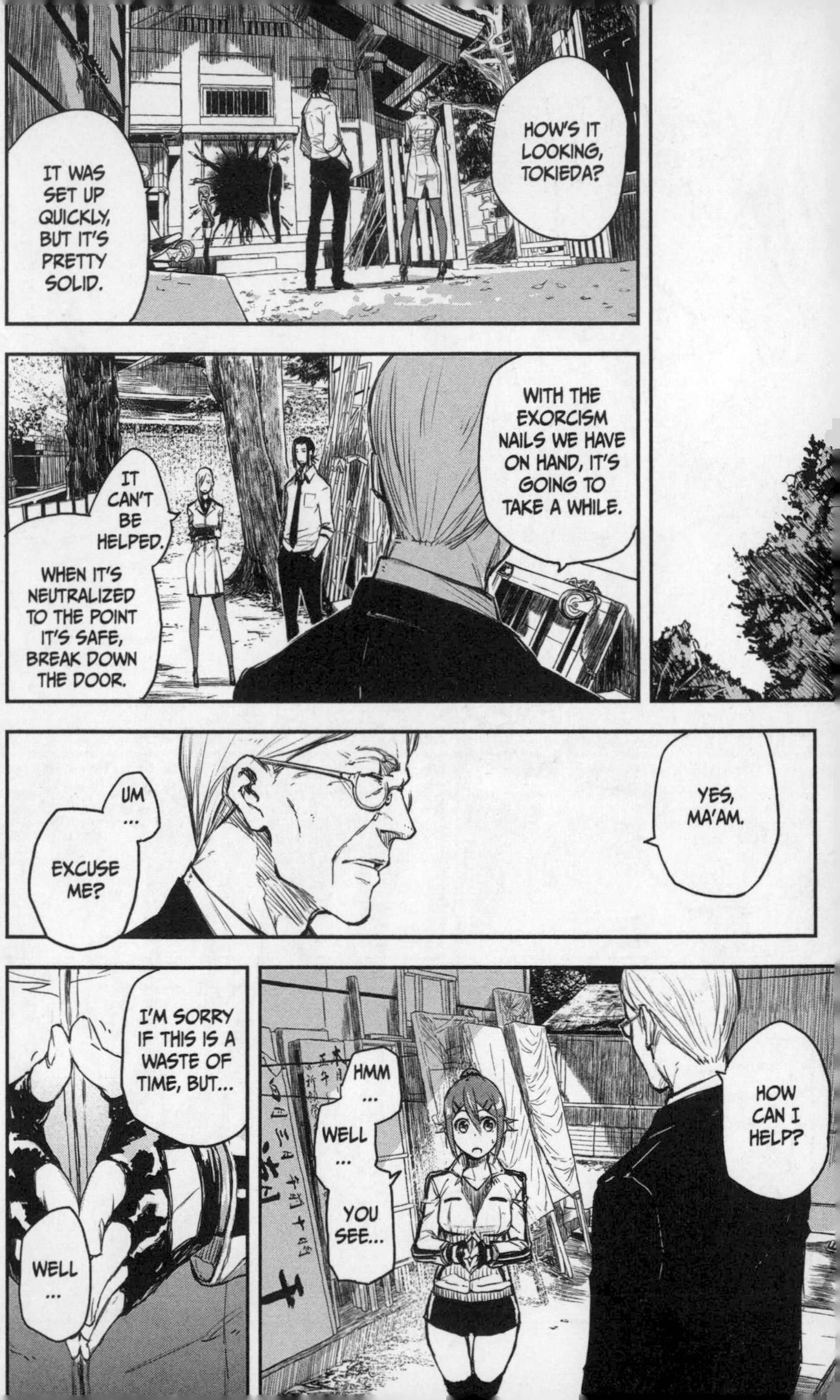
HOW'S IT LOOKING, TOKIEDA?
IT WAS SET UP QUICKLY, BUT IT'S PRETTY SOLID.
WITH THE EXORCISM NAILS WE HAVE ON HAND, IT'S GOING TO TAKE A WHILE.
IT CAN'T BE HELPED.
WHEN IT'S NEUTRALIZED TO THE POINT IT'S SAFE, BREAK DOWN THE DOOR.
YES, MA'AM.
UM ...
EXCUSE ME?
HOW CAN I HELP?
HMM ...
WELL ...
YOU SEE...
I'M SORRY IF THIS IS A WASTE OF TIME, BUT...
WELL ...

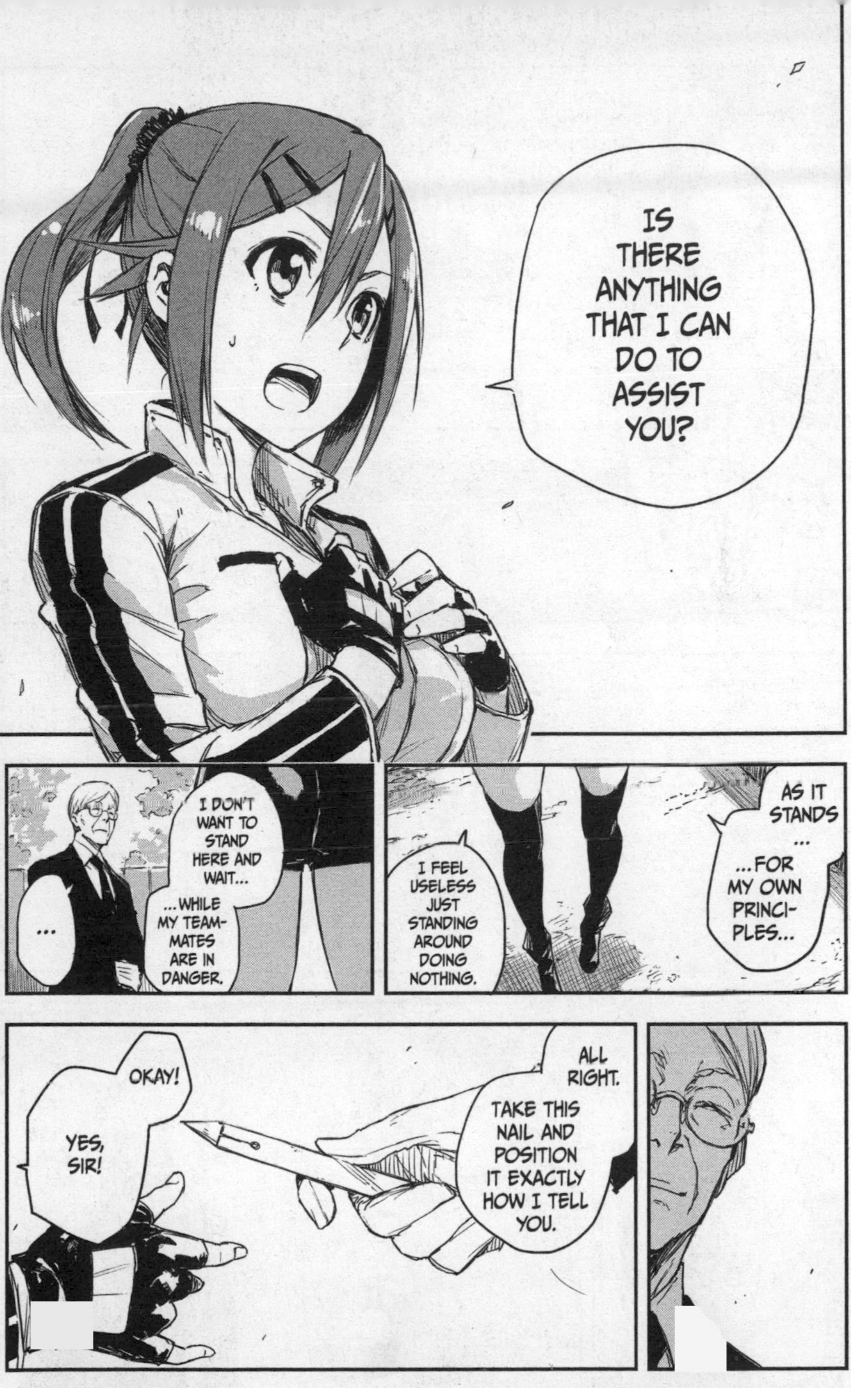
IS THERE ANYTHING THAT I CAN DO TO ASSIST YOU?
AS IT STANDS ...
...FOR MY OWN PRINCIPLES...
I FEEL USELESS JUST STANDING AROUND DOING NOTHING.
I DON'T WANT TO STAND HERE AND WAIT...
...WHILE MY TEAMMATES ARE IN DANGER.
...
ALL RIGHT.
TAKE THIS NAIL AND POSITION IT EXACTLY HOW I TELL YOU.
OKAY!
YES, SIR!

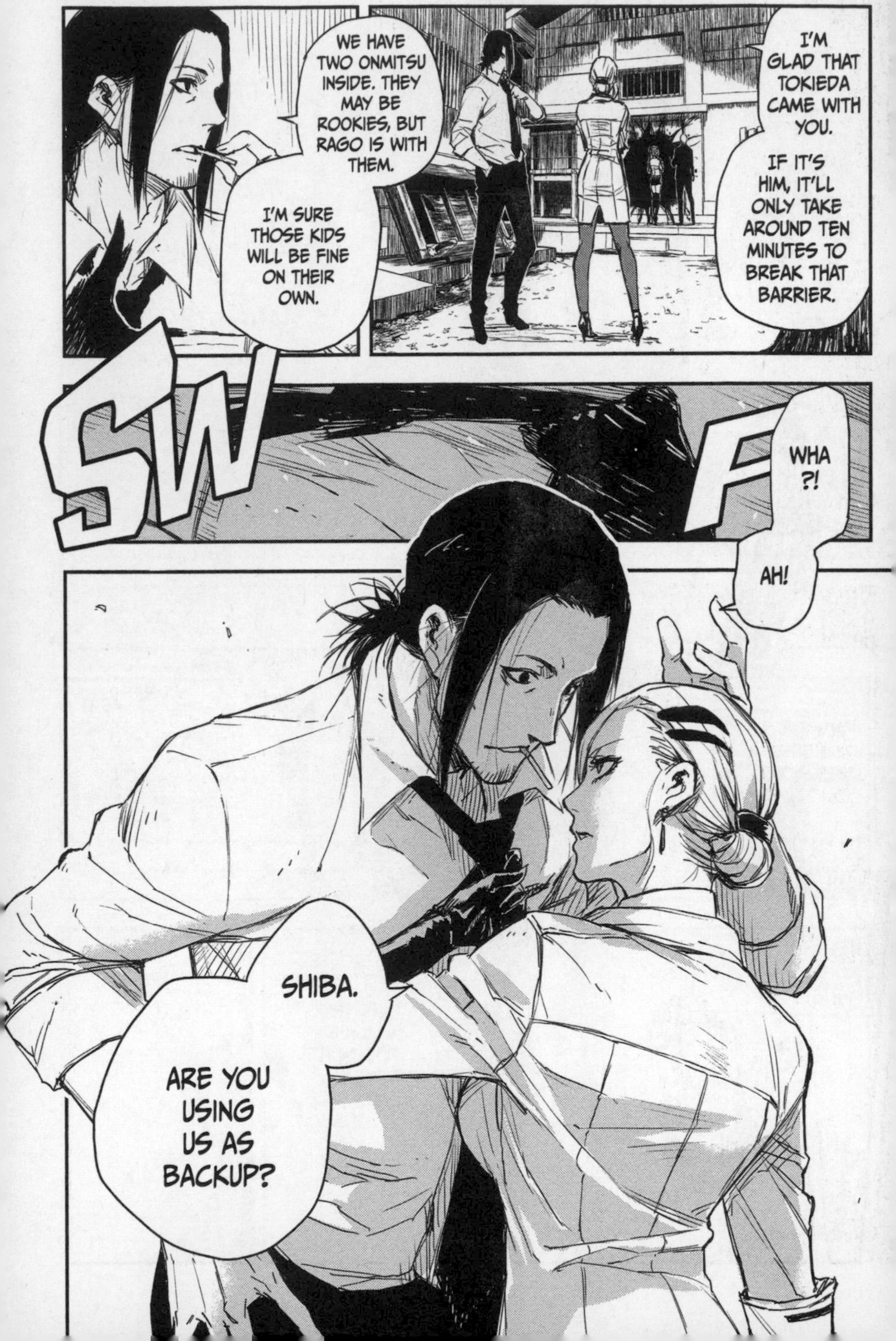
I'M GLAD THAT TOKIEDA CAME WITH YOU.
IF IT'S HIM, IT'LL ONLY TAKE AROUND TEN MINUTES TO BREAK THAT BARRIER.
WE HAVE TWO ONMITSU INSIDE. THEY MAY BE ROOKIES, BUT RAGO IS WITH THEM.
I'M SURE THOSE KIDS WILL BE FINE ON THEIR OWN.
SWF
WHA ?!
AH!
SHIBA.
ARE YOU USING US AS BACKUP?

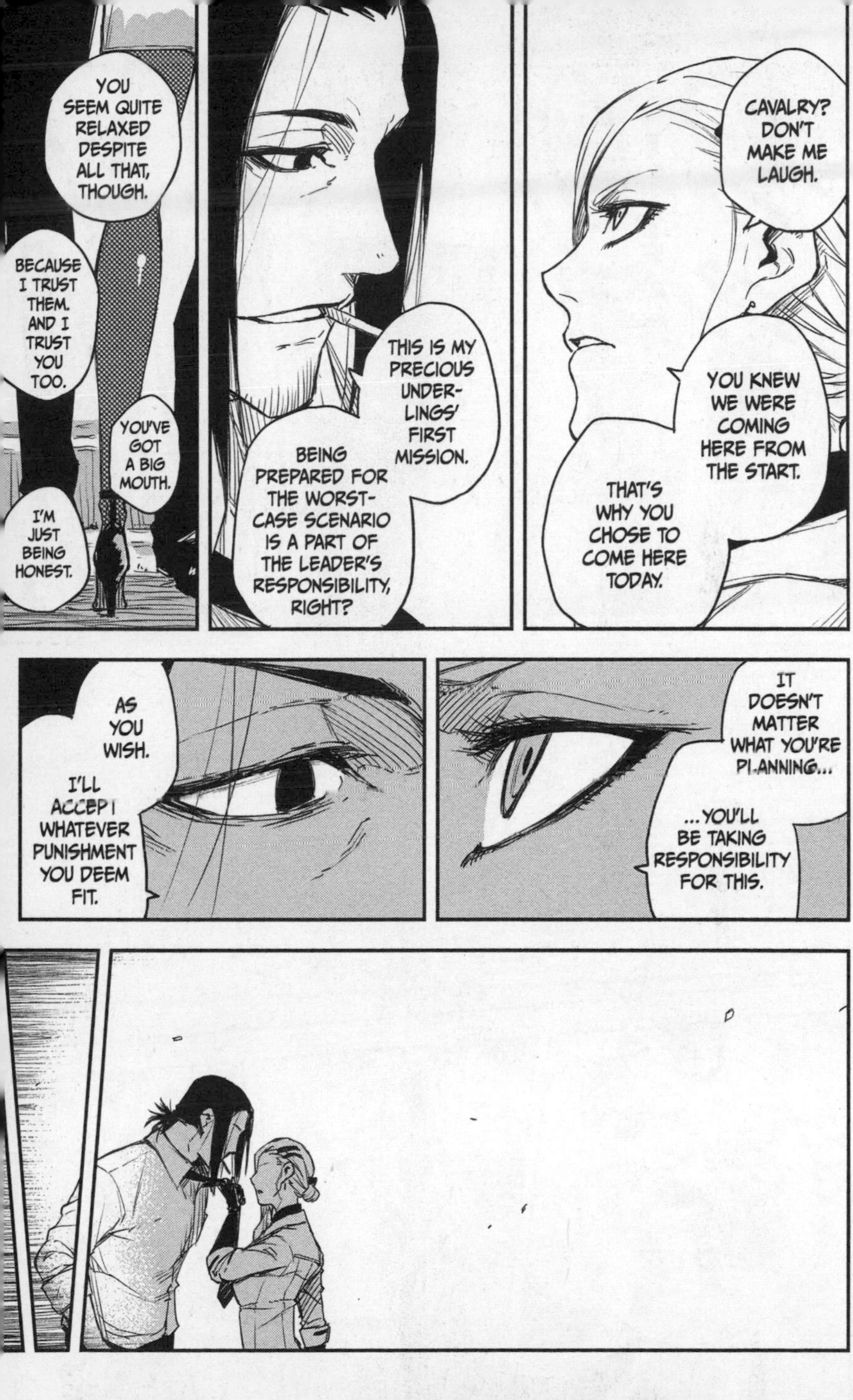
CAVALRY? DON'T MAKE ME LAUGH.
YOU KNEW WE WERE COMING HERE FROM THE START.
THAT'S WHY YOU CHOSE TO COME HERE TODAY.
THIS IS MY PRECIOUS UNDER-LINGS' FIRST MISSION.
BEING PREPARED FOR THE WORST-CASE SCENARIO IS A PART OF THE LEADER'S RESPONSIBILITY, RIGHT?
YOU SEEM QUITE RELAXED DESPITE ALL THAT, THOUGH.
BECAUSE I TRUST THEM. AND I TRUST YOU TOO.
YOU'VE GOT A BIG MOUTH.
I'M JUST BEING HONEST.
IT DOESN'T MATTER WHAT YOU'RE PLANNING...
...YOU'LL BE TAKING RESPONSIBILITY FOR THIS.
AS YOU WISH.
I'LL ACCEPT WHATEVER PUNISHMENT YOU DEEM FIT.

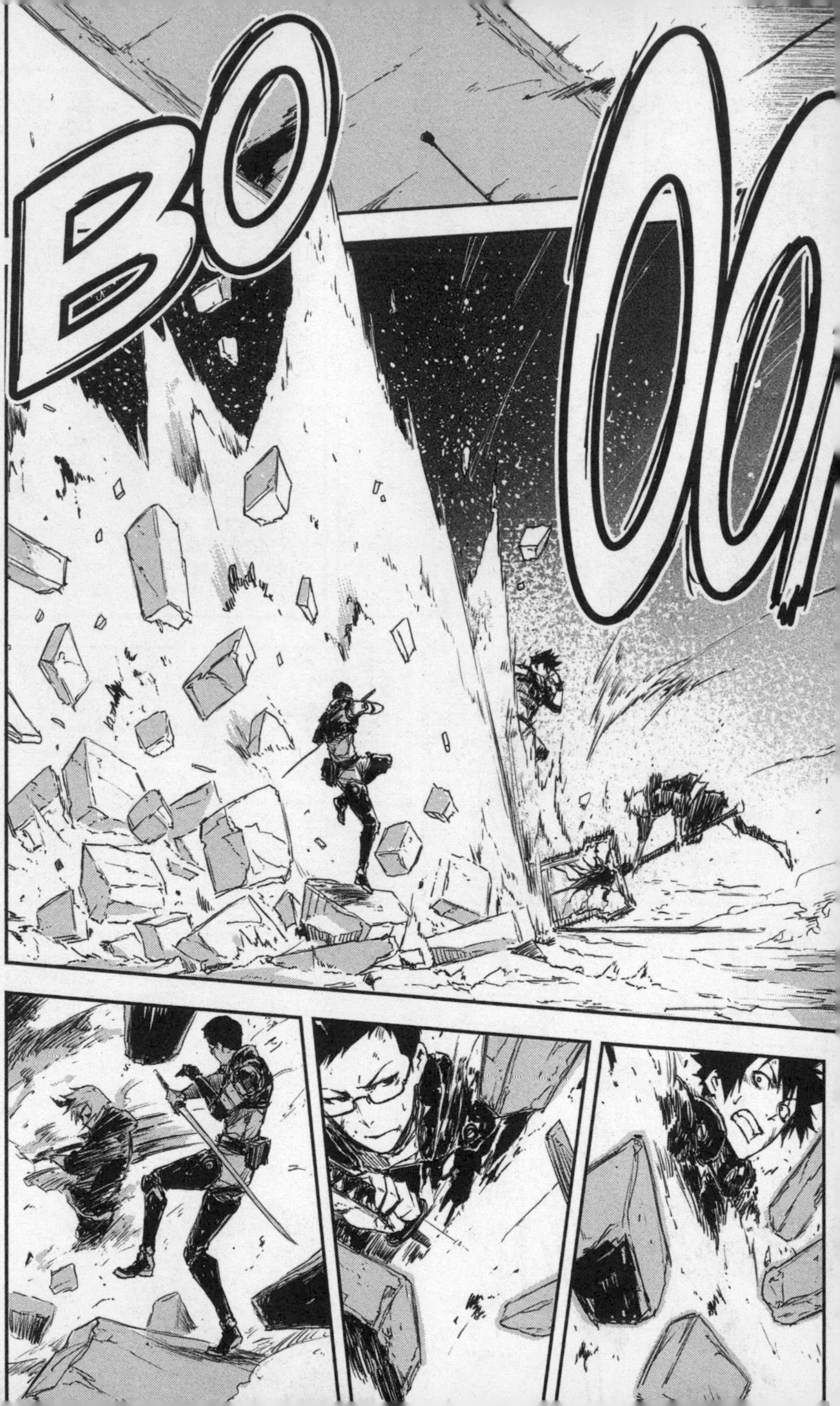
BOOO

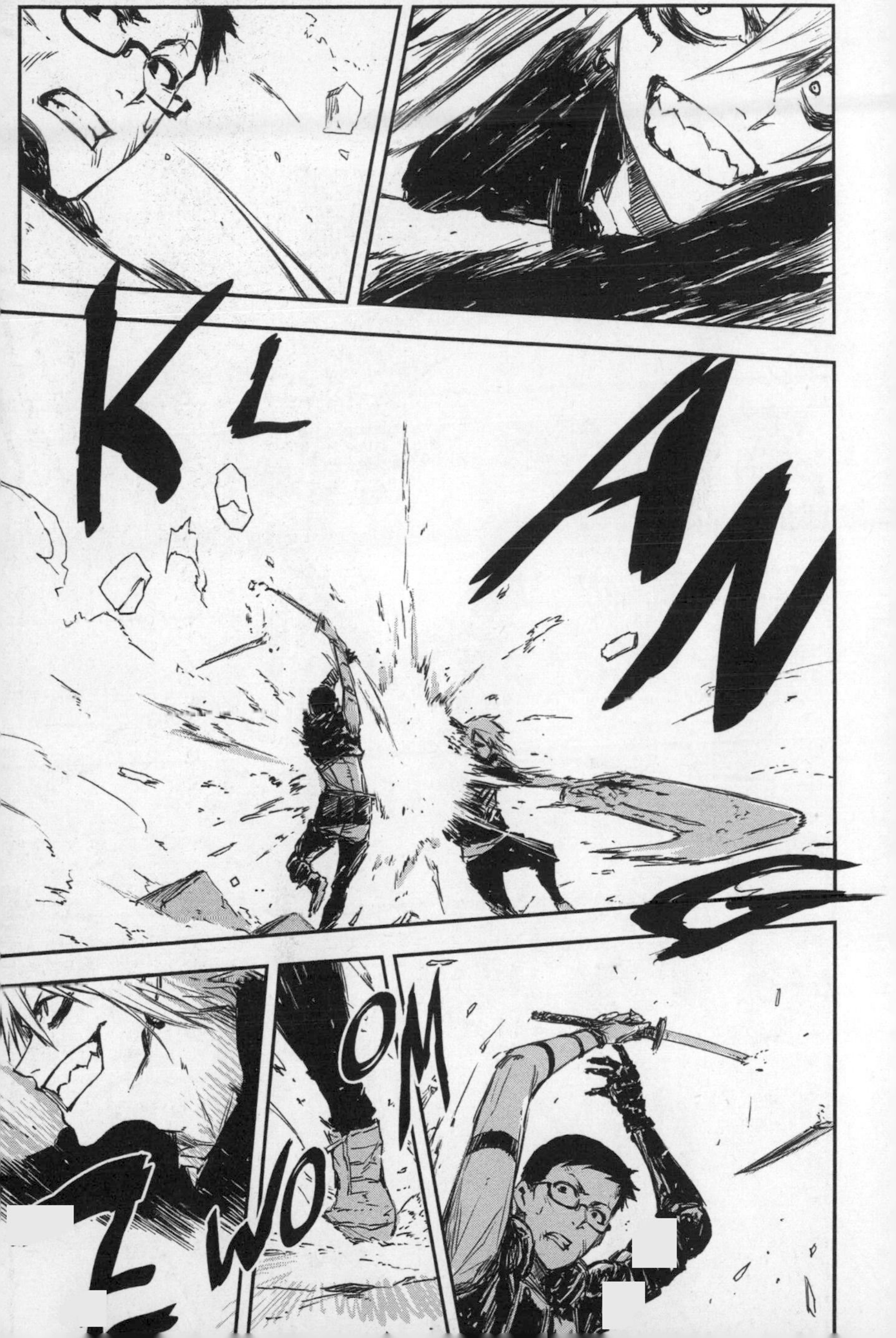
KLANG
WOOM

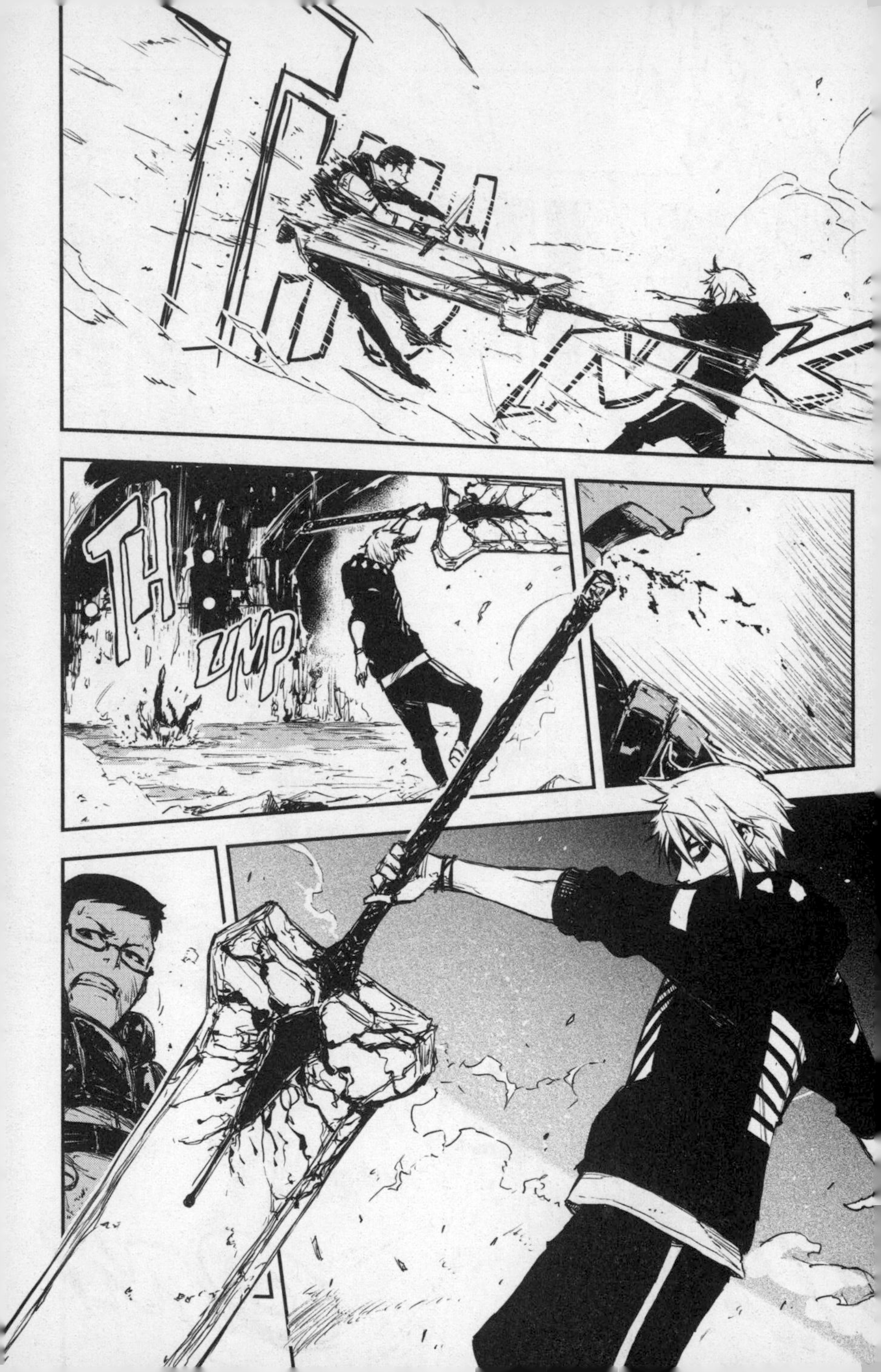
THUMP

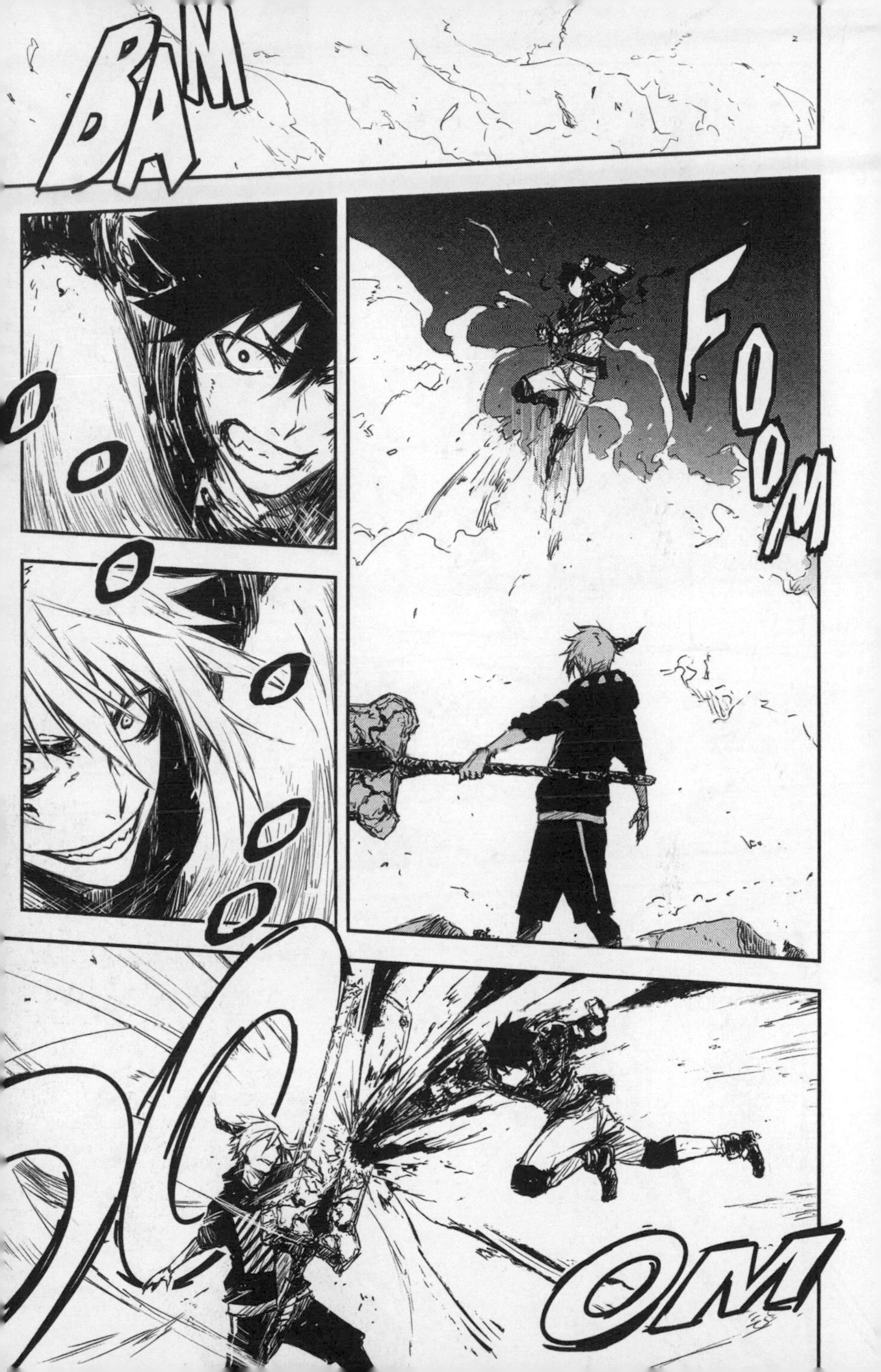
BAM
FOOM
OM

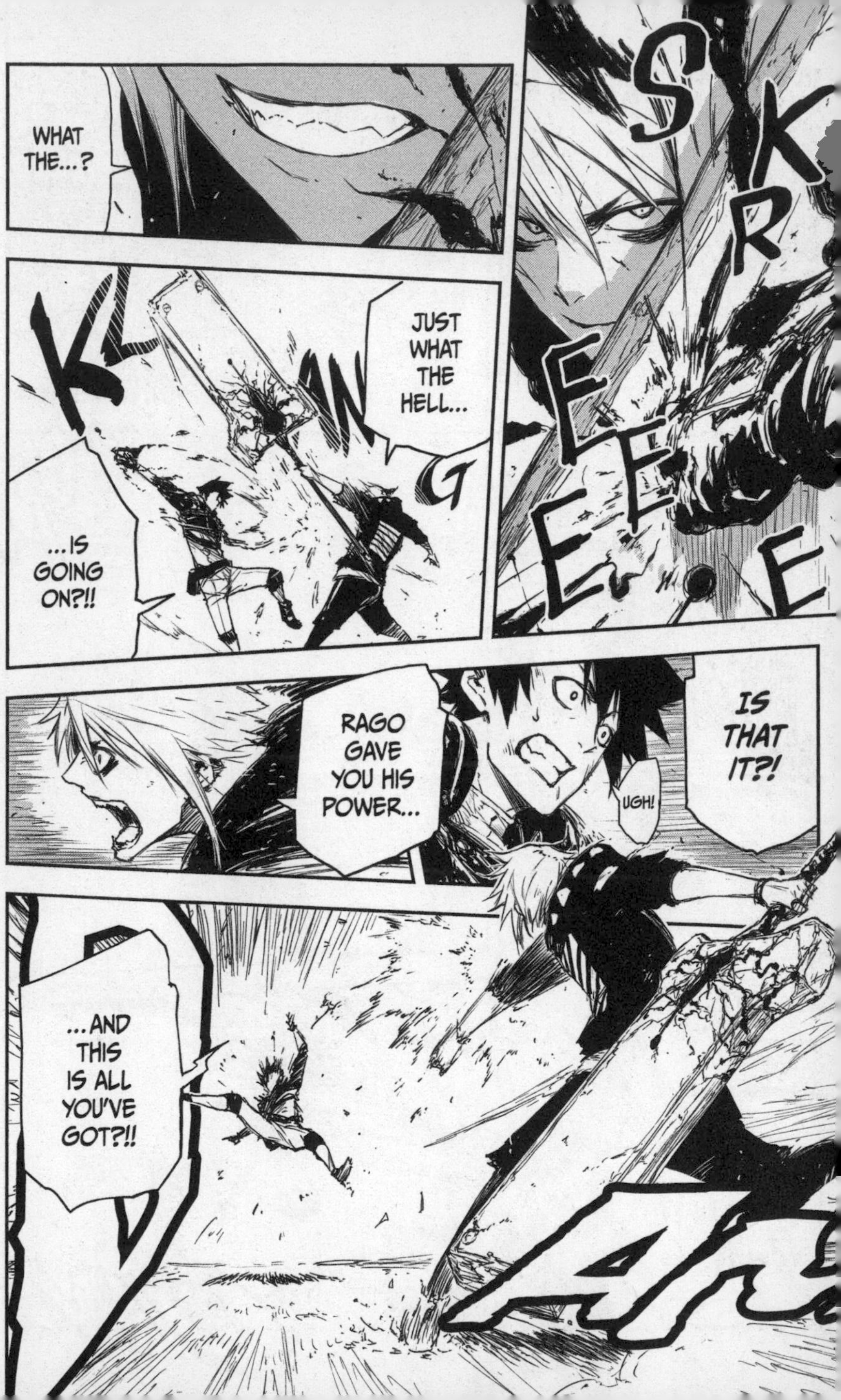
SKREEEE
WHAT THE...?
KLANG
JUST WHAT THE HELL...
...IS GOING ON?!!
IS THAT IT?!
UGH!
RAGO GAVE YOU HIS POWER...
...AND THIS IS ALL YOU'VE GOT?!!

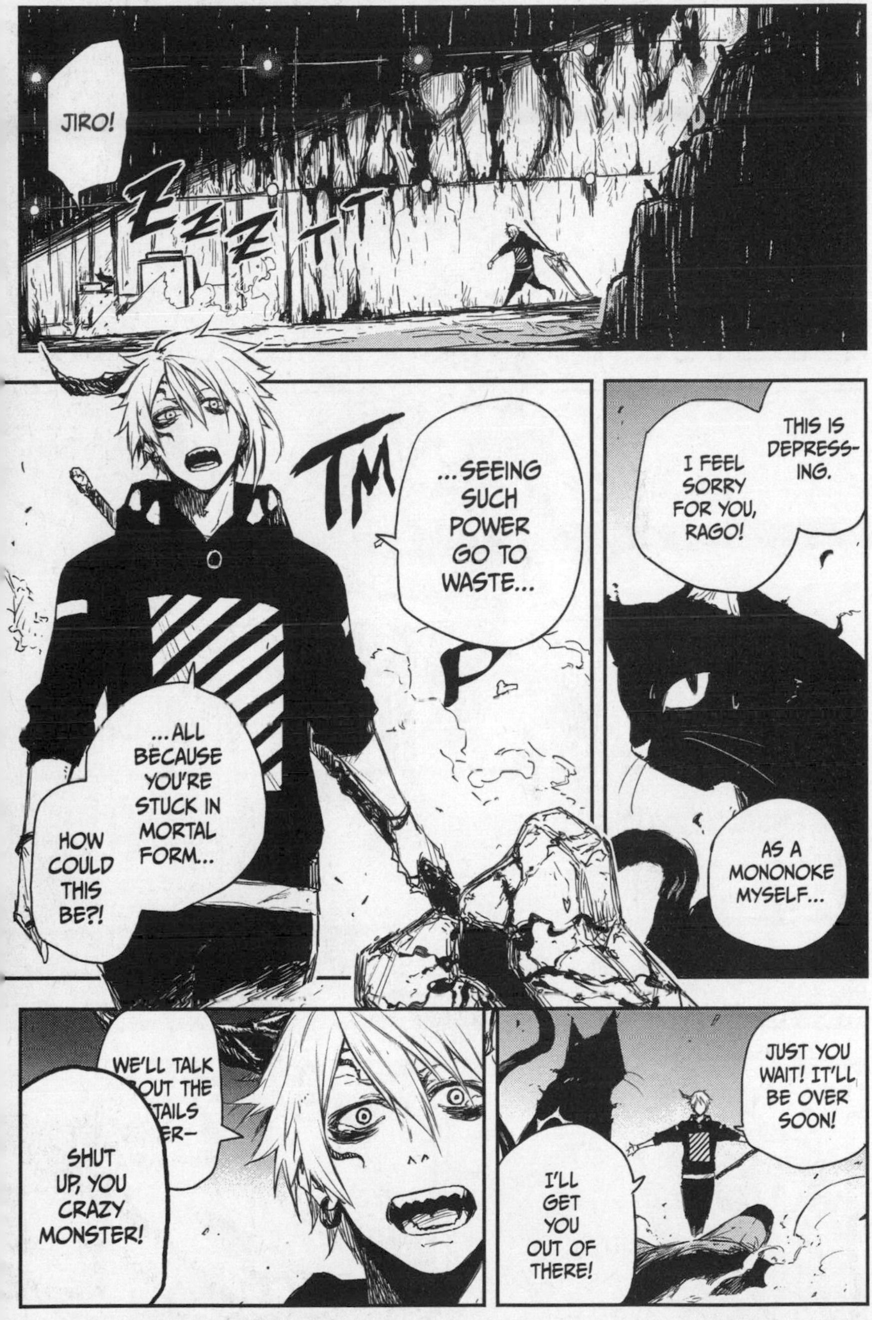
JIRO!
ZZZTT
THIS IS DEPRESS-ING.
I FEEL SORRY FOR YOU, RAGO!
AS A MONONOKE MYSELF...
TMP
...SEEING SUCH POWER GO TO WASTE...
...ALL BECAUSE YOU'RE STUCK IN MORTAL FORM...
HOW COULD THIS BE?!
JUST YOU WAIT! IT'LL BE OVER SOON!
I'LL GET YOU OUT OF THERE!
WE'LL TALK BOUT THE TAILS ER–
SHUT UP, YOU CRAZY MONSTER!

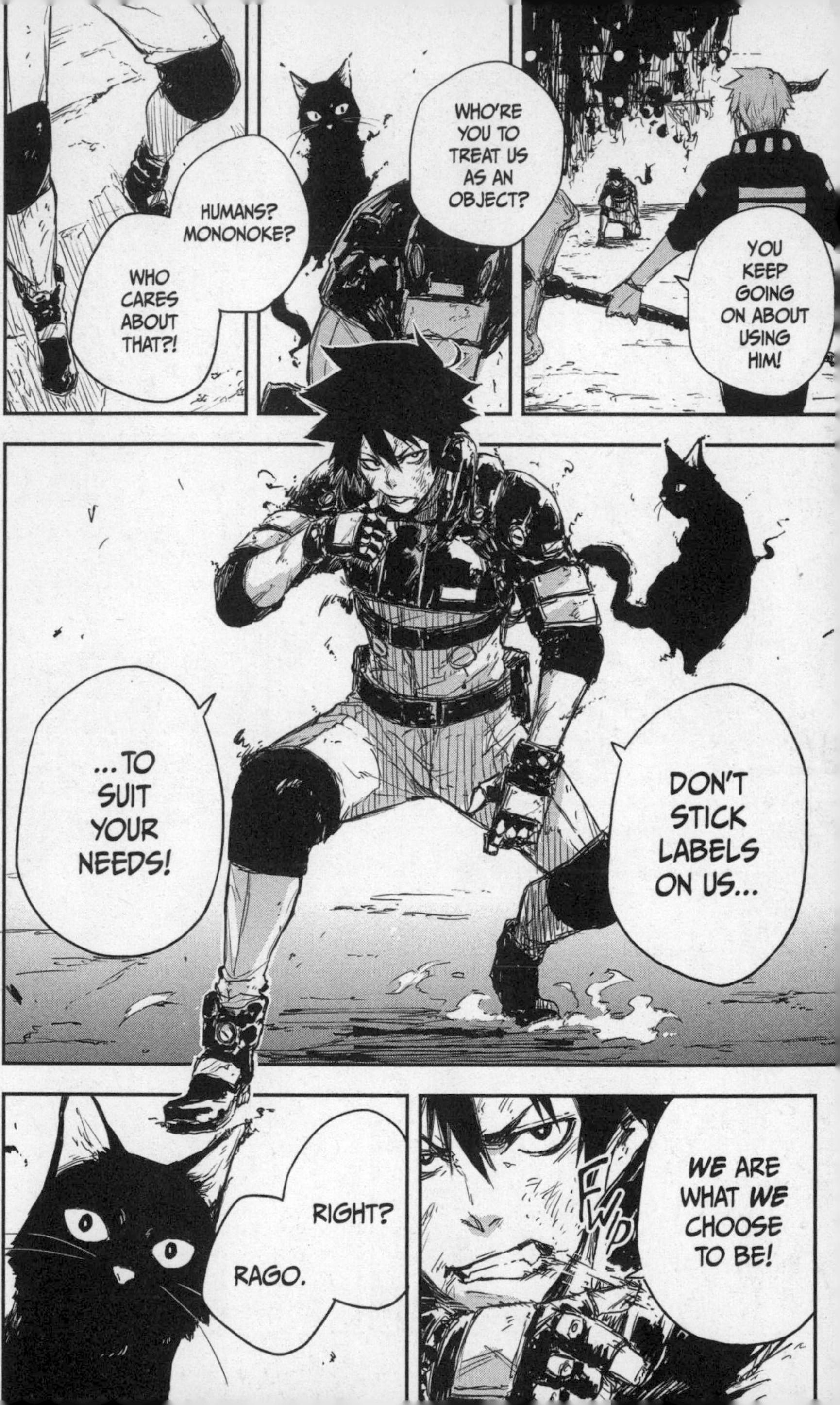
YOU KEEP GOING ON ABOUT USING HIM!
WHO'RE YOU TO TREAT US AS AN OBJECT?
HUMANS? MONONOKE?
WHO CARES ABOUT THAT?!
DON'T STICK LABELS ON US...
...TO SUIT YOUR NEEDS!
WE ARE WHAT WE CHOOSE TO BE!
FWIP
RIGHT?
RAGO.

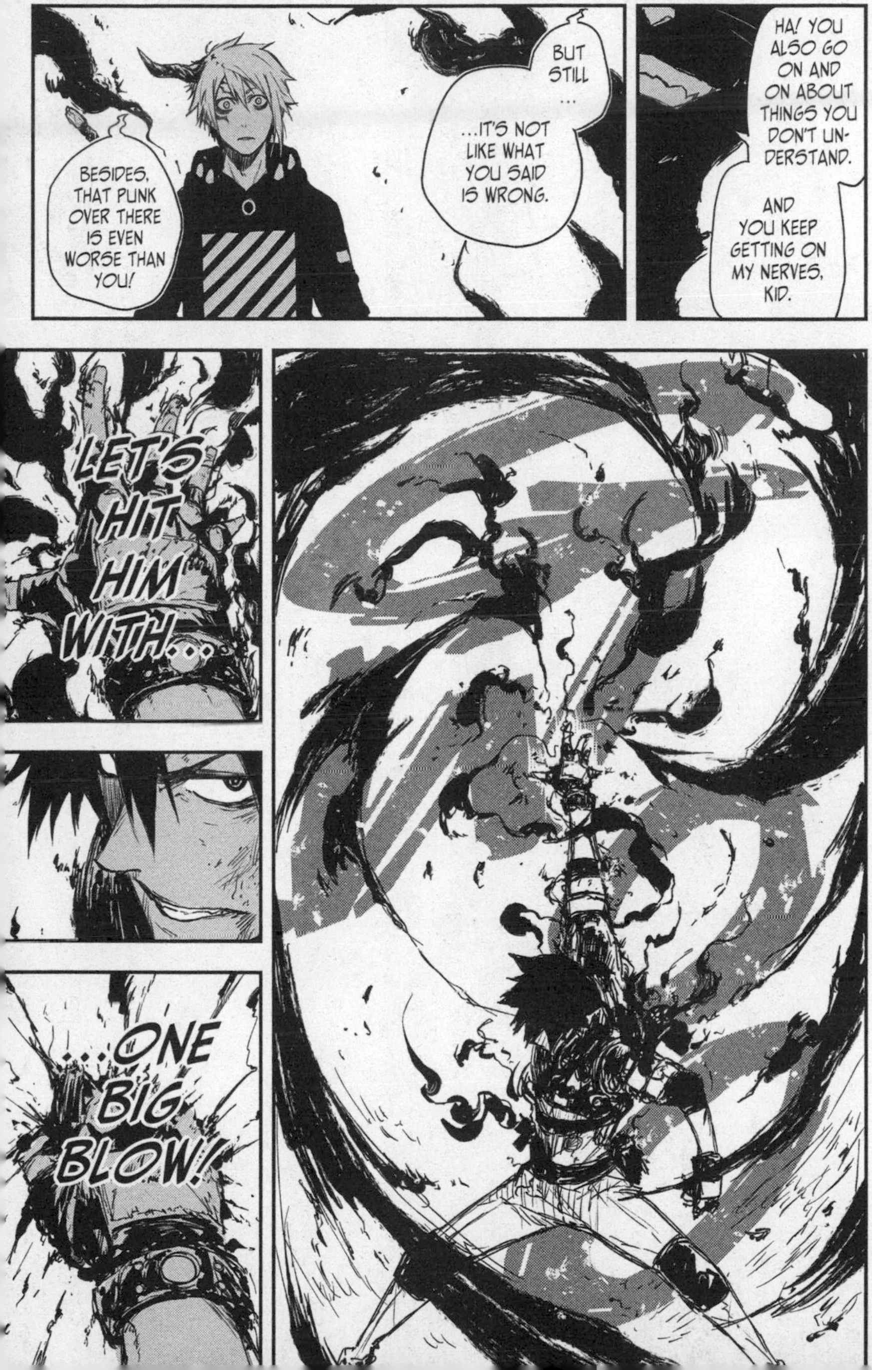
HA! YOU ALSO GO ON AND ON ABOUT THINGS YOU DON'T UNDERSTAND.
AND YOU KEEP GETTING ON MY NERVES, KID.
BUT STILL ...
...IT'S NOT LIKE WHAT YOU SAID IS WRONG.
BESIDES, THAT PUNK OVER THERE IS EVEN WORSE THAN YOU!
LET'S HIT HIM WITH...
...ONE BIG BLOW!

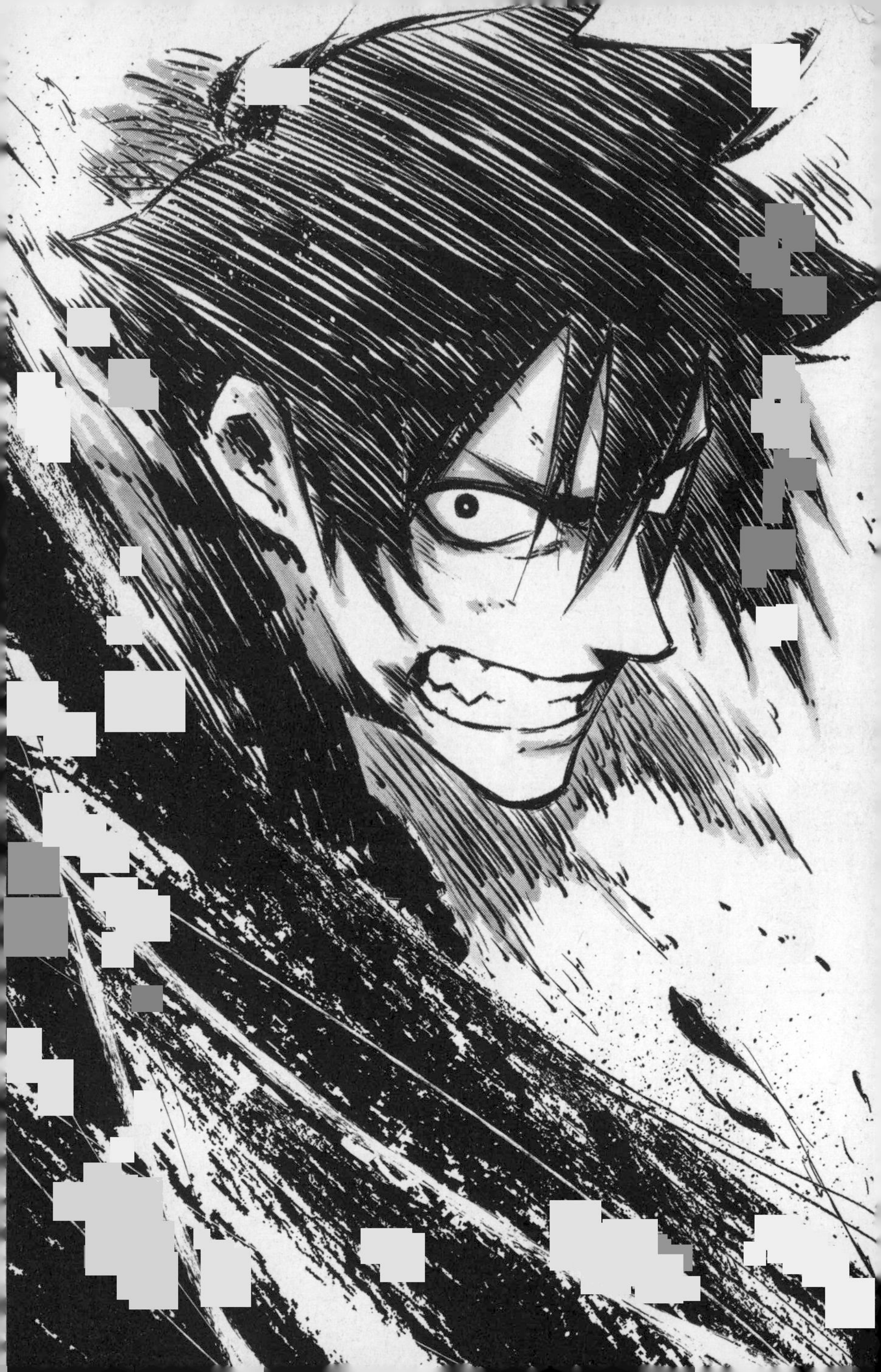

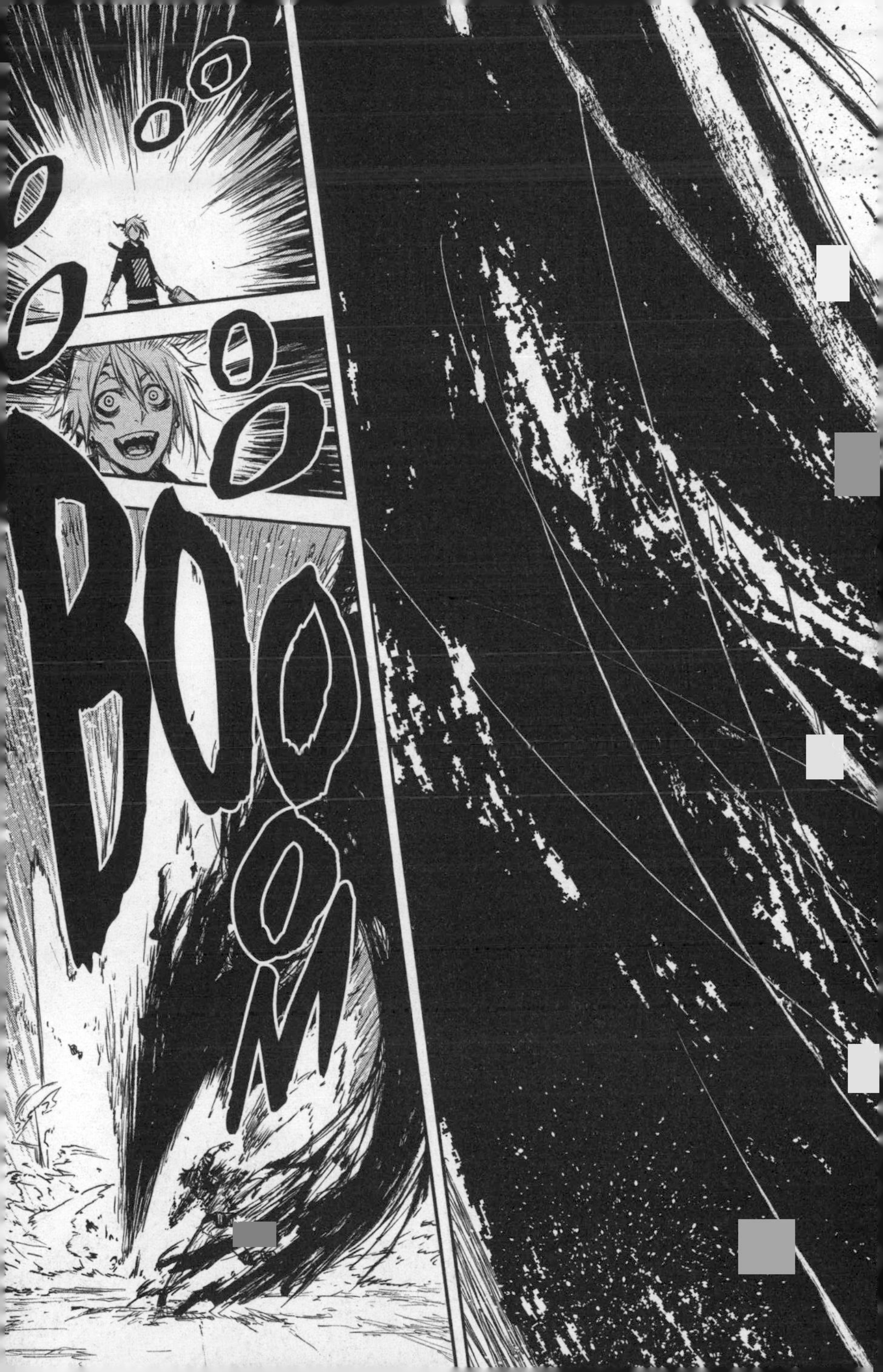
BOOOM

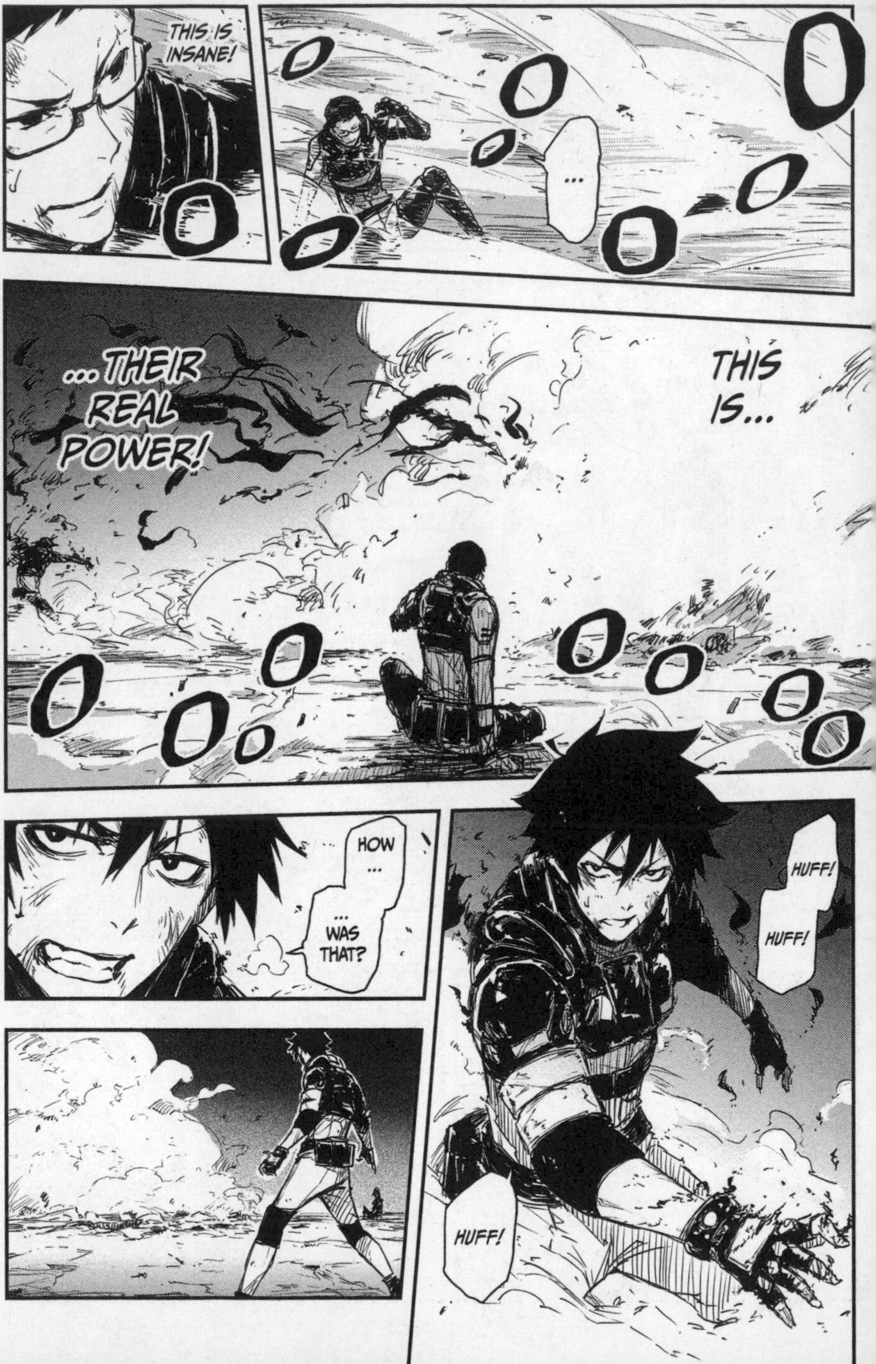
O O O O O O O O
...
THIS IS INSANE!
THIS IS...
...THEIR REAL POWER!
O O O O O O O O O
HUFF!
HUFF!
HUFF!
...HOW...
...WAS THAT?

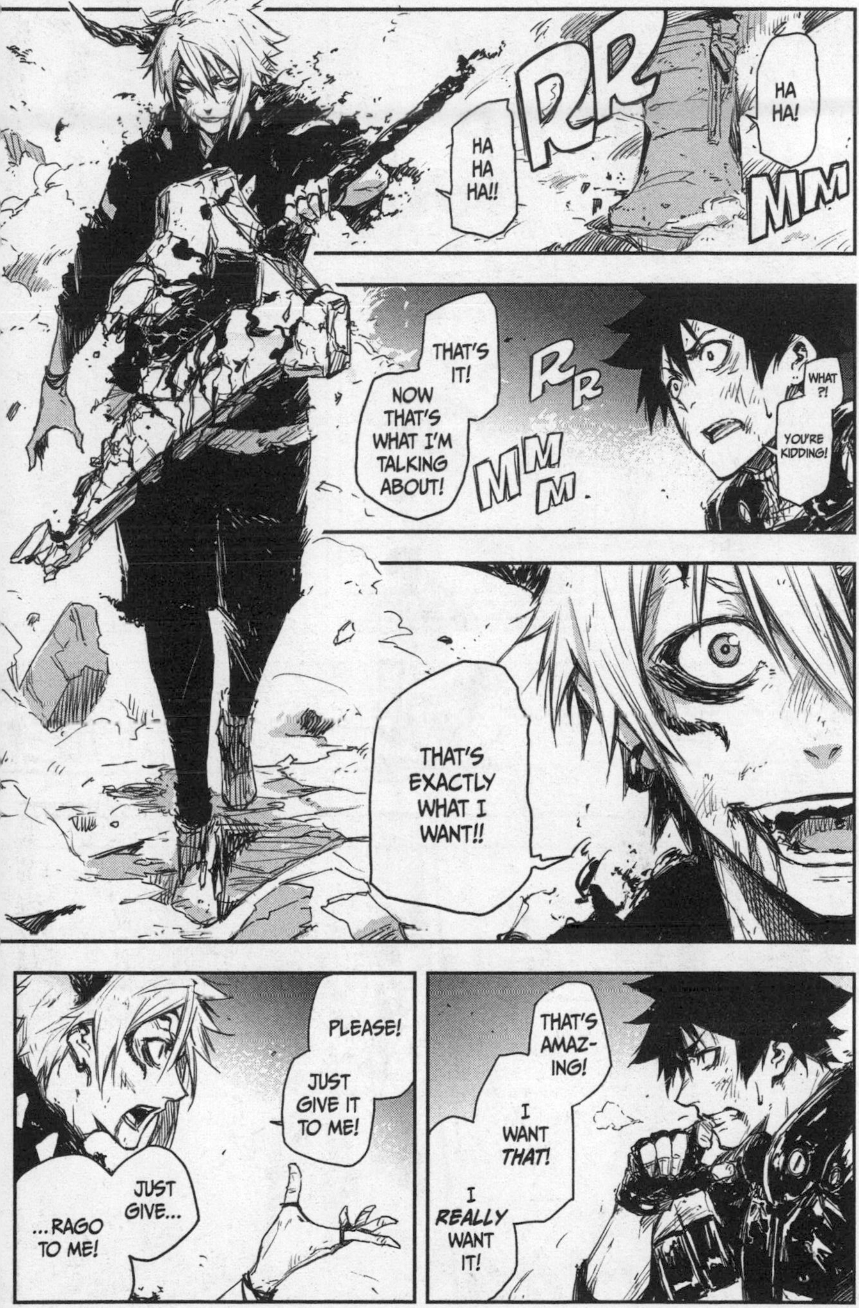
RR
MM
HA HA!
HA HA HA!!
WHAT?!
YOU'RE KIDDING!
RRMMM.
THAT'S IT!
NOW THAT'S WHAT I'M TALKING ABOUT!
THAT'S EXACTLY WHAT I WANT!!
THAT'S AMAZ-ING!
I WANT *THAT*!
I *REALLY* WANT IT!
PLEASE!
JUST GIVE IT TO ME!
JUST GIVE...
...RAGO TO ME!

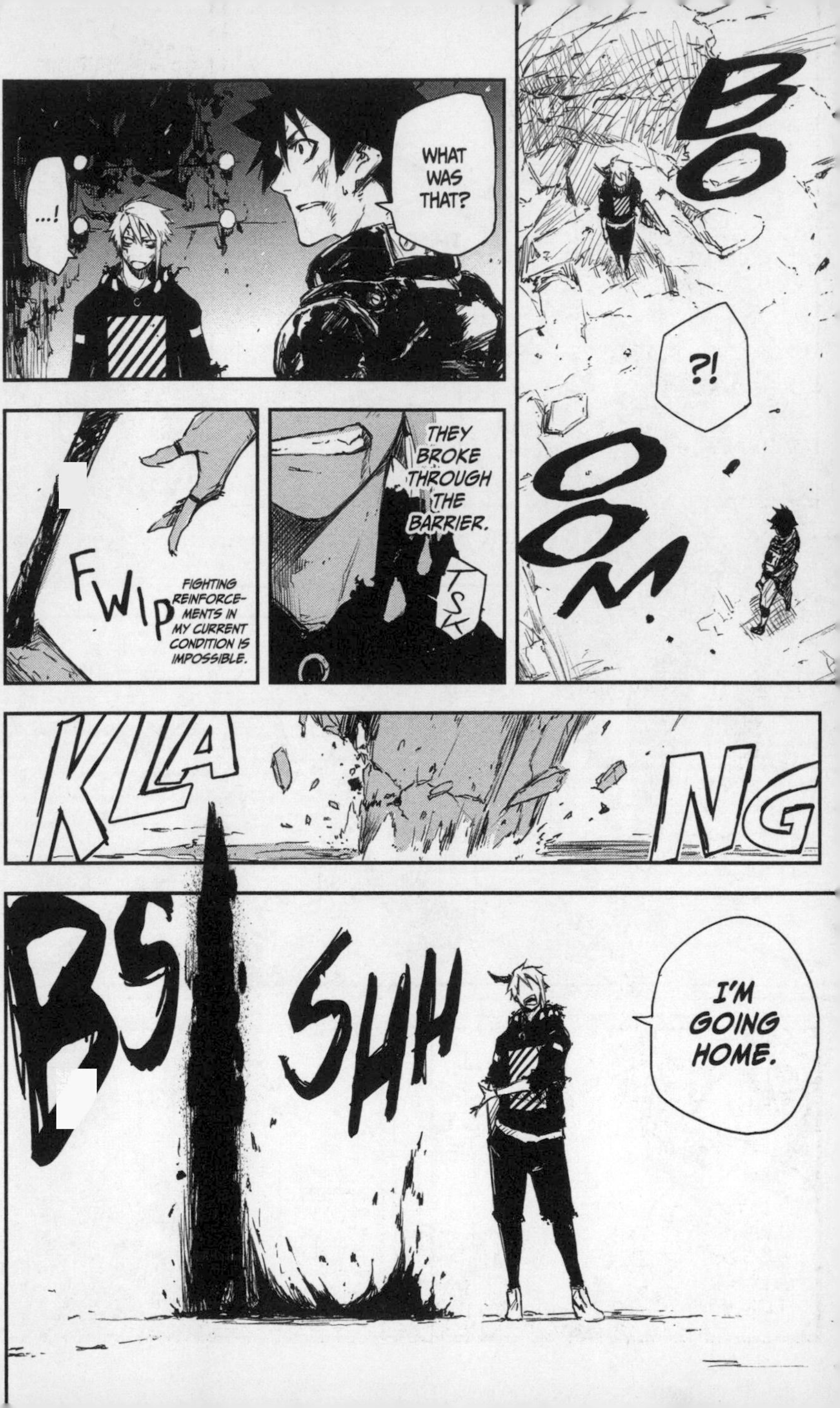
BO
?!
OOM
WHAT WAS THAT?
...!
THEY BROKE THROUGH THE BARRIER.
TSK
FWIP
FIGHTING REINFORCEMENTS IN MY CURRENT CONDITION IS IMPOSSIBLE.
KLA
NG
I'M GOING HOME.
BS
SHH

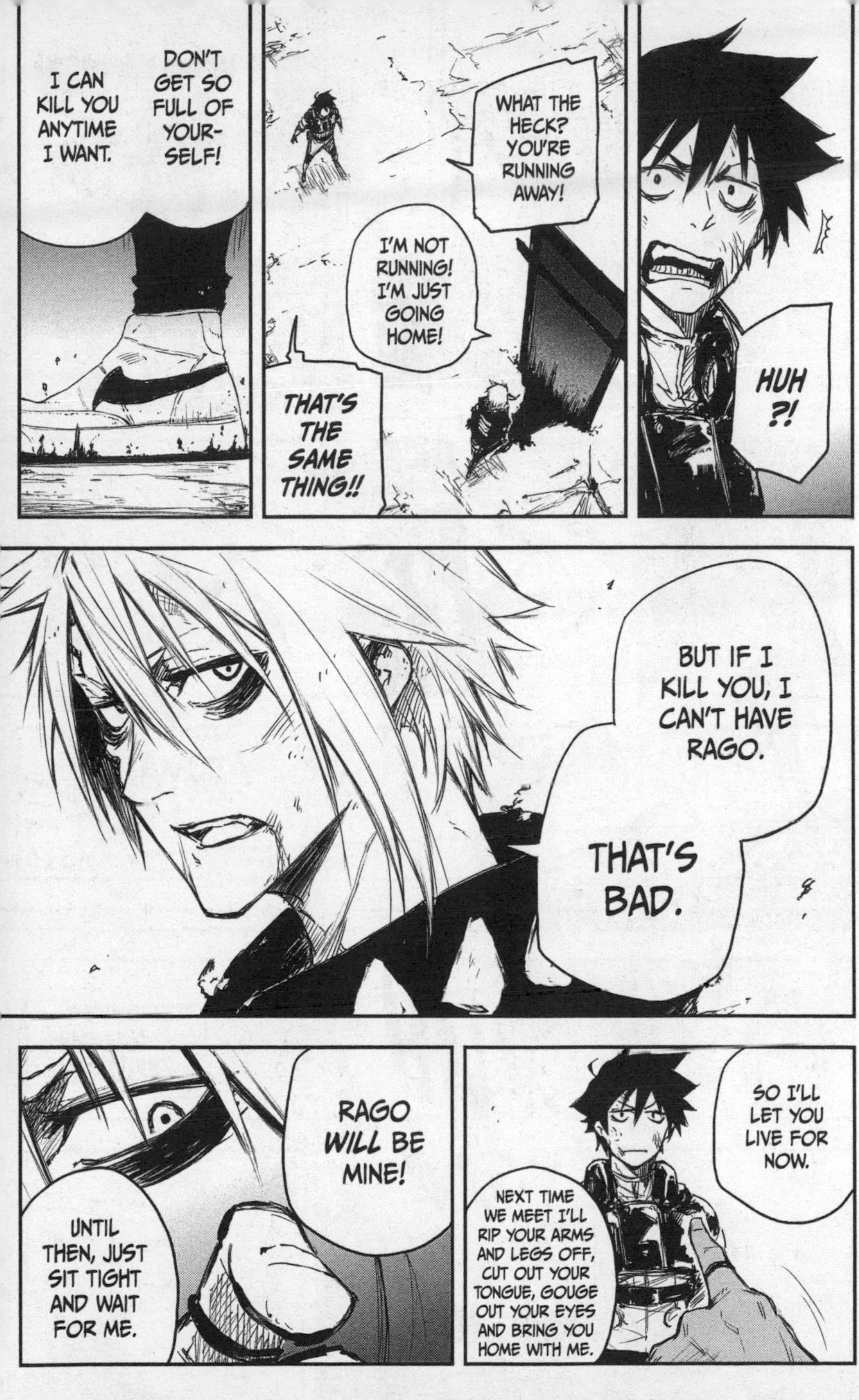
HUH ?!
WHAT THE HECK? YOU'RE RUNNING AWAY!
I'M NOT RUNNING! I'M JUST GOING HOME!
THAT'S THE SAME THING!!
DON'T GET SO FULL OF YOUR-SELF!
I CAN KILL YOU ANYTIME I WANT.
BUT IF I KILL YOU, I CAN'T HAVE RAGO.
THAT'S BAD.
SO I'LL LET YOU LIVE FOR NOW.
NEXT TIME WE MEET I'LL RIP YOUR ARMS AND LEGS OFF, CUT OUT YOUR TONGUE, GOUGE OUT YOUR EYES AND BRING YOU HOME WITH ME.
RAGO WILL BE MINE!
UNTIL THEN, JUST SIT TIGHT AND WAIT FOR ME.

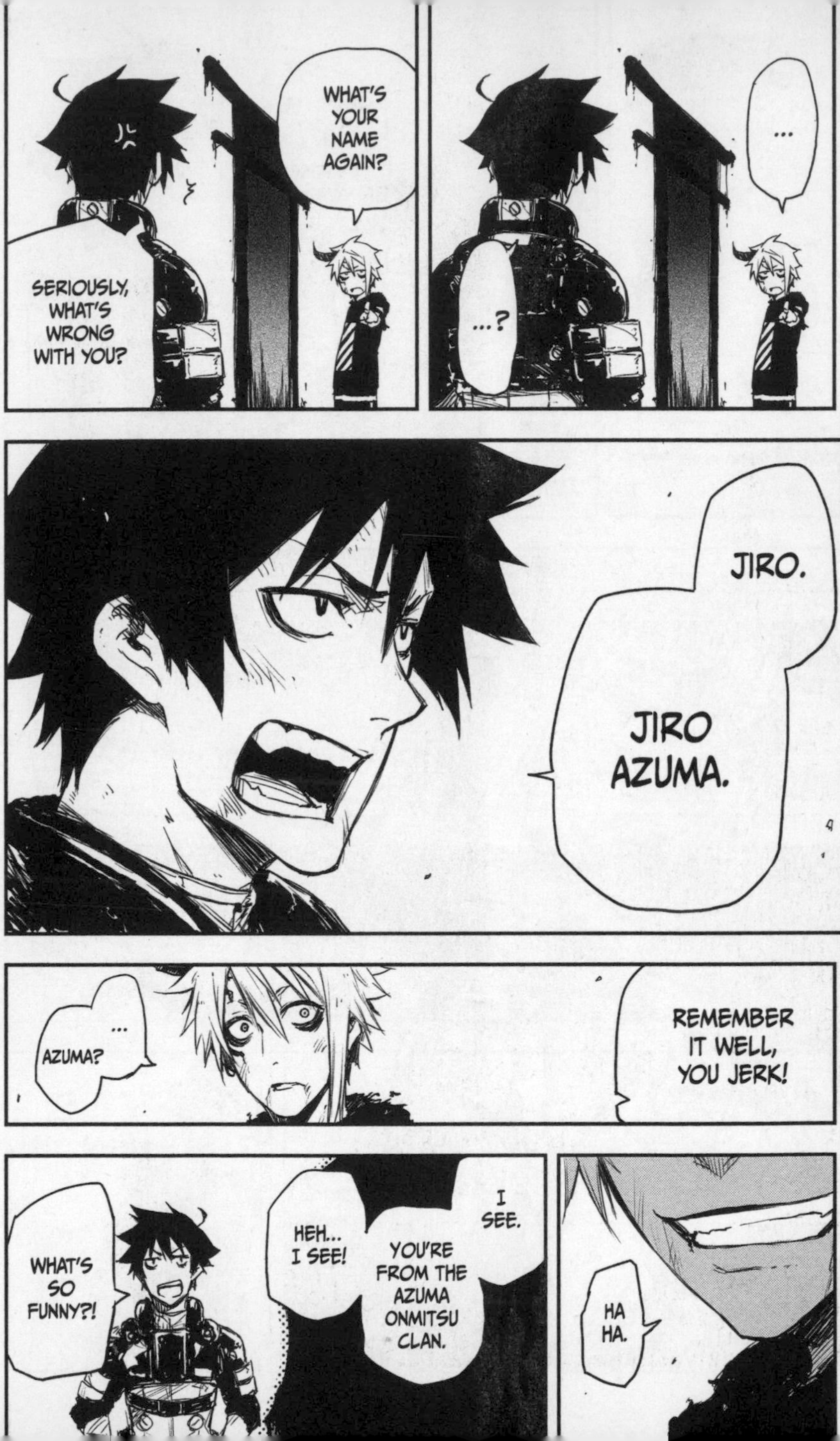
...
...?
WHAT'S YOUR NAME AGAIN?
SERIOUSLY, WHAT'S WRONG WITH YOU?
JIRO.
JIRO AZUMA.
REMEMBER IT WELL, YOU JERK!
... AZUMA?
HA HA.
I SEE.
HEH... I SEE!
YOU'RE FROM THE AZUMA ONMITSU CLAN.
WHAT'S SO FUNNY?!

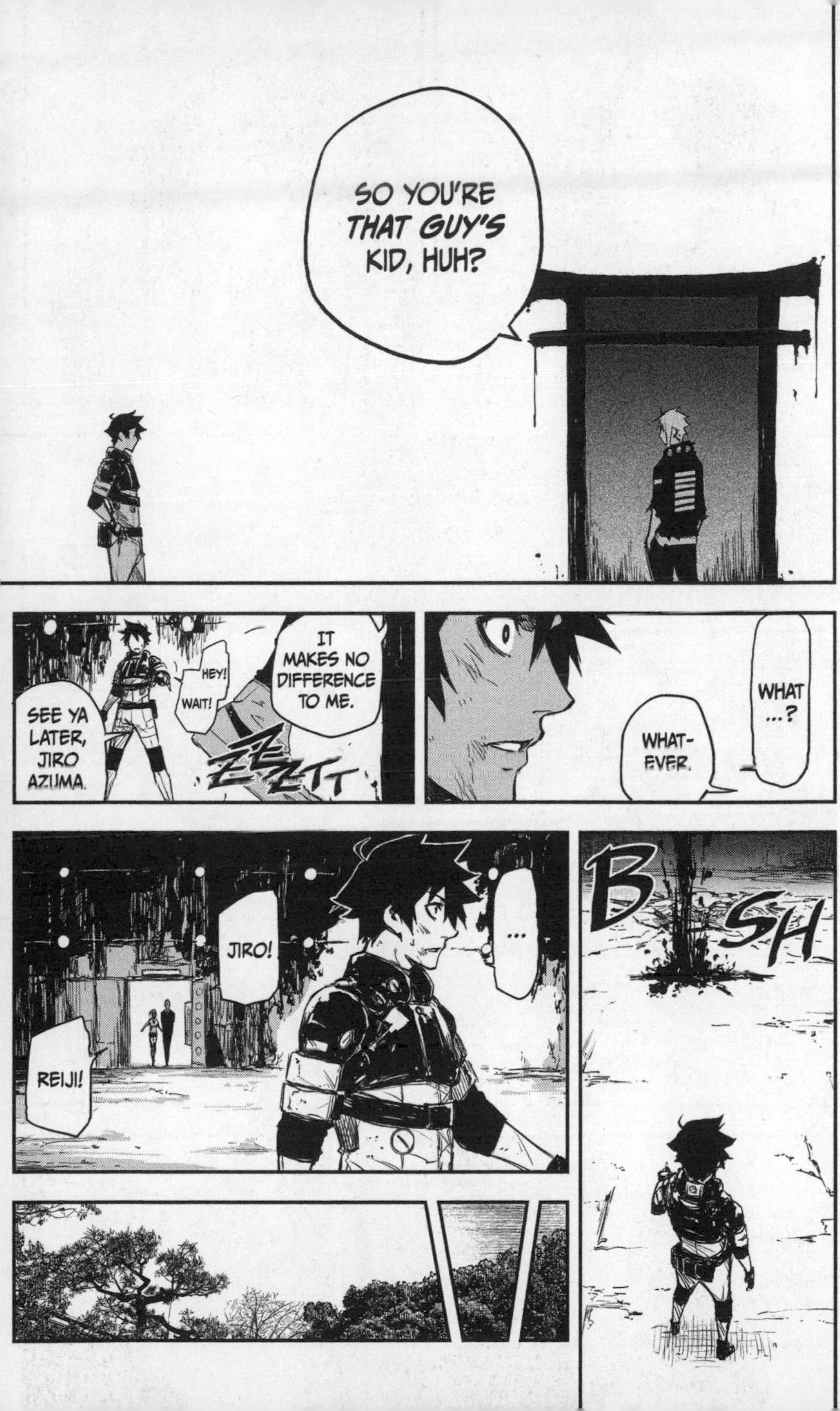
SO YOU'RE THAT GUY'S KID, HUH?
WHAT ...?
WHAT-EVER.
IT MAKES NO DIFFERENCE TO ME.
HEY!
WAIT!
SEE YA LATER, JIRO AZUMA.
BSH
...
JIRO!
REIJI!

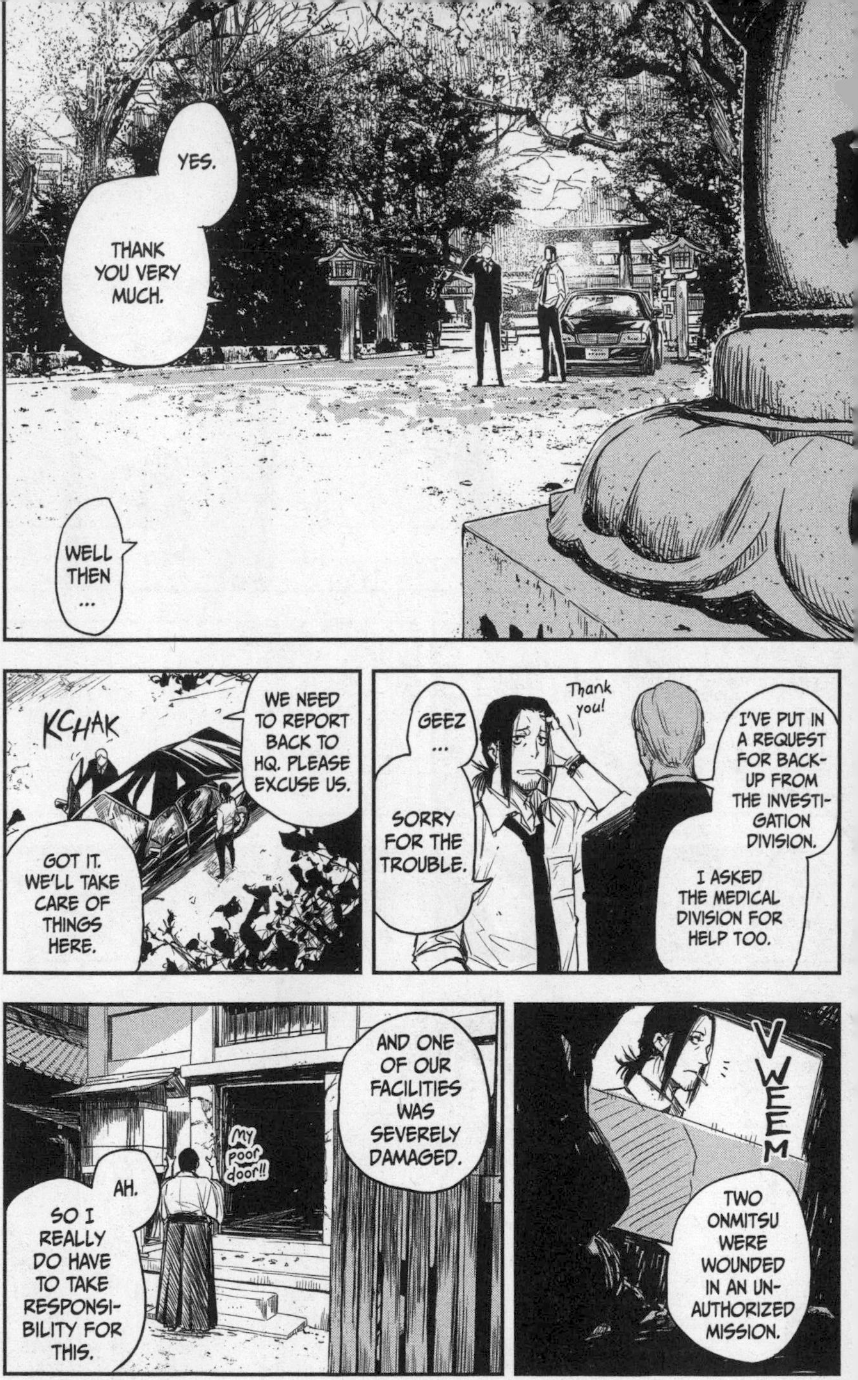
YES.
THANK YOU VERY MUCH.
WELL THEN ...
I'VE PUT IN A REQUEST FOR BACK-UP FROM THE INVESTIGATION DIVISION.
I ASKED THE MEDICAL DIVISION FOR HELP TOO.
Thank you!
GEEZ ...
SORRY FOR THE TROUBLE.
KCHAK
WE NEED TO REPORT BACK TO HQ. PLEASE EXCUSE US.
GOT IT. WE'LL TAKE CARE OF THINGS HERE.
VWEEM
TWO ONMITSU WERE WOUNDED IN AN UNAUTHORIZED MISSION.
AND ONE OF OUR FACILITIES WAS SEVERELY DAMAGED.
My poor door!!
AH.
SO I REALLY DO HAVE TO TAKE RESPONSIBILITY FOR THIS.

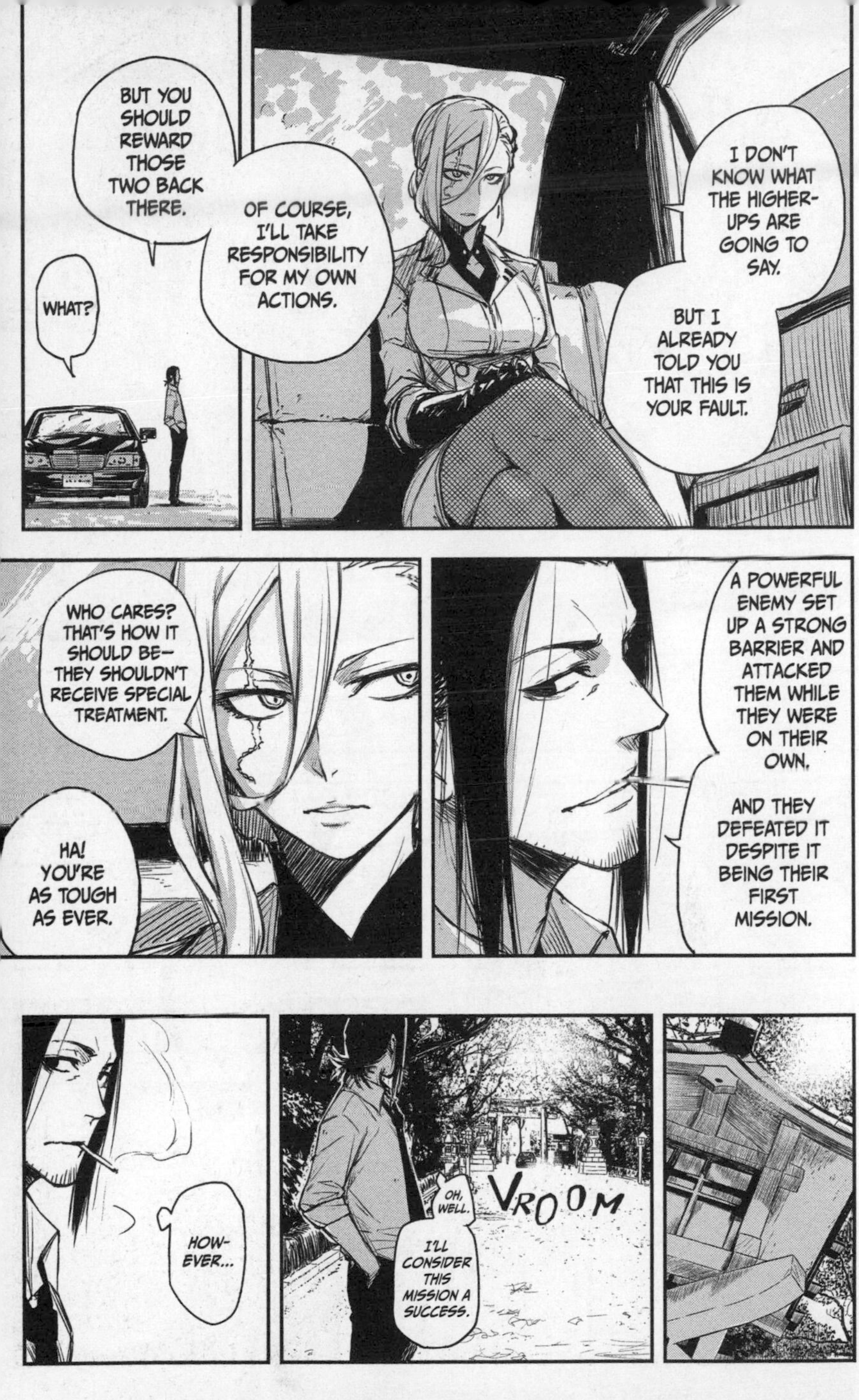
I DON'T KNOW WHAT THE HIGHER-UPS ARE GOING TO SAY.
BUT I ALREADY TOLD YOU THAT THIS IS YOUR FAULT.
OF COURSE, I'LL TAKE RESPONSIBILITY FOR MY OWN ACTIONS.
BUT YOU SHOULD REWARD THOSE TWO BACK THERE.
WHAT?
A POWERFUL ENEMY SET UP A STRONG BARRIER AND ATTACKED THEM WHILE THEY WERE ON THEIR OWN.
AND THEY DEFEATED IT DESPITE IT BEING THEIR FIRST MISSION.
WHO CARES? THAT'S HOW IT SHOULD BE—THEY SHOULDN'T RECEIVE SPECIAL TREATMENT.
HA! YOU'RE AS TOUGH AS EVER.
VROOM
OH, WELL.
I'LL CONSIDER THIS MISSION A SUCCESS.
HOW-EVER...

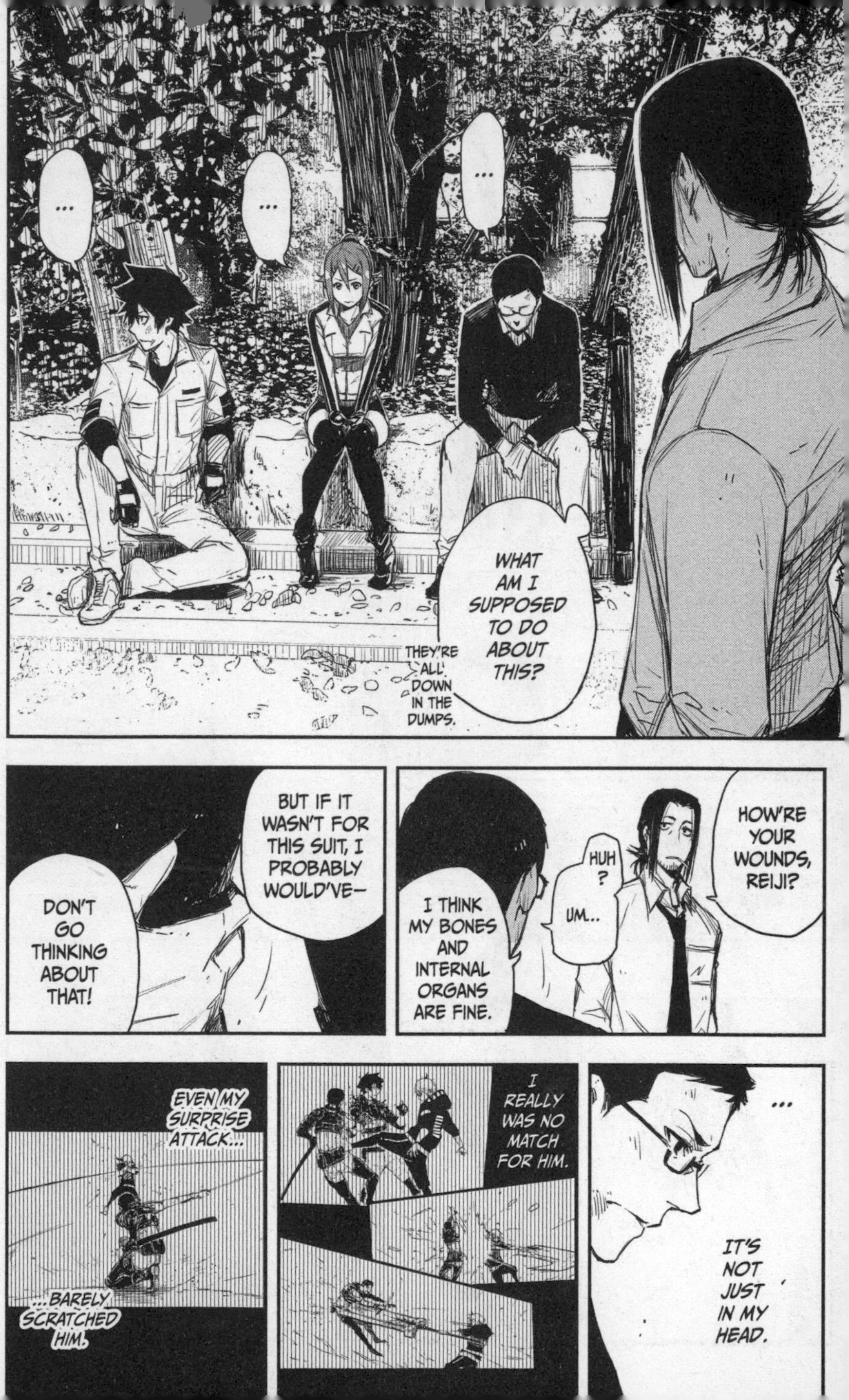
...
...
...
WHAT AM I SUPPOSED TO DO ABOUT THIS?
THEY'RE ALL DOWN IN THE DUMPS.
HOW'RE YOUR WOUNDS, REIJI?
HUH?
UM...
I THINK MY BONES AND INTERNAL ORGANS ARE FINE.
BUT IF IT WASN'T FOR THIS SUIT, I PROBABLY WOULD'VE—
DON'T GO THINKING ABOUT THAT!
...
IT'S NOT JUST IN MY HEAD.
I REALLY WAS NO MATCH FOR HIM.
EVEN MY SURPRISE ATTACK...
...BARELY SCRATCHED HIM.

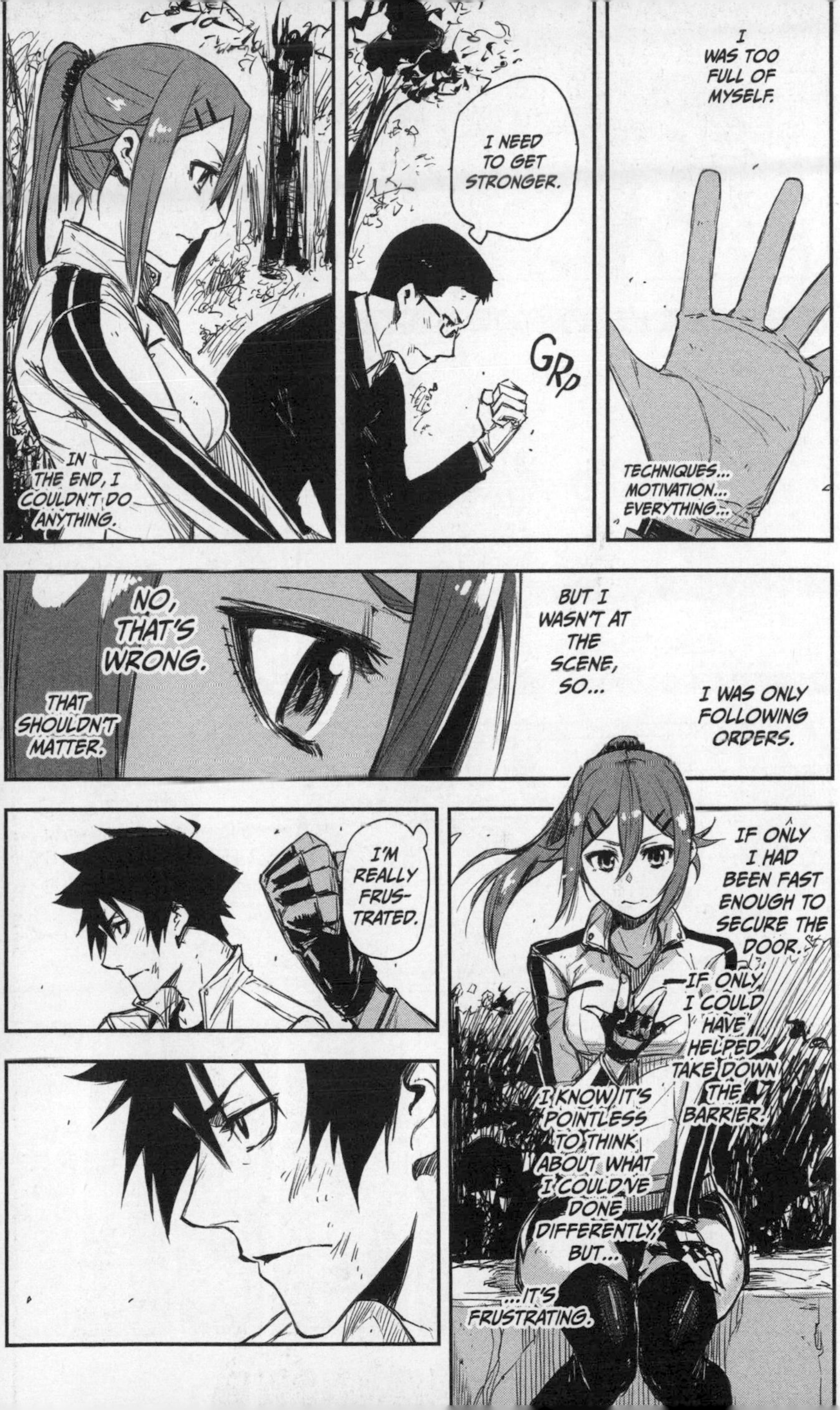
I WAS TOO FULL OF MYSELF.
TECHNIQUES... MOTIVATION... EVERYTHING...
I NEED TO GET STRONGER.
GRP
IN THE END, I COULDN'T DO ANYTHING.
I WAS ONLY FOLLOWING ORDERS.
BUT I WASN'T AT THE SCENE, SO...
NO, THAT'S WRONG.
THAT SHOULDN'T MATTER.
IF ONLY I HAD BEEN FAST ENOUGH TO SECURE THE DOOR.
IF ONLY I COULD HAVE HELPED TAKE DOWN THE BARRIER.
I KNOW IT'S POINTLESS TO THINK ABOUT WHAT I COULD'VE DONE DIFFERENTLY, BUT...
...IT'S FRUSTRATING.
I'M REALLY FRUS-TRATED.

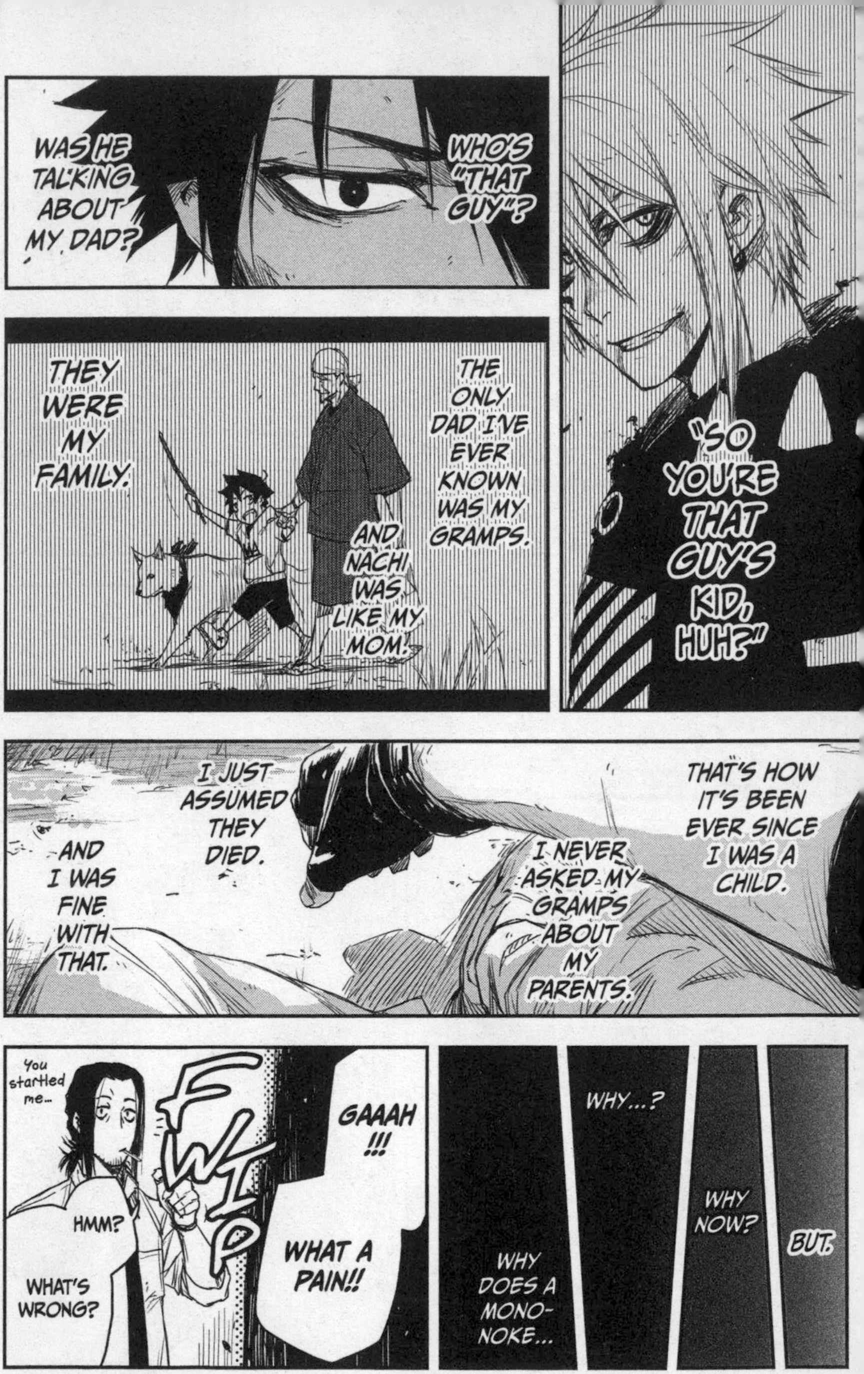
"SO YOU'RE THAT GUY'S KID, HUH?"
WHO'S "THAT GUY"?
WAS HE TALKING ABOUT MY DAD?
THE ONLY DAD I'VE EVER KNOWN WAS MY GRAMPS.
AND NACHI WAS LIKE MY MOM.
THEY WERE MY FAMILY.
THAT'S HOW IT'S BEEN EVER SINCE I WAS A CHILD.
I NEVER ASKED MY GRAMPS ABOUT MY PARENTS.
I JUST ASSUMED THEY DIED.
AND I WAS FINE WITH THAT.
BUT.
WHY NOW?
WHY...?
WHY DOES A MONO-NOKE...
GAAAH!!!
WHAT A PAIN!!
FWIP
You startled me...
HMM?
WHAT'S WRONG?

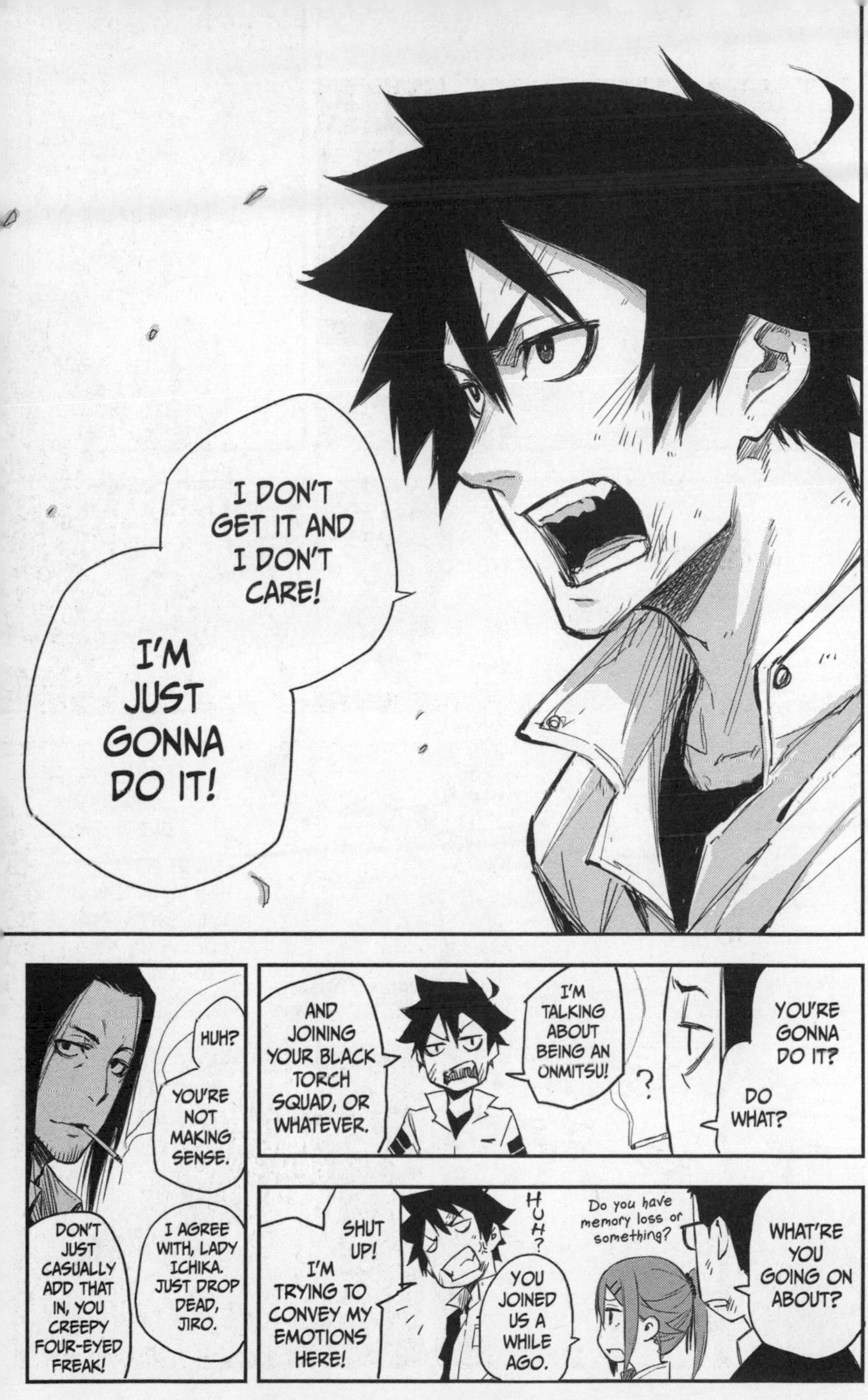
I DON'T GET IT AND I DON'T CARE!
I'M JUST GONNA DO IT!
YOU'RE GONNA DO IT?
DO WHAT?
I'M TALKING ABOUT BEING AN ONMITSU!
?
AND JOINING YOUR BLACK TORCH SQUAD, OR WHATEVER.
WHAT'RE YOU GOING ON ABOUT?
Do you have memory loss or something?
HUH?
YOU JOINED US A WHILE AGO.
SHUT UP!
I'M TRYING TO CONVEY MY EMOTIONS HERE!
HUH?
YOU'RE NOT MAKING SENSE.
I AGREE WITH, LADY ICHIKA. JUST DROP DEAD, JIRO.
DON'T JUST CASUALLY ADD THAT IN, YOU CREEPY FOUR-EYED FREAK!

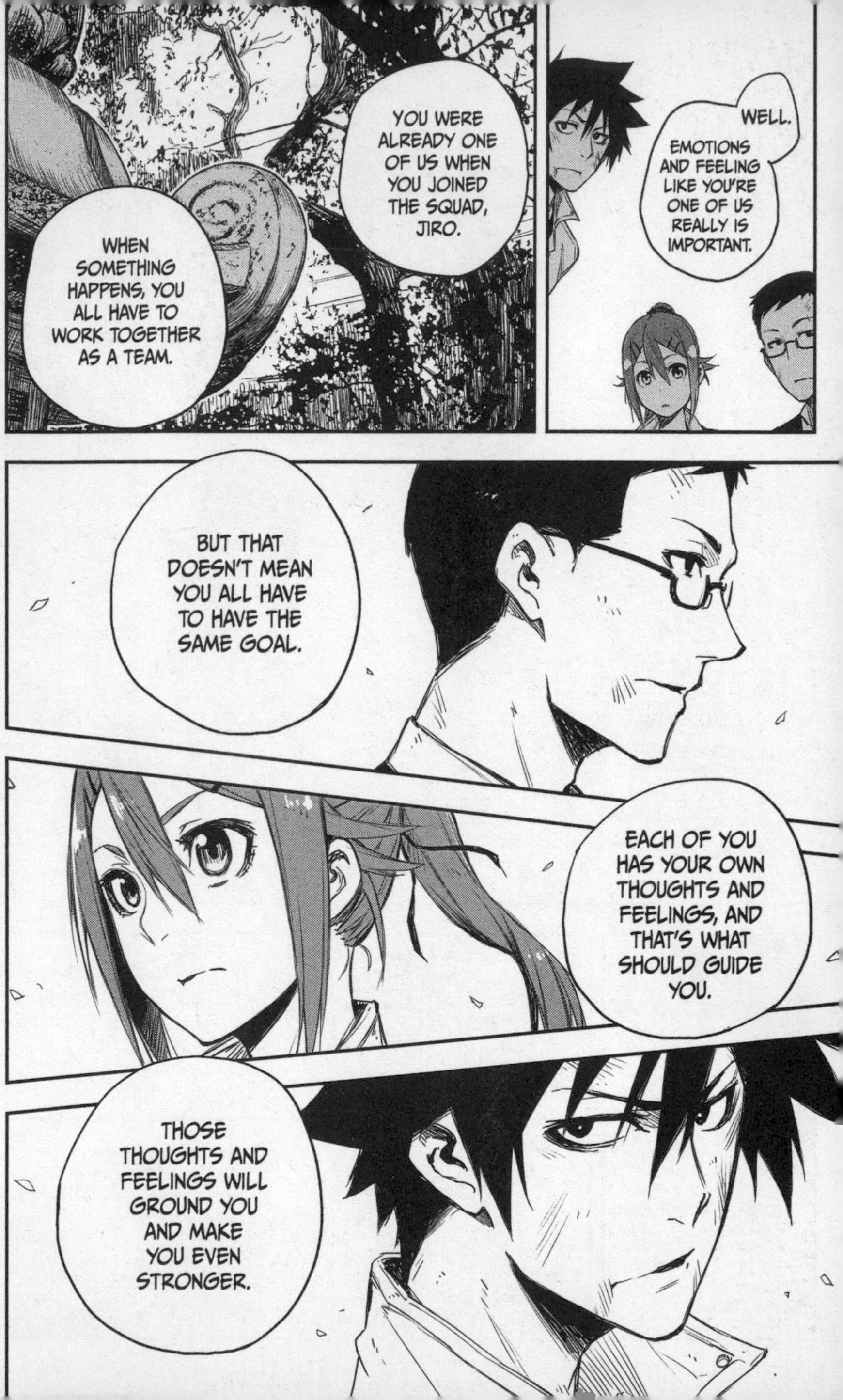
WELL.
EMOTIONS AND FEELING LIKE YOU'RE ONE OF US REALLY IS IMPORTANT.
YOU WERE ALREADY ONE OF US WHEN YOU JOINED THE SQUAD, JIRO.
WHEN SOMETHING HAPPENS, YOU ALL HAVE TO WORK TOGETHER AS A TEAM.
BUT THAT DOESN'T MEAN YOU ALL HAVE TO HAVE THE SAME GOAL.
EACH OF YOU HAS YOUR OWN THOUGHTS AND FEELINGS, AND THAT'S WHAT SHOULD GUIDE YOU.
THOSE THOUGHTS AND FEELINGS WILL GROUND YOU AND MAKE YOU EVEN STRONGER.

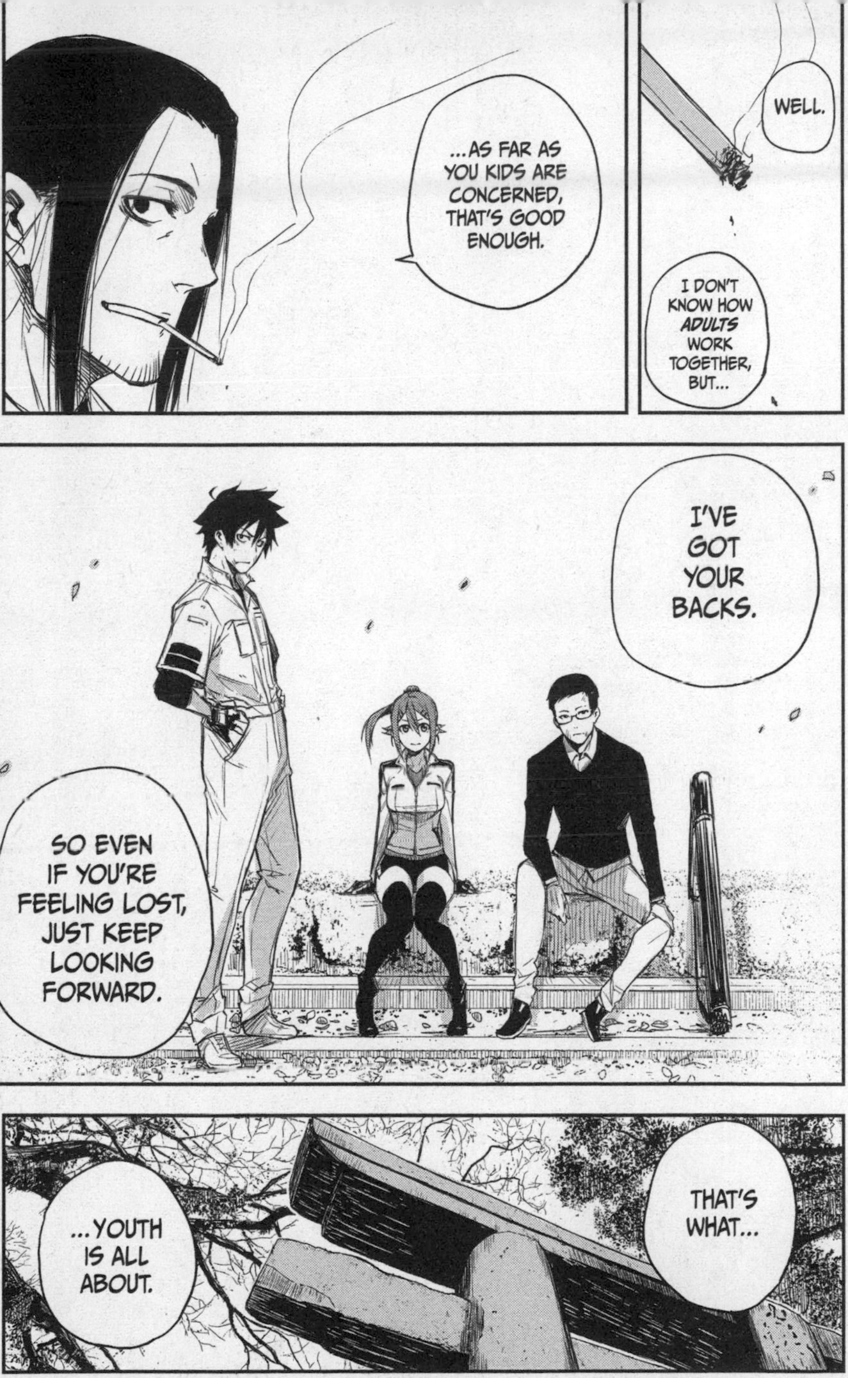
WELL.
I DON'T KNOW HOW ADULTS WORK TOGETHER, BUT...
...AS FAR AS YOU KIDS ARE CONCERNED, THAT'S GOOD ENOUGH.
I'VE GOT YOUR BACKS.
SO EVEN IF YOU'RE FEELING LOST, JUST KEEP LOOKING FORWARD.
THAT'S WHAT...
...YOUTH IS ALL ABOUT.

BLACK TORCH

#7 BLACK BOX

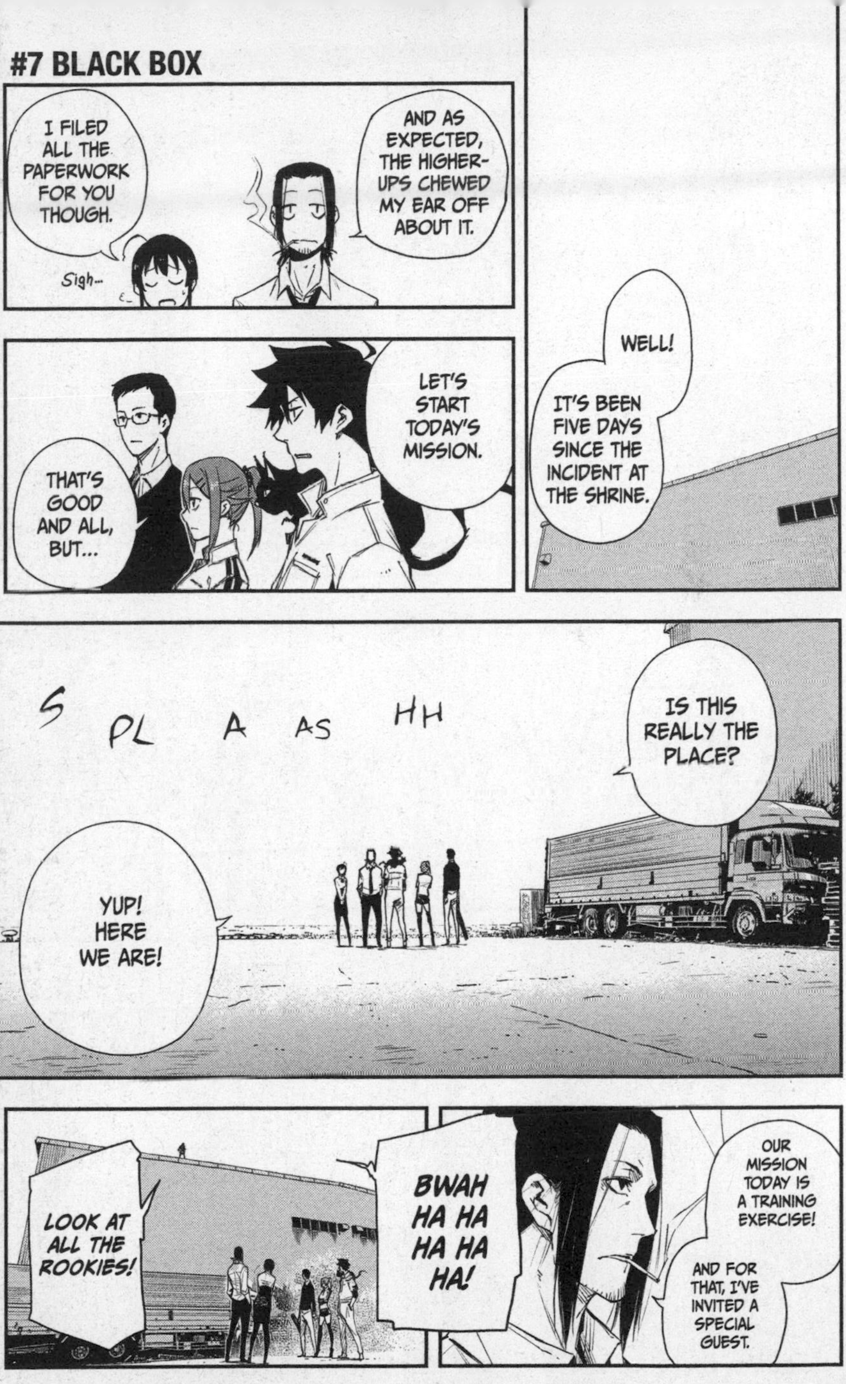
WELL!
IT'S BEEN FIVE DAYS SINCE THE INCIDENT AT THE SHRINE.
AND AS EXPECTED, THE HIGHER-UPS CHEWED MY EAR OFF ABOUT IT.
I FILED ALL THE PAPERWORK FOR YOU THOUGH.
Sigh...
LET'S START TODAY'S MISSION.
THAT'S GOOD AND ALL, BUT...
IS THIS REALLY THE PLACE?
SPLAASHH
YUP! HERE WE ARE!
OUR MISSION TODAY IS A TRAINING EXERCISE!
AND FOR THAT, I'VE INVITED A SPECIAL GUEST.
BWAH HA HA HA HA HA!
LOOK AT ALL THE ROOKIES!

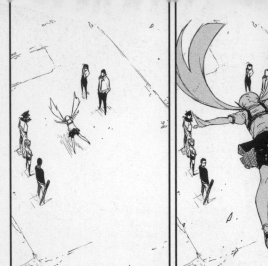

HAH !!

TUP

THUD

SHF

S-SORRY TO KEEP YOU WAITING!

WHO THE HECK ARE YOU?!

...

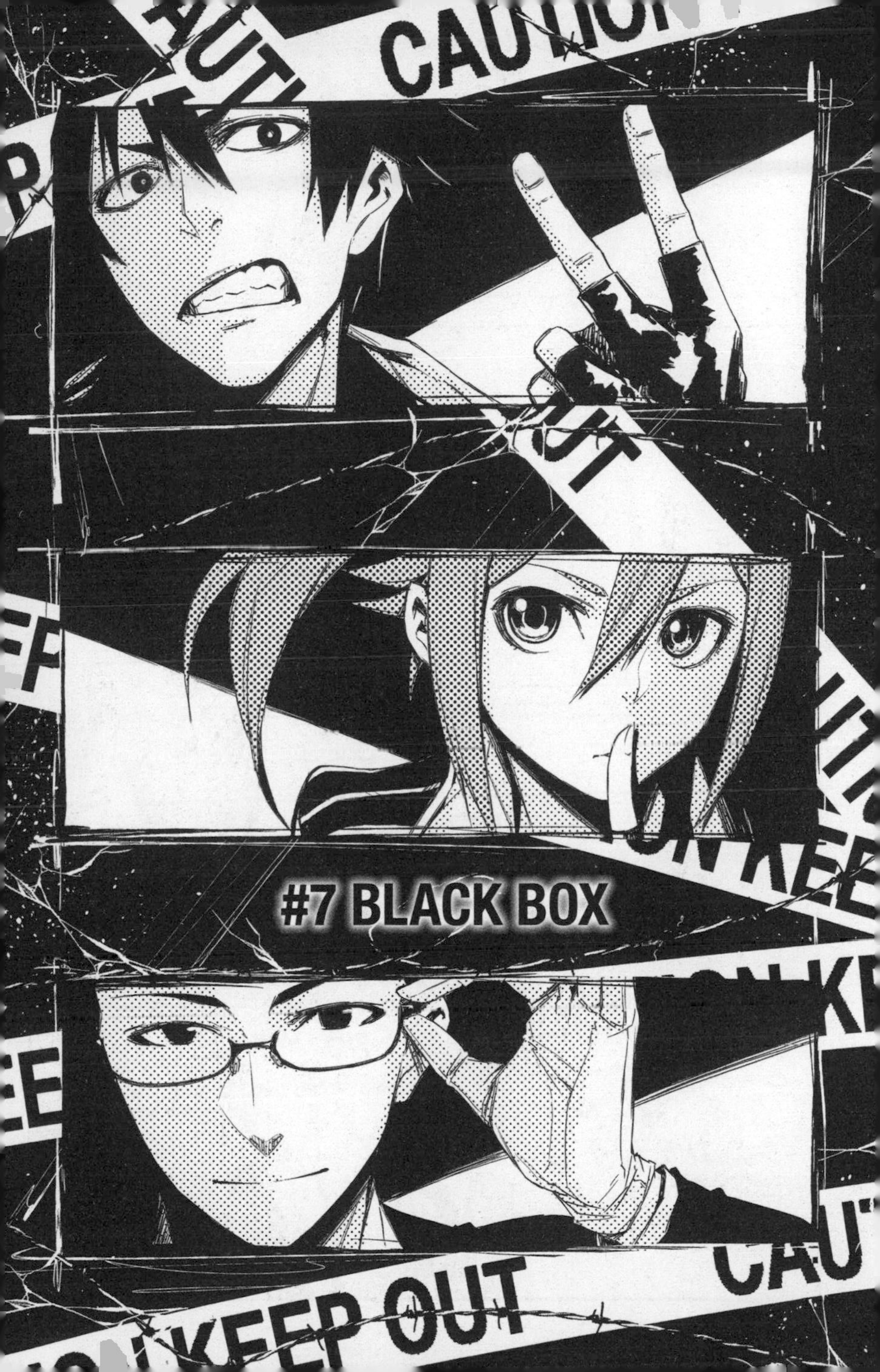
#7 BLACK BOX
CAUTION
KEEP OUT

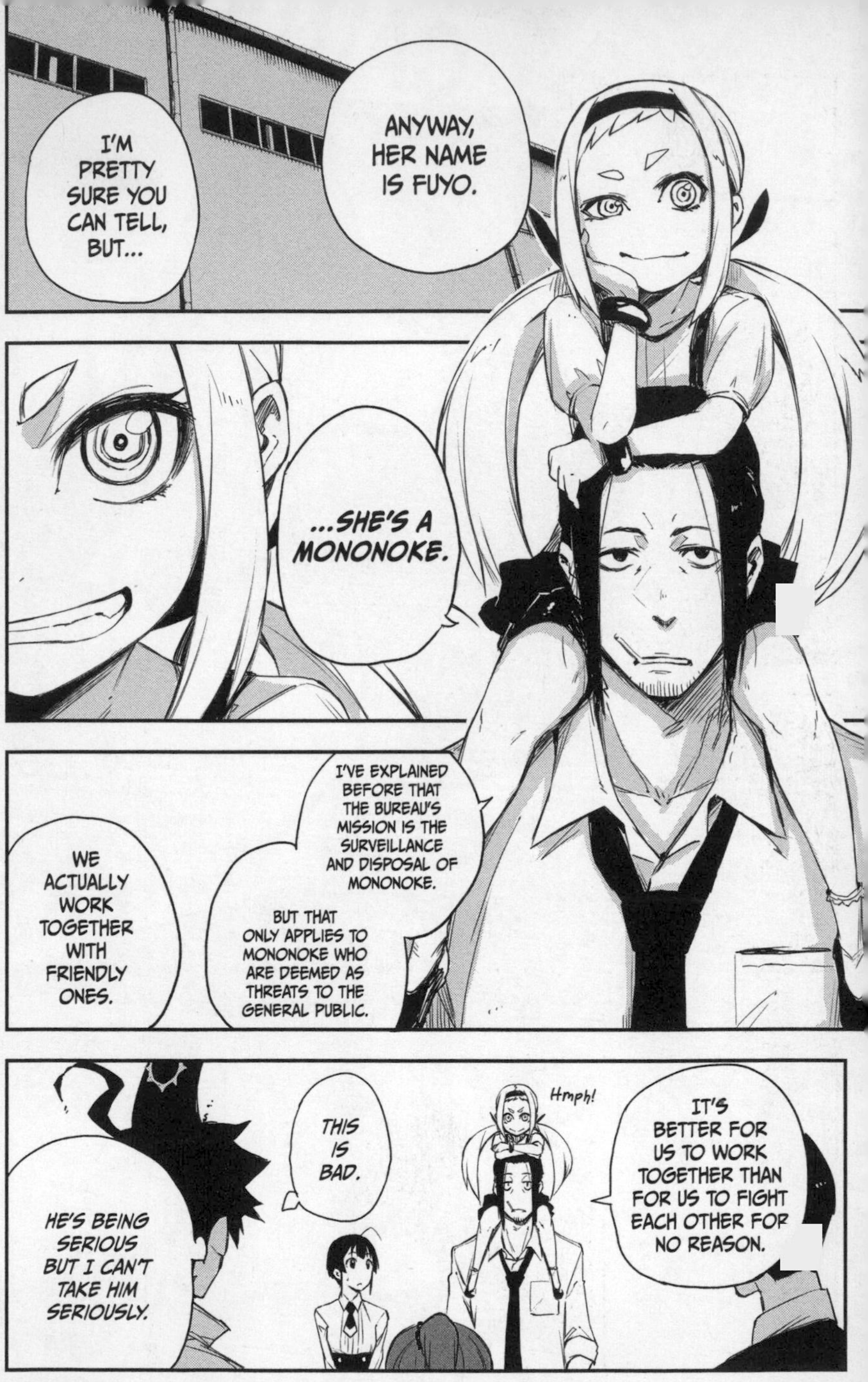
ANYWAY, HER NAME IS FUYO.
I'M PRETTY SURE YOU CAN TELL, BUT...
...SHE'S A MONONOKE.
I'VE EXPLAINED BEFORE THAT THE BUREAU'S MISSION IS THE SURVEILLANCE AND DISPOSAL OF MONONOKE.
BUT THAT ONLY APPLIES TO MONONOKE WHO ARE DEEMED AS THREATS TO THE GENERAL PUBLIC.
WE ACTUALLY WORK TOGETHER WITH FRIENDLY ONES.
IT'S BETTER FOR US TO WORK TOGETHER THAN FOR US TO FIGHT EACH OTHER FOR NO REASON.
Hmph!
THIS IS BAD.
HE'S BEING SERIOUS BUT I CAN'T TAKE HIM SERIOUSLY.

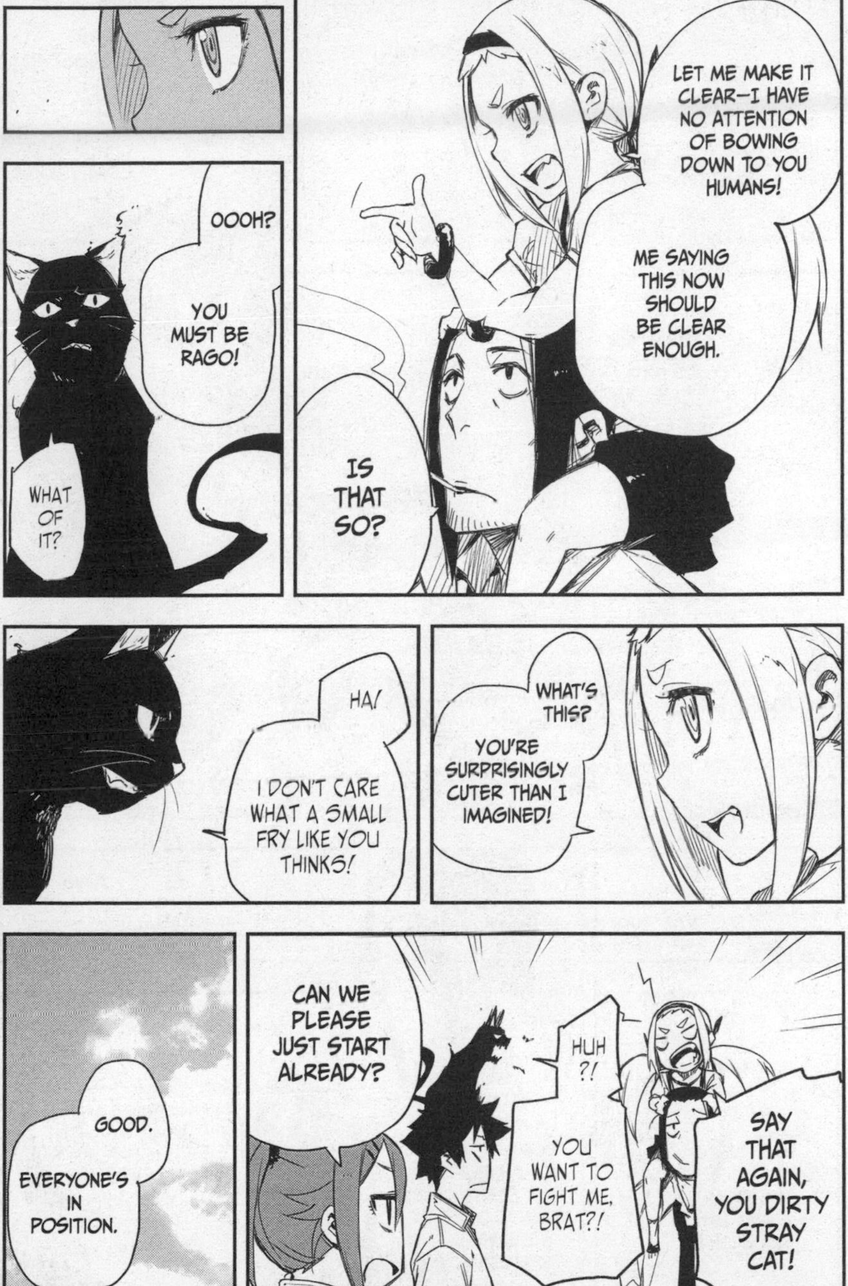
LET ME MAKE IT CLEAR—I HAVE NO ATTENTION OF BOWING DOWN TO YOU HUMANS!
ME SAYING THIS NOW SHOULD BE CLEAR ENOUGH.
IS THAT SO?
OOOH?
YOU MUST BE RAGO!
WHAT OF IT?
WHAT'S THIS?
YOU'RE SURPRISINGLY CUTER THAN I IMAGINED!
HA!
I DON'T CARE WHAT A SMALL FRY LIKE YOU THINKS!
SAY THAT AGAIN, YOU DIRTY STRAY CAT!
HUH?!
YOU WANT TO FIGHT ME, BRAT?!
CAN WE PLEASE JUST START ALREADY?
GOOD.
EVERYONE'S IN POSITION.

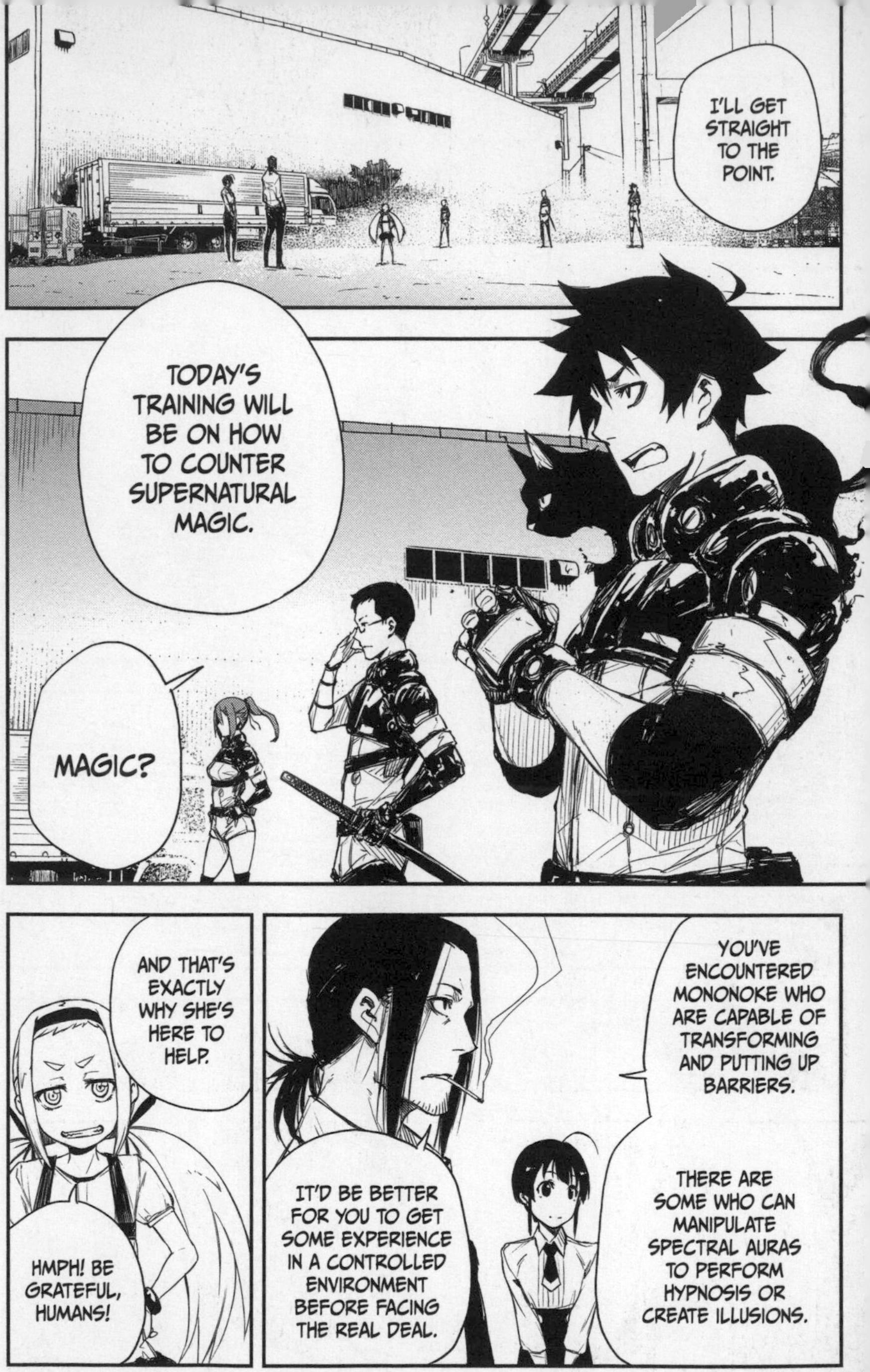
I'LL GET STRAIGHT TO THE POINT.
TODAY'S TRAINING WILL BE ON HOW TO COUNTER SUPERNATURAL MAGIC.
MAGIC?
YOU'VE ENCOUNTERED MONONOKE WHO ARE CAPABLE OF TRANSFORMING AND PUTTING UP BARRIERS.
THERE ARE SOME WHO CAN MANIPULATE SPECTRAL AURAS TO PERFORM HYPNOSIS OR CREATE ILLUSIONS.
IT'D BE BETTER FOR YOU TO GET SOME EXPERIENCE IN A CONTROLLED ENVIRONMENT BEFORE FACING THE REAL DEAL.
AND THAT'S EXACTLY WHY SHE'S HERE TO HELP.
HMPH! BE GRATEFUL, HUMANS!

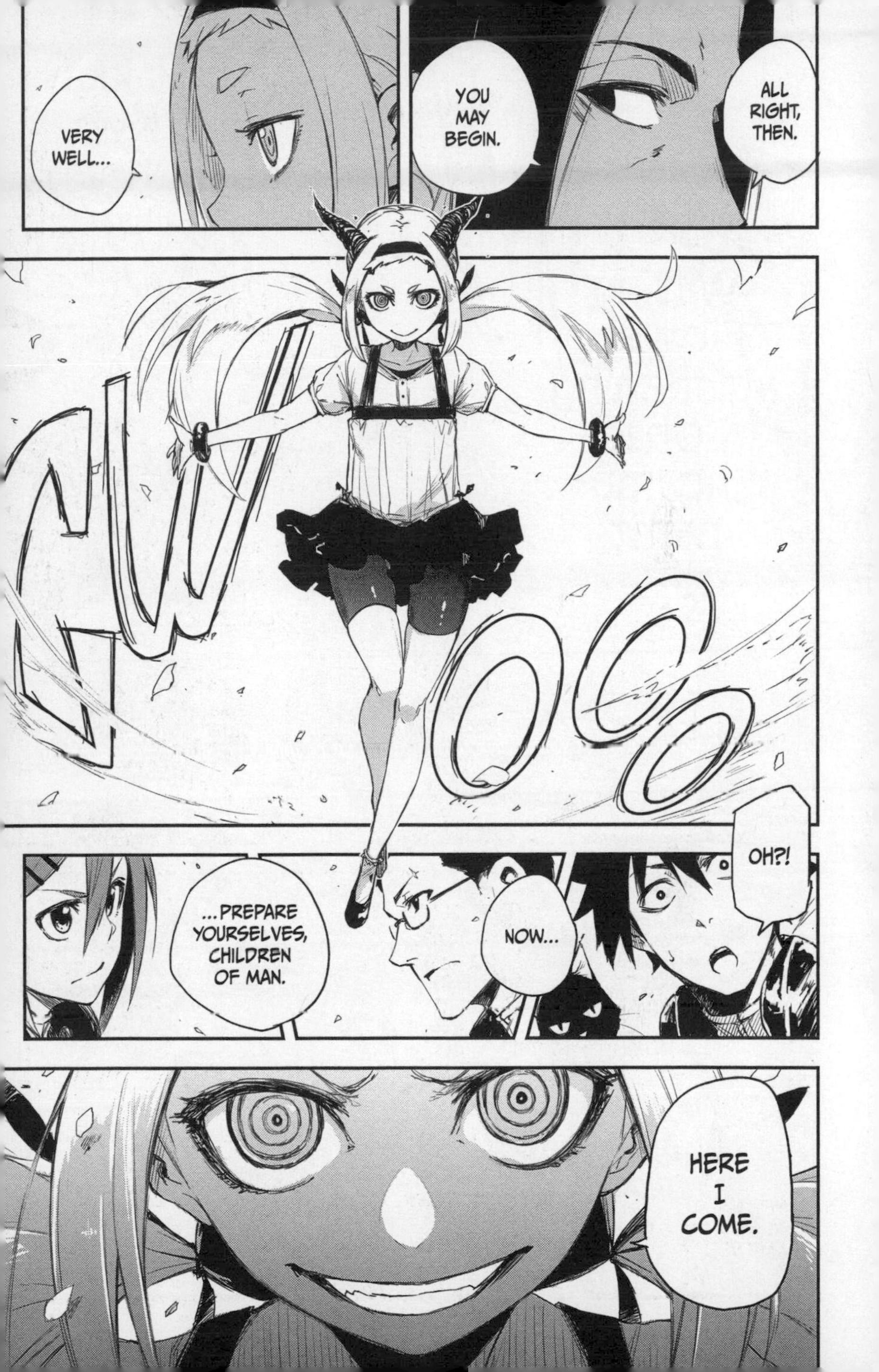
ALL RIGHT, THEN.
YOU MAY BEGIN.
VERY WELL...
GWOOO
OH?!
NOW...
...PREPARE YOURSELVES, CHILDREN OF MAN.
HERE I COME.

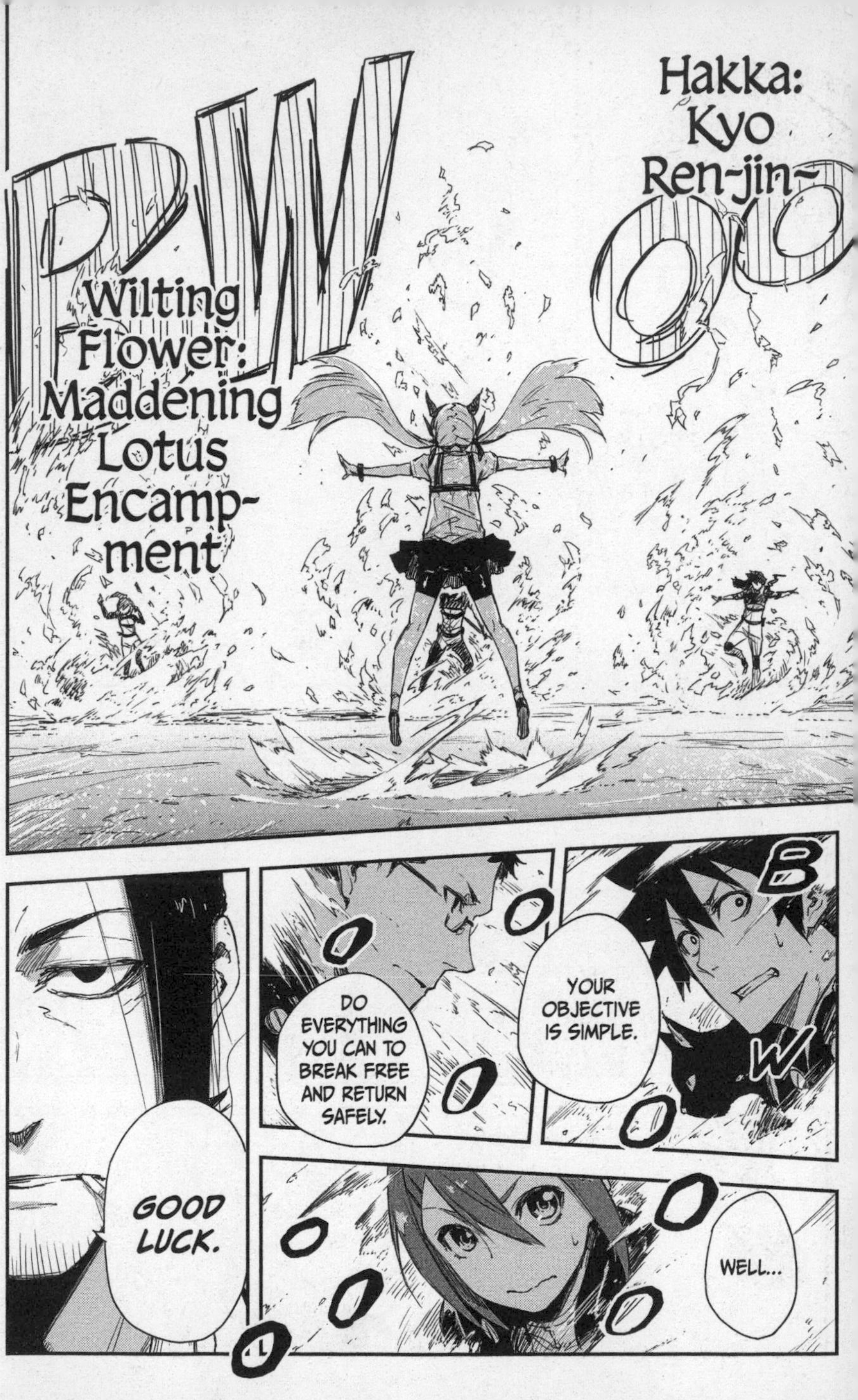
Hakka: Kyo Ren-jin-
OO
PW
Wilting Flower: Maddening Lotus Encampment
BW
YOUR OBJECTIVE IS SIMPLE.
DO EVERYTHING YOU CAN TO BREAK FREE AND RETURN SAFELY.
WELL...
GOOD LUCK.

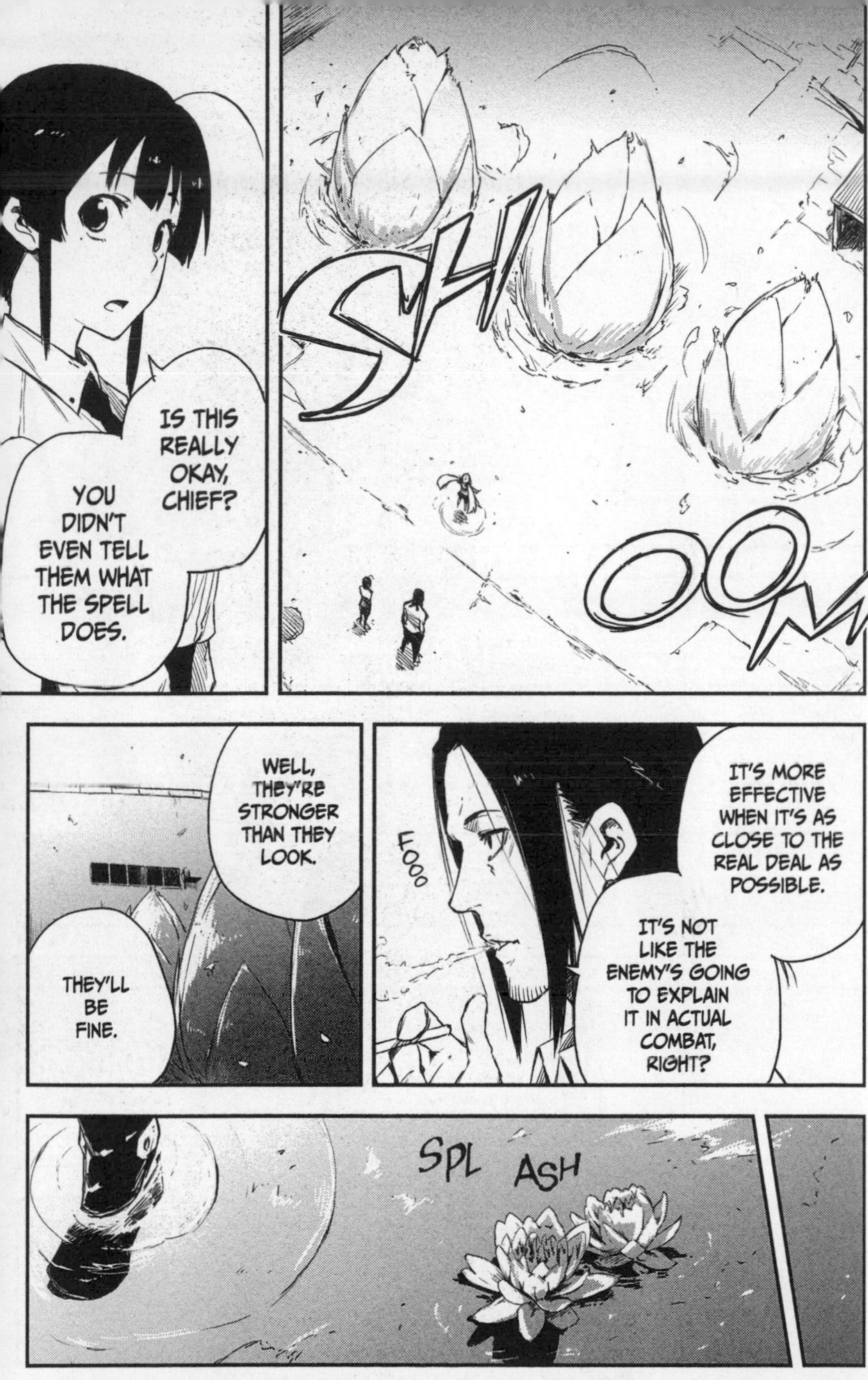
SHOOOM
IS THIS REALLY OKAY, CHIEF?
YOU DIDN'T EVEN TELL THEM WHAT THE SPELL DOES.
IT'S MORE EFFECTIVE WHEN IT'S AS CLOSE TO THE REAL DEAL AS POSSIBLE.
IT'S NOT LIKE THE ENEMY'S GOING TO EXPLAIN IT IN ACTUAL COMBAT, RIGHT?
FOOO
WELL, THEY'RE STRONGER THAN THEY LOOK.
THEY'LL BE FINE.
SPL ASH

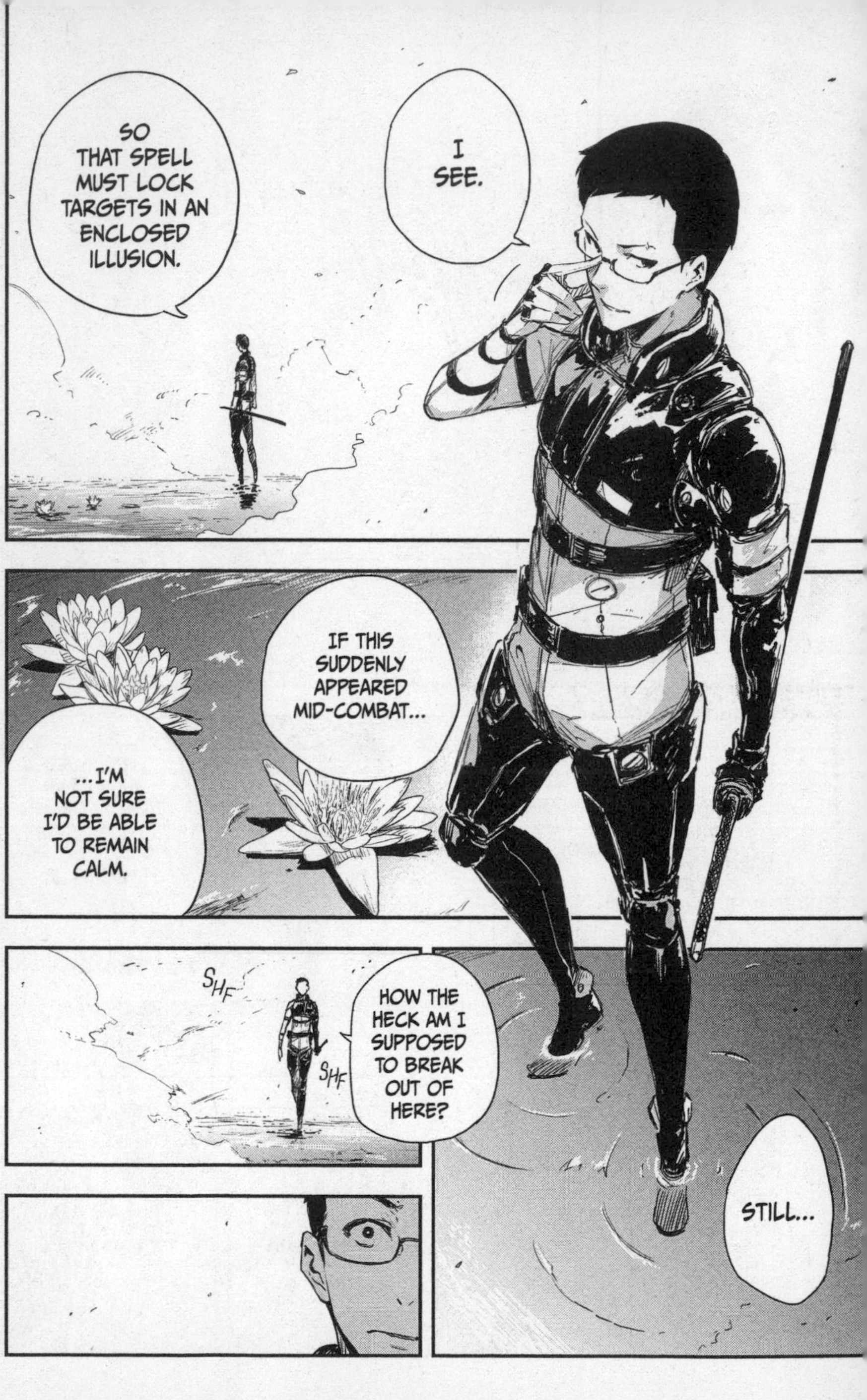
I SEE.
SO THAT SPELL MUST LOCK TARGETS IN AN ENCLOSED ILLUSION.
IF THIS SUDDENLY APPEARED MID-COMBAT...
...I'M NOT SURE I'D BE ABLE TO REMAIN CALM.
STILL...
SHF
HOW THE HECK AM I SUPPOSED TO BREAK OUT OF HERE?
SHF

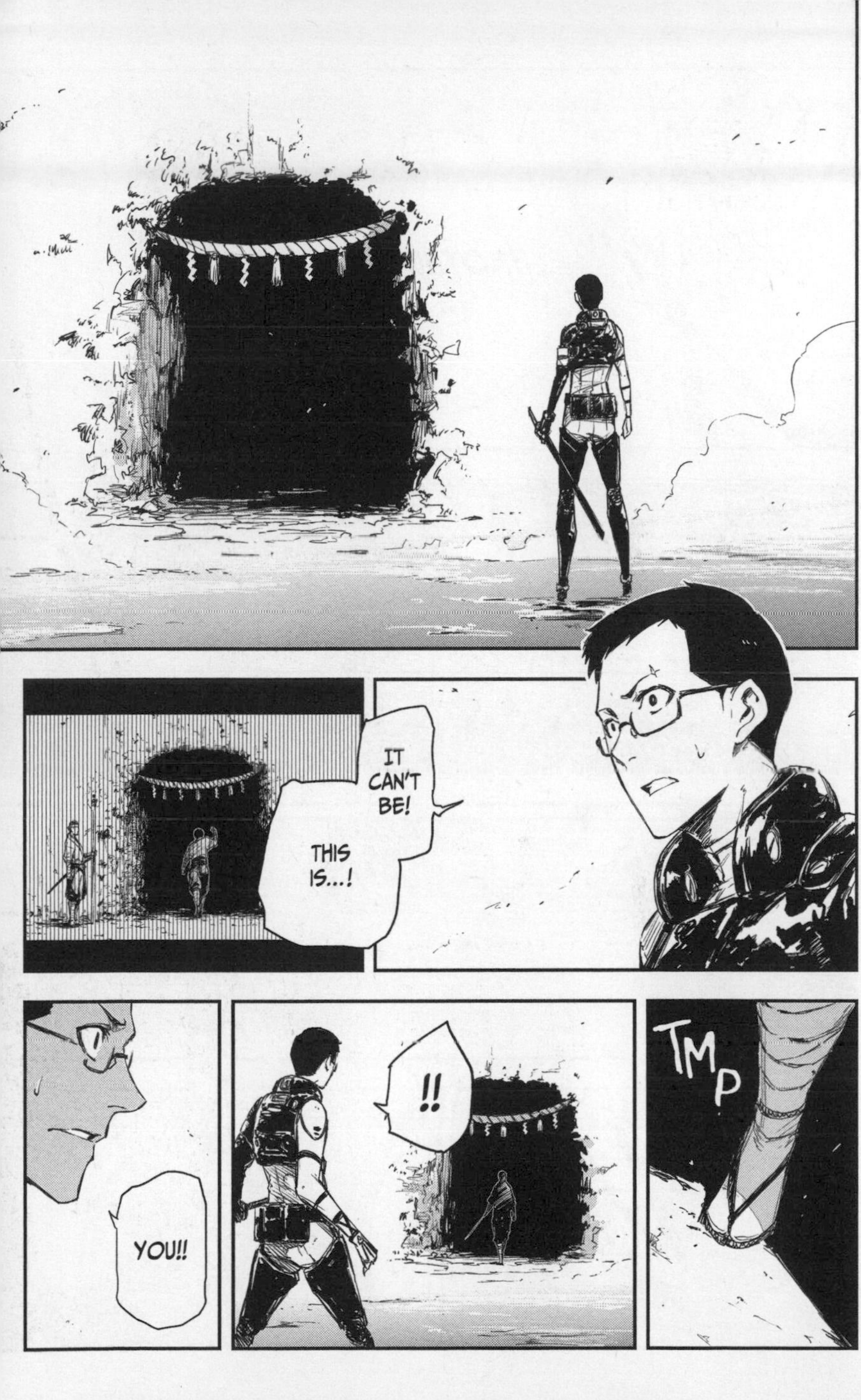
IT CAN'T BE!
THIS IS...!
TMP
!!
YOU!!

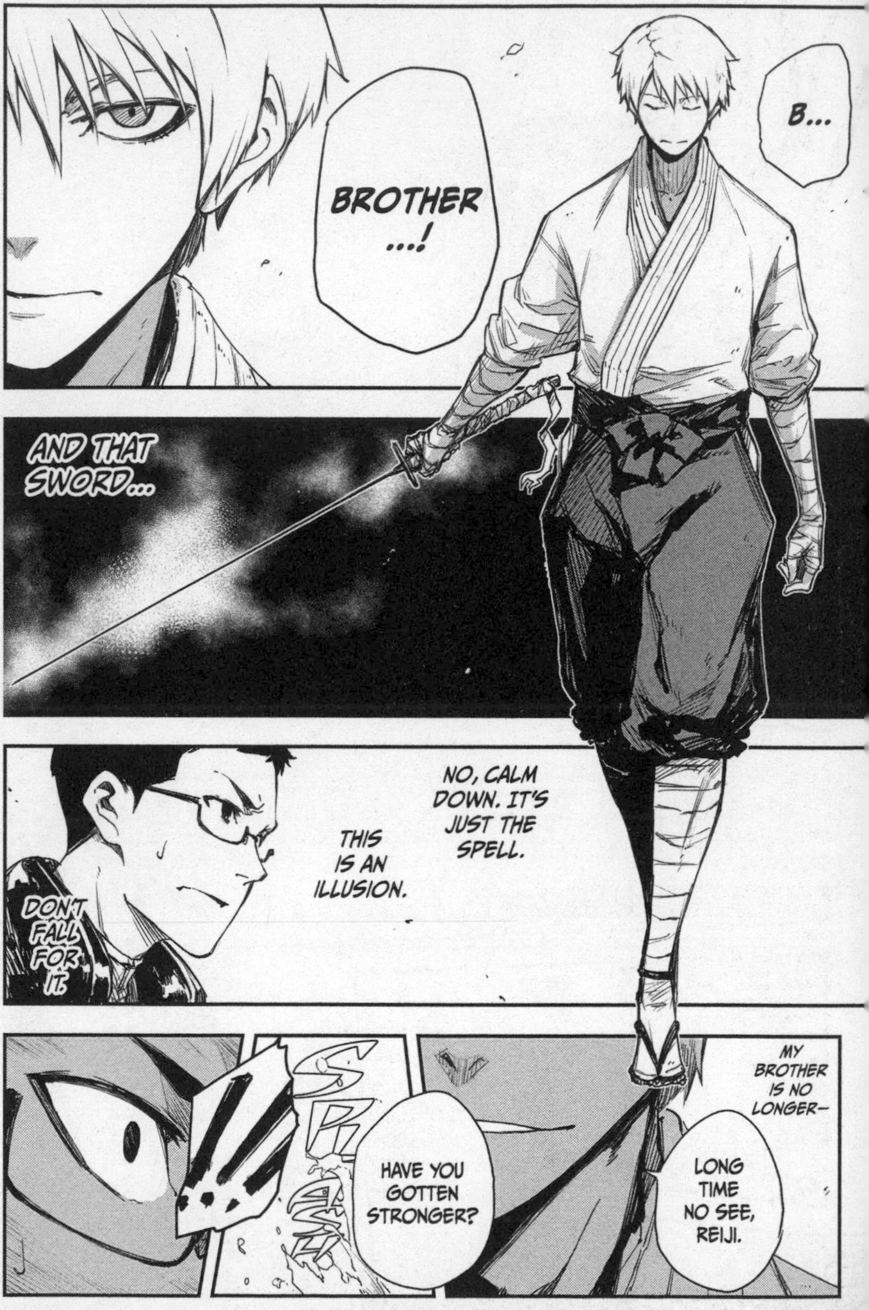
B...
BROTHER ...!
AND THAT SWORD...
NO, CALM DOWN. IT'S JUST THE SPELL.
THIS IS AN ILLUSION.
DON'T FALL FOR IT.
MY BROTHER IS NO LONGER—
LONG TIME NO SEE, REIJI.
HAVE YOU GOTTEN STRONGER?

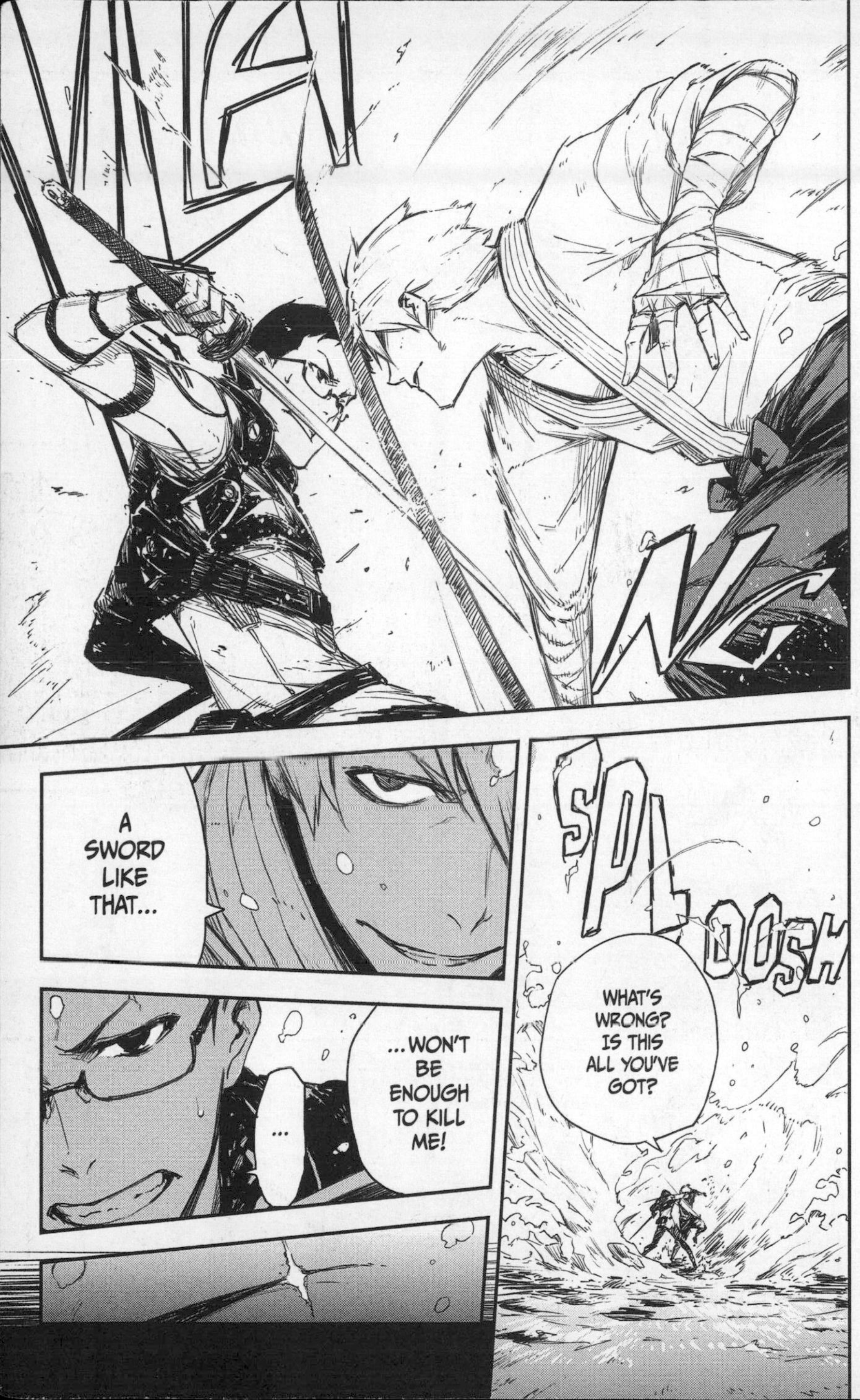
SPLOOSH
WHAT'S WRONG? IS THIS ALL YOU'VE GOT?
A SWORD LIKE THAT...
...WON'T BE ENOUGH TO KILL ME!
...

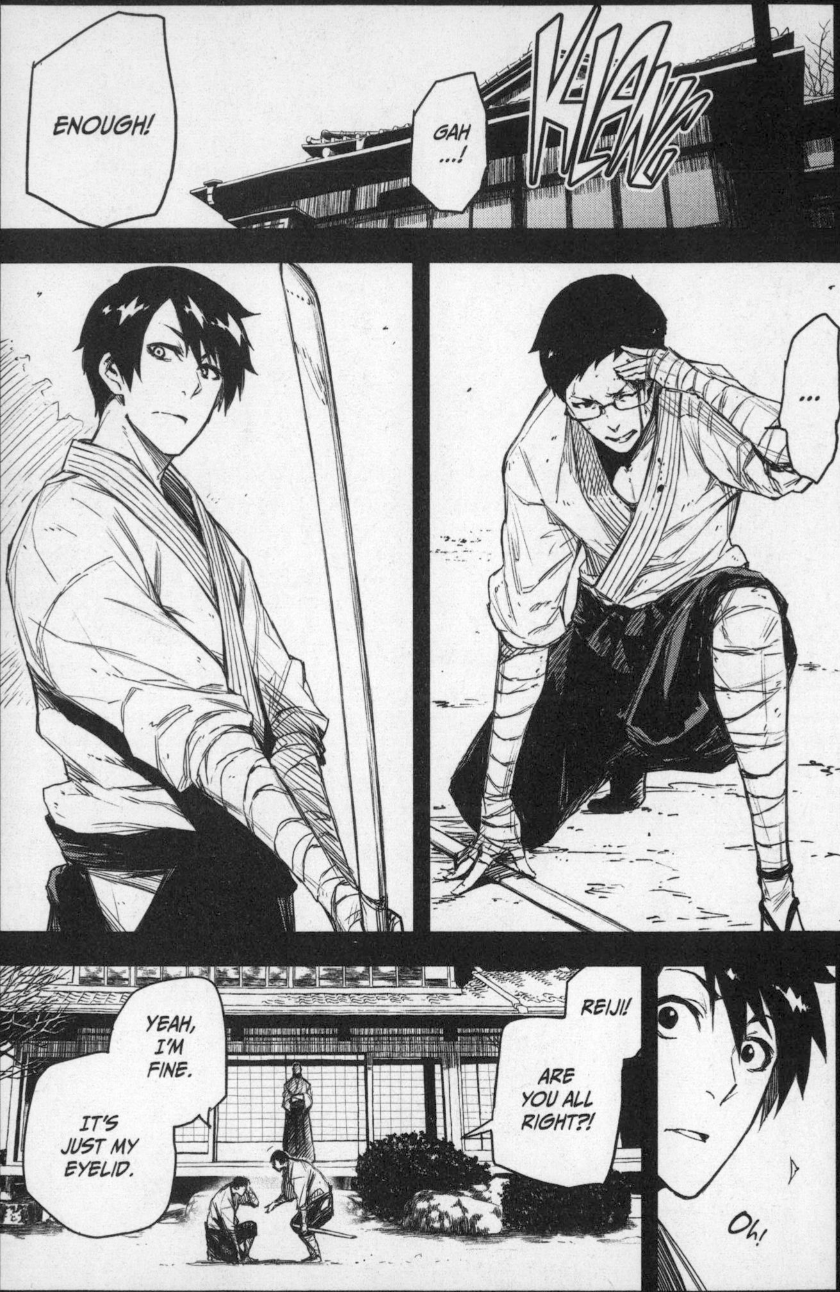
GAH ...!
ENOUGH!
...
GAH ...!
Oh!
REIJI!
ARE YOU ALL RIGHT?!
YEAH, I'M FINE.
IT'S JUST MY EYELID.

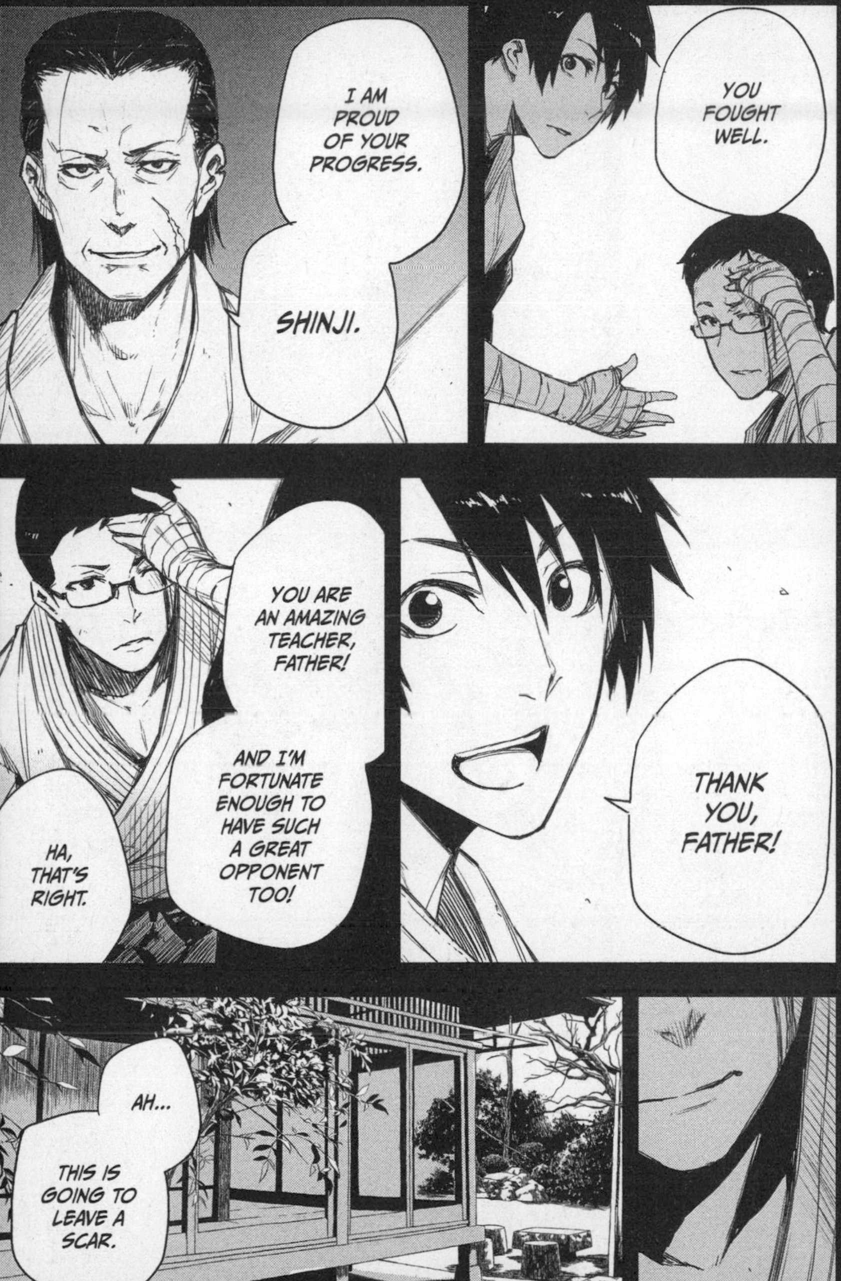
YOU FOUGHT WELL.
I AM PROUD OF YOUR PROGRESS.
SHINJI.
THANK YOU, FATHER!
YOU ARE AN AMAZING TEACHER, FATHER!
AND I'M FORTUNATE ENOUGH TO HAVE SUCH A GREAT OPPONENT TOO!
HA, THAT'S RIGHT.
AH...
THIS IS GOING TO LEAVE A SCAR.

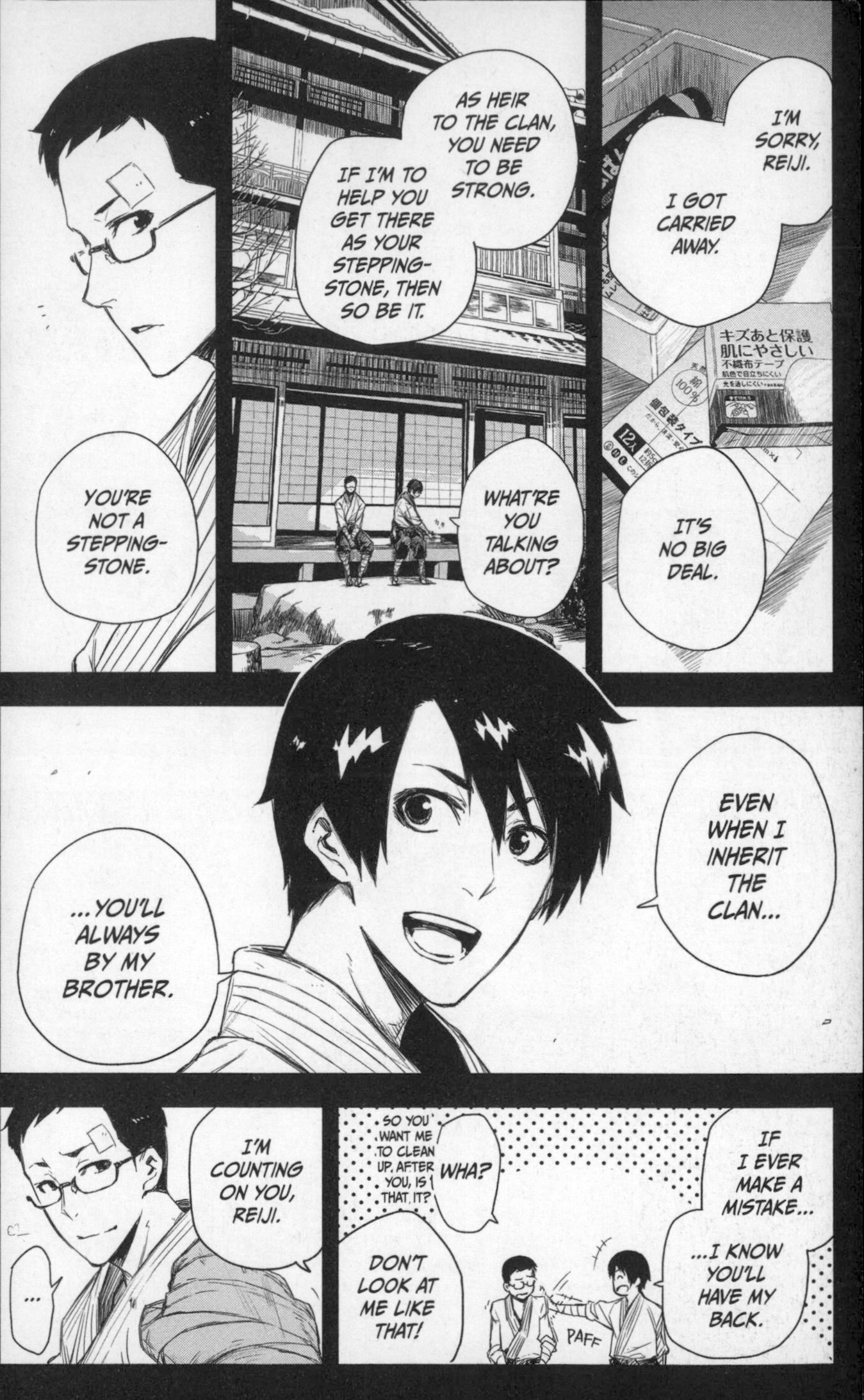
I'M SORRY, REIJI.
I GOT CARRIED AWAY.
キズあと保護
肌にやさしい
不織布テープ
綿100%
個包装タイプ
IT'S NO BIG DEAL.
AS HEIR TO THE CLAN, YOU NEED TO BE STRONG.
IF I'M TO HELP YOU GET THERE AS YOUR STEPPING-STONE, THEN SO BE IT.
WHAT'RE YOU TALKING ABOUT?
YOU'RE NOT A STEPPING-STONE.
EVEN WHEN I INHERIT THE CLAN...
...YOU'LL ALWAYS BY MY BROTHER.
IF I EVER MAKE A MISTAKE...
...I KNOW YOU'LL HAVE MY BACK.
WHA?
SO YOU WANT ME TO CLEAN UP AFTER YOU, IS THAT IT?
DON'T LOOK AT ME LIKE THAT!
PAFF
I'M COUNTING ON YOU, REIJI.
...

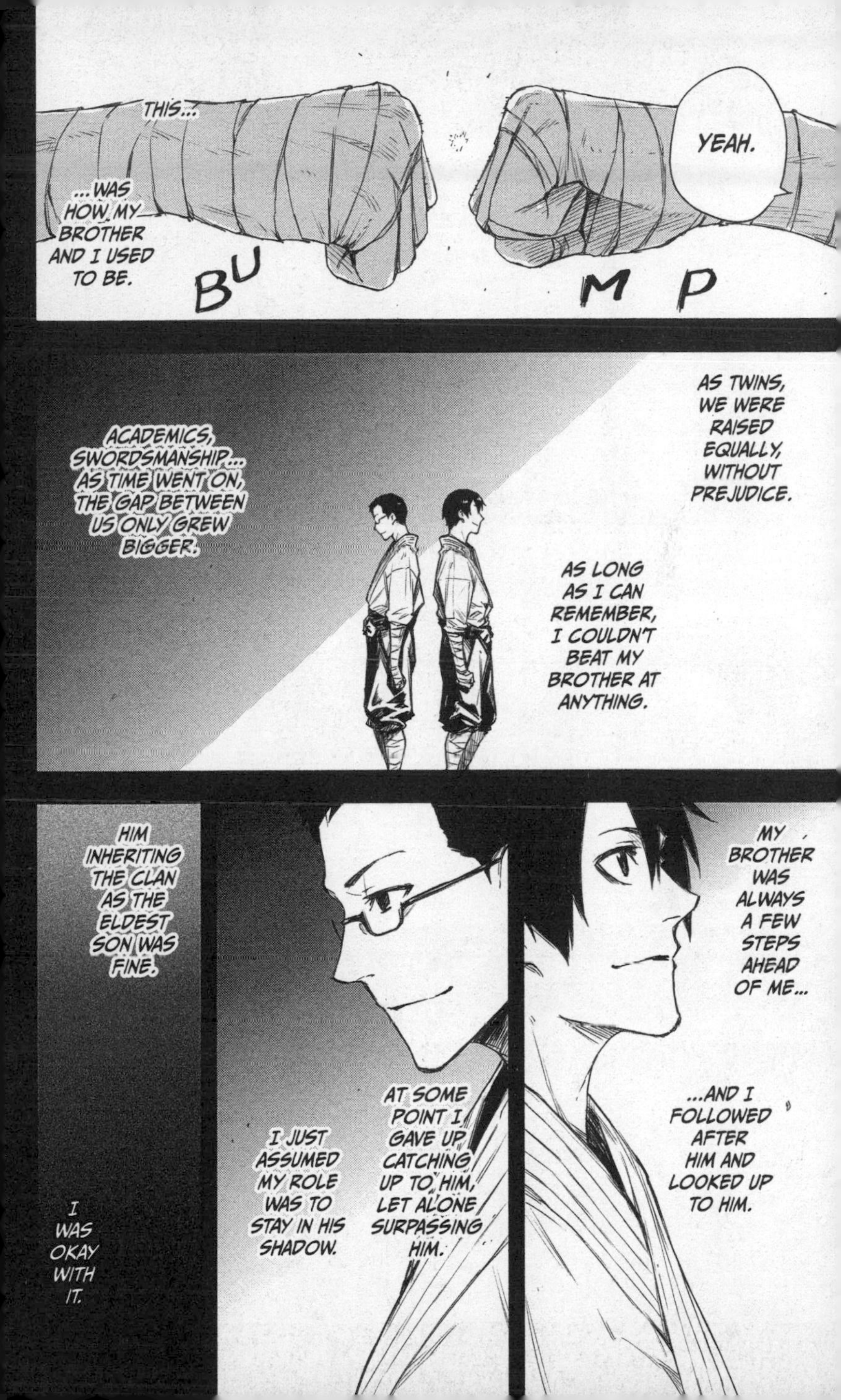
YEAH.
THIS...?
...WAS HOW MY BROTHER AND I USED TO BE.
BU M P
AS TWINS, WE WERE RAISED EQUALLY, WITHOUT PREJUDICE.
AS LONG AS I CAN REMEMBER, I COULDN'T BEAT MY BROTHER AT ANYTHING.
ACADEMICS, SWORDSMANSHIP... AS TIME WENT ON, THE GAP BETWEEN US ONLY GREW BIGGER.
MY BROTHER WAS ALWAYS A FEW STEPS AHEAD OF ME...
...AND I FOLLOWED AFTER HIM AND LOOKED UP TO HIM.
AT SOME POINT I GAVE UP CATCHING UP TO HIM, LET ALONE SURPASSING HIM.
I JUST ASSUMED MY ROLE WAS TO STAY IN HIS SHADOW.
HIM INHERITING THE CLAN AS THE ELDEST SON WAS FINE.
I WAS OKAY WITH IT.

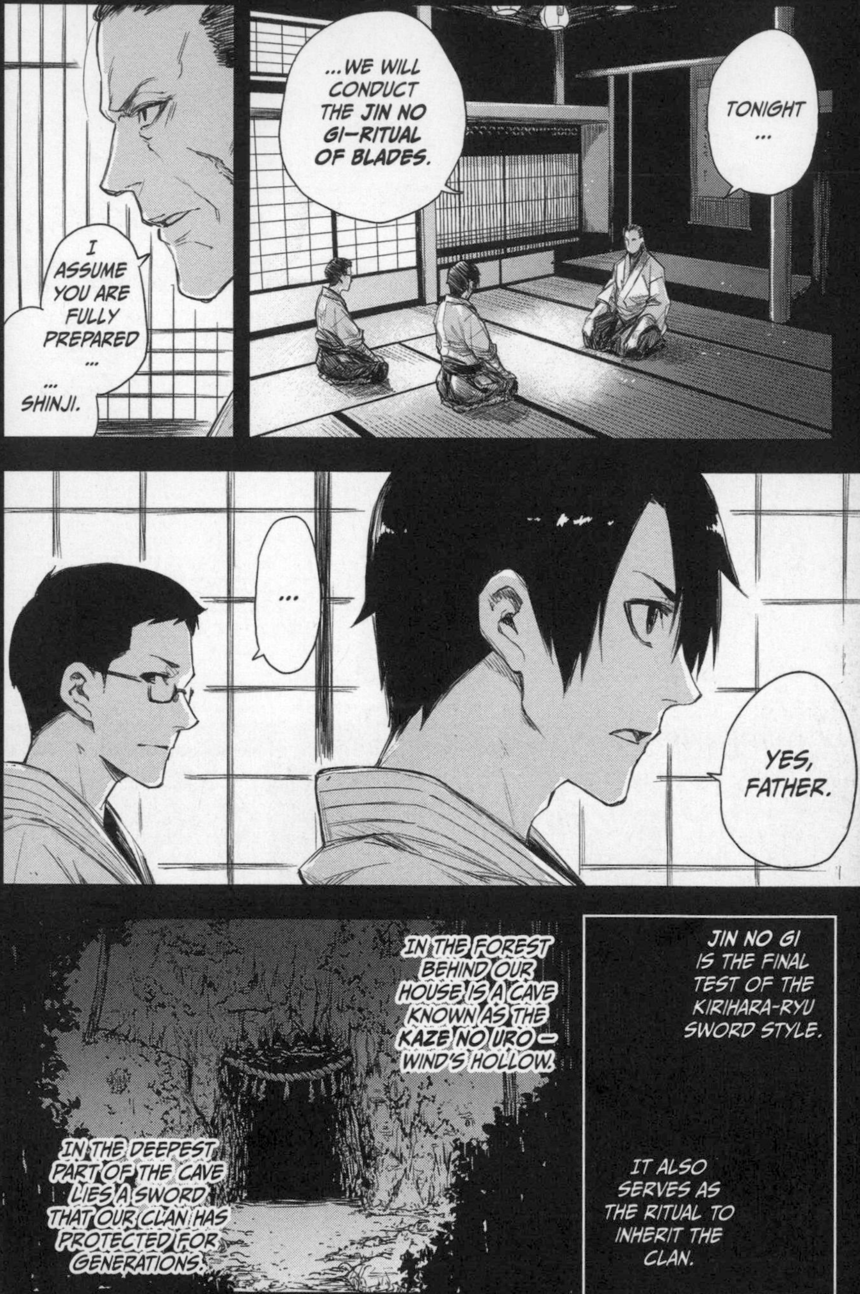
TONIGHT ...
...WE WILL CONDUCT THE JIN NO GI—RITUAL OF BLADES.
I ASSUME YOU ARE FULLY PREPARED ...
... SHINJI.
YES, FATHER.
...
JIN NO GI IS THE FINAL TEST OF THE KIRIHARA-RYU SWORD STYLE.
IT ALSO SERVES AS THE RITUAL TO INHERIT THE CLAN.
IN THE FOREST BEHIND OUR HOUSE IS A CAVE KNOWN AS THE KAZE NO URO— WIND'S HOLLOW.
IN THE DEEPEST PART OF THE CAVE LIES A SWORD THAT OUR CLAN HAS PROTECTED FOR GENERATIONS.

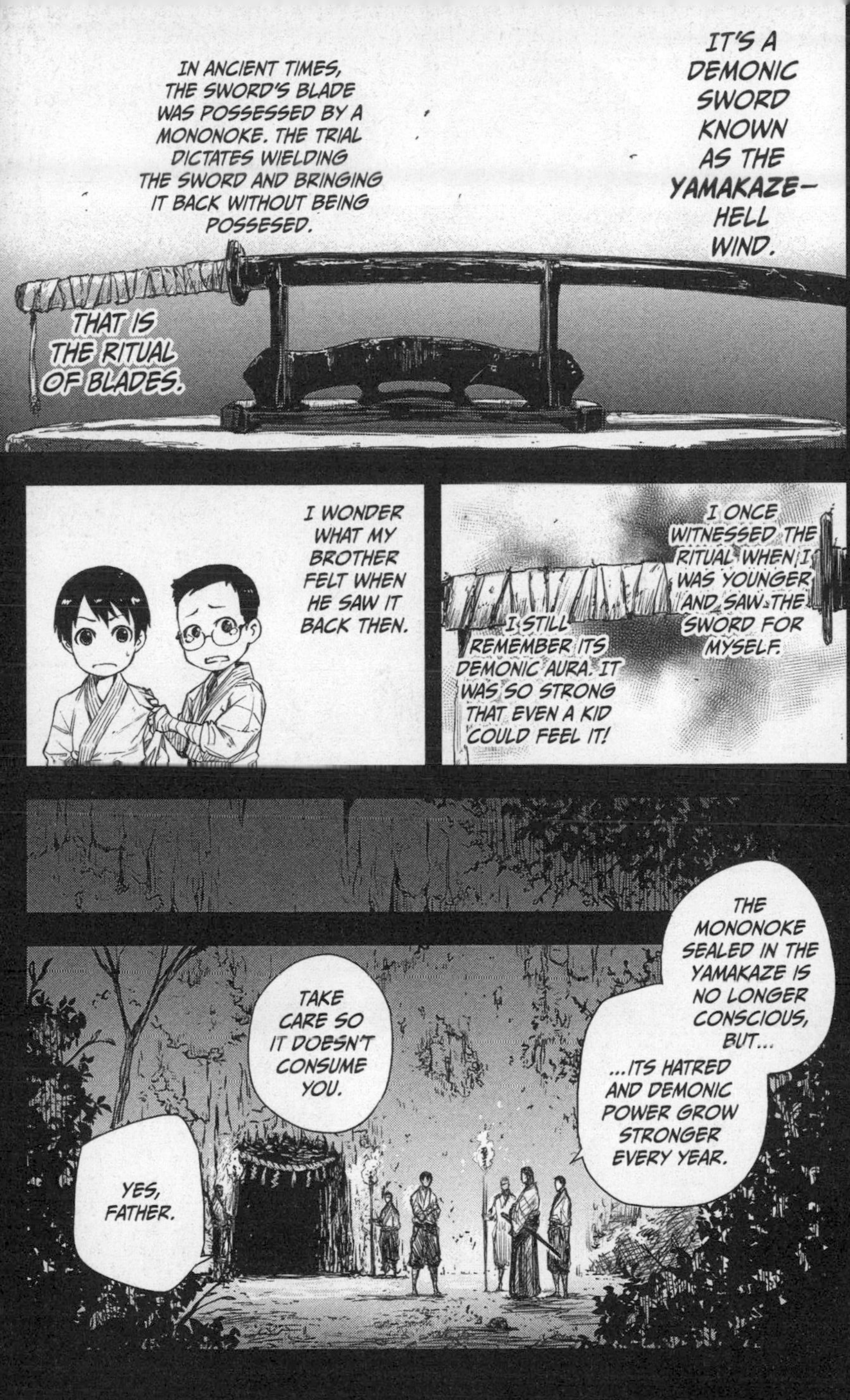
IT'S A DEMONIC SWORD KNOWN AS THE YAMAKAZE— HELL WIND.
IN ANCIENT TIMES, THE SWORD'S BLADE WAS POSSESSED BY A MONONOKE. THE TRIAL DICTATES WIELDING THE SWORD AND BRINGING IT BACK WITHOUT BEING POSSESED.
THAT IS THE RITUAL OF BLADES.
I ONCE WITNESSED THE RITUAL WHEN I WAS YOUNGER AND SAW THE SWORD FOR MYSELF.
I STILL REMEMBER ITS DEMONIC AURA. IT WAS SO STRONG THAT EVEN A KID COULD FEEL IT!
I WONDER WHAT MY BROTHER FELT WHEN HE SAW IT BACK THEN.
THE MONONOKE SEALED IN THE YAMAKAZE IS NO LONGER CONSCIOUS, BUT...
...ITS HATRED AND DEMONIC POWER GROW STRONGER EVERY YEAR.
TAKE CARE SO IT DOESN'T CONSUME YOU.
YES, FATHER.

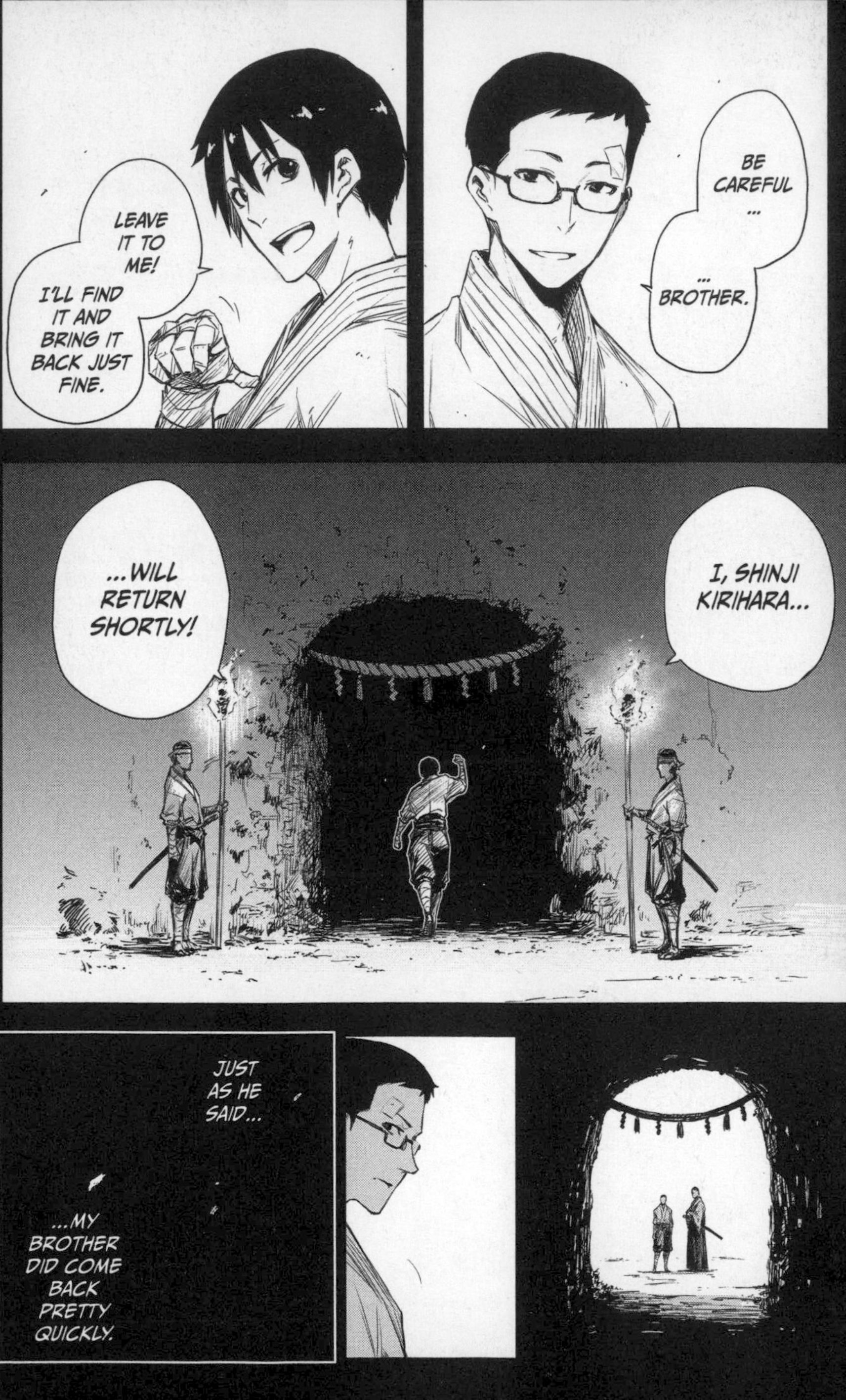
BE CAREFUL ...
... BROTHER.
LEAVE IT TO ME!
I'LL FIND IT AND BRING IT BACK JUST FINE.
I, SHINJI KIRIHARA...
...WILL RETURN SHORTLY!
JUST AS HE SAID...
...MY BROTHER DID COME BACK PRETTY QUICKLY.

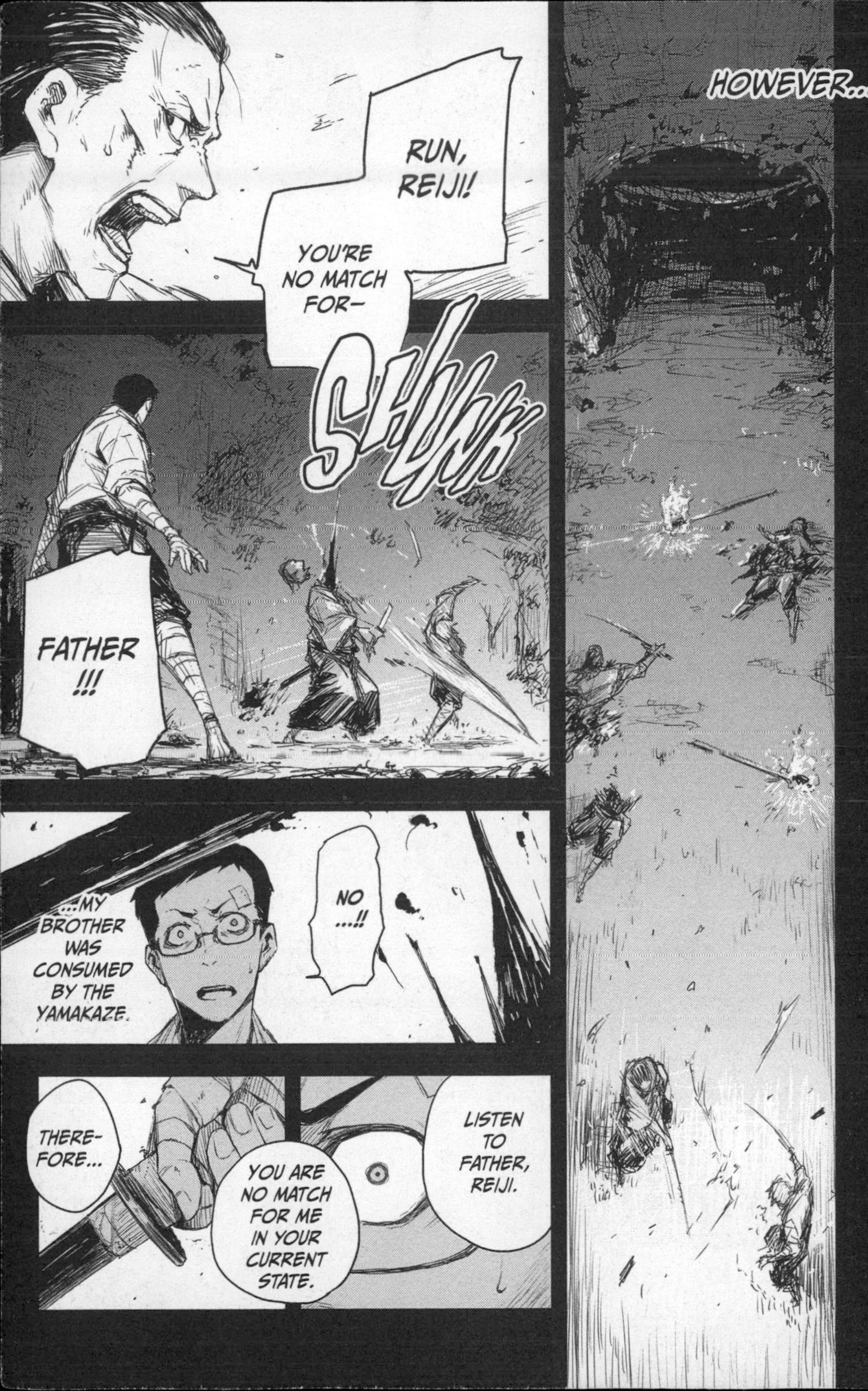
HOWEVER...
RUN, REIJI!
YOU'RE NO MATCH FOR–
SHUNK
FATHER !!!
NO ...!!
...MY BROTHER WAS CONSUMED BY THE YAMAKAZE.
LISTEN TO FATHER, REIJI.
YOU ARE NO MATCH FOR ME IN YOUR CURRENT STATE.
THERE-FORE...

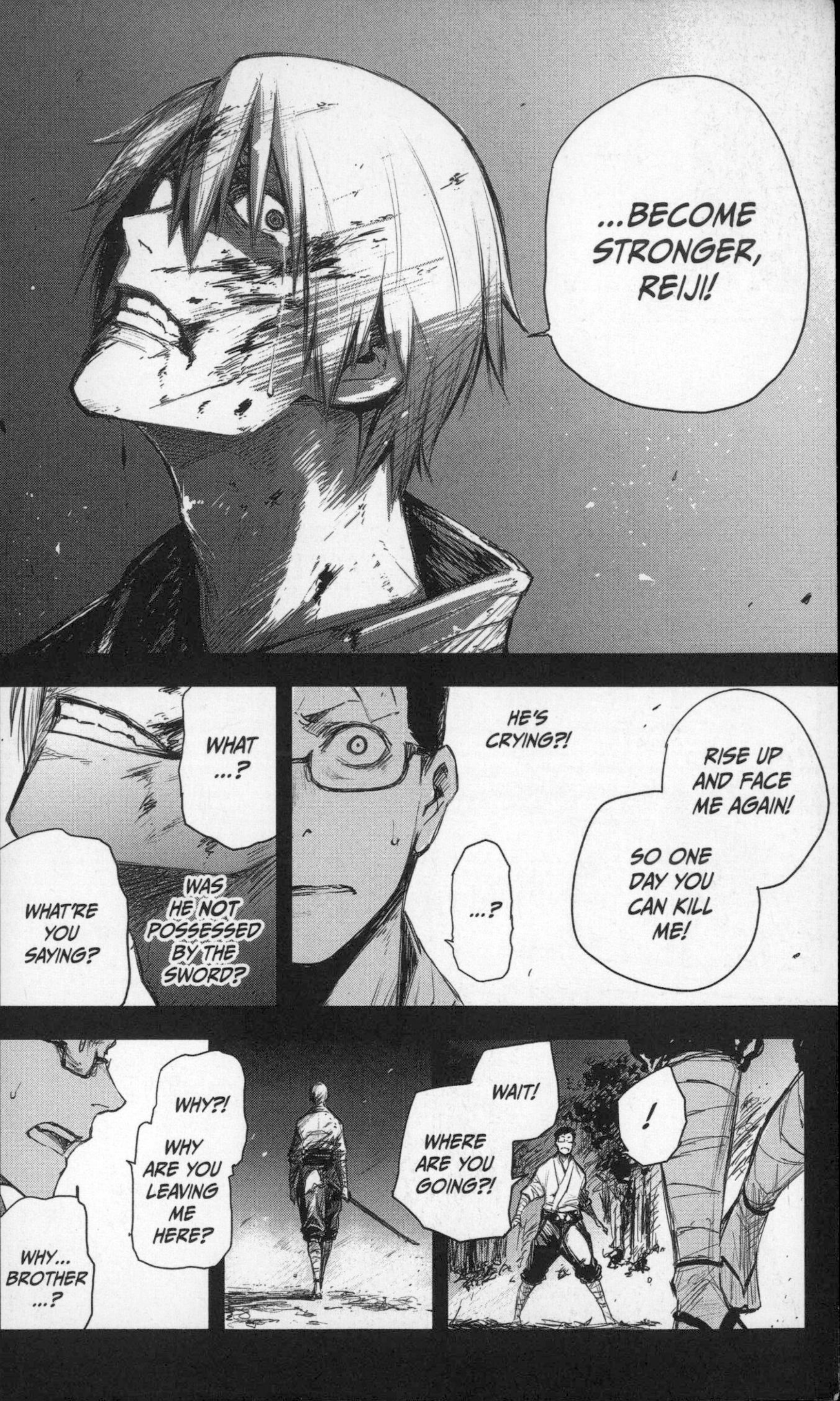
...BECOME STRONGER, REIJI!
RISE UP AND FACE ME AGAIN!
SO ONE DAY YOU CAN KILL ME!
HE'S CRYING?!
...?
WHAT ...?
WAS HE NOT POSSESSED BY THE SWORD?
WHAT'RE YOU SAYING?
!
WAIT!
WHERE ARE YOU GOING?!
WHY?!
WHY ARE YOU LEAVING ME HERE?
WHY... BROTHER ...?

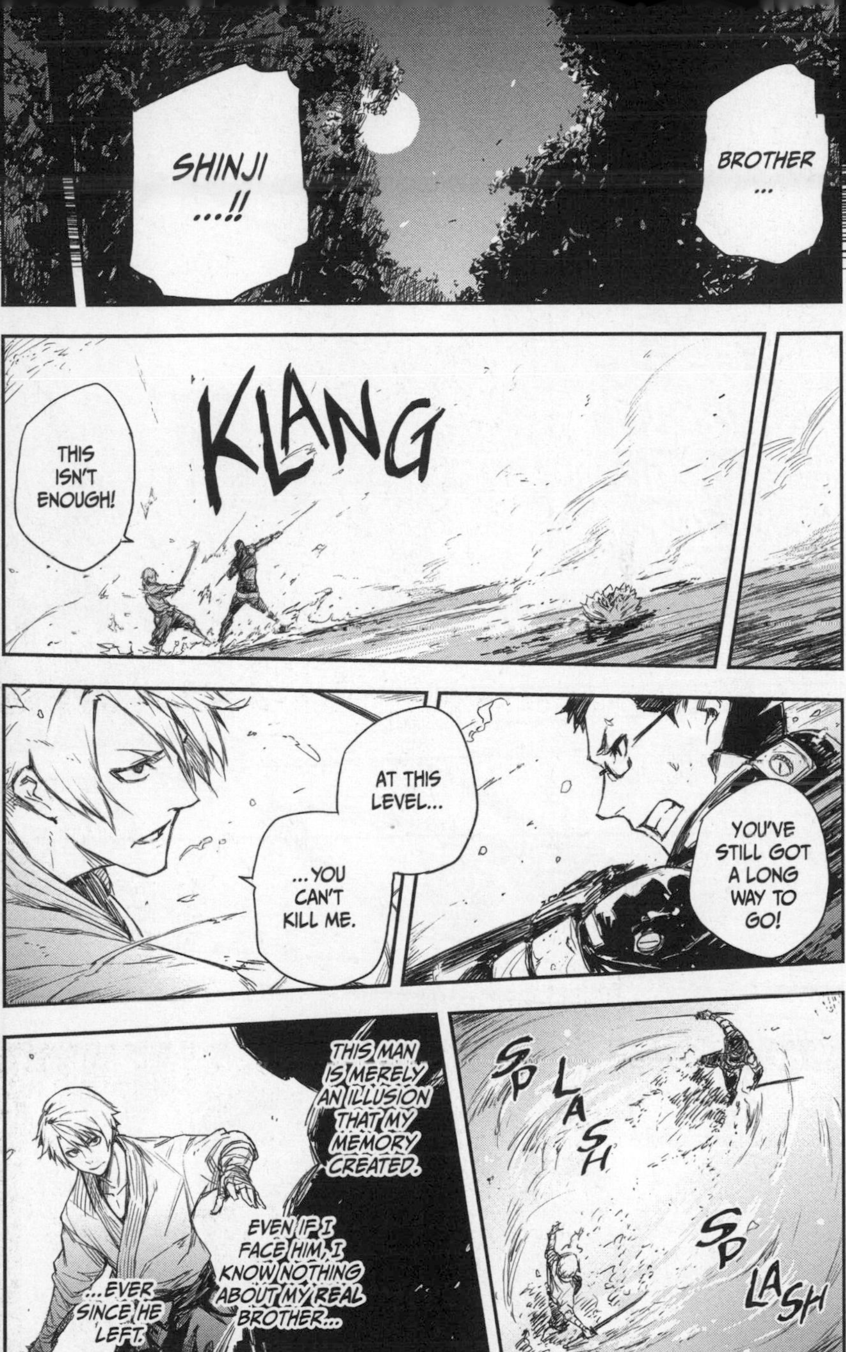
BROTHER ...
SHINJI ...!!
KLANG
THIS ISN'T ENOUGH!
YOU'VE STILL GOT A LONG WAY TO GO!
AT THIS LEVEL...
...YOU CAN'T KILL ME.
SPLASH
SPLASH
THIS MAN IS MERELY AN ILLUSION THAT MY MEMORY CREATED.
EVEN IF I FACE HIM, I KNOW NOTHING ABOUT MY REAL BROTHER...
...EVER SINCE HE LEFT.

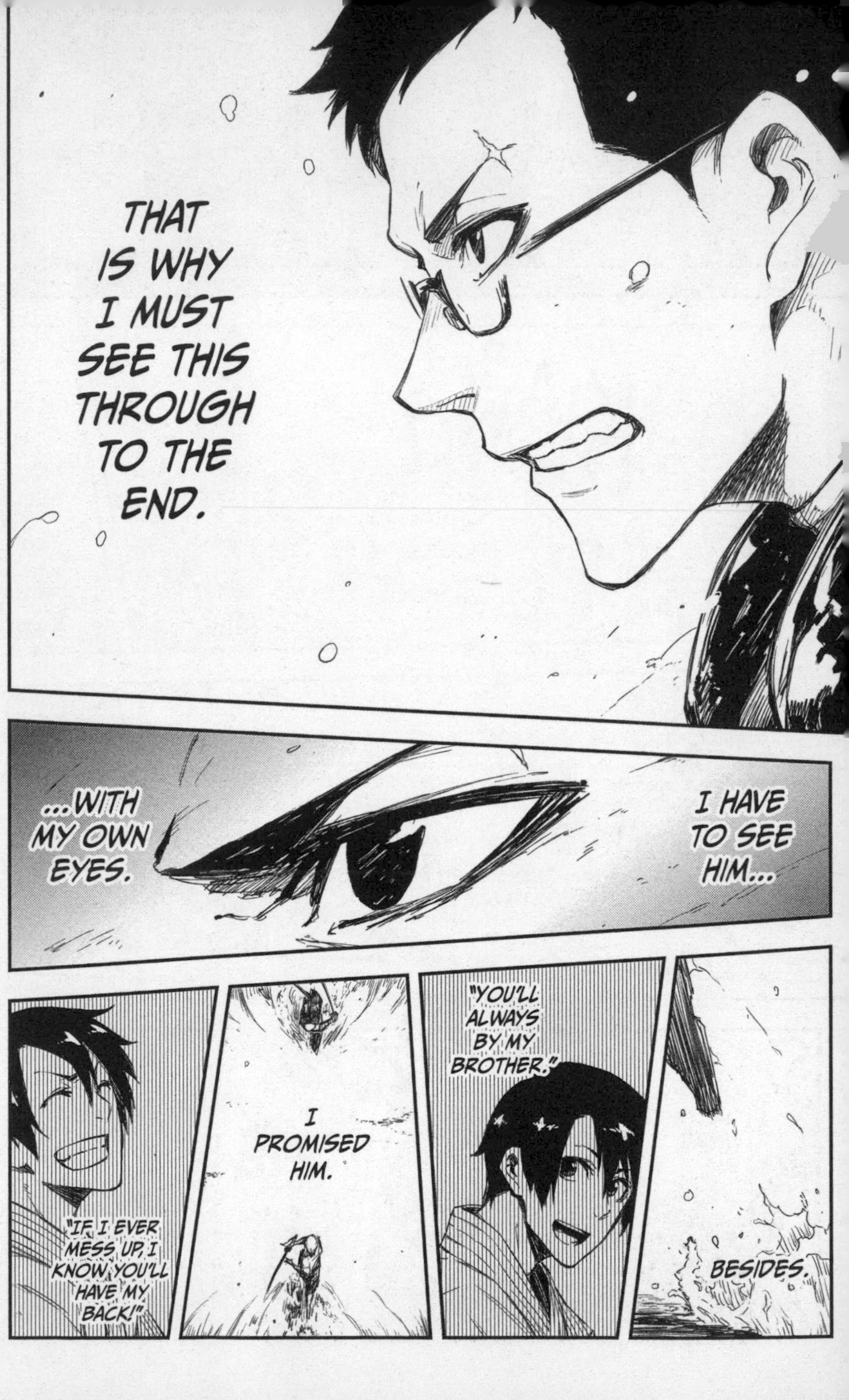
THAT IS WHY I MUST SEE THIS THROUGH TO THE END.
I HAVE TO SEE HIM...
...WITH MY OWN EYES.
BESIDES.
"YOU'LL ALWAYS BY MY BROTHER."
I PROMISED HIM.
"IF I EVER MESS UP, I KNOW YOU'LL HAVE MY BACK!"

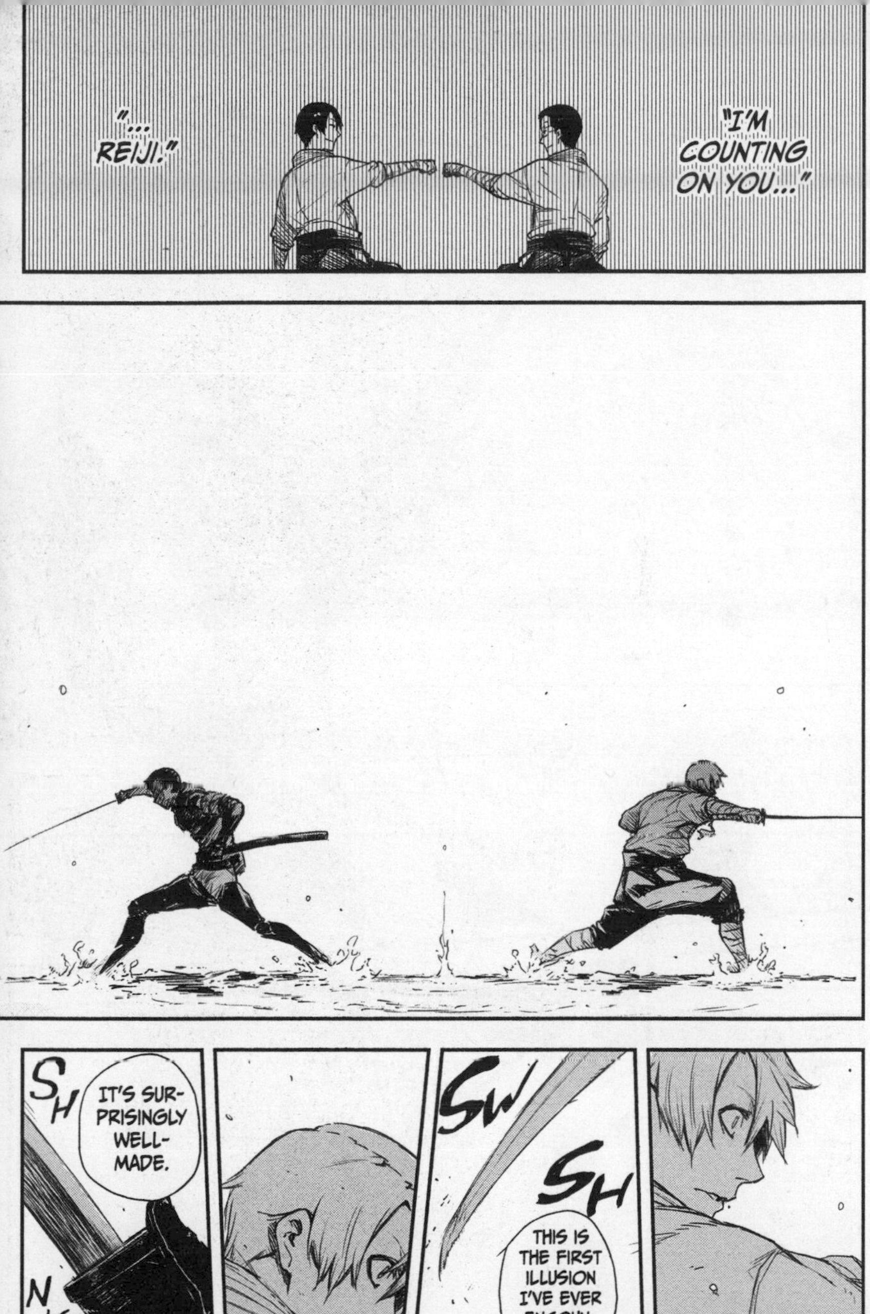
"I'M COUNTING ON YOU..."
"...REIJI."
SW
SH
THIS IS THE FIRST ILLUSION I'VE EVER ENCOUNTERED.
SH
NK
IT'S SURPRISINGLY WELL-MADE.

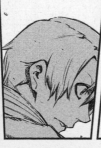

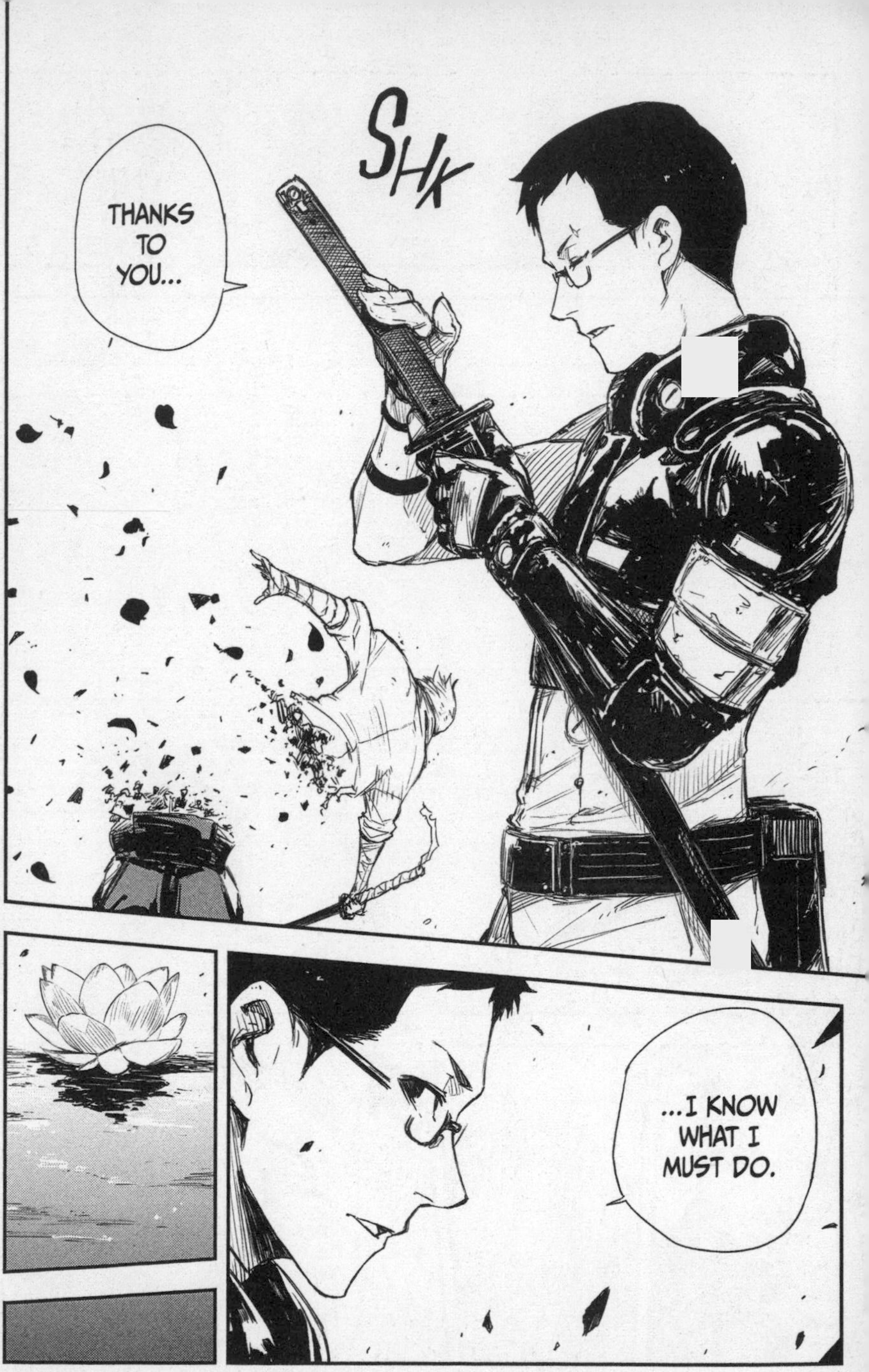
SHK
THANKS TO YOU...
...I KNOW WHAT I MUST DO.

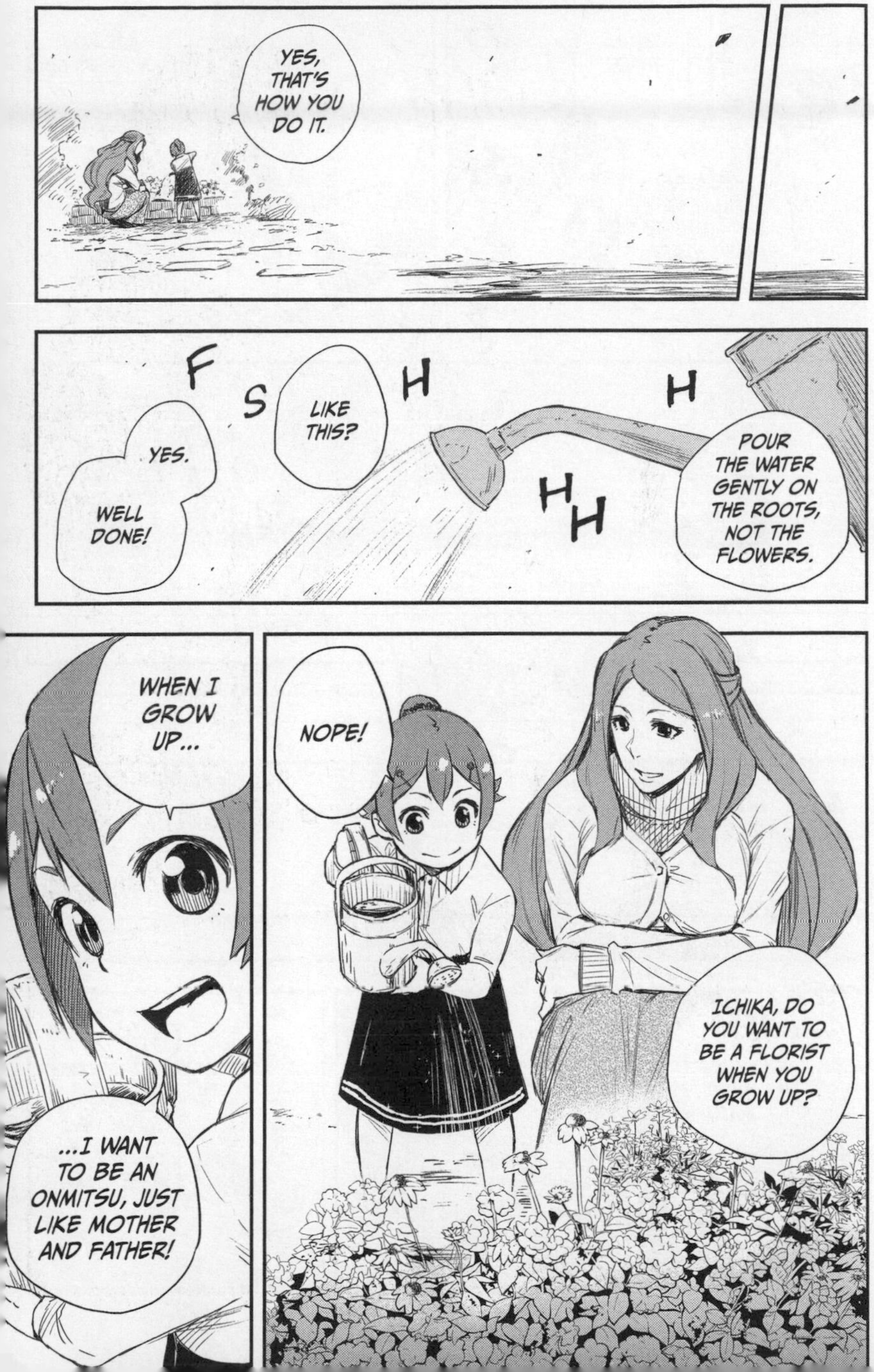
YES, THAT'S HOW YOU DO IT.
POUR THE WATER GENTLY ON THE ROOTS, NOT THE FLOWERS.
FSHHHH
LIKE THIS?
YES.
WELL DONE!
ICHIKA, DO YOU WANT TO BE A FLORIST WHEN YOU GROW UP?
NOPE!
WHEN I GROW UP...
...I WANT TO BE AN ONMITSU, JUST LIKE MOTHER AND FATHER!

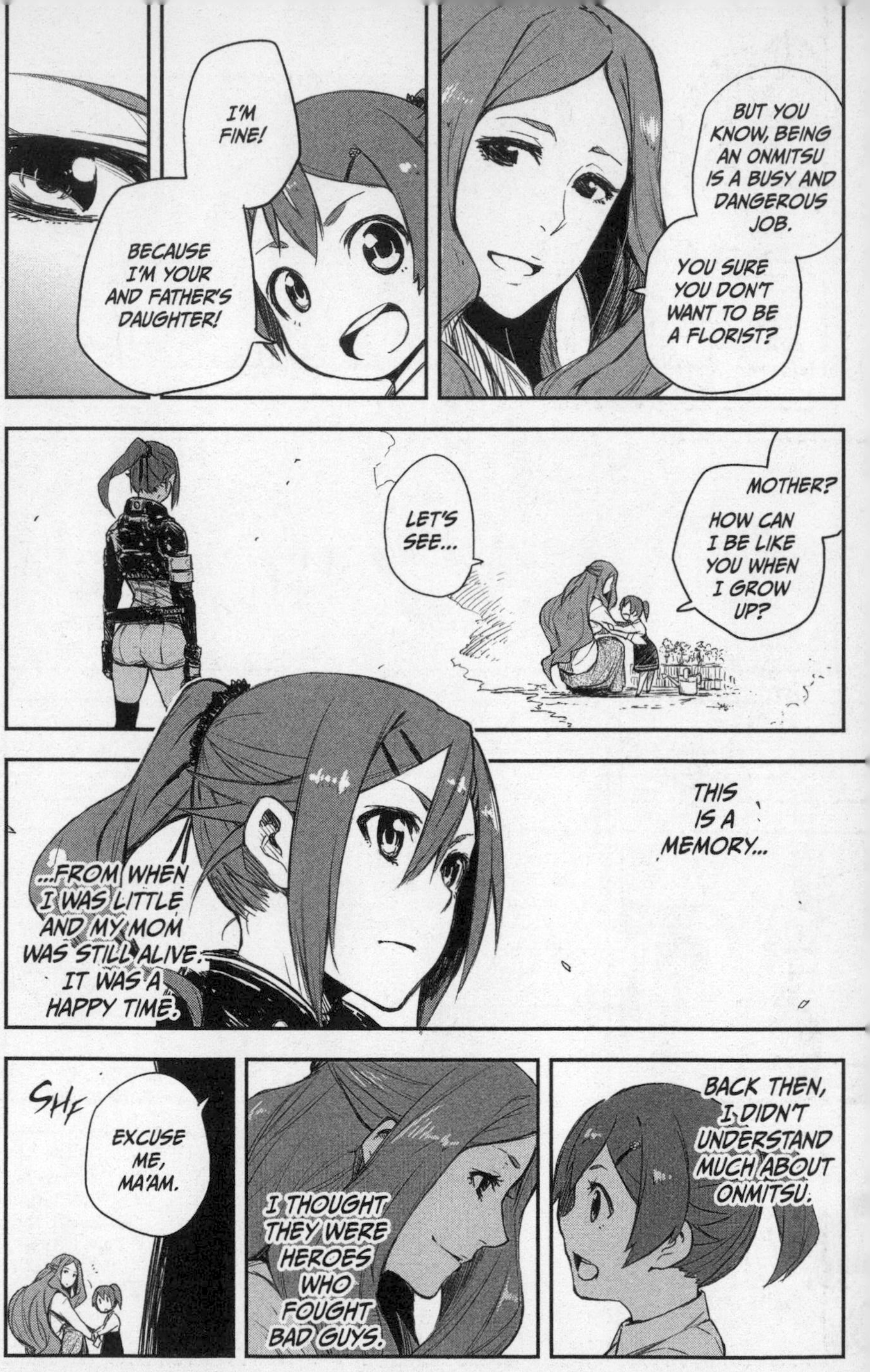
BUT YOU KNOW, BEING AN ONMITSU IS A BUSY AND DANGEROUS JOB.
YOU SURE YOU DON'T WANT TO BE A FLORIST?
I'M FINE!
BECAUSE I'M YOUR AND FATHER'S DAUGHTER!
MOTHER?
HOW CAN I BE LIKE YOU WHEN I GROW UP?
LET'S SEE...
THIS IS A MEMORY...
...FROM WHEN I WAS LITTLE AND MY MOM WAS STILL ALIVE. IT WAS A HAPPY TIME.
BACK THEN, I DIDN'T UNDERSTAND MUCH ABOUT ONMITSU.
I THOUGHT THEY WERE HEROES WHO FOUGHT BAD GUYS.
SHF
EXCUSE ME, MA'AM.

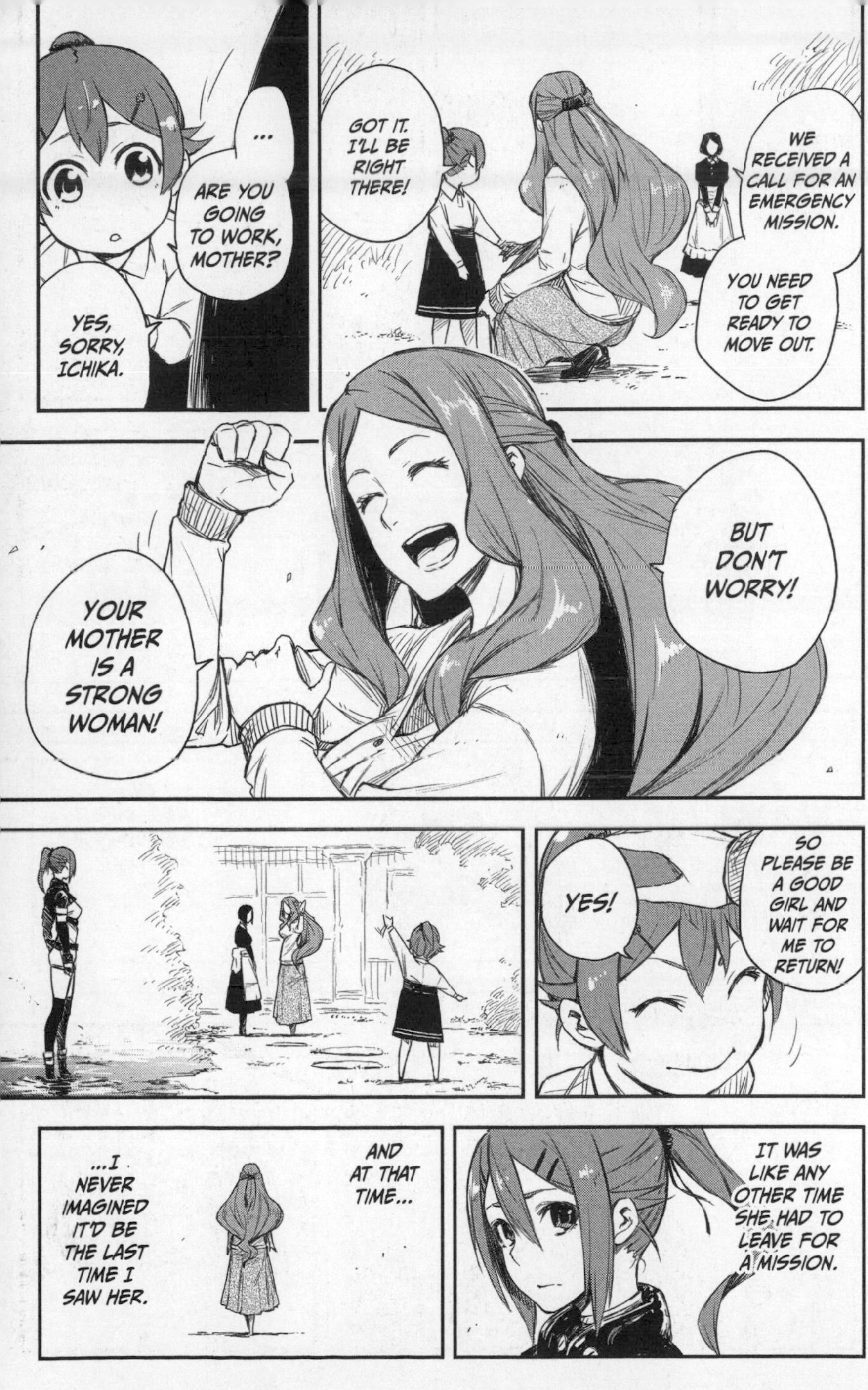
WE RECEIVED A CALL FOR AN EMERGENCY MISSION.
YOU NEED TO GET READY TO MOVE OUT.
GOT IT. I'LL BE RIGHT THERE!
...
ARE YOU GOING TO WORK, MOTHER?
YES, SORRY, ICHIKA.
BUT DON'T WORRY!
YOUR MOTHER IS A STRONG WOMAN!
SO PLEASE BE A GOOD GIRL AND WAIT FOR ME TO RETURN!
YES!
IT WAS LIKE ANY OTHER TIME SHE HAD TO LEAVE FOR A MISSION.
AND AT THAT TIME...
...I NEVER IMAGINED IT'D BE THE LAST TIME I SAW HER.

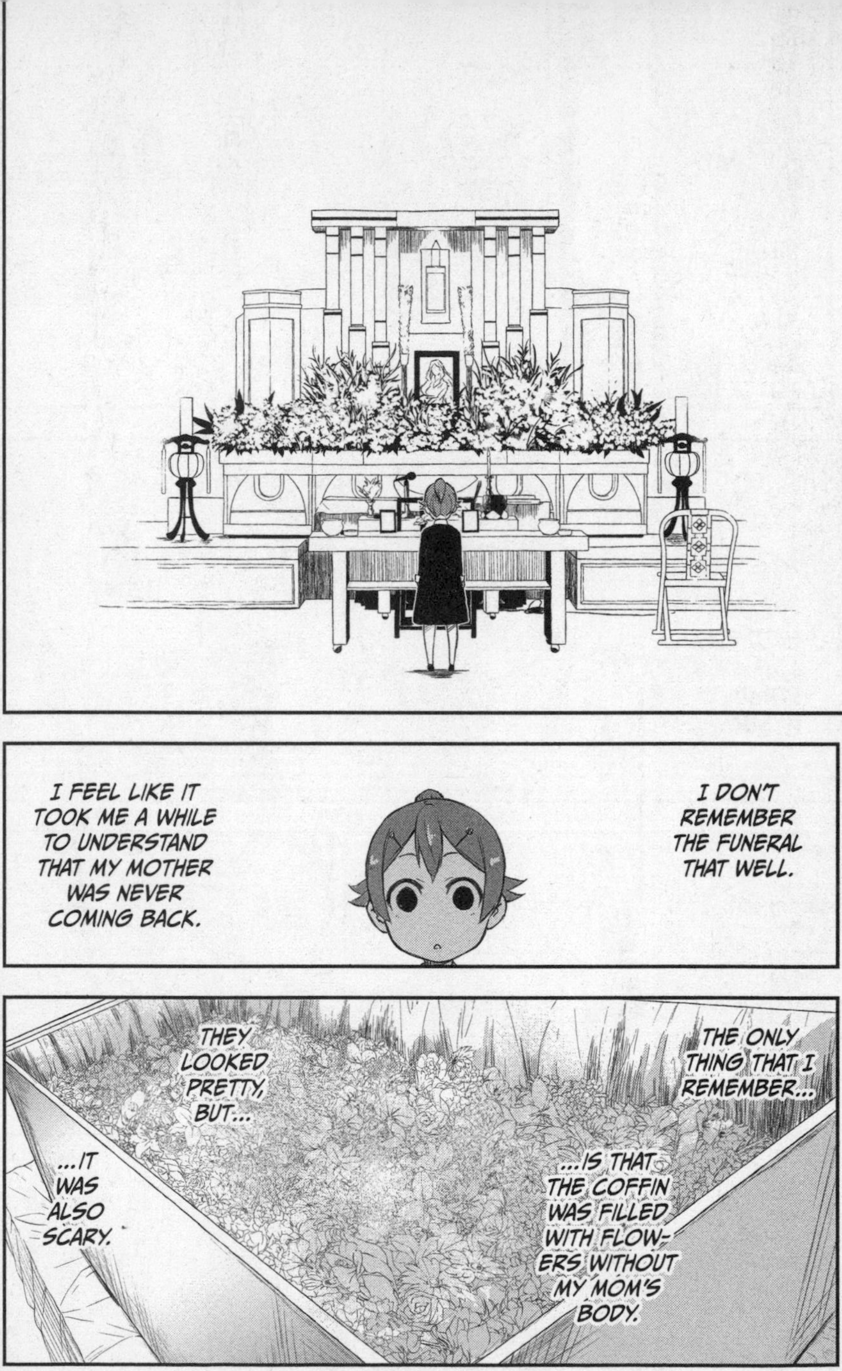
I DON'T REMEMBER THE FUNERAL THAT WELL.
I FEEL LIKE IT TOOK ME A WHILE TO UNDERSTAND THAT MY MOTHER WAS NEVER COMING BACK.
THE ONLY THING THAT I REMEMBER...
...IS THAT THE COFFIN WAS FILLED WITH FLOWERS WITHOUT MY MOM'S BODY.
THEY LOOKED PRETTY, BUT...
...IT WAS ALSO SCARY.

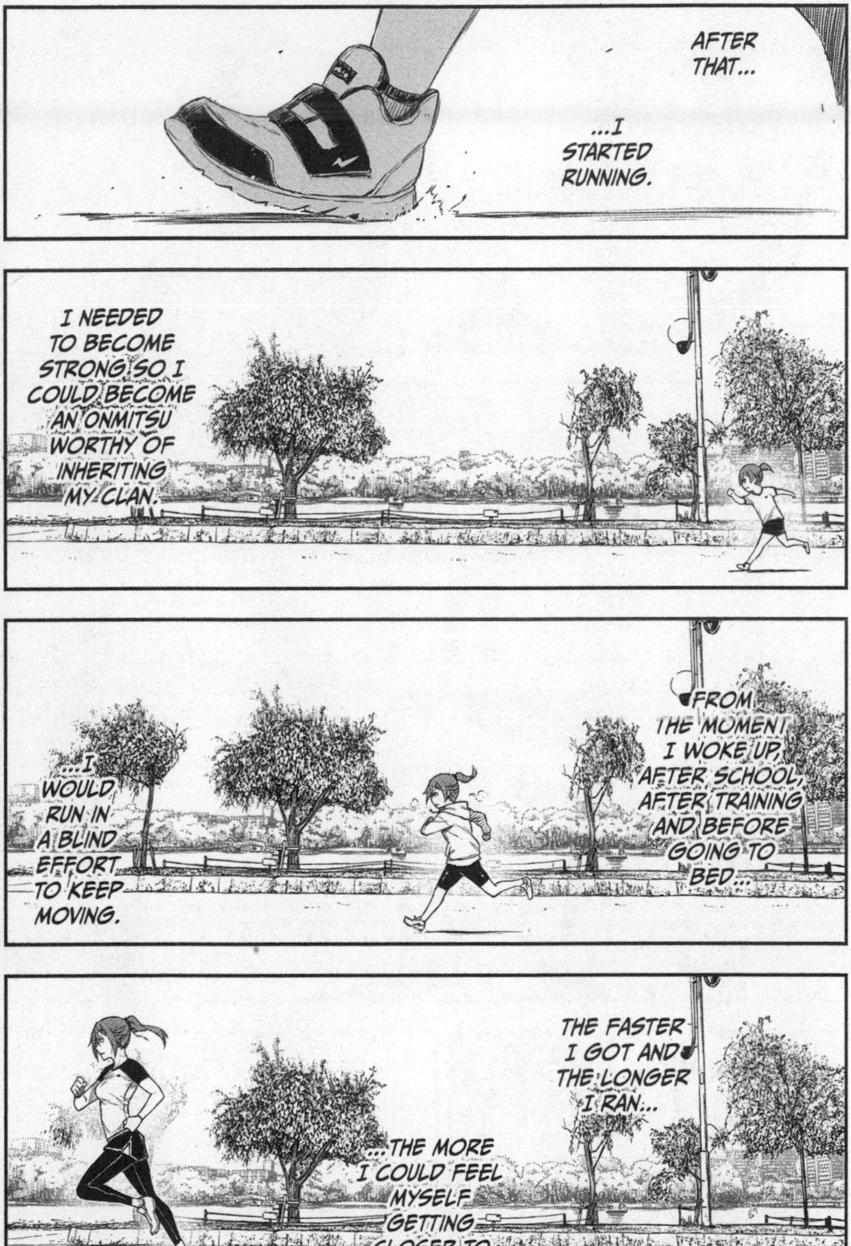
AFTER THAT...
...I STARTED RUNNING.
I NEEDED TO BECOME STRONG SO I COULD BECOME AN ONMITSU WORTHY OF INHERITING MY CLAN.
FROM THE MOMENT I WOKE UP, AFTER SCHOOL, AFTER TRAINING AND BEFORE GOING TO BED...
...I WOULD RUN IN A BLIND EFFORT TO KEEP MOVING.
THE FASTER I GOT AND THE LONGER I RAN...
...THE MORE I COULD FEEL MYSELF GETTING CLOSER TO MY MOM.

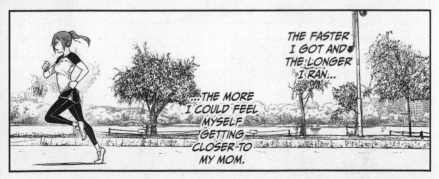

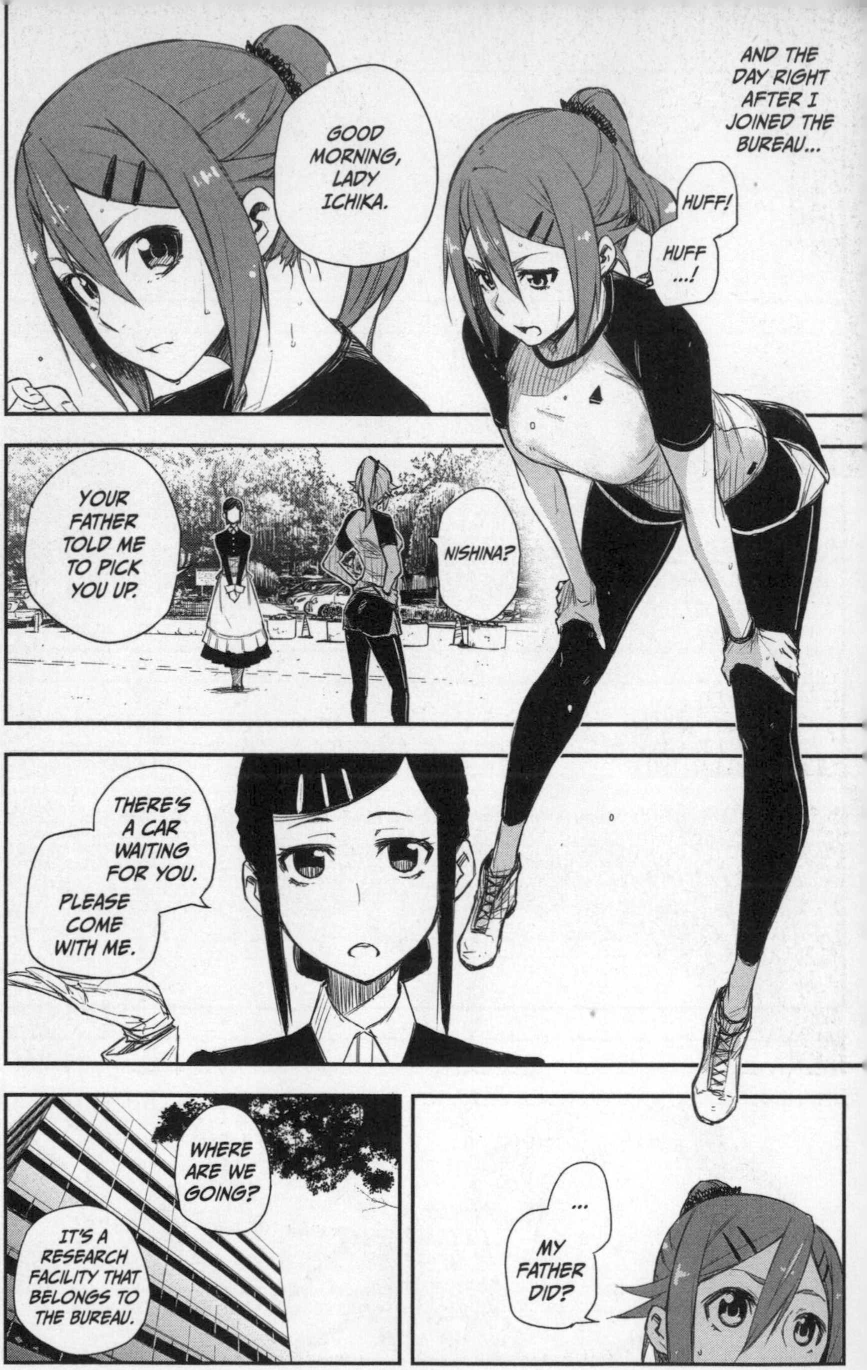
AND THE DAY RIGHT AFTER I JOINED THE BUREAU...
HUFF!
HUFF ...!
GOOD MORNING, LADY ICHIKA.
NISHINA?
YOUR FATHER TOLD ME TO PICK YOU UP.
THERE'S A CAR WAITING FOR YOU.
PLEASE COME WITH ME.
...
MY FATHER DID?
WHERE ARE WE GOING?
IT'S A RESEARCH FACILITY THAT BELONGS TO THE BUREAU.

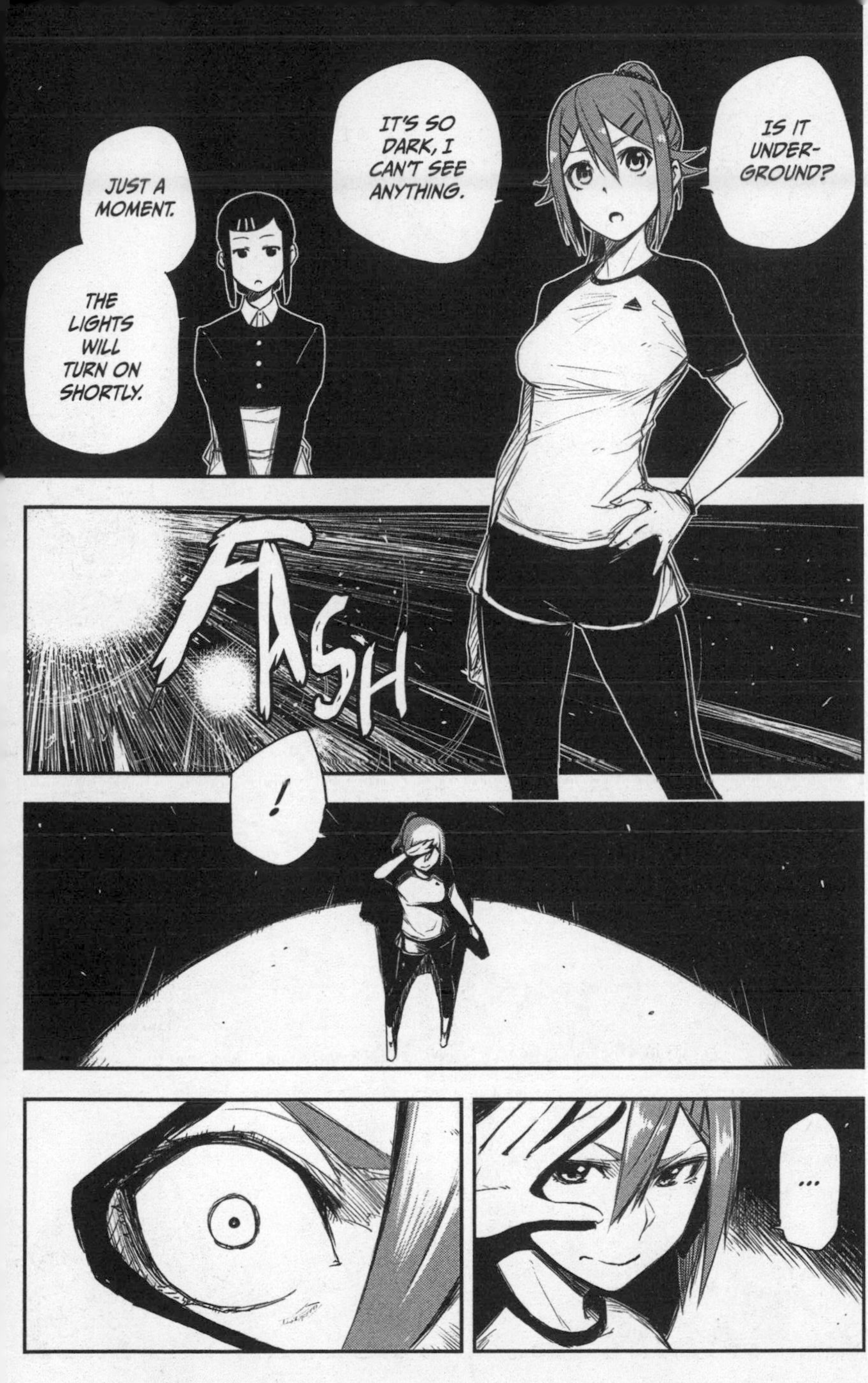
IS IT UNDER-GROUND?
IT'S SO DARK, I CAN'T SEE ANYTHING.
JUST A MOMENT.
THE LIGHTS WILL TURN ON SHORTLY.
FASH
!
...

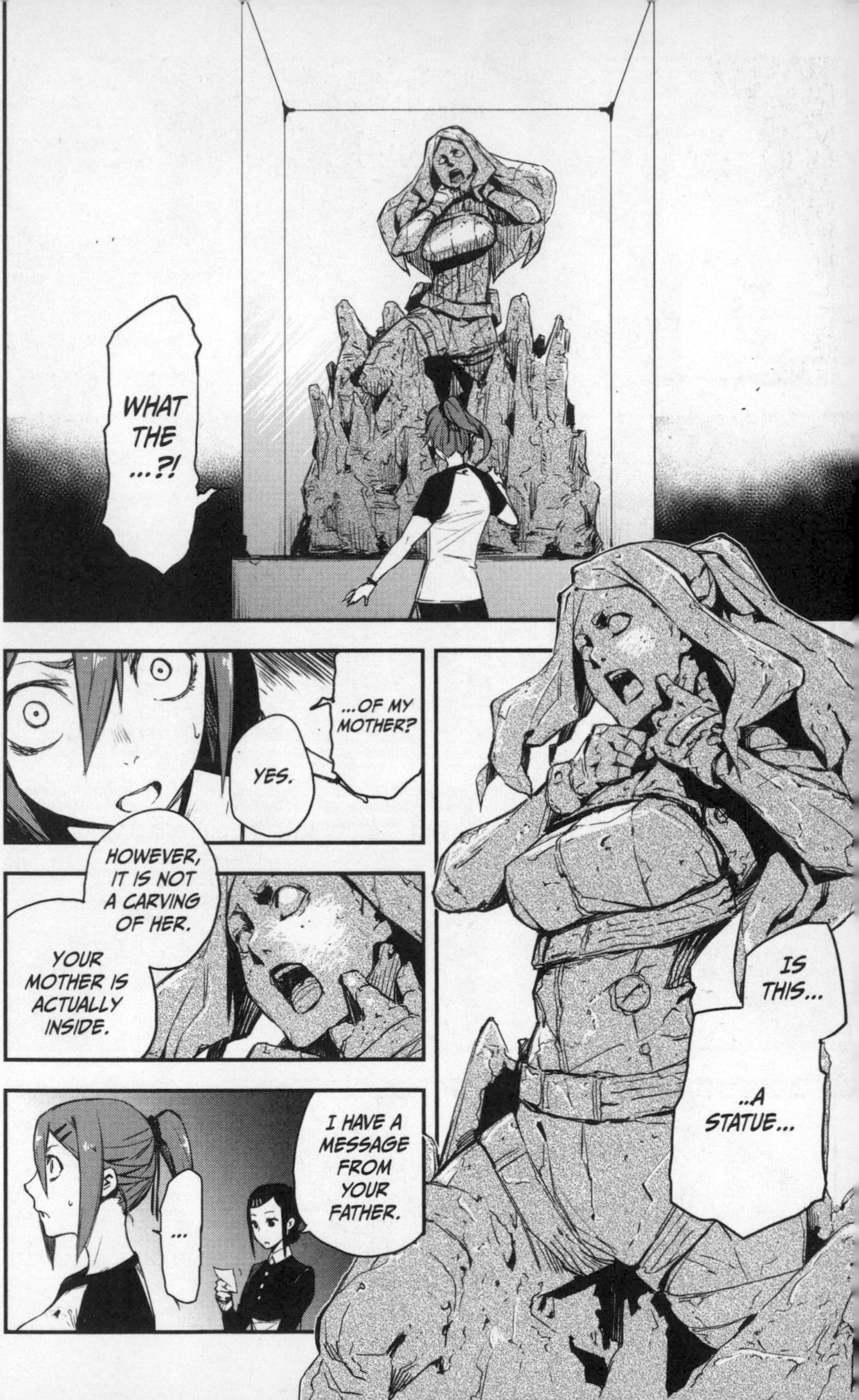
WHAT THE ...?!
IS THIS...
...A STATUE...
...OF MY MOTHER?
YES.
HOWEVER, IT IS NOT A CARVING OF HER.
YOUR MOTHER IS ACTUALLY INSIDE.
I HAVE A MESSAGE FROM YOUR FATHER.
...

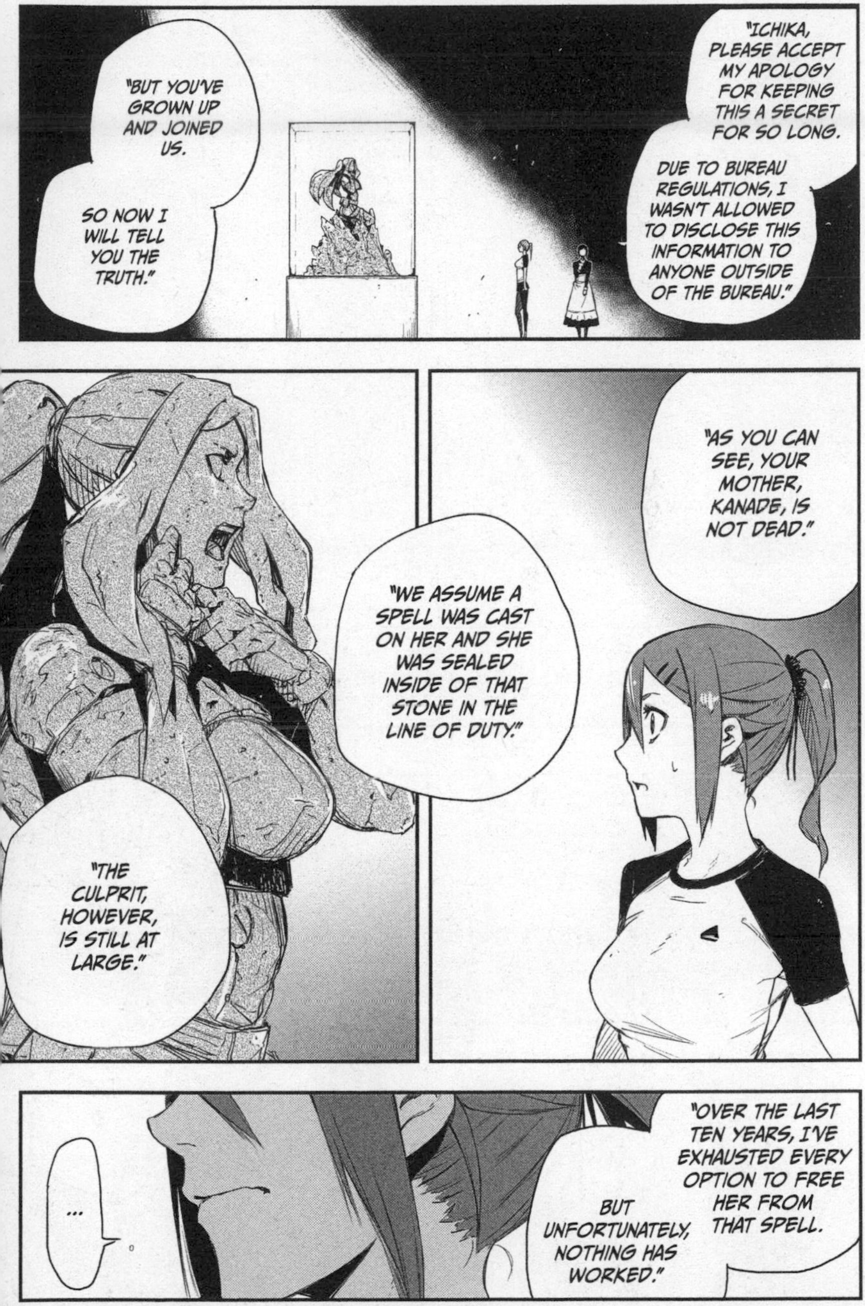
"ICHIKA, PLEASE ACCEPT MY APOLOGY FOR KEEPING THIS A SECRET FOR SO LONG.
DUE TO BUREAU REGULATIONS, I WASN'T ALLOWED TO DISCLOSE THIS INFORMATION TO ANYONE OUTSIDE OF THE BUREAU."
"BUT YOU'VE GROWN UP AND JOINED US.
SO NOW I WILL TELL YOU THE TRUTH."
"AS YOU CAN SEE, YOUR MOTHER, KANADE, IS NOT DEAD."
"WE ASSUME A SPELL WAS CAST ON HER AND SHE WAS SEALED INSIDE OF THAT STONE IN THE LINE OF DUTY."
"THE CULPRIT, HOWEVER, IS STILL AT LARGE."
"OVER THE LAST TEN YEARS, I'VE EXHAUSTED EVERY OPTION TO FREE HER FROM THAT SPELL.
BUT UNFORTUNATELY, NOTHING HAS WORKED."
...

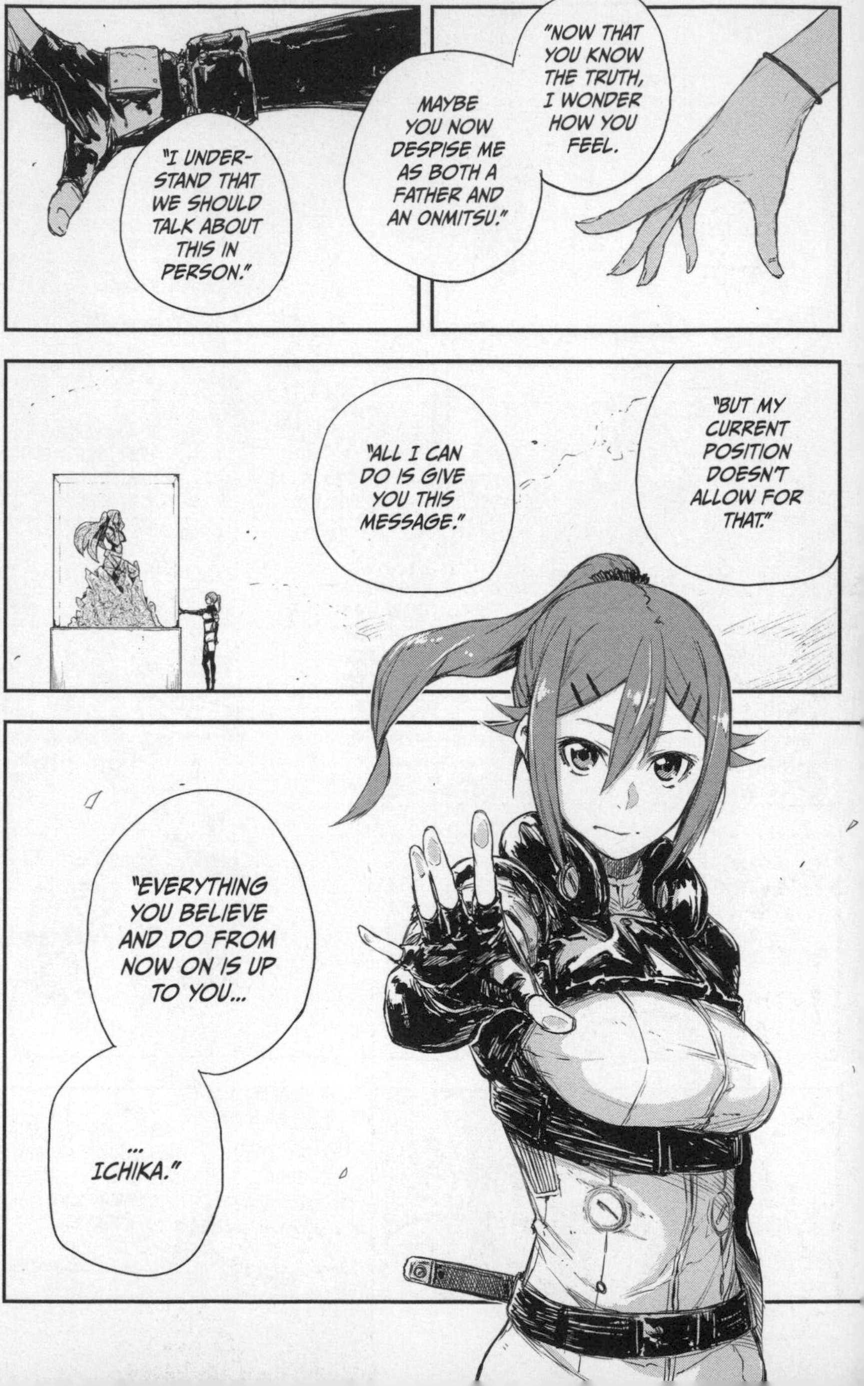
"NOW THAT YOU KNOW THE TRUTH, I WONDER HOW YOU FEEL.
MAYBE YOU NOW DESPISE ME AS BOTH A FATHER AND AN ONMITSU."
"I UNDER-STAND THAT WE SHOULD TALK ABOUT THIS IN PERSON."
"BUT MY CURRENT POSITION DOESN'T ALLOW FOR THAT."
"ALL I CAN DO IS GIVE YOU THIS MESSAGE."
"EVERYTHING YOU BELIEVE AND DO FROM NOW ON IS UP TO YOU...
... ICHIKA."

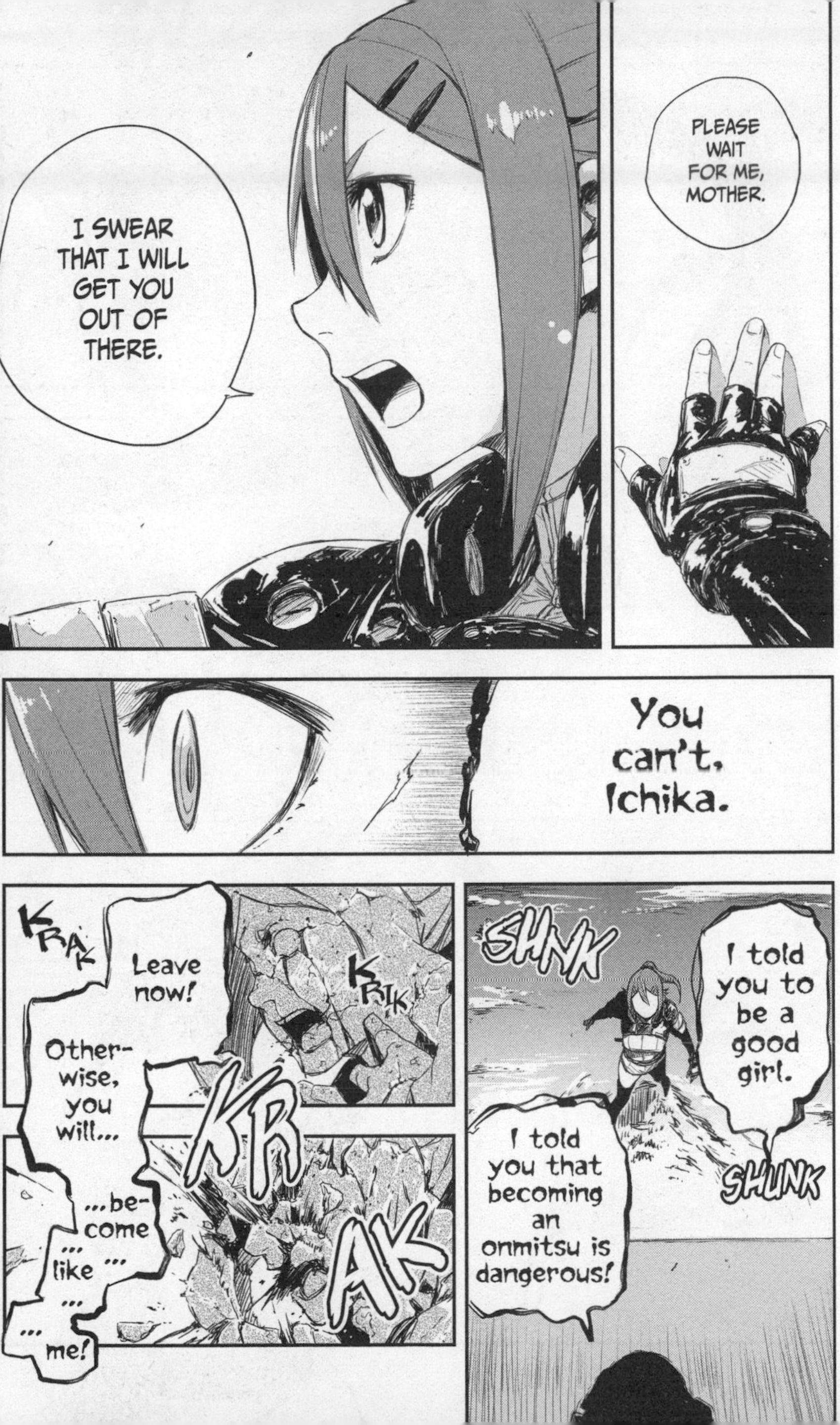
PLEASE WAIT FOR ME, MOTHER.
I SWEAR THAT I WILL GET YOU OUT OF THERE.
You can't, Ichika.
SHNK
I told you to be a good girl.
SHUNK
I told you that becoming an onmitsu is dangerous!
KRAK
Leave now!
KRIK
Other-wise, you will...
KRAK
...be-come ... like ... ...me!

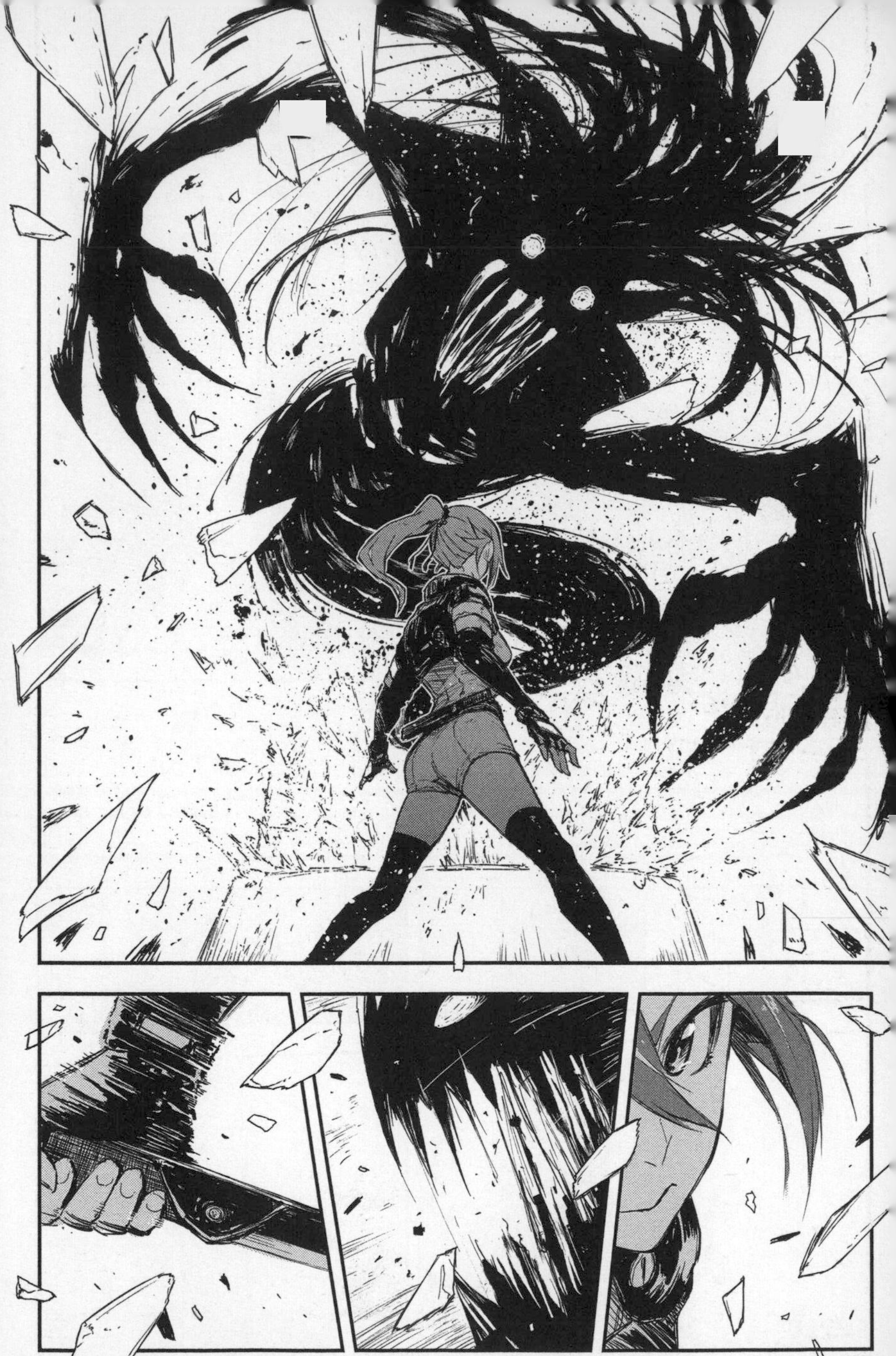

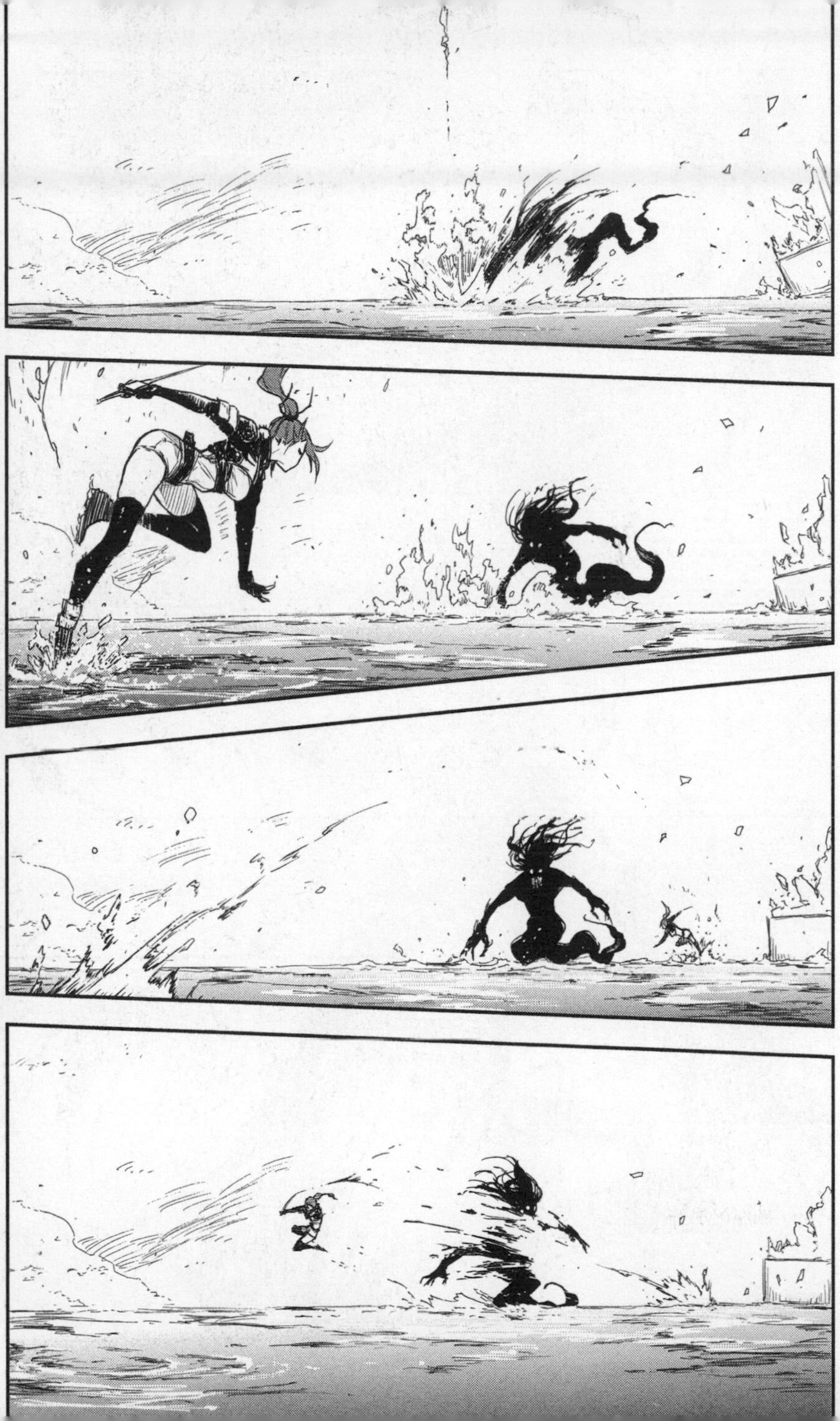

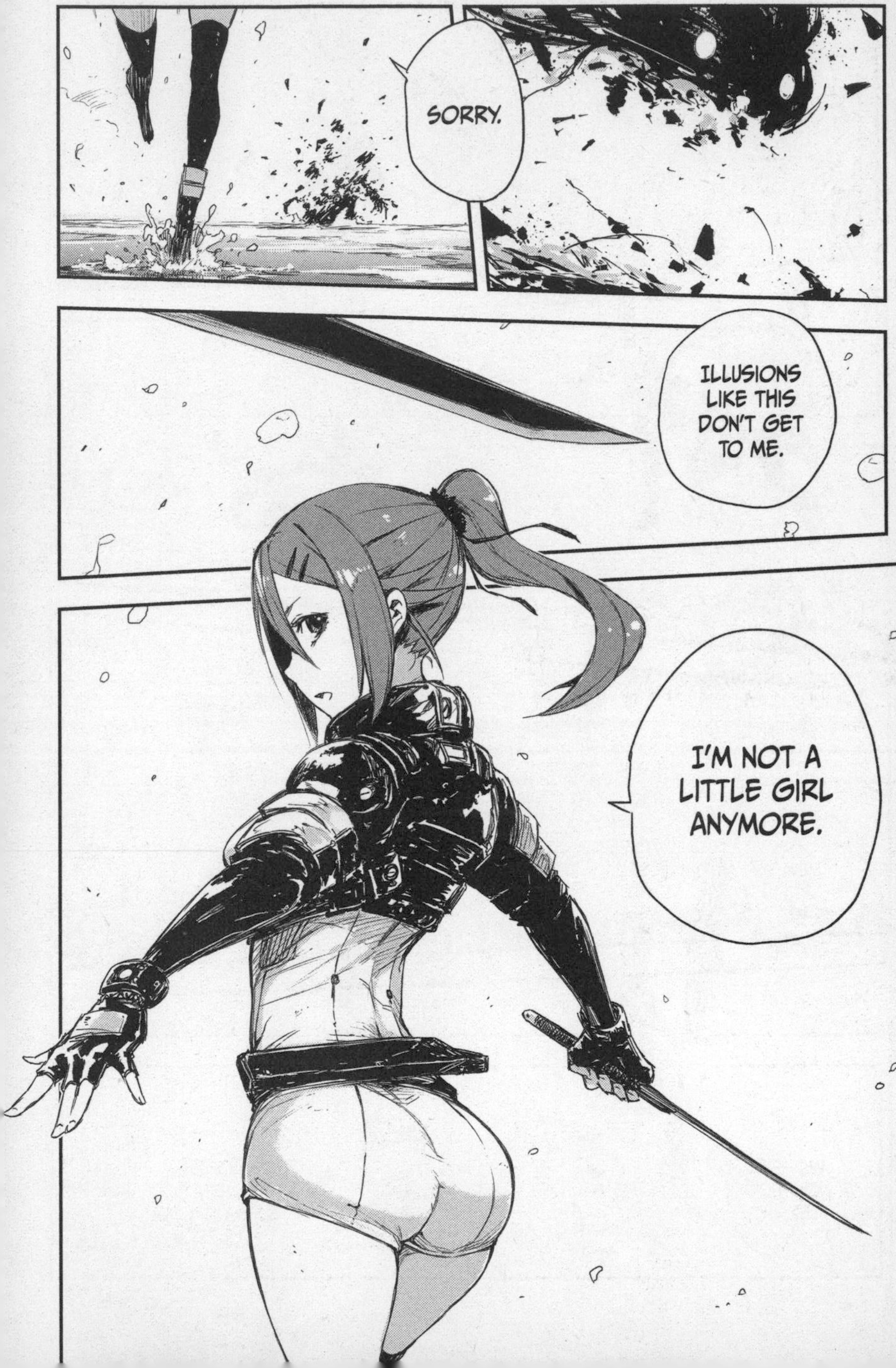
SORRY.
ILLUSIONS LIKE THIS DON'T GET TO ME.
I'M NOT A LITTLE GIRL ANYMORE.

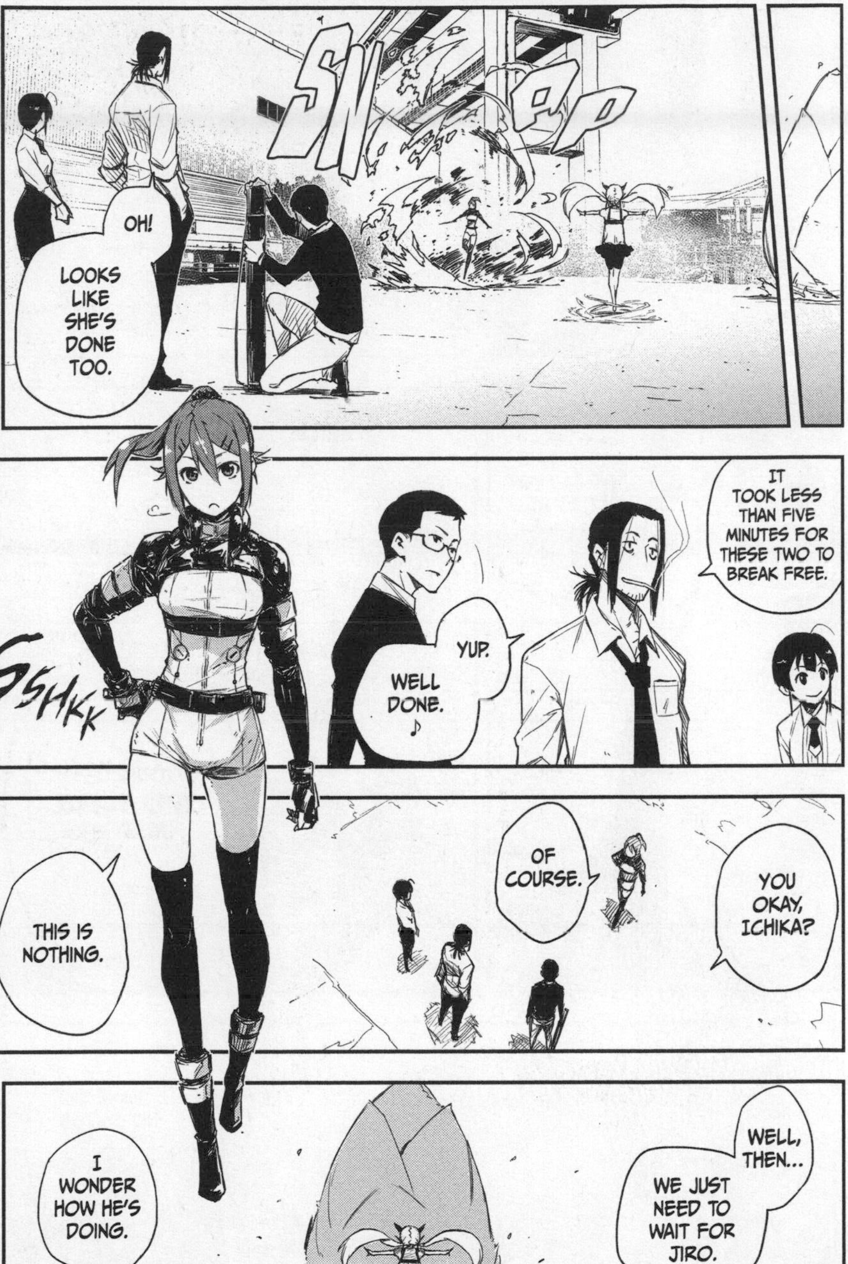
SNAP
OH!
LOOKS LIKE SHE'S DONE TOO.
IT TOOK LESS THAN FIVE MINUTES FOR THESE TWO TO BREAK FREE.
YUP.
WELL DONE. ♪
SSHKK
YOU OKAY, ICHIKA?
OF COURSE.
THIS IS NOTHING.
WELL, THEN...
WE JUST NEED TO WAIT FOR JIRO.
I WONDER HOW HE'S DOING.

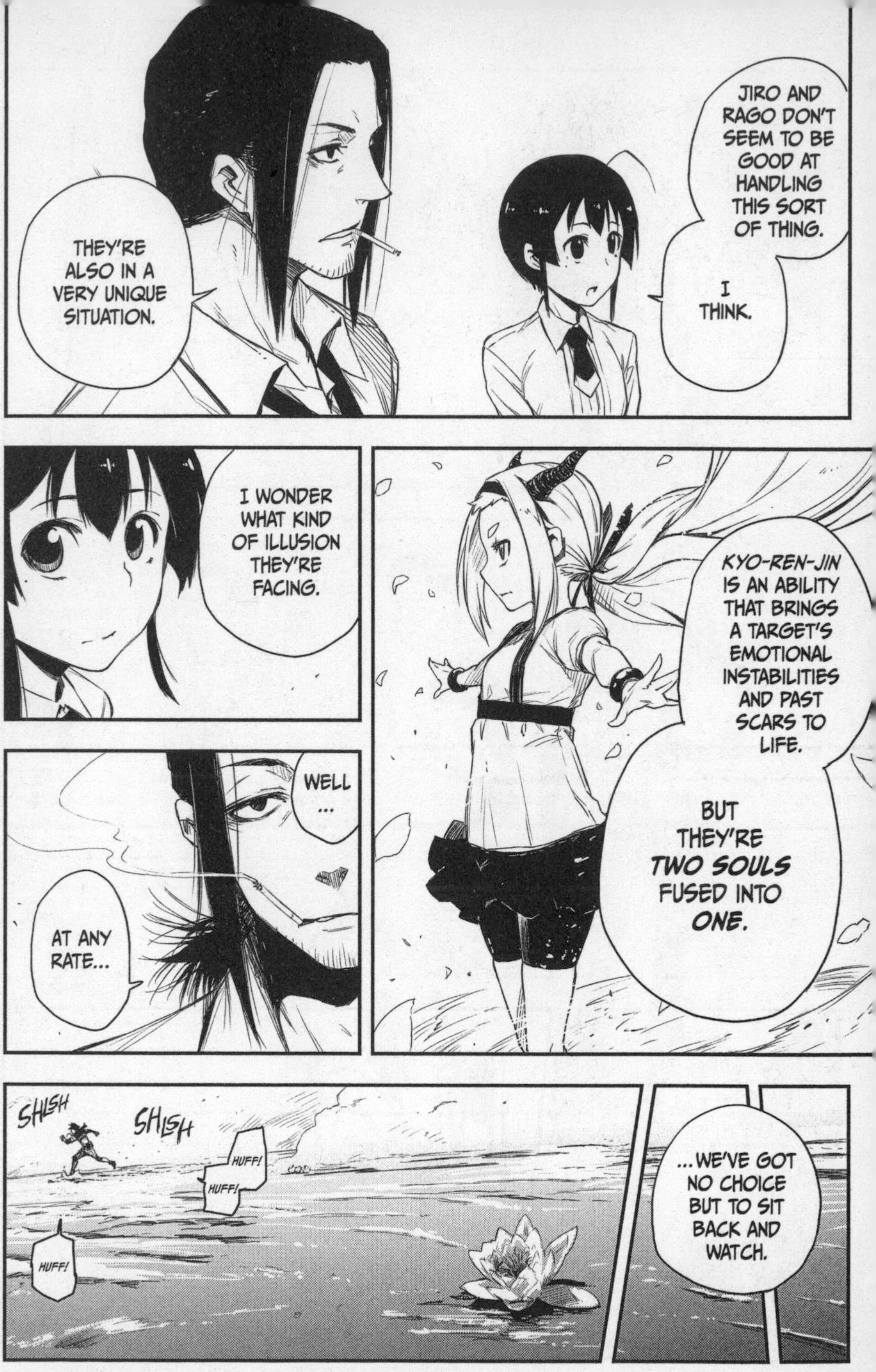
JIRO AND RAGO DON'T SEEM TO BE GOOD AT HANDLING THIS SORT OF THING.
I THINK.
THEY'RE ALSO IN A VERY UNIQUE SITUATION.
KYO-REN-JIN IS AN ABILITY THAT BRINGS A TARGET'S EMOTIONAL INSTABILITIES AND PAST SCARS TO LIFE.
BUT THEY'RE ***TWO SOULS*** FUSED INTO ***ONE***.
I WONDER WHAT KIND OF ILLUSION THEY'RE FACING.
WELL...
AT ANY RATE...
...WE'VE GOT NO CHOICE BUT TO SIT BACK AND WATCH.
SHLSH
SHLSH
HUFF!
HUFF!
HUFF!

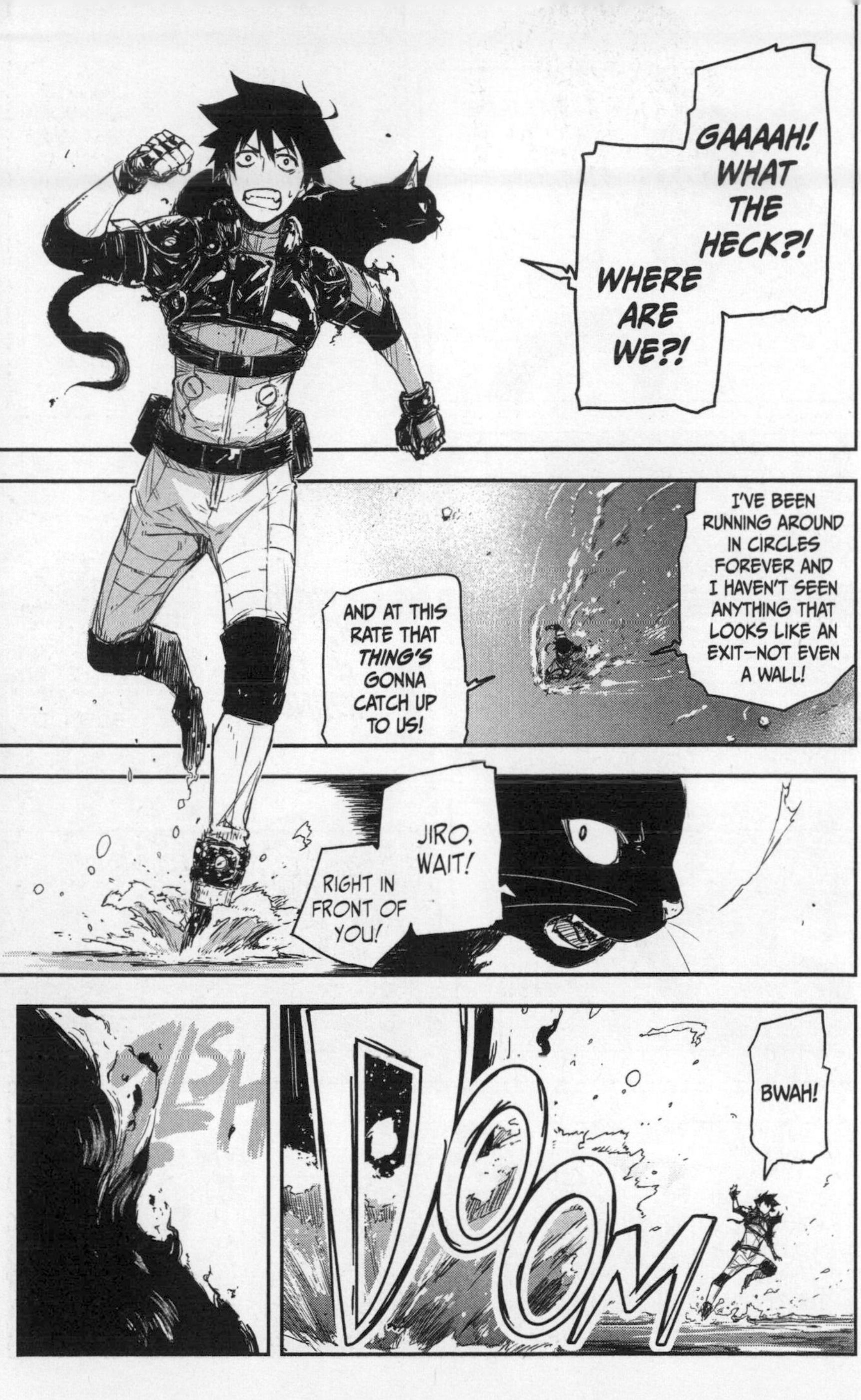
GAAAAH! WHAT THE HECK?! WHERE ARE WE?!
I'VE BEEN RUNNING AROUND IN CIRCLES FOREVER AND I HAVEN'T SEEN ANYTHING THAT LOOKS LIKE AN EXIT—NOT EVEN A WALL!
AND AT THIS RATE THAT *THING'S* GONNA CATCH UP TO US!
JIRO, WAIT!
RIGHT IN FRONT OF YOU!
BWAH!
DOOM

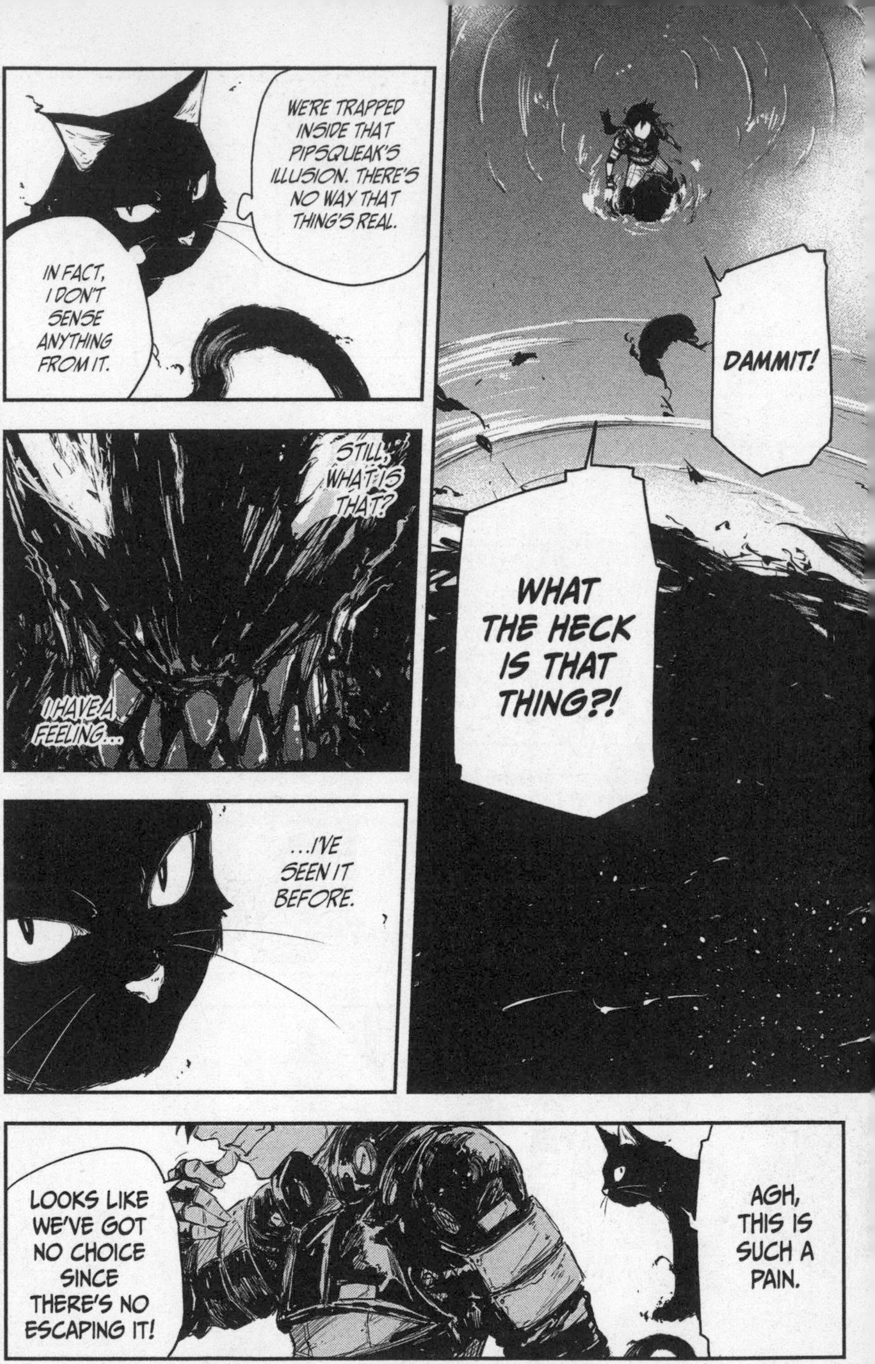
DAMMIT!
WHAT THE HECK IS THAT THING?!
WE'RE TRAPPED INSIDE THAT PIPSQUEAK'S ILLUSION. THERE'S NO WAY THAT THING'S REAL.
IN FACT, I DON'T SENSE ANYTHING FROM IT.
STILL, WHAT IS THAT?
I HAVE A FEELING...
...I'VE SEEN IT BEFORE.
AGH, THIS IS SUCH A PAIN.
LOOKS LIKE WE'VE GOT NO CHOICE SINCE THERE'S NO ESCAPING IT!

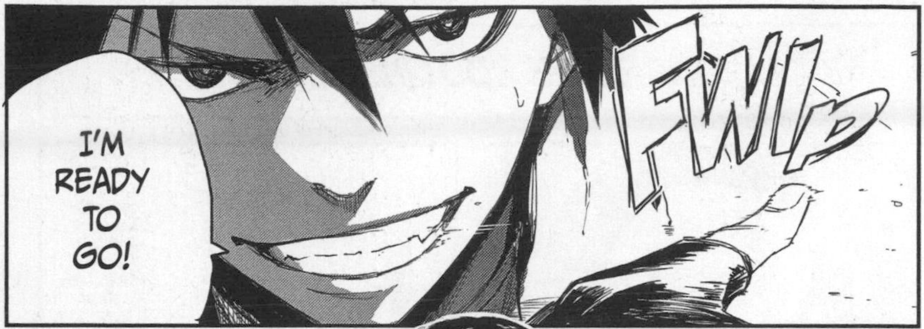
FWIP
I'M READY TO GO!

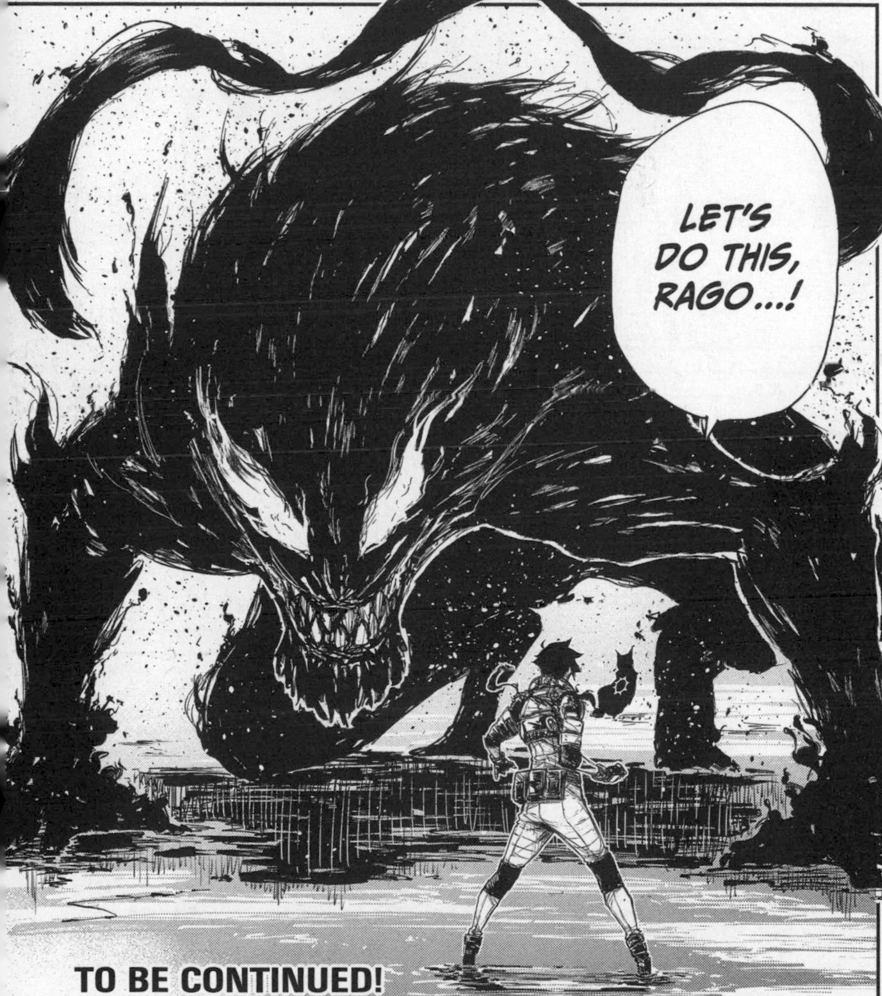
LET'S DO THIS, RAGO...!
TO BE CONTINUED!

MORNING ROUTINE: JIRO

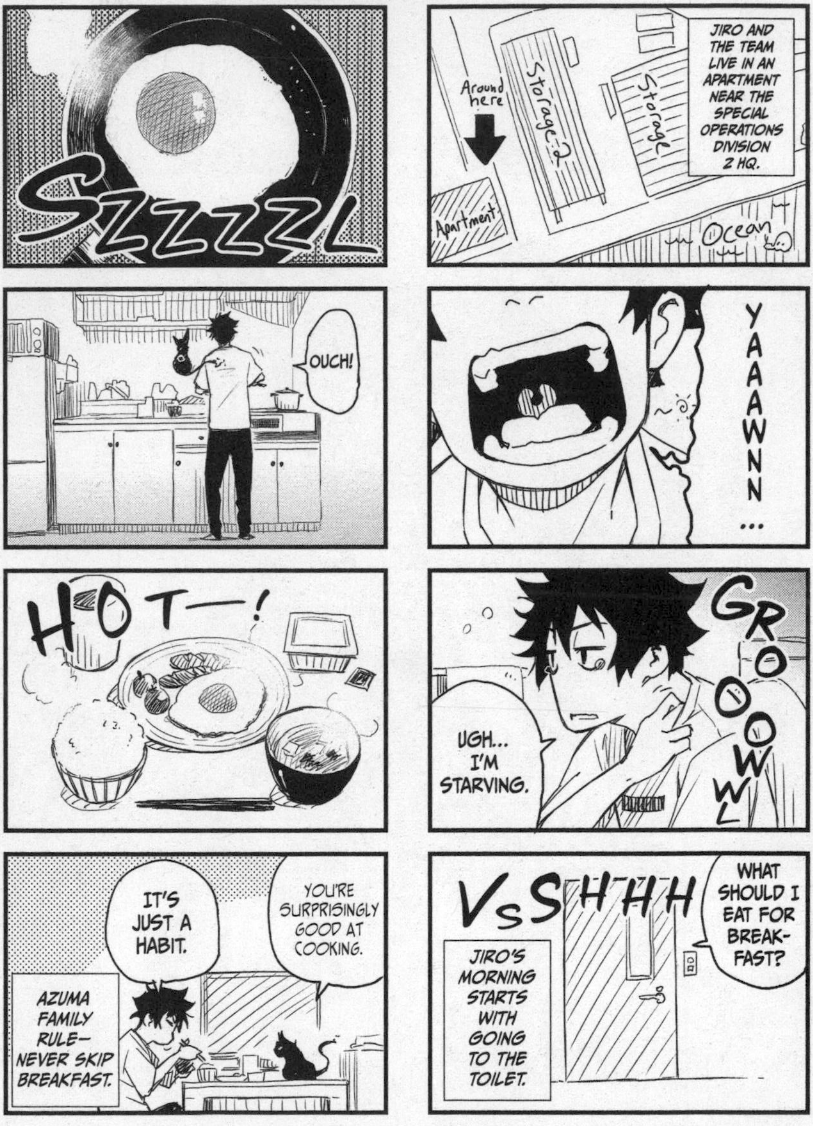
JIRO AND THE TEAM LIVE IN AN APARTMENT NEAR THE SPECIAL OPERATIONS DIVISION 2 HQ.
Storage
Storage 2
Around here
Apartment
Ocean
YAAAWNN...
GROOOOWL
UGH... I'M STARVING.
WHAT SHOULD I EAT FOR BREAK-FAST?
VSSHHH
JIRO'S MORNING STARTS WITH GOING TO THE TOILET.
SZZZZL
OUCH!
HOT—!
YOU'RE SURPRISINGLY GOOD AT COOKING.
IT'S JUST A HABIT.
AZUMA FAMILY RULE—NEVER SKIP BREAKFAST.

MORNING ROUTINE: ICHIKA

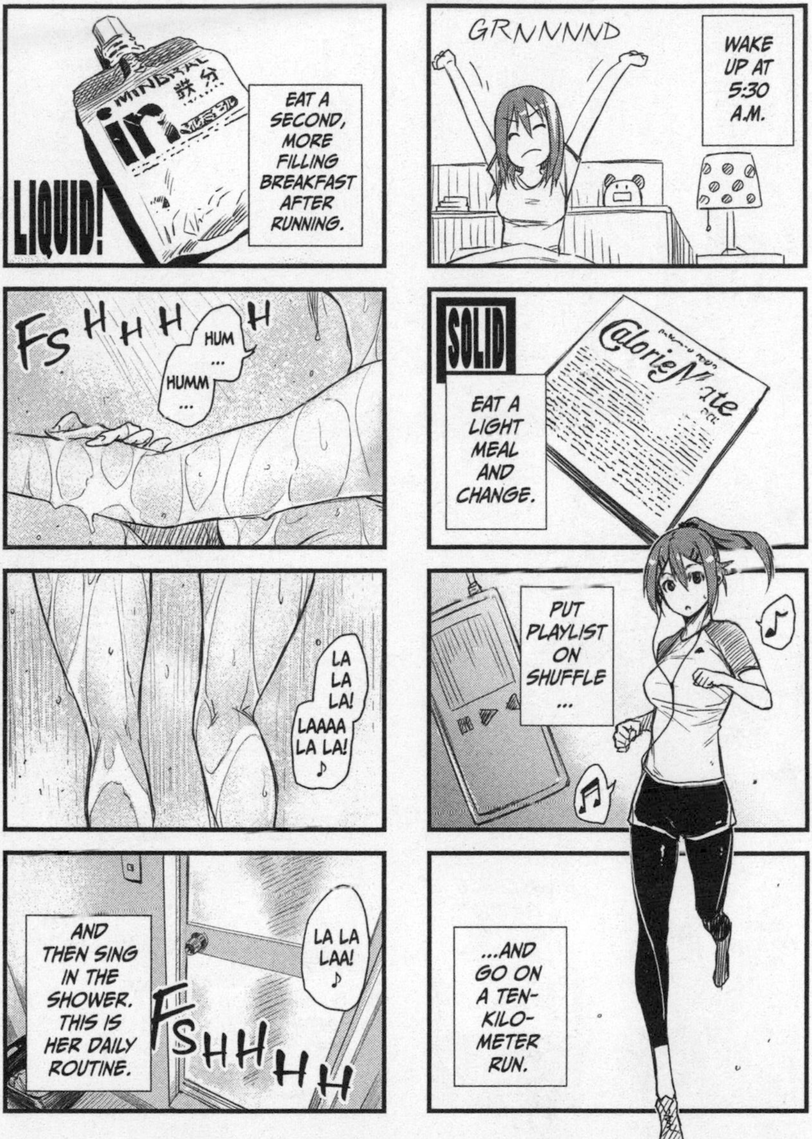
WAKE UP AT 5:30 A.M.
GRNNNND
SOLID
EAT A LIGHT MEAL AND CHANGE.
PUT PLAYLIST ON SHUFFLE ...
...AND GO ON A TEN-KILOMETER RUN.
EAT A SECOND, MORE FILLING BREAKFAST AFTER RUNNING.
MINERAL
in
LIQUID!
HUM ... HUMM ...
FSHHHHH
LA LA LA! LAAAA LA LA! ♪
LA LA LAA! ♪
AND THEN SING IN THE SHOWER. THIS IS HER DAILY ROUTINE.
FSHHHHH

MORNING ROUTINE: REIJI

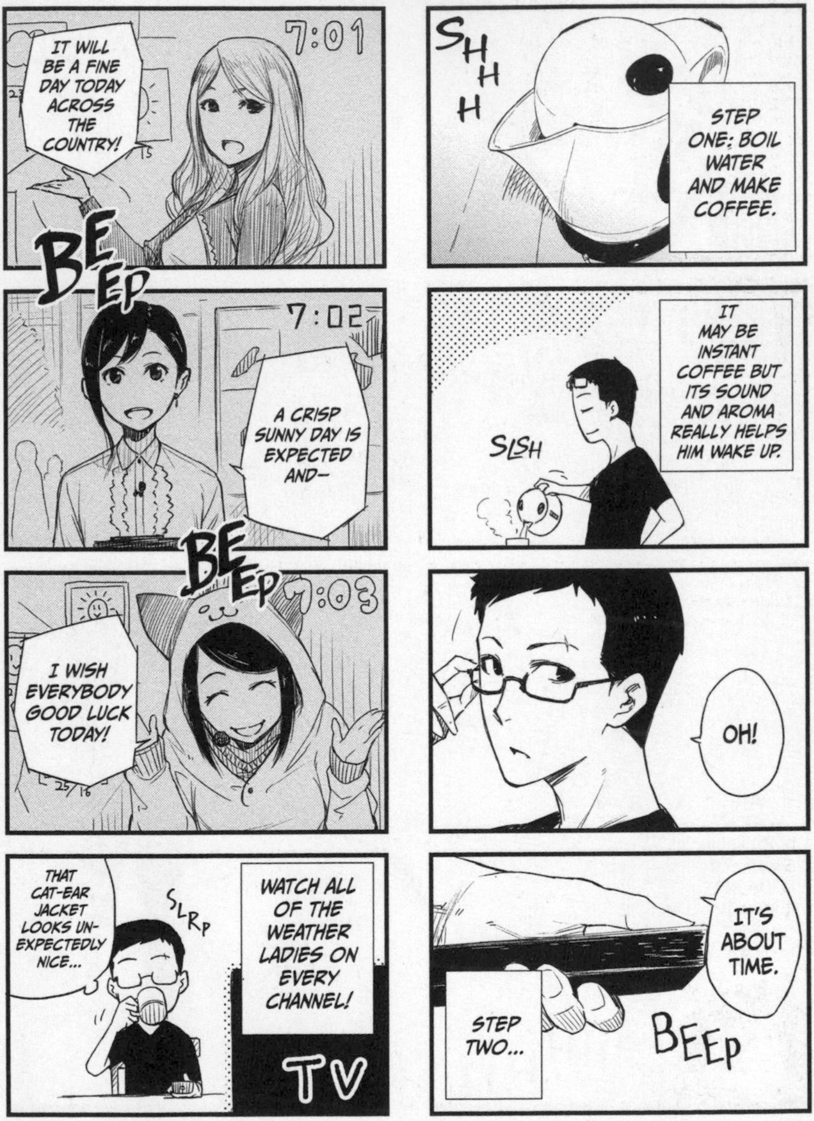
SHHH
STEP ONE: BOIL WATER AND MAKE COFFEE.
IT MAY BE INSTANT COFFEE BUT ITS SOUND AND AROMA REALLY HELPS HIM WAKE UP.
SLSH
OH!
IT'S ABOUT TIME.
BEEP
STEP TWO...
7:01
IT WILL BE A FINE DAY TODAY ACROSS THE COUNTRY!
BEEP
7:02
A CRISP SUNNY DAY IS EXPECTED AND—
BEEP
7:03
I WISH EVERYBODY GOOD LUCK TODAY!
WATCH ALL OF THE WEATHER LADIES ON EVERY CHANNEL!
TV
THAT CAT-EAR JACKET LOOKS UN-EXPECTEDLY NICE...
SLRP

MORNING ROUTINE: SHIBA

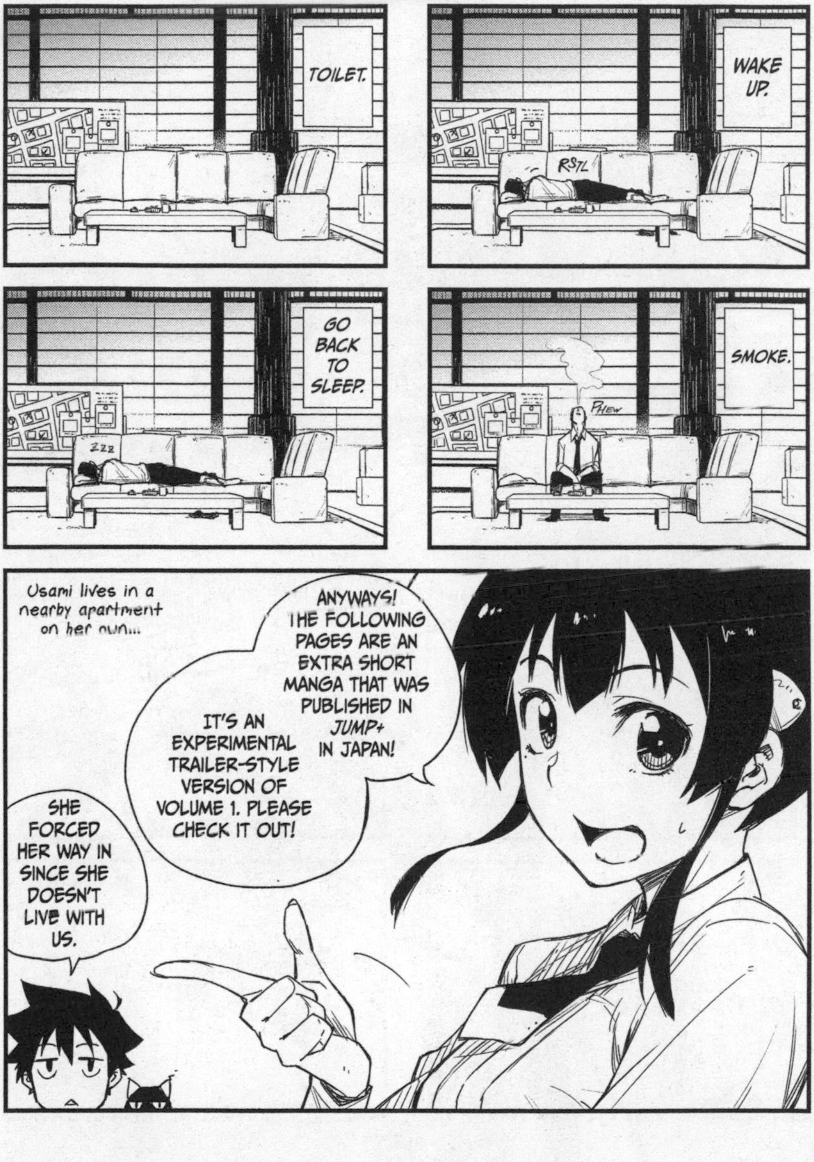

WAKE UP.
RSTL
TOILET.
SMOKE.
PHEW
GO BACK TO SLEEP.
ZZZ
ANYWAYS! THE FOLLOWING PAGES ARE AN EXTRA SHORT MANGA THAT WAS PUBLISHED IN JUMP+ IN JAPAN!
IT'S AN EXPERIMENTAL TRAILER-STYLE VERSION OF VOLUME 1. PLEASE CHECK IT OUT!
Usami lives in a nearby apartment on her own...
SHE FORCED HER WAY IN SINCE SHE DOESN'T LIVE WITH US.

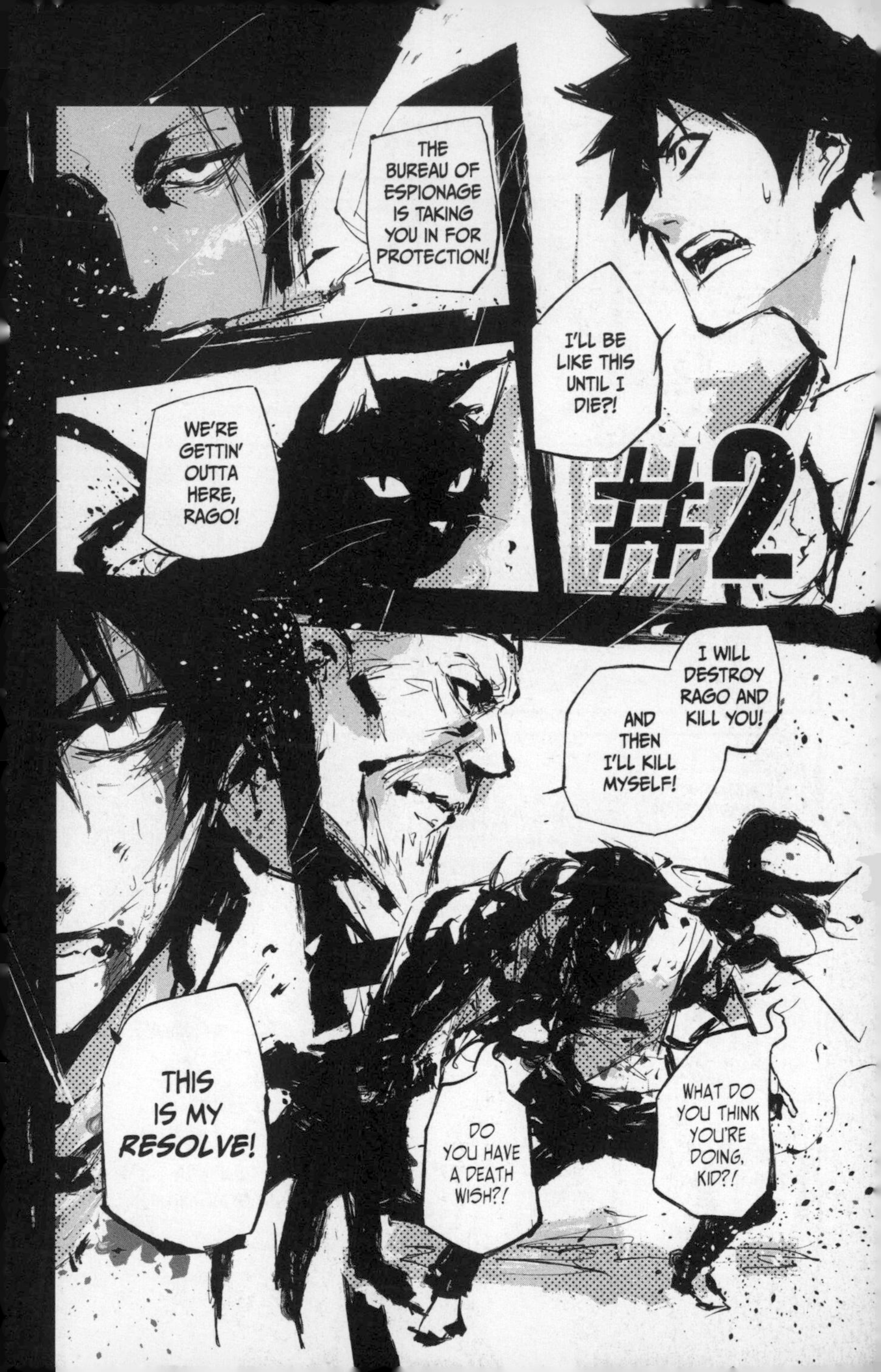
I'LL BE LIKE THIS UNTIL I DIE?!
#2
THE BUREAU OF ESPIONAGE IS TAKING YOU IN FOR PROTECTION!
WE'RE GETTIN' OUTTA HERE, RAGO!
I WILL DESTROY RAGO AND KILL YOU!
AND THEN I'LL KILL MYSELF!
WHAT DO YOU THINK YOU'RE DOING, KID?!
DO YOU HAVE A DEATH WISH?!
THIS IS MY *RESOLVE*!

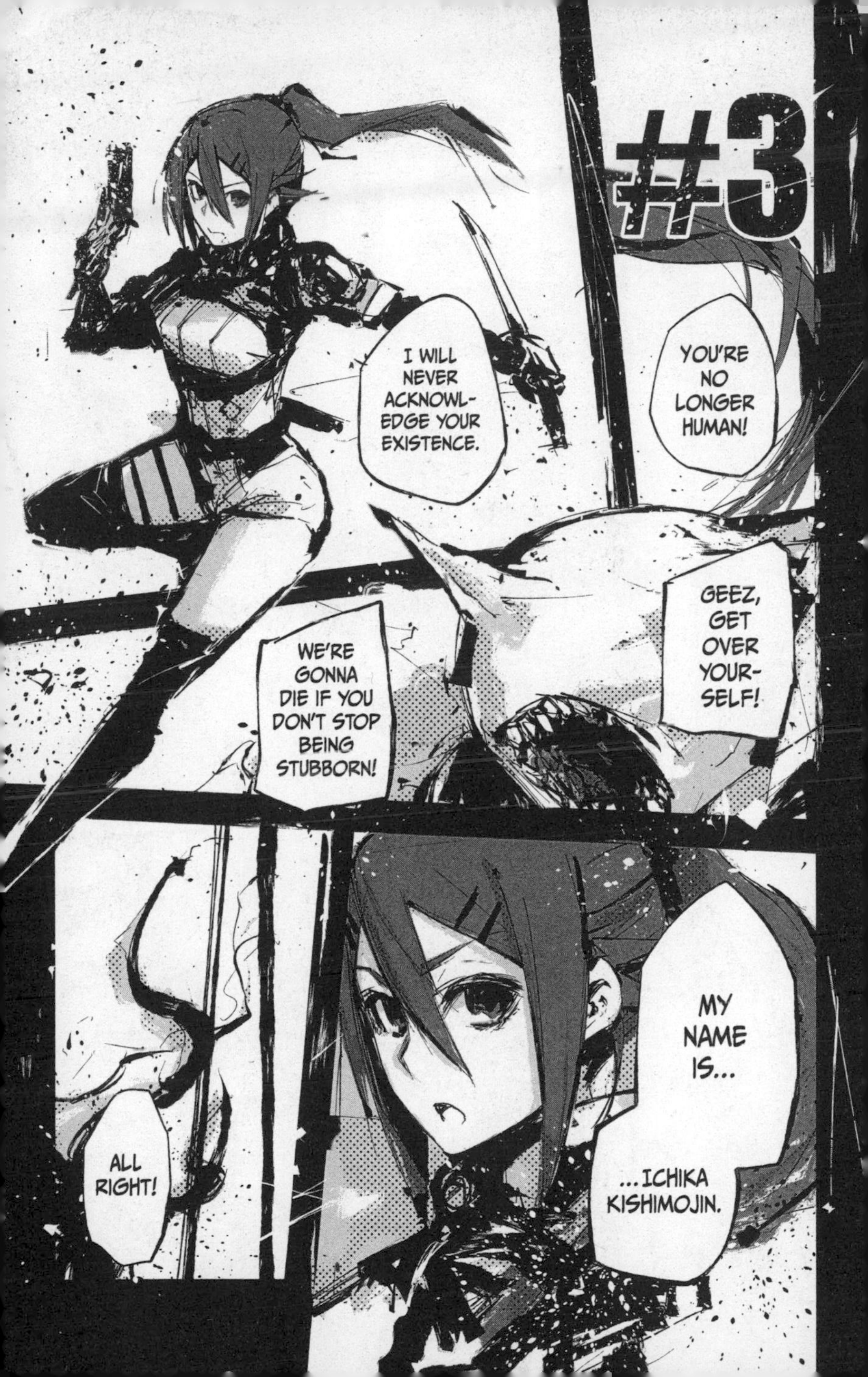
#3
YOU'RE NO LONGER HUMAN!
I WILL NEVER ACKNOWLEDGE YOUR EXISTENCE.
GEEZ, GET OVER YOURSELF!
WE'RE GONNA DIE IF YOU DON'T STOP BEING STUBBORN!
MY NAME IS...
...ICHIKA KISHIMOJIN.
ALL RIGHT!

BLACK TORCH

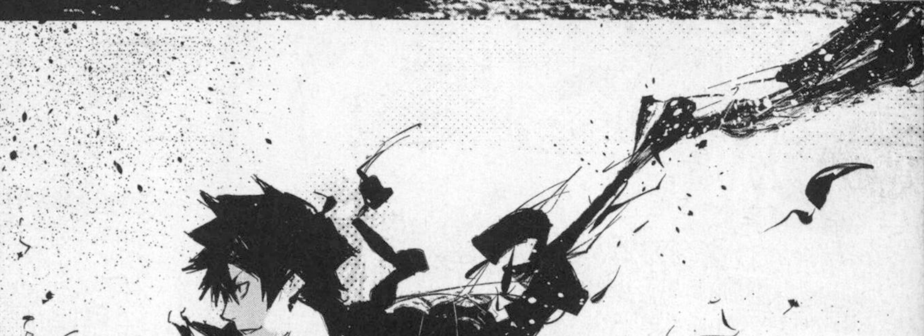
LET'S DO THIS, PARTNER!

Check out Volume 1!

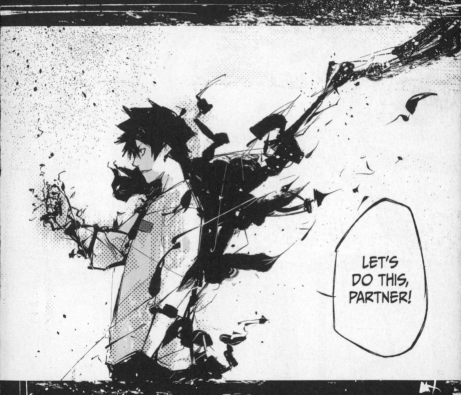

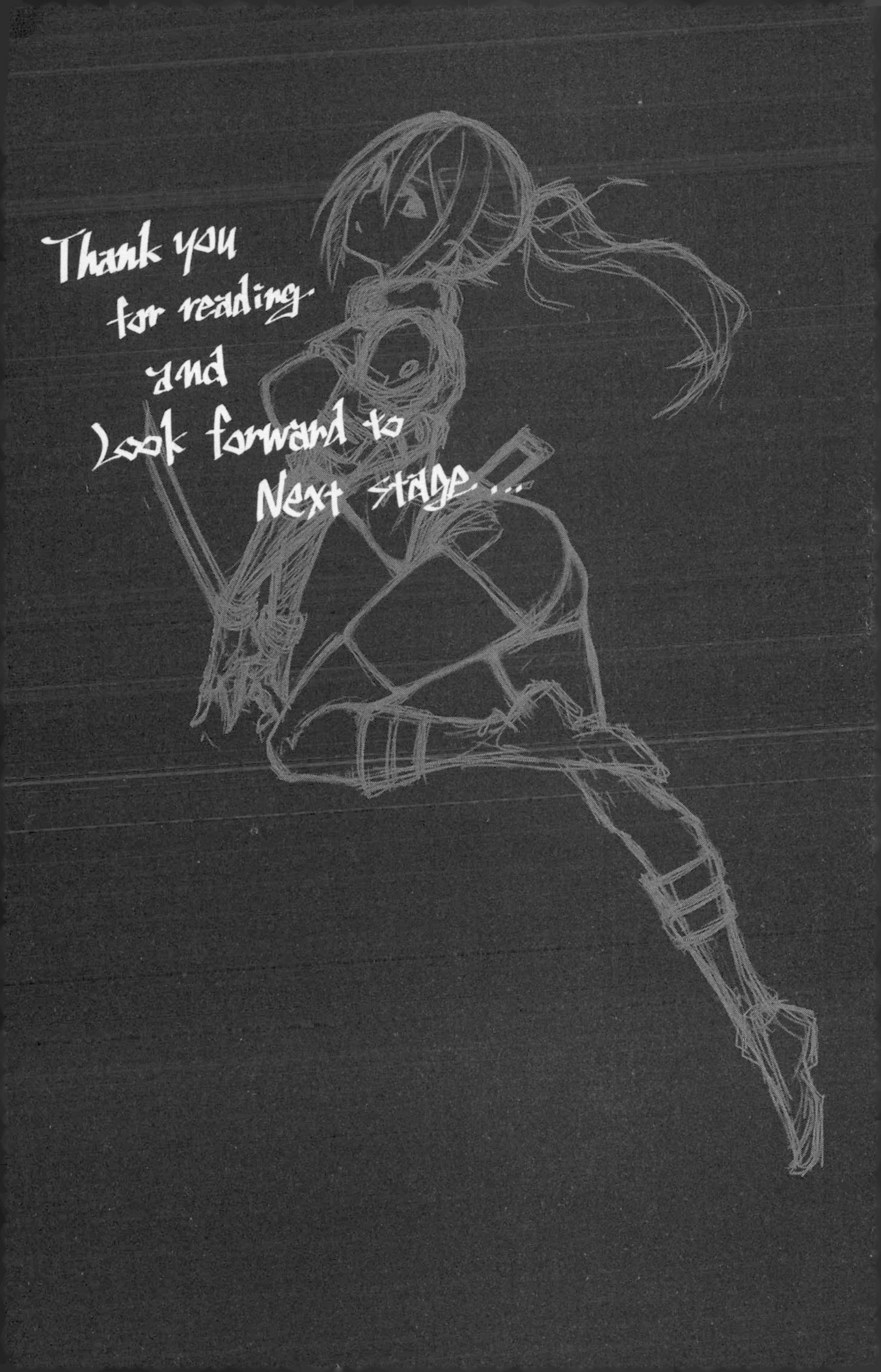
Thank you
for reading
and
Look forward to
Next stage...

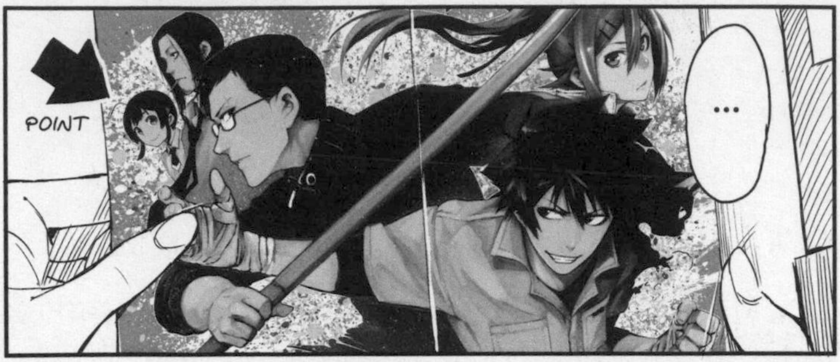
...
POINT

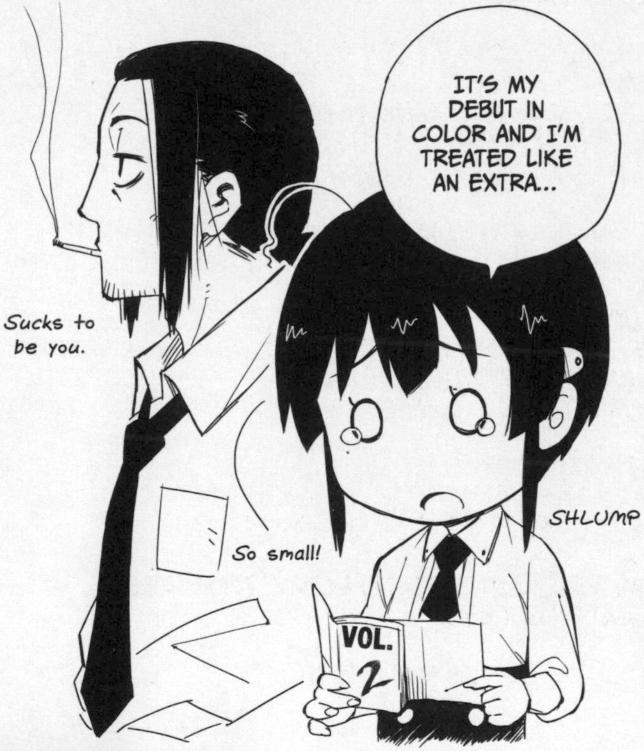
IT'S MY DEBUT IN COLOR AND I'M TREATED LIKE AN EXTRA...
Sucks to be you.
SHLUMP
So small!
VOL. 2

BLACK TORCH 2

STORY & ART
TSUYOSHI TAKAKI

POORLY WRITTEN AFTERWORD!

IT'S NICE TO SEE YOU AGAIN! THANK YOU FOR MAKING YOUR WAY TO THE END OF THE BOOK!

TIME FLEW BY AND WE'RE ALREADY AT VOLUME 2! HALF A YEAR HAS PASSED SINCE THE SERIES STARTED AND A LOT OF THINGS HAVE CHANGED. ONE MAJOR CHANGE IS ALL THE FEEDBACK I'VE RECEIVED ON THIS SERIES!

IN THE PAST, THE ONLY PEOPLE WHO EVER COMMENTED ON MY WORK WERE MY FAMILY AND FRIENDS. BUT SINCE THE SERIES STARED, ESPECIALLY AFTER VOLUME ONE WAS RELEASED, MANY PEOPLE STARTED TO TWEET AT ME AND REPLY TO ME ON TWITTER ABOUT THE SERIES AND IT REALLY CHEERED ME UP! I'D LIKE TO EXPRESS MY SINCEREST GRATITUDE TO EVERYONE WHO HAS REACHED OUT TO ME!

IT'S A GREAT MORALE BOOSTER FOR A CREATOR LIKE ME SINCE IT'S NICE KNOWING THAT THERE ARE PEOPLE OUT THERE WHO READ MY WORK. IT REALLY MAKES ME HAPPY!

IN ADDITION TO SOCIAL MEDIA, THERE ARE READERS WHO RESPOND DIRECTLY TO THE MAGAZINE IN THE FORM OF LETTERS OR QUESTIONNAIRES AND IT ALSO DRIVES ME TO WORK HARDER! EVEN IN THE GLORY DAYS OF THE INTERNET, THOSE LETTERS AND QUESTIONNAIRES STILL HAVE AN IMPACT!

THEREFORE, IF SOME OF YOU READ THIS COMMENT AND THOUGHT, "OKAY, THEN WORK HARDER BECAUSE I'M NOW SUPPORTING YOU!" PLEASE SEND SOMETHING TO THE *JUMP SQ* EDITORIAL TEAM TO GIVE TO ME. IT'LL MAKE MY DAY!

OKAY, THIS IS TURNING LESS INTO A COMMENT AND MORE INTO MY PERSONAL DIARY. I'LL JUST FINISH IT HERE.

SEE YOU NEXT VOLUME!

4:36 A.M. July 2017

Tsuyoshi Takaki

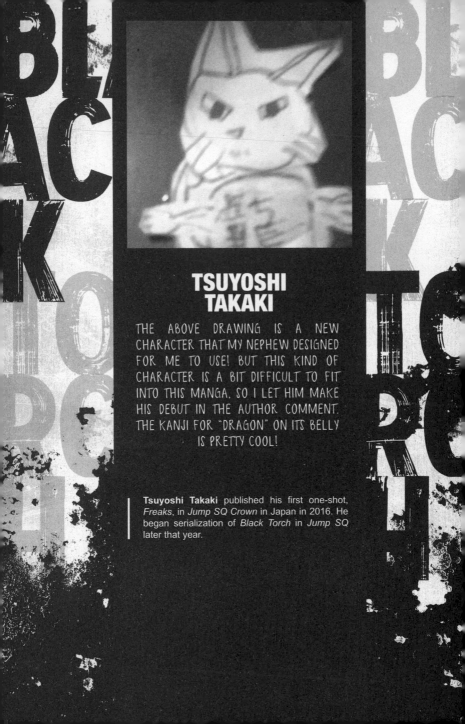

TSUYOSHI TAKAKI

THE ABOVE DRAWING IS A NEW
CHARACTER THAT MY NEPHEW DESIGNED
FOR ME TO USE! BUT THIS KIND OF
CHARACTER IS A BIT DIFFICULT TO FIT
INTO THIS MANGA, SO I LET HIM MAKE
HIS DEBUT IN THE AUTHOR COMMENT.
THE KANJI FOR "DRAGON" ON ITS BELLY
IS PRETTY COOL!

Tsuyoshi Takaki published his first one-shot,
Freaks, in *Jump SQ Crown* in Japan in 2016. He
began serialization of *Black Torch* in *Jump SQ*
later that year.

BLACK TORCH
VOLUME 2

SHONEN JUMP Manga Edition

STORY AND ART BY **TSUYOSHI TAKAKI**

Translation/Toshikazu Aizawa and Colin Leigh
Touch-Up Art & Lettering/Annaliese Christman
Design/Julian [JR] Robinson
Additional Translation & Editing/Marlene First

Published by VIZ Media, LLC
P.O. Box 77010
San Francisco, CA 94107

Printed in the U.S.A.

10 9 8 7 6 5 4 3 2 1
First printing, November 2018

VIZ MEDIA
viz.com

ratings.viz.com RATED T+ OLDER TEEN

PARENTAL ADVISORY
BLACK TORCH is rated T+ for Older Teen and is recommended for ages 16 and up. This volume contains violence and gore.

Black ✤ Clover

STORY & ART BY YŪKI TABATA

Asta is a young boy who dreams of becoming the greatest mage in the kingdom. Only one problem—he can't use any magic! Luckily for Asta, he receives the incredibly rare five-leaf clover grimoire that gives him the power of anti-magic. Can someone who can't use magic really become the Wizard King? One thing's for sure—Asta will never give up!

SHONEN JUMP

VIZ media
www.viz.com

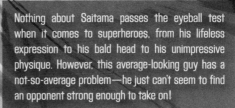

YOU ARE READING THE WRONG WAY

Black Torch reads from right to left, starting in the upper-right corner. Japanese is read from right to left, meaning that action, sound effects, and word-balloon order are completely reversed from English order.

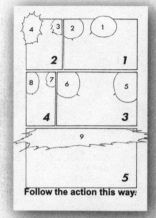

Follow the action this way: